CONSTRUCTING OUTDOOR FURNITURE
WITH 99 PROJECTS

CONSTRUCTING OUTDOOR FURNITURE
WITH 99 PROJECTS

BY PERCY W. BLANDFORD

TAB TAB BOOKS Inc.
BLUE RIDGE SUMMIT, PA. 17214

FIRST EDITION

SECOND PRINTING

Printed in the United States of America

Library of Congress Cataloging in Publication Data

Blandford, Percy W.
Constructing outdoor furniture, with 99 projects.

Includes index.
1. Outdoor furniture.   I. Title.   II. Title: Con-
structing outdoor furniture, with ninety-nine projects.
TT197.5.09B58 1983   684.1′8   82-19367
ISBN 0-8306-0454-5
ISBN 0-8306-1454-0 (pbk.)

Cover illustration by Al Cozzi.

Contents

Other TAB books by the author:

Introduction

AN ATTRACTION OF MAKING OUTDOOR FURNIture individually is that you are producing just one item that need not be like anything else. Much of what we buy is mass produced. It can be attractive, but a great many other people will have identical things. A quantity-produced piece of outdoor furniture can give us ideas, but there is no need to copy it slavishly. It was designed to suit factory methods. You ought to be able to produce something better by giving it individual attention.

Of course, there is nothing wrong with using machines. There is no virtue in doing heavy work by hand if a machine can do it for you. But when it comes to making joints and providing finishing touches, it might be better to use hand tools.

Not much is said about the choice of wood in this book. There are materials lists for most projects, but it is advisable to consult your local lumber yard about the choice of wood. Some woods will be prohibitively expensive in some places yet readily available at lower prices in a different part of the country. Explain to your supplier what the wood is for and accept his advice.

The construction of much indoor furniture now includes many manufactured boards as well as the common plywood. Some of the manufactured furniture boards are unsuitable for outside use. Some plywood is described as for exterior use or for boatbuilding. These grades can be used for outdoor furniture, but other plywood would quickly delaminate in damp conditions. In general, it is best to make outdoor furniture from solid wood.

A few items in this book can be considered hammer-and-nail projects, but most items have more advanced construction. Most people who handle tools want to show their skill in properly cut joints and other features that give their work an individual stamp. The materials lists give finished widths and thicknesses, but lengths are full to allow for final trimming. Very small parts are not listed; they can be cut from oddments.

For most projects, there are working drawings—giving one or two elevations and a plan—drawn to scale. There can be slight variations when drawings are reduced for reproduction, but for sizes that are not immediately obvious, you can compare with something on the same view that is dimensioned. Unless otherwise marked, all sizes are in inches. Where a view is symmetrical and only part of it is shown, the centerline is indicated by the draftsman's broken line of long and short dashes.

Familiarize yourself with the early chapters before going on to individual projects. If you want to know more about making furniture, you can refer to my other TAB books. They include No. 860, *The Woodworker's Bible* (covers tool handling, joints, and woodworking); No. 1004, *The Upholsterer's Bible* (deals comprehensively with that subject); No. 1044, *The Woodturner's Bible* (covers all aspects of using a lathe); No. 1188, *66 Children's Furniture Projects* (includes outdoor as well as indoor items).

Overview

I F THE CLIMATE WHERE YOU LIVE ALLOWS YOU to spend time outdoors for worthwhile periods, you need furniture intended for use in the open air. It might be possible to improvise or occasionally use indoor furniture, but it is always better to have furniture especially intended for outdoor use.

For outdoor activities in your yard or garden or on a deck or patio, you will find that your main need is for chairs and tables. Other items are often important, but they come second to the seats and tables.

Outdoor furniture can take many forms and be made from many materials. In Victorian days, there was a vogue for cast-iron outdoor furniture—often elaborately decorated. Despite the decoration, we would not regard it as beautiful. Was it comfortable? Usually not. It might have matched the rather staid times and general shunning of comfort of the period, but it has little place now. In any case, cast iron is not the material for an amateur or individual craftsman who wants to make outdoor furniture. Wrought ironwork offers more scope and is sometimes used with wood, but few people have facilities for working iron or steel.

Wooden furniture blends well into natural surroundings. If the woods and construction techniques are carefully chosen, wooden outdoor furniture can be expected to have a long life. With some woods, appearance improves with age.

Another attraction of wood is that it can be worked with simple or elaborate equipment. It is possible to make satisfactory outdoor furniture with a very limited tool kit, yet a more advanced craftsman can exercise all his skill and draw on the resources of a well-equipped shop.

Outdoor furniture is a specialized subject. It is not really an extension of indoor furniture. Indoor furniture should be of good quality, but it is not designed to stand up to outdoor conditions, particularly the effects of rain and strong sunlight. Nor is indoor furniture intended to withstand heavy usage given outdoor furniture. Taking indoor furniture outside is not recommended.

The wood used for outdoor furniture is usually of larger sections than that used for indoor furniture. Joints are often simple but they are strong. Frequent use is made of nails and screws (with bolts where needed). At one time glue was rarely used in furniture making, but with modern, fully waterproof glues available, extra strength comes from using glue with metal fastenings. Outdoor furniture mostly would not look right indoors because it gets its beauty outdoors from its functional and strong appearance. Fitness for purpose is a much more obvious requirement of a piece of outdoor furniture.

Seating can range from a simple plank bench, suitable for a brief rest, to something with all the upholstery needed for comfort and positions that allow for sitting upright or anywhere between that and reclining fully. Chairs can have backs and legs in a basically similar configuration to indoor chairs or there can be some arrangements not seen indoors. There can be provisions for removable arms and cushions.

There are many types of seats that will accommo-date more than one person. Such longer benches can be regarded as wayside seats along a path, but they also can be attractive in your yard. The craftsman will be attracted by the fact that there is little more work in making a seat for two or three than in making it for one.

Tables might not seem to have so many variations, but this book shows that there are a great many ways of achieving the desired result of a level flat surface at a suitable height. Tables can be combined with seating as in the almost universal picnic table. Tables and chairs can be made to fold for storage or transport. Making combined furniture or folding furniture requires more thought and attention to detail, but the skill required should be within the capabilities of most amateur craftsmen.

Chapter 1

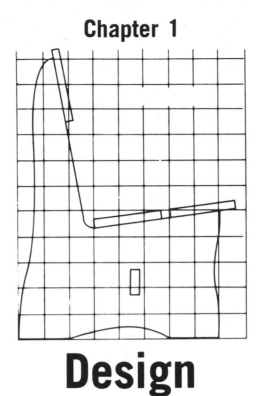

Design

FURNITURE FOR OUTDOOR USE SERVES MANY OF the same purposes as furniture for use indoors but presents several special considerations as well. It might occasionally be possible to use indoor furniture outdoors, but you will soon discover that it is not the best for the purpose. Outdoor furniture tends to get rough treatment. Quality indoor furniture would suffer if used very much outdoors. Indoor furniture is not usually designed to withstand dampness and dirt. Excessive sunlight will damage its finish. This is particularly true for any upholstery. The finish put on indoor furniture will not always stand up to outdoor conditions and the glue used might soon deteriorate.

Outdoor furniture should be specially designed. There might be a few items that you could take indoors for use, but it is better to regard open air as outdoor furniture's normal environment. That does not mean outdoor furniture should be massive and crude. Some of it fits that description, but other items qualify as fine specimens of cabinetwork as much as indoor furniture. Outdoor furniture does not have to be uncomfortable. Some of it can be simple and rather basic, but if its proportions are right, it will give all the comfort you

need. Attached upholstery cannot be used on furniture that will have to stay outside in rain, but much can be done with cushions that can be taken indoors.

SIZES AND PROPORTIONS

No matter how much skill is lavished on a piece of furniture it is no use, for instance, if a chair is too high to allow your feet to reach the ground or a table is too high or low to be used when you are seated. Sizes and proportions have to be right. Fortunately, most of us are near an average size and a furniture size that is right for the majority will suit us. One advantage of making your own furniture is that you can alter sizes to suit individuals. If you have someone very tall or very short in the family, you can alter the dimensions to afford them the same comfort that the average person gets with average equipment.

For sitting upright, the support should be around 16 inches from the floor. You might reduce this to as low as 12 inches or go up an inch or so, but the height is about right when your thighs are horizontal. For something like fishing or tending a camp fire—where you have to lean forward or reach the ground—the height can come down

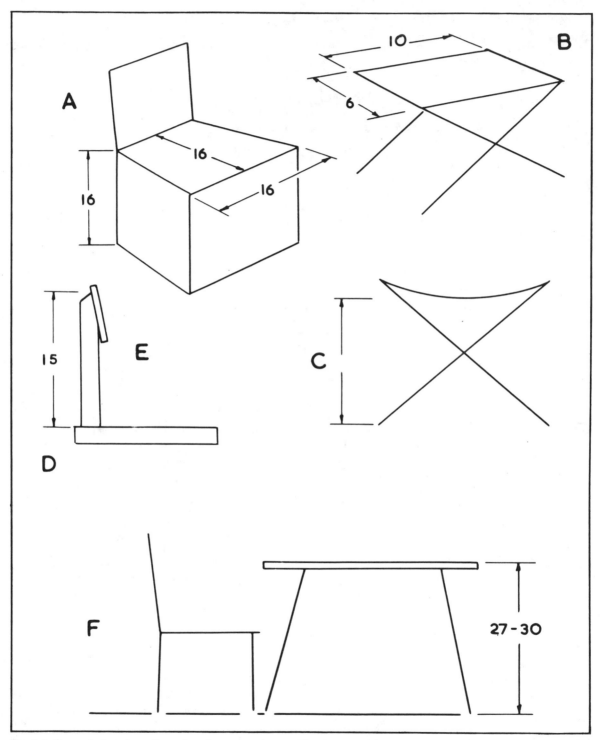

Fig. 1-1. Suggested average dimensions for various types of furniture.

to perhaps 10 inches, but that is not the height you want to sit at for long periods. Remember to allow for the thickness of a cushion, if one is to be used, but it is the compressed thickness that counts. Even quite a thick cushion goes down to about 1 inch under body weight.

If you are to sit upright for eating or working at a table, the seat should be big enough. At the front it can be 16 inches wide or more, and about the same back to front, but it could be an inch or two narrower at the rear (Fig. 1-1A). If you measure one of your indoor chairs the proportions will be found to be much the same.

It is possible to manage with a smaller seat, but you will not want to sit on it too long. Stools should have tops no more than 10×6 inches. This is particularly true if they are intended to fold very compactly. Such a support could be valued as an alternative to standing or sitting on the ground, but it is a compromise (Fig. 1-1B).

If it is a rigid seat, you can allow for some padding. If it is a slung seat, made of canvas or other flexible material, the important height is near the point of greatest sag (Fig. 1-1C). The sling must support you under and around those two bits of hard bone in your posterior. It is surprising how little area of seat is needed.

In an upright position, most people want support for their backs if they are to sit for long. Stools or other backless seats are unsuitable for long use. You could have a chair back reaching high enough to support your shoulder blades, but for most outdoor furniture support at the small of your back is sufficient. This means having the top about 15 inches above the seat (Fig. 1-1D). Then you have to consider its angle. A level seat and an upright back would not be comfortable. It is the angle of the part that fits into your back that counts. The arrangement of its support is not so important providing that is clear of your back. The part you rest against needs to slope back slightly; 10 degrees past vertical is about right (Fig. 1-1E).

With that sort of upright chair there will be a matching table. For a comfortable working or eating height, it will be somewhere between 27 inches and 30 inches from the floor (Fig. 1-1F). This will be just below the level of your elbows, when sitting, so you can reach comfortably over the table.

There are variations. If you make small folding stools and want a folding table to use with them, it will have to be low to match their heights. You can bring it down to as low as 20 inches (particularly if compactness of folding is important).

The table area will be determined by your needs, but it should not be too small in relation to the height if it is to be free-standing; otherwise it will be unstable. If it is to be attached to the ground, that problem does not arise. For a free-standing table, particularly of lightweight construction, it is advisable to make its top sizes no less than the table height. In other words, the minimum size occupies a cube.

LOUNGING SEATS

Much sitting in the open air can be described as lounging. If you do not want to sit at a table, the requirements of

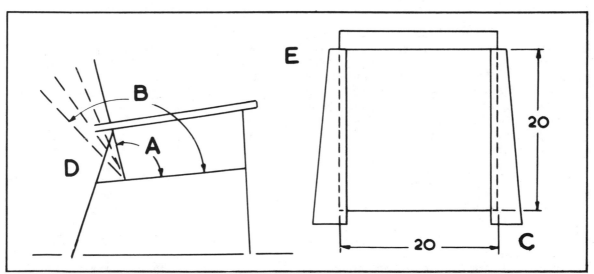

Fig. 1-2. An armchair can have different back angles and the legs can slope to give stability. The seat of an armchair is usually bigger than for a chair without arms.

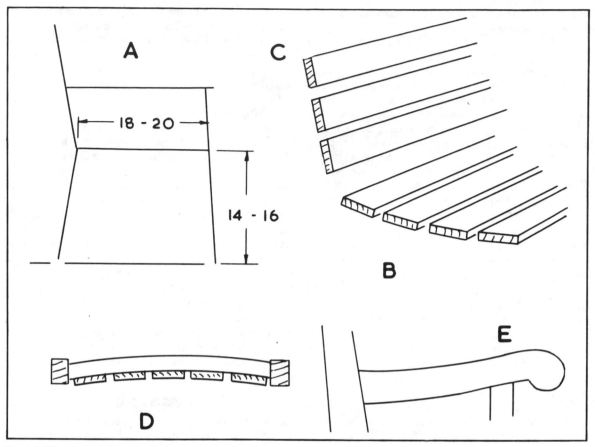

Fig. 1-3. The general sizes of a chair can be developed to allow for a curved seat, a slat back, and curves in the back and arms.

seating are very different. You do not need to sit so high and you will want to lean back. It is the angle of your thighs that is crucial for comfort. The front edge can be nearly as high as for an upright seat, but your thighs slope back. How much of a slope depends on the degree of lounging. Back to front can be up to about 20 inches (or more) if cushions are to be included. Ideally the slope of the back of the chair should be adjustable. In the most upright position, the back should be 10 degrees or so more than a right angle to the seat (Fig. 1-2A). Further angular positions can go back some way, depending on how near a horizontal position you want to reach, but 45 degrees past perpendicular to the seat is a reasonable limit (Fig. 1-2B). If it is a fixed back, you will have to settle for a compromise position.

There are lounging chairs without arms, but if you want to lean back and read or sew there is an advantage in having a chair with arms. The area contained in the arms and back needs to be large enough to allow body movement. If someone wants to curl up with their legs under them, there should be room. In any case, you do not want anything like a form-fitting chair. If the seat is 20 inches square, that is about right, but it could be a few inches wider (Fig. 1-2C).

Usually the seat is parallel, but it could be slightly narrower at the back. The arms can be about 10 inches above the seat and can be slightly nearer it at the back (Fig. 1-2D). Many chairs have seat and arms parallel in side view. The arms should not restrict the seat, so they are usually parallel with it on their inner edges. They can taper back on the outer edges; this is largely for the sake of appearance (Fig. 1-2E).

BENCHES

Wider seats for two or three people have much in common with arm chairs or lounging seats, but they are usually arranged rather more upright. They are not as upright as chairs for use with tables—unless that is their purpose. The seat height is comparatively low, say 14 inches to 16 inches, and deeper back to front than some chairs (probably 18 inches to 20 inches). The back is given a comfortable slope and can go higher than a simple chair (Fig. 1-3A).

Comfort in a seat can be increased by giving it a curve. Some plastics are molded almost to figure form, but it is impractical to make a double curvature in wood. Instead, there can be a curve back to front; this is usually made up with laths (Fig. 1-3B). Back supports are usually made of slats straight across (Fig. 1-3C). Shoulders accept straight support where a posterior is better fitted with a curve. There can be a curve across a back if slats are vertical on hollowed supports (Fig. 1-3D).

Arms do not have to be straight. Some shaping in side view improves appearance and actually conforms better to your arm resting with the elbow in the hollow and your wrists and hands over the curve. How much shaping depends on the available equipment for cutting curves in fairly thick wood (Fig. 1-3E).

STABILITY

A chair, table, lounger, or other piece of furniture that will not stand steadily could be just an inconvenience or a definite danger. The design must always have regard for stability. If you are making things that will be attached to

the ground, that takes care of stability—as far as falling over is concerned—but the structure could still be so fragile that it collapses.

On the whole, it is safe to assume that the supports of anything should cover at least the same floor area as the top. Unfortunately, users of furniture do not just sit with their weight thrusting downward. You have to design furniture so that just about whatever the user does it ought to stand up to it. Leaning back heavily in a chair is usual. Tilting a seat on two legs is common. Leaning or sitting on a table must be expected.

Examination of chairs in your home will show how they are designed to remain steady. Front legs need not be quite as far forward as the front of the seat (Fig. 1-4A). People do not tend to tilt chairs forward. Rear legs should go further back (Fig. 1-4B). The higher the chair back the more leverage is applied by anyone leaning back heavily, and the further the legs should go to resist this. Obviously, there are limits and excessive leg projection has to be avoided. Even then, some outdoor chairs have their rear legs much further back than would be usual indoors. This applies to all kinds of seating that is not held down. Several people pressing back together on an unsecured bench will put on a considerable tilting strain.

When viewed from the front, there is less need for a great spread of legs because there is less tendency for a user to put on sideways loads. Nevertheless, it helps to have the spread of feet greater than the seat (Fig. 1-4C).

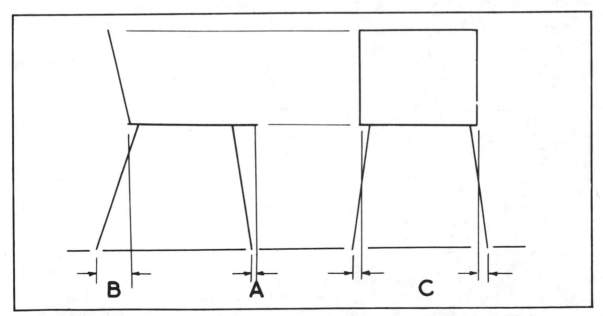

Fig. 1-4. The seat of a chair is arranged for convenience in use, but the legs splay outward to give stability in use.

This is particularly true if the seat is not very wide. A broad-arm chair is more stable because of its width.

Table supports should spread to come under the corners of the top, or very near that, whether there are separate corner legs, slab ends, or some other means of support. Much depends on size. A large tabletop will be tolerant of feet further in from the corners than would a small table that needs all the spread for stability that can be given.

Weight affects rigidity and stability. A massively constructed piece of furniture gains stability by its sheer weight, providing it is of reasonable proportion. Examples are picnic tables with bench seats included alongside (all supported on heavy crossed legs). Some almost require a crane to move them.

RIGIDITY

Rigidity is the resistance of a structure to unintentionally fold or collapse. Stability is the resistance to tipping over. They are related, but rigidity is more the consideration of producing a structure where the parts provide mutual support, without necessarily being heavy—unless that is a requirement.

Resistance to deflection comes from triangulating. If you have a three-sided frame with loose joints (Fig. 1-5A), you cannot push it out of shape. If you have four pieces similarly joined, you can alter the shape easily (Fig. 1-5B). If you make the shape into two triangles by adding a diagonal, its shape cannot be altered (Fig. 1-5C). This is the principle that governs keeping structures in shape. It also applies to standing on uneven ground. A tripod will stand without wobbling. Four or more legs will not always stand firm with equal load on all legs. Tables and chairs do not lend themselves to three-legged construction, but three-legged stools are possibilities and a round table tabletop can have three legs.

Light frames can be held in shape with diagonal braces. A pair of legs can have one brace straight across near the feet and a diagonal above that (Fig. 1-5D). A diagonal at about 45 degrees provides the best bracing. That is not always possible. A better bracing has two diagonal strips (Fig. 1-5E).

Some assemblies will appear to have four-sided frames, so there is no apparent triangulation, but that is not so if the joints are rigid. There is the effect of triangulation in the rails (Fig. 1-5F). The deeper a rail and its joints the more the triangulating effect. There is usually more than one rail so triangulating occurs at both levels.

If the whole panel is solid wood, it obviously cannot be pushed out of shape (Fig. 1-5G). In effect it is multiple

triangulating. If a seat is made with many slats, each held by a single screw, the assembly could be pushed out of shape (Fig. 1-5H). If the joints are glued and two screws are spread at each joint (Fig. 1-5J), the assembly has a good resistance to distortion. A diagonal brace below would have a similar effect, but that might not be practical. Corner blocks (Fig. 1-5K) would also resist distortion.

Crossed legs will be seen to have a triangulating effect in themselves (Fig. 1-6A). Under a table they can be symmetrical, but they also can be altered to get better stability under a chair (Fig. 1-6B), with the rear foot coming further back.

If rails are added to an assembly, their stiffening effect can be judged. Suppose a lower rail or stretcher is to come low down between the ends of a table or bench. It might be put flat or on edge. In resistance to distorting the assembly lengthwise, it would be better on edge (Fig. 1-6C), where the triangulating effect would be wider. A flat rail would have negligible resistance (Fig. 1-6D).

CONVENIENCE

Some outdoor furniture might look good and be well made, yet not fulfill its purpose because it is impossible or inconvenient to use. Lower rails are necessary in many assemblies to give rigidity. Rails between front and back legs of a chair are not in the way of a sitter's legs, at whatever level they are put (Fig. 1-7A). Neither would a back rail, but a low front rail—particularly in a chair used for sitting upright—would be a nuisance. A front rail could be high (Fig. 1-7B). The top rail could be deep to give stiffness without the need for a lower one (Fig. 1-7C). Another arrangement has a crosswise rail between the side rails instead of the front legs (Fig. 1-7D) so that it is far enough back not to interfere with swinging legs.

A similar problem occurs with table rails. With slab ends, all the necessary bracing can come from a central stretcher (Fig. 1-7E). This leaves clearance for sitters' feet at each side. The crossed-leg sawbuck arrangement can also get all the stiffness needed from a central rail (Fig. 1-7F).

With corner table legs it is possible to stiffen with deep top rails only and dispense with lower rails. But then there is another problem. A sitter might not be able to get his knees under a deep rail. With the usual chairs and normal tables, you cannot have top rails deeper than about 5 inches without meeting this problem.

Diagonal lower rails are kept away from feet (Fig. 1-7G), but then there are problems of strength on the

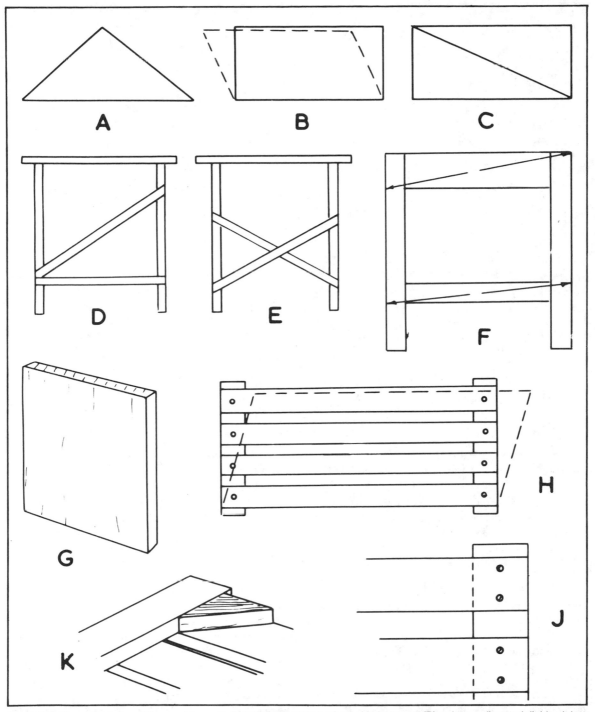

Fig. 1-5. A triangular frame (A) cannot be pushed out of shape, but a four-sided one can (B) unless a diagonal divides it into triangles (C). This is seen in framing (D and E), but construction can provide an internal triangulation or the arrangement of nails or screws does the same (F through K).

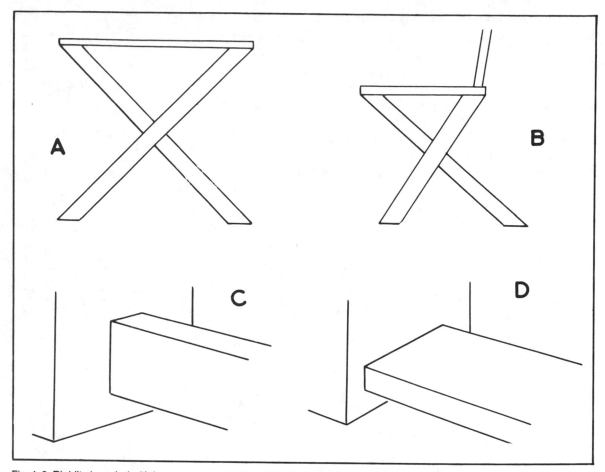

Fig. 1-6. Rigidity is varied with leg arrangements (A and B). An upright stretcher (C) stiffens a table better than a flat one (D).

crossing and the joints to the legs. Otherwise there can be similar arrangement to the chair, with the rail one way between the rails the other way, or even double rails (Fig. 1-7H). That still leaves rails far enough out to interfere with the feet of anyone sitting at the ends.

APPEARANCE

Fitness for purpose is the main consideration in making outdoor furniture. Fortunately, if an item is functional and looks right, you can consider its appearance to be acceptable. In making furniture for use in the garden or yard, there is certainly no need to decorate for the sake of decoration.

There are some design considerations. A square is not considered as good looking as a rectangle. If you are making something that has a boxlike configuration, it looks better if all of its surfaces are longer one way than

the other, and at no angle of viewing does the outline appear to be a square. You may not consider that important in a functional piece of furniture, but if you will get your results just as well with a rectangle as with a square, choose to make the item rectangular.

Curves are considered better looking than straight lines. You will have to include many straight lines—wood construction is more easily done with straight pieces of wood—but consider adding curves. The arms of a chair can include curves. As they are the most prominent feature, the curves will have a softening effect on the whole design. The top of a chair back could be cut with a curve and it will look better than with a straight edge. It is possible to cut curves into straight edges. This can also be functional, as at the bottom of a bench end, where the curve produces feet at the corners. A rectangular cutout would be less pleasing.

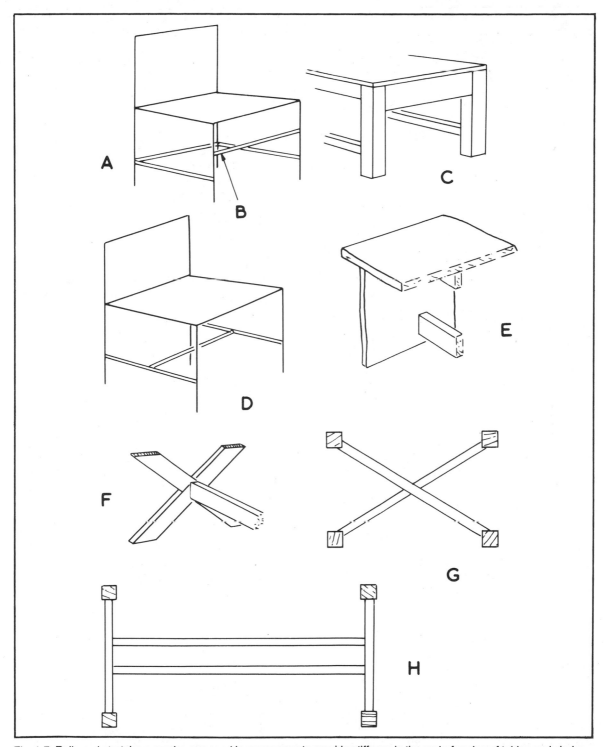

Fig. 1-7. Rails and stretchers can be arranged in many ways to provide stiffness in the underframing of tables and chairs.

Color has a place in design. Do you want to draw attention to the piece of furniture or would you rather it was inconspicuous? Most hardwoods left untreated will soon weather so they blend into their surroundings. At the other extreme, you might want to paint the wood in bright colors. Against the mainly green background of foliage, red and yellow are the colors that stand out. Paint your work bright red if you want it to shout "Look, I made it!" Such a color might match the paintwork of an adjoining building and be justified.

More usual colors for furniture in a formal or cultivated garden or on a well-kept lawn are white and green. White looks attractive and inviting, but it needs to be kept clean and you will have to touch up the paint frequently. Fortunately, there is no problem in matching the color. Green can be more of a problem for touching up. Supposedly there are more shades of green than any other color.

There are treatments with linseed and other oils that will preserve the wood as well as give it a mellow appearance. But oil takes some time to dry and you will not be thanked if someone gets it on their clothes. Varnish is another finish that lets you see the wood grain, but it must be the best quality outdoor varnish. That means asking for boat varnish. Then give the wood at least three coats. Be prepared to touch up as necessary or the wood rubbed bare will stain and you cannot put that right.

FOLDING

All of the design considerations affecting rigid furniture have to be kept in mind when you are planning furniture to take apart or fold. Usually folding furniture has to be light for portability. Select wood with reasonably straight grain and without flaws. There will be little margin to take care of weak parts.

The important thing concerning folding furniture is that there must be no fear of it folding or collapsing in use. When you are using it, you should be able to treat it in the same way as rigid furniture. Whatever locks the parts in place must always do so. Ideally there should be no loose parts. Loose pegs and other things can be lost and then the assembly cannot be put together. Worse are nuts and bolts that have to be taken out and wrenches are needed to tighten them.

Some folding furniture is never disassembled. Before making anything with the inherent complication of folding, consider if a rigid item might serve just as well.

PRACTICALITY

Designs in this book cover all manner of construction. If you do not think your skill is up to one thing, you might find a simpler construction technique for something serving the same purpose. When you design something yourself, think through all the steps in construction. Much of the skill in making anything is in anticipating the move after the next. Will you have all the tools needed for what you want to do? If not, it might be possible to buy wood already machined to suit or you might have to pay someone to do work for you. Will that be worthwhile or is there some other way of achieving the same ends with your own tools and skills?

It is very easy to come up with a design that needs a different section of wood for almost every part. If you have your own circular saw and jointer, that might not matter, but if you have to pay for wood to be machined to many sizes it will be expensive. It is better to discover what stock sizes your supplier can provide and design at least most of the project around those sizes. Remember that bought planed wood is usually about ⅛ inch under the specified size. It will not matter, for instance, if wood is 2⅞ inch wide or 3 inch wide, but if you insist on a finished size of 3 inches you will pay much more for it.

Do not underrate your own skill. If you have the tools necessary, tackle work you have not done before. It will take much longer for you to cut a particular joint than it would take an expert, but having plenty of time is an advantage for an amateur. You will experience a greater sense of achievement from being able to look at a piece of craftsmanship that incorporates a new skill than if you accepted some simpler alternative.

Chapter 2

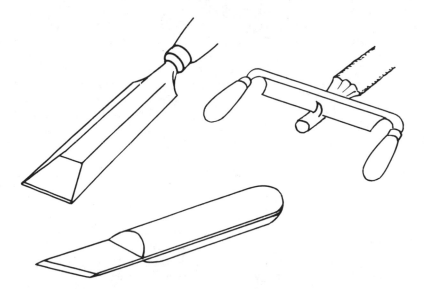

Tools and Materials

THE MAKING OF OUTDOOR FURNITURE IS A branch of woodworking that embraces a large range of methods of construction. There are considerable variations in the skills needed as well as in the equipment required. There are opportunities for using woods that would not be suitable for use indoors. It is possible to use wood almost straight from the tree. At the other extreme are pieces of outdoor furniture made of woods that might also be used for indoor furniture. Some of the first woods can be made into crude, but satisfactory, furniture with very few tools and little precision. These tools and techniques would not be suitable for high-class work done with lumber that has been seasoned, planed, and made with cabinetwork joints.

There is no one tool kit to be recommended to anyone planning to make outdoor furniture. You have to consider what sort of work you intend to do. Tools of all kinds are always worth having. If you have assembled a shop with many power tools and a large range of hand tools, you will probably find uses for all things in making outdoor furniture. If you are starting with no more than common household tools, it is still possible to produce some types of furniture, but you will have to be selective.

This chapter is not intended to contain a guide to all basic woodworking tools. It does provide an indication of what tools will be particularly useful for this sort of woodworking.

Most homeowners will have a hammer, a saw, a screwdriver, and a few other tools that have been accumulated. There will be a use for these, whatever their condition. If you buy tools, get the best. Price is usually a good guide to quality. This is particularly so with edge tools (the ones that cut). If a tool is to be sharpened and keep its edge, it has to be made of quality steel that has been properly hardened and tempered. That is what you pay for. A poor tool might never take a good edge. If it does, it might quickly lose it as soon as you try to cut with it.

In general, you will do better work with a small collection of good tools than you will with a larger number of inferior ones. This is also a consideration when there is a choice of tool for the same purpose. For instance, you can buy a pump-action screwdriver that certainly puts screws in quickly. For the same price, you could buy several plain screwdrivers of different sizes, that would be of more use to you. This reasoning could apply to many other tools with chromium plating, special brass facings, and similar extras that make very attractive tools. For the work you are planning, you probably can manage with inexpensive, plain tools. A boxed kit of tools might seem an attractive way to get together what you need, but it will almost certainly get you some tools you will never use and others of sizes that you would have chosen as individual tools.

SAWS

Most of the cutting to size will be done by hand. If you have a circular saw, either a portable one or one mounted in a saw bench, it will be useful, but it would not be a first priority in buying. Instead a good *handsaw* or *panel saw* about 20 inches long and with about 8 teeth per inch will do most cutting (Fig. 2-1A). Notice that the teeth are set in alternate directions so the groove they cut is wider than the metal from which the saw is made. This *kerf* prevents the saw from binding in a deep cut and it is particularly important if there is still sap in the wood. Normal teeth are a diamond shape and these are designed for cutting across the grain. There are *ripsaws* that look the same, but their teeth are more upright on their leading edges so they cut more efficiently along the grain. It should not be necessary to get one of these. The small amount of cutting along the grain can be done with cross-grain teeth.

For finer work there is a *backsaw*, 10 inches or 12 inches long, with a stiffening piece along the back. Teeth can be as fine as 16 per inch. A backsaw is the bench saw. It does not tear the grain much. If you want to cut grooves across wood or make mortise and tenon joints, you must have a backsaw.

A panel saw is best used with the wood supported at about knee height. You can make a trestle or use an old chair. Then you can hold the wood with one knee while making cuts downward. Some sawing with the panel saw can be better done with the wood upright in a vise. Joint cutting with a backsaw can be done with the wood in a vise or held against a bench hook (Fig. 2-1B). Such a hook is easily made. A bench with a good vise helps in doing of accurate work. Any table-size structure will do. What you need is rigidity and a front edge stiff enough and strong enough to stand up to hammering and planing.

If you want to make furniture from natural wood—either slabs cut from logs or pieces of poles—the wood will probably still have sap in it and a saw suitable for dry, seasoned wood would not cut far without binding and coming to a halt. The saw teeth have to be fairly coarse and be given more set than the other saws so that they make a wider kerf as they progress through the wood. It is also best to provide deep gullets at intervals to clear away sawdust (Fig. 2-1C). Saws are made with these teeth that look like panel saws, but it is more usual to have the blade narrow and tensioned in a tubular frame (Fig. 2-2). Even if you are mainly interested in furniture made from prepared dry wood, one of these saws will be useful for cutting back branches or otherwise preparing the place you intend to site the furniture.

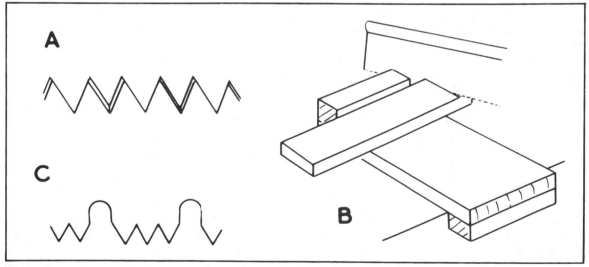

Fig. 2-1. Crosscut saw teeth are sharpened to points opposite ways to sever wood fibers (A). A bench hook is convenient for sawing small parts (B). Saws for green wood can have gullets between groups of teeth to clear sawdust (C).

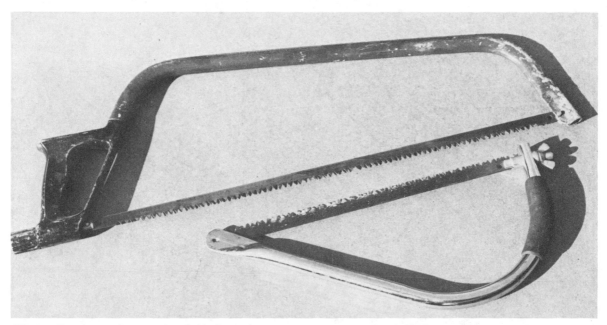

Fig. 2-2. Frame saws have teeth suitable for cutting unseasoned or newly felled wood.

CHISELS AND KNIVES

For any sort of furniture you will need edge-cutting tools. In most situations, the tool most easily controlled to do what you want is a chisel. They are available in many widths. The general-purpose ones can be described as *firmer* chisels. Long thin ones are *paring* chisels; these are not meant to be hit and you are unlikely to need them. If you are buying new chisels, start with ½-inch wide and 1-inch wide chisels. The simplest chisels have square edges. Others have wide bevel edges. The simplest chisels have square edges. See Fig. 2-3A. If there is little difference in price, get bevel edges because they will do all the square edges will and get closer into corners that are less than square.

If you will be cutting mortise and tenon joints, it is helpful to have chisels the same width as the mortises. Usually, mortises are one-third the width of the wood. Much of your wood will be between 2 inches and 3 inches wide. There will be uses for ⅝-inch and ¾-inch chisels. A very wide chisel is useful for paring broad surfaces and you might want one that is 1½ inches wide.

Modern chisels mostly have plastic handles that can be hit with a hammer without much risk of damage. Wood handles are better hit with a wooden mallet. In any case, a mallet has uses during assembly of many structures. The mallet can be quite crude and it can be homemade.

A tool dealer has many different types of chisels.

You will probably never need most of the special ones. A chisel curved in cross section is called a *gouge*. Delay buying one until you find a definite need for it. If it is sharpened on the inside of the curve, it is called *in-canelled* and is used for paring concave edges. If it is sharpened on the outside it is *out-canelled* and is used for removing waste from hollows.

There are uses for a good knife. It might be a hunting knife or a clasp knife. The important thing is that it can be kept sharp enough for whittling cuts. If you want to do upholstery with foam filling, a carving knife is the tool for cutting that material.

In some types of outdoor furniture, natural poles have to be tapered to go into holes to make something like a dowel joint. The traditional tool for tapering the ends is a *draw knife* (Fig. 2-4). The wood has to be held in a vise or by other means. Then the tool is used in both hands to make cuts toward you (Fig. 2-3B). The edge is bevelled on one side—like a chisel. If it is used with the bevel downward, you can regulate the depth of cut by altering the angle of the handles.

If that is not the type of woodwork you want to do, but would prefer the cutting of joints in prepared wood, there is a use for a *marking knife*. It has its cutting edge at the end and could be made from a broken table knife (Fig. 2-3C). This is used, instead of a pencil, when marking a part of a joint that has to be sawn across the grain. As the

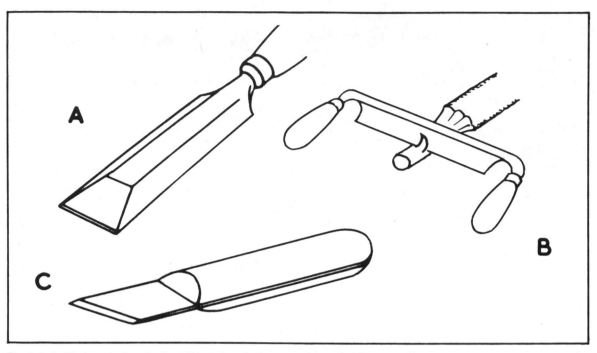

Fig. 2-3. A chisel can be bevel-edged (A). A draw knife cuts as it is pulled (B). A marking knife is sharpened on its end (C).

knife severs the grain fibers, a much cleaner edge is left if the saw kerf is arranged against the waste side of the line.

PLANES

Whether you need many planes or not depends on the types of furniture you want to make and in what state you obtain the wood. If you have a jointer or other power planer, you can deal with wood bought from the saw. You could buy your wood already planed. If you only want to make rustic furniture from poles, you will not need a

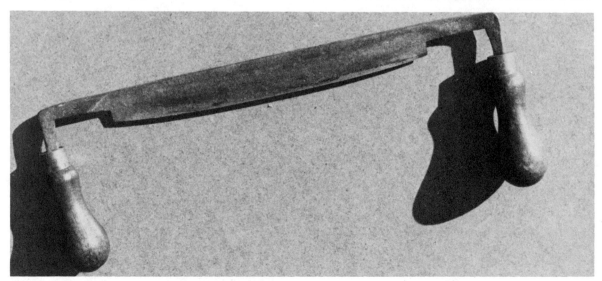

Fig. 2-4. A draw knife cuts when pulled with both hands.

14

plane. But even then you will find uses for it if you have a plane.

Machine-planed wood has a series of tiny ridges across the grain. How big they are depends on the coarseness of cut and how fast the wood was passed over the cutters. For much furniture, that sort of finish is all that is needed. If you want a better surface, you will have to hand plane the power plane marks away.

The most commonly used hand plane is the Stanley or Record *smoothing plane* (described as 4 inches or 4½ inches for a wider one). That should be the first plane you buy (Fig. 2-5). It is intended for planing along the grain with fine cuts, but you can use it for trimming across the grain. With its mouth adjusted widely, it can be set coarse to take off thick shavings.

If you want to plane surfaces and edges straight, the plane should have a longer sole, to span inequalities. A very long plane is called a *fore* or *jointer*, but your second plane could be the intermediate size called a *jack plane*. There will be occasions when you need to straighten edges. That is easier to do with a long plane than with the shorter smoothing plane.

Another useful plane is the little *block plane*. There are several versions, but all are intended to be used in one hand. The block plane is used for dealing with a ragged end or to take the sharpness off the angle between two surfaces. You often will find yourself picking it up for small cuts.

A *spokeshave* is something like a plane. Its blade is in a narrow surface controlled by a handle at each side. It is the tool for following curves, such as the shaped edge of a board. The modern metal version works like a plane, but an older type has a blade something like a small draw knife and it makes more of a slicing cut.

SHARPENING

Everyone who has cutting tools should have the means of sharpening them and know how to sharpen. A common fault with beginners is to try to carry on with a blunt tool. A skilled man will pause for sharpening much more frequently.

Most edge tools, of the plane and chisel type, will have two bevels (Fig. 2-6A). The long bevel is put there by grinding. The short bevel is made on an *oilstone* or *whetstone*. The edge can be revived a great many times on the oilstone, but when its bevel gets very long the tool is ground again. Therefore, you start with just a narrow bevel again on the oilstone.

Fig. 2-5. Smoothing planes are useful, general-purpose levelling tools.

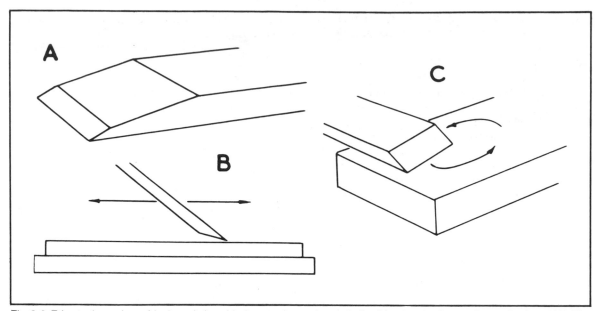

Fig. 2-6. Edge tools, such as chisels and plane blades, can have a long grinding bevel and a shorter sharpening bevel (A). The latter is maintained on an oilstone (B) and any wire edge is removed by rubbing flat (C).

Grinding can be done on a high-speed electric stone, but care is needed to avoid overheating and to keep the bevel true. Dip frequently in water to cool the steel. If rainbow colors appear on the steel, that is a sign of overheating which has drawn the temper (softened the steel). Professional grinding is done on a slower, larger stone that is kept wet. The need for grinding is so infrequent that you might prefer to pay for it and only sharpen on the oilstone yourself.

Plane blades and chisels are only sharpened on one side. The other side should be kept flat. The usual sharpening stone for these tools is a block about $8 \times 2 \times 1$ inches and it can be mounted in a wood case. There are degrees of coarseness obtainable. A coarse stone cuts quickly, but the edge given to the tool reflects the size of the grit and would appear to be like a saw edge under a lens. That sort of edge would be good enough for some rough work, but it is better to follow with a finer stone. It is possible to get combination stones, with fine and coarse grits on opposite sides, but most craftsmen prefer separate stones.

Most coarser stones are manufactured grits, but the finest stones are natural (such as Washita and Arkansas). For most outdoor furniture planing, there is no need to go down to the finest stones that are more appropriate to edges for finishing quality hardwoods in cabinetwork.

To sharpen a chisel or plane blade, have a thin oil on the stone. Light lubricating oil or kerosene is better than motor oil (which would make a barrier between the steel and the stone). Have the bevel angled downward with one hand holding higher up and the fingers of the other hand applying pressure (Fig. 2-6B). Rub the tool at a constant angle along and about the surface of the stone. The stone, as well as the steel, wears away. Keep it level and rub it all over the surface. The greatest difficulty, at first, is maintaining a steady angle along the length of the stone. But that comes with practice.

Wipe the oil off the stone and feel the edge on the flat side. If there is a roughness there, that is a *wire edge*. This is a tiny sliver of steel rubbed off the sharp edge, but still clinging to it. It indicates that the edge is sharp. Put the flat of the steel on the stone (Fig. 2-6C) and give it a few circular rubs. That should remove the wire edge. If it does not, slice the edge across a piece of scrap wood.

If that sharpening was on a coarse stone and you want to follow with a finer stone, make sure the edge is clean. Then repeat all the sharpening on the fine stone. You only need to rub long enough to remove the scratches from the coarse stone.

To sharpen a knife, note the angle toward the edge at each side and hold the blade at that angle on the stone. Again control with one hand while the other puts on pressure. Move about if it is a curved edge, but maintain the angle. After rubbing well on one side, turn the knife over and do the same on the other side. Continue until you can feel a wire edge and then slice across a piece of scrap wood to remove it.

MARKING OUT

A pencil is your best general marking tool or you can use a knife for precision cuts across the grain. Measuring presents no problems, but remember that a rule is only a means of comparing things. If you can bring two parts together for marking, that is better than using a rule. If several parts have to be given similar distance marks, even if overall lengths are different, it is easier to put the required distances on the edge of a strip of wood—called a *rod*—than to rely on a rule.

You will have to mark squarely at right angles. A try square that can be pushed against a straightedge, while you mark along its blade, is the standard tool, but there is a limit to its size. There are several other things that can be used. A sheet of plywood can be assumed to have square corners. Even the corner of a magazine page should be square. Other methods of squaring are described in Chapter 3.

An adjustable square can be used with a pencil for marking lines parallel with an edge (Fig. 2-7). Its blade is adjusted to the distance and a pencil held against the end is pulled along with it. The tool made specially for this purpose is a *marking gauge*, with a steel spur projecting to scratch from the stem. For mortise and tenon joints, there are mortise gauges with two adjustable spurs to mark both lines at the same time. One of these will be worth having if you plan to make many of these joints. Otherwise, you can mark with two settings of a plain marking gauge.

If you are planing wood true and to width and thickness, the first side is called the *face side* and the first edge, square to it, is the *face edge*. In subsequent marking out, you should work from these surfaces and there are conventional marks to pencil on them to indicate what they are (Fig. 2-8).

HOLES

If you have only one power tool, it should be an electric drill. But it will not do all your drilling. Holes up to about ⅜ of an inch for screws and bolts can be made with drills originally intended for metal. Above that it is better to use drills designed for wood. Some will fit the electric drill, but you will reach a stage where you must use a brace to drill by hand. If you buy one, it is worthwhile

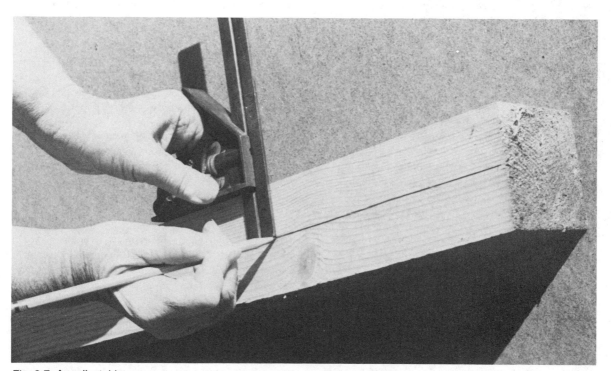

Fig. 2-7. An adjustable square can be used with a pencil to draw a line parallel to an edge.

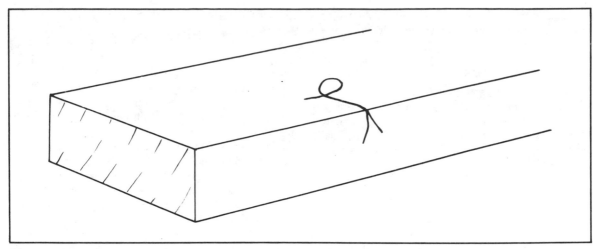

Fig. 2-8. Marks are penciled to indicate face side and face edge as wood is prepared by planing.

paying a little more for a ratchet brace. It will allow you to work in a restricted space where you cannot sweep a complete circle with the handle. Besides making holes, the brace can be used with a screwdriver bit for the many large screws used in outdoor furniture. It will also countersink holes for screw heads or just to take off roughness.

A particularly useful tool for the holes needed in rural construction using natural poles is an *auger*. This is a bit extended to have its own lever handle (Fig. 2-9). The working end is like a woodworking twist bit, but it is usually longer so it can be used for deeper holes. It is not an essential tool, but if you can find one it is useful.

WOOD

The types of trees that produce wood suitable for making things run into thousands. Fortunately, trees are a renewable resource. Despite the extensive felling going on, wood is likely to be available for a very long time. Nevertheless, some species must be conserved. This is particularly true for those that can take a hundred years to reach a stage when they can usefully be converted to lumber.

Wood used for making furniture is broadly divided into *hardwoods* and *softwoods*. The names indicate the differences in most cases, but there are actually hardwoods softer than some softwoods. The names really indicate if the tree loses its leaves in the winter (as well as the general types of leaves). Coniferous trees with needle leaves produce softwoods. Hardwoods come from broad-leafed trees and most of these lose their leaves in the winter in temperate climates.

Most hardwoods are considerably stronger, harder, and heavier than most softwoods. Mostly they are more durable, but some hardwoods are prone to rot quite quickly. Some softwoods that contain plenty of resin are quite durable. Local suppliers will be able to suggest suitable woods. Local woods are probably less expensive than imported ones. One of the most durable woods for outside use is teak (which has to be imported). There are a few substitutes for it. The oaks are durable but beech is not.

As a tree grows, it increases in girth with the production of annual rings (Fig. 2-10A). As the tree gets older, the inner part becomes more compacted and that is the *heartwood*. The outer rings are the *sapwood*. The heartwood is stronger and more durable. Some woods can show little difference between sapwood and heartwood. Where there is any choice, use the heartwood for outdoor furniture.

The lifeblood of the tree is its sap. There is less of it in the winter and that is the best time for felling. Newly cut wood is quite wet with sap. Drying this out to an acceptable level is called *seasoning*. For natural seasoning, a log is cut into boards. Then the boards are stacked, with spacers between, and left for a long time. The usual allowance is one year for each 1 inch of thickness of the boards. There are artificial ways of hastening seasoning and most wood we get today has gone through one of these processes. There must be some sap left, but it has to be a controlled, small amount.

As wood is dried it shrinks. For practical purposes that can be regarded as mostly in the direction of the annual rings. Therefore, a board cut radially will get thinner, but remain flat (Fig. 2-10B). One cut further out will warp because shrinking is around the curve of the rings. See Fig. 2-10C. Controlled seasoning minimizes the problem, but looking at the end of a board allows you to estimate what will happen to it with changes in moisture content.

As it is a natural product, wood is not a consistent material. Flaws must be accepted. The most common flaws are knots. These occur where branches leave the trunk. If the knot is small and solid with the surrounding wood, it does not matter. If there is a black edge to the knot, it will probably fall out and the wood will be weakened, probably only slightly. Avoid wood with knots half the width or more. A knot is a break in the lengthwise grain and does not provide much strength in itself.

Cracks, called *shakes*, occur in the growing tree. Small ones might not matter, but if they are large you will have to cut the wood to avoid them. Resin pockets in some softwoods can be a nuisance; they will not have much effect on strength. Straight grain will be less liable to warp and twist than grain that curves all over the place.

There are some woods where you will never get much straight grain.

Some trees grown in forests have quite straight trunks, due to all the trees thrusting upward to compete for sunlight at the top, but other trees will be far from straight. This is particularly true for some hardwoods grown away from other trees. When boards are cut across a log, the extreme edges follow a varying curved outline. This is called a *waney edge* (Fig. 2-11). If the wood is being used for indoor woodwork, a straight cut to remove this edge has to be made. This often leaves quite wide pieces with one straight and one waney edge that will be wasted and might be large enough for use in some rustic furniture. It might be obtainable free or at firewood prices. Other wide boards retaining their waney edges on one or both sides might also be valued for making outdoor furniture.

Bark on the outside of the tree normally should be removed. There are a few trees where bark is so tight that leaving it on will not matter and it might be considered a design feature. Where bark tends to loosen as

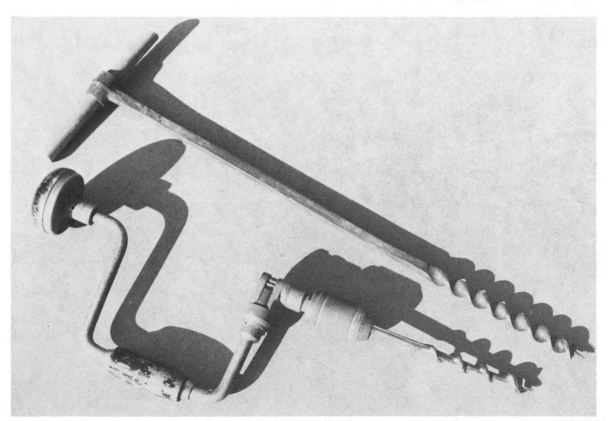

Fig. 2-9. An auger, with its own handle, compared with a bit in a brace.

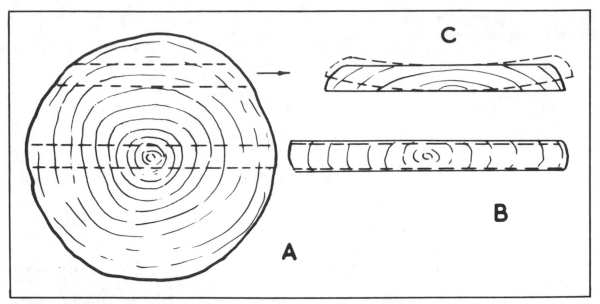

Fig. 2-10. When boards are cut across a log (A), shrinkage occurs in the direction of the annual rings (B) and can cause warping in boards cut further from the center (C).

Fig. 2-11. Waney-edged boards, shown here on a pair of doors, have many uses in the construction of outdoor furniture.

the wood dries, it will harbor insects and moisture. Both of these can attack the wood. Normally you should remove bark. The board will still have all the features of the waney edge and might need little treatment except the removal of sharp edges.

NAILS AND SCREWS

Many joints in outdoor furniture are made with nails, screws, or bolts. You have to consider the effects of corrosion. Pure iron has a good resistance to corrosion. Its initial light coating of rust resists further rusting. Very little pure iron is available now. What we loosely call "iron" is actually "mild steel." This is iron with a small amount of carbon in it. Rust on mild steel is an ongoing thing. Unprotected mild steel in damp conditions will eventually rust away.

Copper has a good resistance to corrosion, but it is soft and therefore not of much use. It can be alloyed with zinc to make brass or with tin to make bronze. Both of these alloys have a good resistance to the effects of moisture. Aluminum also resists moisture, but in its pure state it is soft. Other metals alloyed with it give hardness, but sometimes with reduced corrosion resistance. So-called stainless steel is not immune to all kinds of attack, but it can be alloyed to resist certain liquids. The

usual variety should be satisfactory in normal weather. Salt in the atmosphere will often attack metals.

Mild steel can be protected by plating. There is no need for some of the expensive plated finishes for outdoor furniture, but zinc gives fairly inexpensive protection. One such treatment is called *galvanizing*. Mild steel bolts buried in wood can have a long enough life. This is particularly true if their exposed ends are painted. There are rust-inhibiting fluids that can be used on steel fastenings before driving them and before painting.

Nails are best described by their length. The *penny system* of grading can be confusing if you are unfamiliar with it. For most furniture, you will need fairly large nails with standard heads. Diameters vary with length and you will not have any choice. Nails of other sections and with different heads are meant for other purposes and are not for your sort of woodwork.

Barbed ring nails have teeth cut around them that resist pulling out (Fig. 2-12A). They can be obtained in mild steel, possibly galvanized, but they are also made in bronze for boatbuilding. Both types are useful where you need a firm attachment, yet there is not much depth for holding or space for many nails.

Screws are made in many lengths and in thicknesses described by a gauge number (the higher the number, the

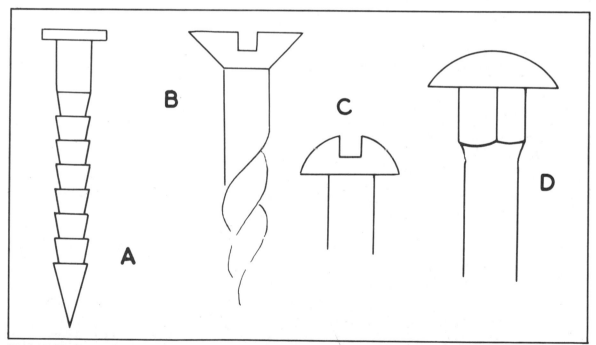

Fig. 2-12. The grip of a nail can be improved with annular rings (A). Screws can have flat (B) or round heads (C). A square neck under a bolt head prevents it turning in wood (D).

thicker the screw). Sizes start with tiny screws, smaller than you will need, and go up to quite large ones. The usual screw has a flat or countersunk head (Fig. 2-12B). You might sometimes need round-head screws (Fig. 2-12C), but for most purposes flat heads are all you will require. Screw length varies with the wood surface. Within each length there will be at least three gauge thicknesses available. In general, you want the thicker ones. In any case, avoid slender screws that will shear off when being driven. Typical useful sizes are: 8 gauge by 1½ inches, 10 or 12 gauge by 2 inches, 12 or 14 gauge by 3 inches. In longer screws, you will not usually need too much larger than 14 gauge. Brass screws are not as strong as steel ones. Therefore, they will have to be thicker or you could drive a steel screw first, withdraw it, and then replace it with the brass screw.

Care is needed in drilling for screws. See Chapter 4. Long nails can bend when driven. Undersize holes help them to enter and prevent bending. If a nail bends, you can straighten it, but is then prone to buckle again.

In heavy construction, the best fastening method is to bolt right through. The term *bolt* means a fastening with a screw thread only a short distance from the end. If the thread goes for nearly all the length, it is an *engineering screw*. To avoid confusion, the screws for driving into wood can be called *wood screws*. More information on bolts is given in Chapter 4.

Quoted lengths are from the surface, which would be under a hexagonal or square head, but from the top of a countersunk one. A coach bolt is particularly intended for woodwork. It has a shallow "snap" head and a square neck under it (Fig. 2-12D). The square pulls into the top of the drilled hole and resists turning when the nut is tightened on the other end. Normal bolts require a wrench at both ends. When choosing bolts, it is usually better to have one large bolt through a joint than several smaller ones. Quoted diameters are fractional. You will not usually need ¼ inch bolts. The general sizes are ⅜ inch or ½ inch, but for large work you will have to choose larger bolts.

GLUE

Not so long ago, the use of glue on outdoor woodwork would not have been considered because there were no glues able to withstand moisture for more than brief periods. Many modern glues are unsuitable even though claims for some of them might imply otherwise. Nevertheless, there are glues developed particularly for boatbuilding that can be used on outdoor woodwork.

In most constructions that have to be left outside, it is still common to have metal fastenings as well as glue. The two complement each other. In tenoned construction, glue alone will provide security. It is where parts merely overlap that there should be screws or bolts through. But you can put glue between the parts as well.

It is not always easy to identify a fully waterproof glue because it might only be described by a trade name. If the glue is in two parts to mix before use or apply to meeting surfaces, it is almost certainly waterproof. This is particularly true if it is described as for boatbuilding. A powerful waterproof glue (in two parts) is resorcinol. It leaves a red glue line that normally will not matter for this type of furniture. The strongest of these glues is epoxy. Besides wood to wood, it will also join many other materials to themselves and to wood.

Most glues require the surfaces to be in reasonably close contact. If you try to fill a gap with glue, it will not provide any strength. In that case, you can mix sawdust with the glue. This bonds the glue and particles to the surfaces to make a stronger joint. At the other extreme, do not tighten a close-fitting joint so hard that most of the glue is squeezed out. There must be enough glue left to make a bond.

There is not much need for stoppings in outdoor woodwork. The older putty and similar things that set hard have been superseded, but make sure you buy an exterior stopping. Some are only intended for indoor use. For filling holes over punched nails, there are stoppings to press in and sand level. They appear to set hard, but actually they remain slightly flexible to allow for movement of the wood. They can be used in cracks, but larger gaps are better filled with a more flexible stopping sold for the purpose. These synthetic stoppings are superior to any you might mix yourself from older formulae.

In making outdoor furniture there are no uses for cabinetmaking sealers. If you want to limit water absorption via end grain, you can use waterproof glue that is brushed on like paint.

FINISHES

Some woods can be left untreated and they have sufficient resistance to rot to last a long time. They will take on a weathered appearance that you might want. Otherwise you have to apply a finish.

There are wood preservatives available. For them to be most effective, the wood has to be soaked. You can obtain some protection by brushing on the preservative. Some preservatives are clear. Others are colored, often green, but that is translucent and it fades fairly rapidly. It is unwise to rely on the preservative to provide much contribution to appearance. Most preservatives can be followed by paint, but check the directions on the can. Some take a long time to dry before the furniture can be used or before paint should be applied.

Most paints now available are synthetic. They are superior in durability and quality of finish to the older paints made from natural materials. Read the instructions on the can. There might be a limit to the amount of brushing advised. Too much will alter appearance by causing air bubbles. Most paints must dry between coats, but there are some where a further coat must be put on before the earlier one is fully dry. There might be a maximum or a minimum time between coats.

The best protection comes with a gloss finish. This is usually what you want in any case, because it looks good and is easily kept clean. The effectiveness of the finish depends on what is applied underneath as much as on the quality of the final coat.

The first coat on bare or preserved wood has to make a bond with the wood grain. This is a *primer* that is thin so it penetrates. Its color is not important, but is usually white or pink. There might have to be a second coat of primer. This is followed by an undercoat that is a matt finish of a color compatible with the *top coat*. It is better if it is not exactly the same shade as the top coat. Then you can see how you are progressing on the final coat.

It is the undercoat that provides the body in the paint system. You might need to apply two coats because this is where thickness is made (not at the final stage). In some paint systems, the primer is the same as the undercoat—probably thinned. Get thinners recommended by the paint manufacturers and use them sparingly.

If the undercoat is not as smooth as you prefer, use wet-and-dry, medium abrasive paper, with water. The top gloss coat is a once-only coat. You will actually need to buy more undercoat than top coat. If you apply a second top coat, it tends to run on the earlier gloss and finish unevenly. It is inadvisable to mix different makes of paints. Most paint manufacturers recommend complete systems of finishes. Have one and follow it through.

Check that the paint offered is intended for exterior use. The most durable paint is produced for boats and it can be used on furniture. Check that it is intended for use on wood and not fiberglass. There are some boat paints, supplied in two parts, that have to be mixed before use. There is no need to use them on furniture. They make a very hard skin on a boat and they are intended for immersion in water.

Paint obscures the grain of the wood. If you want to protect the wood, but still see the grain details, the usual finish is varnish. Be careful what you use. Some varnish is intended for indoor use only. Avoid anything with shellac in it because it will not stand up to even slight dampness. Like paints, most varnishes are now synthetic. Not only has this given them better protection, but it makes application easier. Some natural varnishes could not be applied in very hot or very cold conditions and even slight humidity altered them. Synthetic varnishes are more tolerant of atmospheric differences.

A varnish described as "exterior" might be satisfactory, but a boat varnish should be even better. Some of it is described as "spar varnish." That has good weather resistance. There are no primers or undercoats for varnish. The first coat should be thinned, using the thinners recommended by the makers, but further coats are made with the varnish as supplied.

Chapter 3

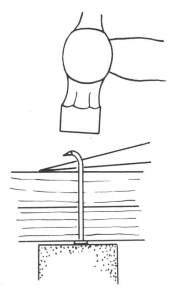

Basic Techniques

T HE MOST BASIC FURNITURE IS FORMED FROM natural poles or slabs of wood. Often the bark is left on and the parts are either nailed or assembled with a simple peg arrangement. Little regard is provided for the niceties of squaring and exact size. Other furniture is comparatively massive and made of wood that has been sawn to squared sections, but not finished in a way that would make it suitable for indoor furniture. Sometimes the wood is used almost directly from the tree and it does not season until after it has been made into furniture. In other situations, the furniture is made of planed, seasoned wood and it would be acceptable to use the items inside the home as well as outside.

There is room in the making of outdoor furniture for a wide range of skills. It is possible to make satisfactory furniture if all you can do is saw wood to length and nail parts together. For that work the range of tools needed is also slight. With more skill and more tools, it is possible to produce more advanced furniture. Anyone experienced in making indoor furniture of good quality will probably feel happier producing outdoor furniture of almost cabinetmaking quality.

The items described in this book cover the whole range of constructions and skills. Most workers can do better than they think if they try. In any case, there are some basic techniques that ought to be mastered and it is worthwhile learning these before you start on your projects.

NAILING

Most people believe they already know how to nail and can hit the nail on its head with a hammer more than they hit their own nail. There is more to it than that. Most nails used in outdoor furniture are fairly large. You must take into consideration other things besides being able to hit the nail every time.

If the wood is not very hard and the nail not too large, you could just position the nail and drive it. If it is near an edge you might split the wood. Usually, if you are dealing with nails 3 inches or more long, it is better to drill a starter hole for each nail. If you are nailing two pieces of wood together it is the grip of the nail in the lower piece clamping the upper piece to it under the nail head (Fig. 3-1A) that counts. You do not gain anything by having the nail tight in the top piece (as it would be if you nailed without drilling). In smaller sizes that does not matter.

For much nailing, you can drill an undersize hole through the top piece and partly into the bottom piece.

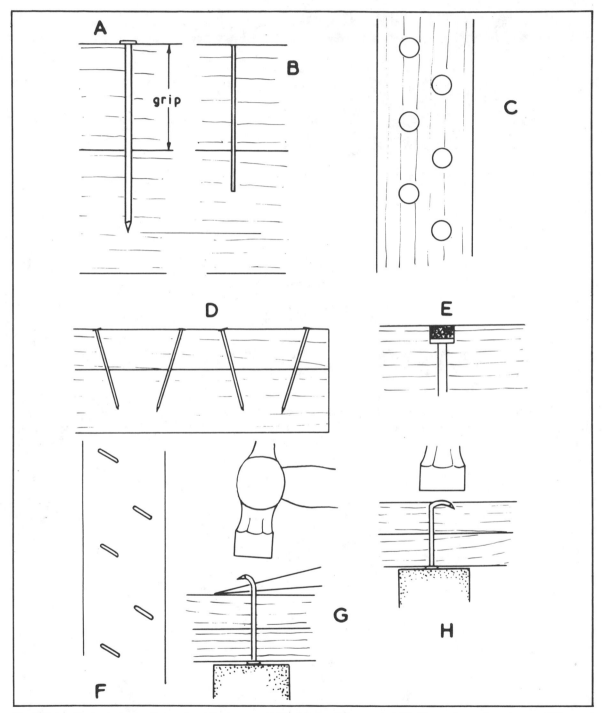

Fig. 3-1. A nail grips between its head and the lower part (A). A hole will be needed (B). Staggering nails reduces splitting and adds strength (C); so does dovetail nailing (D). A nail set below the surface can be covered with stopping (E). Nails can be taken through and clenched (F,G, and H).

How much undersize and how far depends on the size of the nail and the wood. If it is very hard wood, the hole in the top piece can be the same size as the nail and a smaller drill can be used to continue into the bottom piece. Usually one drill size will do (Fig. 3-2B). Even in very hard wood, it is best to stop the drill short so the nail makes its own way into the last short distance. Even if you are dealing with an assembly where you can drive nails without drilling, nail holes near the edge of the board should be drilled so that there is less risk of splitting.

It is not easy to decide on the length of nails and spacing. It is largely a matter of experience. Remember it is the length of nail in the lower piece of wood that provides the grip. About three-fourths of the way through the average board will be about right. About twice the depth of the upper piece of wood is another guide for thinner parts. As for the number of nails, too many is better than too few. Do not drive nails wastefully. A minimum of three nails in any joint should be used, but in many furniture constructions a 2 inch spacing is about right. Try to avoid driving nails close by in the same line of grain. That encourages splitting. If there is space, a zig-zag line (Fig. 3-1C) makes a stronger joint and spreads the nails in the grain. If the lower part of a nail is going into end grain, it should go about twice as far into it as it would in side grain, if possible, or there will have to be more nails going to a lesser depth.

If nails have to be driven in a row, there is a gain in strength if they are driven at alternate angles to provide *dovetail nailing* (Fig. 3-1D). The slope used need not be much. If you are aiming at equal spacing, remember it is the spacing where the boards meet rather than at the heads that is important.

Nail heads normally finish level with the surface. For neatness, the heads can be punched below the surface and then the hole can be filled with a stopping material (Fig. 3-1E). If you are making furniture with wood that has not been fully seasoned, you should assume that a board will probably get thinner as it dries out. In that case, it is advisable to punch nail heads below the surface so that they are not left standing and liable to snag clothing as the wood surface shrinks. For large nails, the punch used should be quite large. It can be made from a piece of iron rod, ½ inch or more thick, filed at one end to about the diameter of the nail head.

In some places, the greatest strength will come from taking the nail right through and turning over the point. This is particularly so where the wood is thin and where there would not be much grip with normal nailing. This *clench nailing* is not just a matter of hitting over the projecting nail end. The neatest way to bury the point is along the grain, but it is stronger to go squarely or diagonally across the lines of grain (Fig. 3-1F).

It is better to bury the point than to merely turn it over. That is stronger and prevents the point from scratching anyone or tearing clothing. This is best done in stages. Drive the nail through. Then support the head with an iron block or a heavy hammer. Put a spike beside the projecting nail point and hammer the end to a curve over it (Fig. 3-1G). Pull out the spike and hammer the nail point into the wood (Fig. 3-1H).

SCREWS

Compared with nailing, screwing parts together has the advantage of exerting a clamping action. The force of hammering at one place can cause nails to loosen at another place. That does not happen with screws. It is possible to pull parts together progressively by going back over screws for further tightening. If it is expected that parts will have to be disassembled later, screws can be withdrawn without damaging the wood. With nails there would be damage even if nails could be pulled out.

For better-class work, screws are always preferable to nails. As with nails, the choice of screw size is largely a matter of experience. Screws have parallel unscrewed necks. The longer the screw the longer this neck. Usually the plain neck goes in the top piece and the screwed part goes into the lower piece. It is only the screwed part in the lower piece of wood that provides the grip. There is nothing to be gained by having it cut a thread in the upper piece. In fact, that could prevent the screw from pulling the upper piece tight to the other piece.

For each length of screw, there are several gauge thicknesses available. For most outdoor work, you should choose the thicker screws. Thicker screws are stronger and they grip better. They need not be spaced as closely. As with nails, avoid getting close screws in the same line of grain (because of the risk of splitting). A zig-zag arrangement can be used.

Screws in the sizes used in building furniture must have starter holes drilled. The clearance hole in the top piece of wood should allow the screw to pass easily and be drilled right through even if part of the screw thread will come within it (Fig. 3-2A). What size and length of hole to drill in the lower piece depends on the screw and the wood. In soft wood, the hole can be quite small in relation to the screw and only be taken about half as far as the screw will go (Fig. 3-2B). In hard wood, it should be bigger and be taken deeper (Fig. 2-3C). But even then leave a short distance for the screw to make its own way.

Large screws are difficult to drive tightly. It helps to rub wax or a candle on a screw before driving. That is

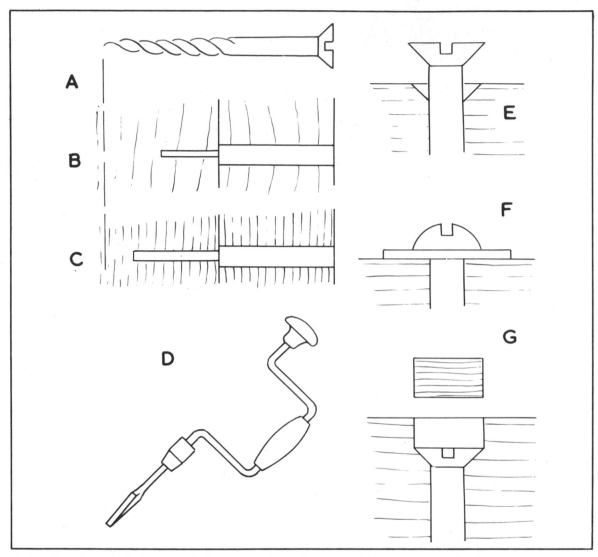

Fig. 3-2. Screws need holes (A,B, and C). A screwdriver bit in a brace is useful for large screws (D). A hole can be countersunk (E). A washer spreads pressure (F). A plug in a counterbored hole hides a screw head (G).

cleaner than using lubricating oil or grease. Even with a large screwdriver, it might be difficult to exert enough torque. In any case, make sure the end of the screwdriver matches the screw head. You will waste a lot of energy if the driver does not match. The best way to get a large screw fully tightened is to use a screwdriver bit in a brace (Fig. 3-2D).

If you are using countersunk screw heads that are to finish flush with the surface, drive one screw as an experiment. In many woods, it will pull its head in withou

any preparation of the top of the hole. If it does not, use a countersink bit to recess the hole. Do not do that as fully as the size of the screw head. Allow for some pulling in (Fig. 3-2E). If you use round head screws, put a washer under each head (Fig. 3-2F). Otherwise the head will partly pull in and it will look untidy.

The neatest finish comes from *counterboring*. With this technique, the screw heads are far enough below the surface for a wood plug to go over each of them (Fig. 3-2G). Because the wood is usually quite thick, there is

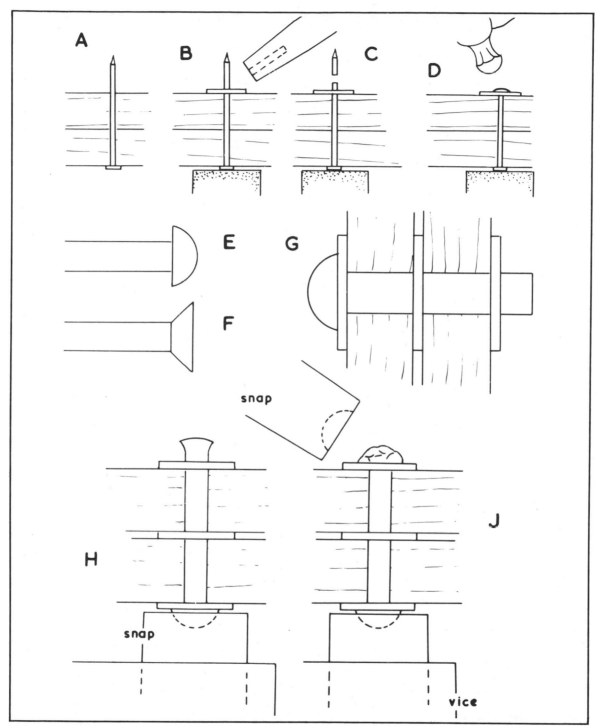

Fig. 3-3. A nail can be rivetted through a washer (A through D). Rivets can go through washers to make pivots for moving parts (E through J).

plenty of depth to allow the heads to be sunk without loss of strength. The size of the counterbored hole depends on the size of plug. The best plugs are cut across the grain with a plug cutter that fits in a drill chuck. This can be used in a drill press or with an electric drill mounted on a stand. Otherwise, a piece of dowel rod could be used.

Sink the screw head about the same depth as the diameter of the plug. After that, drill for the screw in the usual way. Make sure the screw is fully tightened because you will not be able to get at it later. Let the plug stand high so that you can plane it level after the glue has set. If you use a plug cutter on a piece of the same wood used to make the furniture, then put the plug in with its grain the same way as that surrounding it. It will be inconspicuous in the finished work.

RIVETS

In building outdoor furniture, there are not many uses for rivets. Nevertheless, where wood is too thin to provide much grip for screw and bolts would be inappropriate, a rivet is the answer. Where parts of folding furniture have to pivot, a rivet will be preferable to a bolt for the wood parts to turn on.

For joining pieces of wood, the method or riveting is based on a technique used in boatbuilding. A nail is chosen that will go through and project a short distance (Fig. 3-3A). A small washer is driven over the nail. Ideally, it should have a hole that needs forcing on the nail. Therefore, a hollow punch is needed (Fig. 3-3B). The nail head is held by an iron block. Then the end of the nail is cut off a short distance above the washer (Fig. 3-3C). You must judge the amount left as enough for hammering on to the washer. Use a small *ball peen* or *cross peen* hammer to spread the end tightly on to the washer (Fig. 3-3D). Aim to form a rounded head, by hammering around the end, rather than on top only to get a broad flatter head.

In boatbuilding, that kind of riveting is done with copper nails; copper is a metal that spreads easily. Because copper resists weathering, it would be very suitable for joints in trellis or any furniture that has to be left outdoors.

For furniture pivots, the diameter needs to be ¼ inch or more. Therefore, nails cannot be used. Some rivets come with round (Fig. 3-3E) or countersunk heads (Fig. 3-3F) already made on one end. You can usually arrange for the manufactured head to come on the more prominent side; the head you make need not have such a good finish. Never have a rivet head directly on the wood. It will pull in. Always use washers. Try to avoid any slackness at the washer hole. If you try to spread a rivet head over a loose-fitting washer, much of your effort will go into spreading the neck of the rivet to the washer hole size.

Normally there will be washers each side and between the moving parts (Fig. 3-3G). Cut the end of the rivet to allow enough for forming the second head. There are tools called rivet *setts or snaps* that are like punches with hollowed ends to match rivet heads. If one of these is available, the manufactured head can be supported in it while the other end is formed (Fig. 3-3H). Otherwise a lead block is an alternative support that will hold the rivet against hammering without damaging the head. Hammer all round the projecting end to make the new head. For any riveting through wood, do not hammer too hard or you will bend the rivet in the wood. Try to make a head that matches the one on the other side. If you can hammer it approximately to shape you can round it by hitting a rivet snap on it (Fig. 3-3J).

BOLTS

Many parts of outdoor furniture are held together with bolts. If you use bolts with hexagonal or square heads and nuts to match, have washers under the heads and nuts (Fig. 3-4A). If the threaded part extends some way through the nut, it looks better if it is sawn off fairly close in. If the bolt is through moving parts, there is a risk of the nut working loose. The traditional way of locking it is with a locknut. This is a second thinner nut (Fig. 3-4B). Do not merely tighten one on top of the other, but hold the lower nut with a wrench while the other is tightened. Then turn the wrenches toward each other so that the nuts jam.

Locknuts can be used but there are alternatives. It is possible to get nuts with a friction arrangement built in; these are sometimes called *stiffnuts*. They lock well enough without further action (Fig. 3-4C). A simple method of securing is to hammer over the end of the bolt so that the nut cannot come off (Fig. 3-4D). There are epoxy glues intended for locking nuts to threads. The glue is smeared on and left to set. This secures the nut and bolt threads.

Coach bolts are popular for outdoor furniture. The shallow, round head does not project much and the square neck under it pulls into the wood to prevent the bolt from turning as the nut is tightened (Fig. 3-4E). For this and other bolts, drill a hole the same size as the bolt diameter. The square neck will pull in as the nut is tightened.

For some assemblies, you will want a bolt action, but the length will be more than a normal bolt will reach.

In that case, there can be a rod screwed at both ends so that nuts and washers can be used (Fig. 3-4F). If screwing tackle is available, such a rod can be made when required. Otherwise a craftsman could easily make up what you need.

NOTCHED JOINTS

In most outdoor furniture, the joints are not complicated and not many pieces require the careful fitted work of indoor furniture. Although securing parts that cross by resting surfaces against each other and fastening through

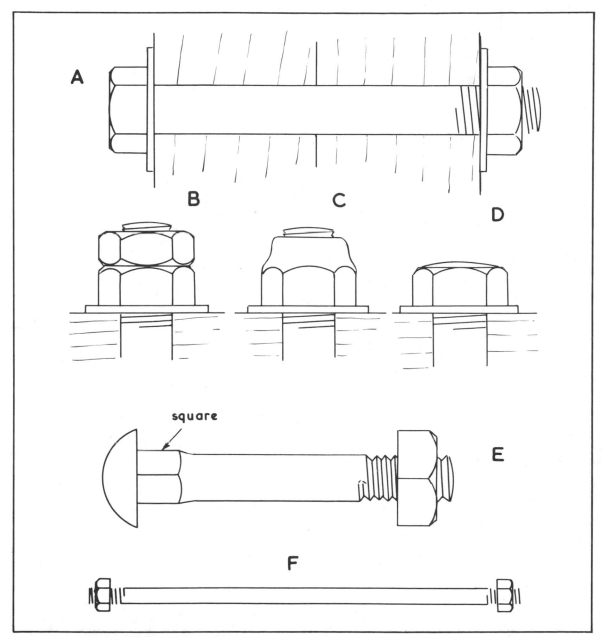

Fig. 3-4. Bolts through wood need washers (A). Nuts can be locked in several ways (B,C, and D). A square neck prevents a bolt turning (E). Threaded rod can be used instead of long bolts.

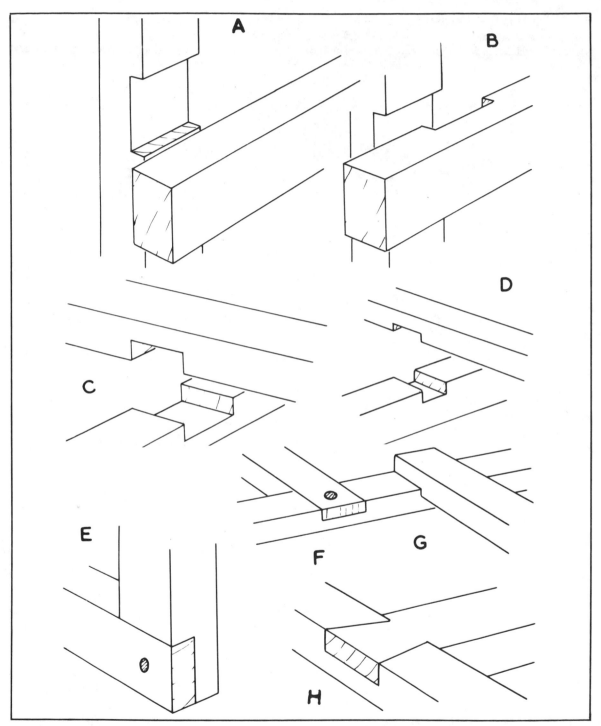

Fig. 3-5. Notching parts together prevents them from sliding over each other and can bring them to the same level. They can be secured by dowels or dovetailing.

will be all that is needed in many places, there are some situations where something more is required to resist movement of one piece over another. This often is done by *notching*.

If the load on one piece will tend to make it slip on another, a notch can resist this tendency much better than any other method of fastening. If a horizontal member will come under load—as it would if supporting a seat—a notch in a vertical or inclined member will hold it (Fig. 3-5A). The notch does not have to be very deep and there can be a bolt to hold the horizontal piece into it. If there is a possibility of movement in both directions, the other part can be notched as well (Fig. 3-5B). Notching deeply would weaken the wood. Notches should be no deeper than necessary (½ inch depth in 2-inch wood is the sort of cut to consider).

In some constructions, it is necessary that the crossing parts are brought to the same level. In such a case, half would have to be cut out of pieces of the same thickness (Fig. 3-5C). That is what a cabinetmaker calls a *halving* or *half-lap joint*. If the pieces that cross are not the same thickness, but one surface has to come to the same level, the joint is stronger if less is cut from the thinner piece (Fig. 3-5D).

Of course, all crossings are not square and joints have to be cut accordingly, but the principle is the same. Another place for halving joints is at corners. If two meeting members have to come in the same plane,

whether they meet squarely or not, half can be cut from each and one or more bolts or dowels can be put through (Fig. 3-5E). A similar joint can be arranged partway along one piece (Fig. 3-5F).

If the crossing parts do not have to be in the same plane, but notching is required to resist sliding, the notching need not be as deep (Fig. 3-5G). In that case, the resistance to sliding is in the direction square to the longer piece, but there is no resistance in the direction away from it (except that provided by bolts). If the joint is to resist pulling apart, the end can be cut as a dovetail (Fig. 3-5H). The slope of the dovetail does not have to be much; about 1 in 7 or 8 will do. For example, in the width of a 4-inch board, the taper could be ½ inch.

To do their job properly, notches should make a reasonably close fit on the other part. Mark the width from the other part. Don't rely on a measurement that it ought to be. Square down the edges and gauge the depth of cut on both sides (Fig. 3-6A). Saw on the waste side of the lines. To be certain of following the lines at both sides, tilt the saw while cutting from one side (Fig. 3-6B). Then go to the other side, saw back, and finally saw straight through. Chop away the waste with a chisel (Fig. 3-6C). If you cut diagonally in a wide notch, it will pare more cleanly. First slope up from both sides, until you have cut almost to the lines (Fig. 3-6D), and then chisel straight across. Ideally you will get the bottom of the notches exactly level.

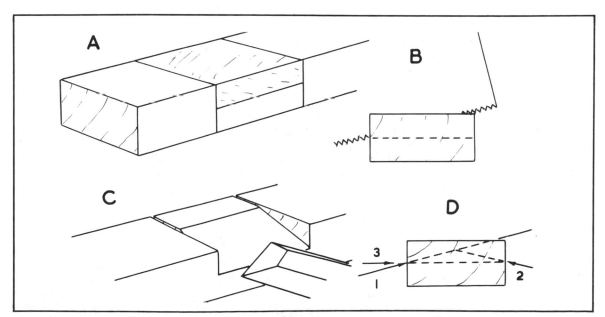

Fig. 3-6. Notches are marked out, and then cut by sawing and chiselling from opposite sides.

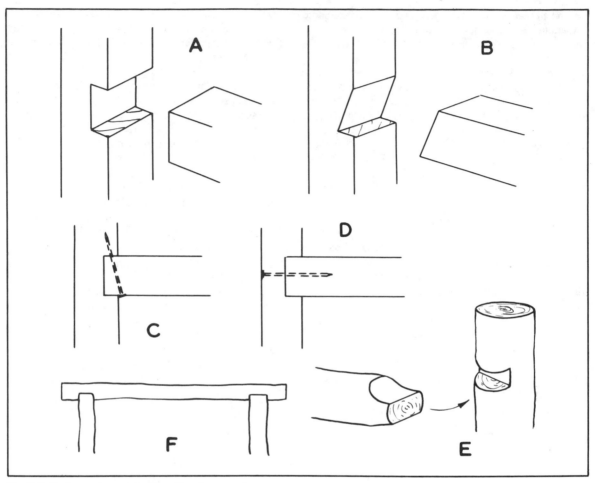

Fig. 3-7. Parts can be notched together in several ways.

Check with a straightedge laid across. Having the center high would interfere with getting the other part bedded down properly. Making it slightly hollow would be better. The best joint will go together with just a little help from a mallet or hammer. Put a piece of scrap wood over the joint and hit on that. This prevents marking the wood and spreads the force of each blow.

A less common notched joint in outdoor furniture is where the end of a piece goes into a notch. For indoor furniture, this would be used to hold a shelf into an upright and it is called a *housing* or *dado joint*. Outside, the parts are not usually as wide as a shelf, but there are occasions where the most convenient joint for a particular purpose is this form (Fig. 3-7A). The notch is made as previously described. Cut the end of the other piece squarely.

A simpler version can be used (Fig. 3-7B). This has the advantage of having all the cuts made by sawing. In both cases, there could be a nail or screw driven diagonally upward (Fig. 3-7C) as a stronger alternative to one driven into the end (Fig. 3-7D).

The parts do not necessarily have to be planed squared wood. Similar joints can be used with natural round rods (Fig. 3-7E). A top crossbar could be notched and nailed downward (Fig. 3-7F).

MORTISE AND TENON JOINTS

In just about all branches of woodwork, the most commonly used joints are mortise and tenons. They are not quite so common in outdoor furniture. A mortise is a rectangular hole into which the projecting tenon on the other part fits. If the parts are the same thickness, the

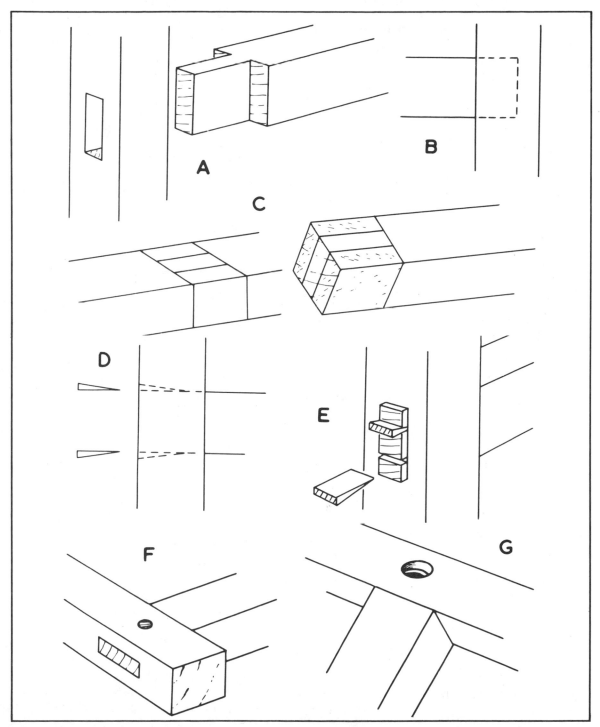

Fig. 3-8. Mortise and tenon joints are commonly used in furniture. They can go through or be stopped and the tenon is often one-third the thickness of the wood (A,B, and C). Wedges or dowels hold and pull the joints together (D through G).

tenon is about one-third of that (Fig. 3-8A). In the simplest form the tenon goes through. If it stops inside the mortised part, it is called a *stopped tenon* or *stub tenon* (Fig. 3-8B).

As with other joints, mark the sizes of one piece on the other directly from the wood, rather than by measurements, whenever possible. Mark all around the wood (Fig. 3-8C). For the finest work, cuts across the grain are marked with a knife and the width of tenon and mortise would be marked with a mortise gauge (which has two adjustable spurs). You could manage with an ordinary marking gauge or by measuring with a rule and pencil.

The shoulder and sides of the tenon can be sawn, preferably with a fine backsaw. Most of the waste in the mortise is best removed by drilling. Usually this is done partly from each side if it is a through mortise. Then the shape is trued with chisels, cutting across the grain first.

Although waterproof glue should be used, it is advisable to further strengthen mortise and tenon joints that are to remain outdoors exposed to all weathers. A mortise can be cut slightly wider so that wedges can be driven at the ends of the tenons (Fig. 3-8D). Probably a better way of wedging is to make saw cuts across the end of the tenon before assembly, and then drive in wedges (Fig.

3-8E). Glue the wedges and the joint. Then plane the ends level after the glue has set.

Tenons can also be held in by dowels (usually one at each joint). Drill across after assembly and drive a dowel through (Fig. 3-8F). It is often difficult to clamp the large structures involved in outdoor woodwork and there is a method of using dowels or pegs that will pull joints together. Before assembly, mark and drill through the mortise and tenon. Locate the hole in the tenon slightly closer to its shoulder so that when the joint goes together the holes do not quite match (Fig. 3-8G). Taper the end of an overlong piece of dowel rod or make a similar peg. Drive it in and the tenon will be drawn tighter.

There are many variations on the mortise and tenon joint that are mostly applicable to indoor furniture. Variations are given as they occur in projects described later in this book.

DOWELING

In the manufacture of indoor furniture, much use of dowel joints is made—usually in places where the older hand craftsman used mortise and tenon joints—because doweling lends itself better to quantity production. There are fewer uses of dowels in outdoor furniture, but there

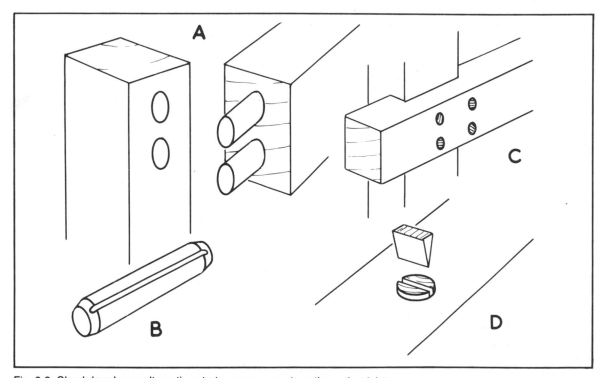

Fig. 3-9. Glued dowels are alternatives to tenons or can strengthen other joints.

are occasions when dowels make the best joint. Prepared dowel rods should be used. They are made of hardwood and they are available in many diameters. For most outdoor furniture, the dowels should be fairly thick. Usually they are near half the thickness of the wood being joined. The use of dowels in securing tenons is described earlier, but there are joints where dowels form the joints themselves.

The typical joint comes where dowels are used instead of tenons (Fig. 3-9A). In planning this sort of joint, the dowels should provide about the same glue area that would be given by a tenon. There should never be less than two dowels in any joint. How deep to take them depends on the wood. Approximately two to three times their diameter is about right, but they could go deeper into end grain.

Always allow for the holes being rather deeper than the dowels will go. A dowel acts like a piston and you must allow air and surplus glue to escape. Otherwise the wood will burst or crack. Taper the dowel ends and saw a groove lengthwise for the air to escape (Fig. 3-9B). Careful marking out is important. There are jigs available for getting holes to match, but these are mostly intended for wood of the smaller sections used in indoor furniture.

There are places in outdoor furniture where dowels can be used instead of screws or bolts, with holes drilled right through (Fig. 3-9C). There can be saw cuts across the ends, so wedges may be driven in, in the same way as suggested for tenons (Fig. 3-9D). Arrange the wedges across the direction of the grain in the surrounding wood.

CLAMPING

Although there will be uses for ordinary C-clamps, bar clamps or other versions of clamps to fit on pipes or the edges of boards, much of the assembly work in outdoor furniture is outside the reach of these devices.

Wedges have some uses. If you have a rigid board longer than the parts to be clamped, you can nail or screw on blocks. Then drive wedges at one or both ends to tighten the joints (Fig. 3-10A). A similar idea employs two long boards and bolts. Then the wedges are driven against the bolts (Fig. 3-10B).

Single wedges do not put on direct pressure and driving them will tend to move the parts. It is better to use pairs of similar wedges called *folding wedges* (Fig. 3-10C). By driving them alternately against each other, a parallel thrust is applied (Fig. 3-10D).

Instead of wood you can use rope. There can be a tight lashing around the work over scrap wood. Then you drive wedges under the wood (Fig. 3-10E).

Another way of using rope is as a *Spanish windlass*. Use one turn of thick rope or many turns of thinner rope with the ends tied together. Put a rod through the rope loops and twist (Fig. 3-10F). This puts a considerable load both on the parts being clamped and on the rope. Make sure the rope is strong enough. Stop the rod against an adjacent part (Fig. 3-10G) or by tying it to the turns (Fig. 3-10H) to keep on the pressure.

The Spanish windlass could go around the four sides of an assembly, such as a seat, as well as be used across a flat frame. Several clamping arrangements might have to be used together to get all parts tight. At the same time, you will have to watch squareness (as described in the following section).

SQUARING

Absolute squareness of all parts of a piece of outdoor furniture might not seem so important as when indoor furniture is being assembled, but it is surprising how lack of truth in some part will become rather obvious. It is worthwhile checking squareness of most things as they are assembled. If possible, work on a flat floor even if the furniture will eventually be used on uneven ground. You can then check that such things as seats and tabletops are parallel with the floor when the legs are standing level. In the final situation, you will know that leveling will bring these important parts true. Without the initial test, you do not have a basis of comparison.

A spirit level is a useful tool. Try it in all directions on a tabletop or anything else that should be level. If it seems to show a persistant error, turn it end for end in case the fault is in the level. The longer the level, the more accurate your result. This is particularly true if you are dealing with a surface that is something less than flat. If you use a small level, put it on a straightedge that will bridge over unevenness.

Where possible, check squareness with a try square; there is a limit because of its size. If you try to extend the blade of a 12-inch try square with a straightedge, the trouble is that a negligible error at its tip becomes a large one at 48 inches, for instance. Corners of sheets of plywood and other manufactured boards can be assumed to be square and you can use one of these sheets to check squareness within its limits of size.

Most assemblies are rectangular. If they are not rectangular they are usually symmetrical. In this case, it is easier to check squareness by comparing diagonals. If you have a four-sided frame that should be square, measure corner to corner or between matching points (Fig. 3-11A). When the frame is square, these measurements

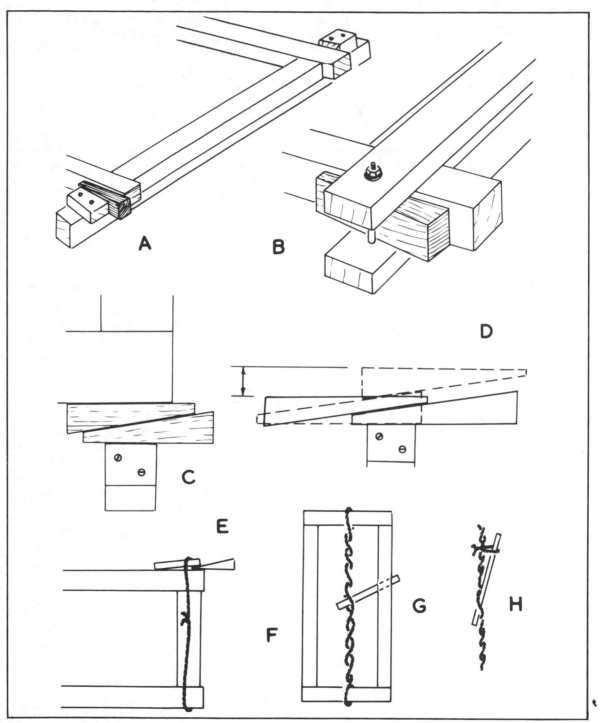

Fig. 3-10. Wedges can provide considerable clamping pressure (A through E). A Spanish windlass made from rope will also serve as a clamp (F, G and H).

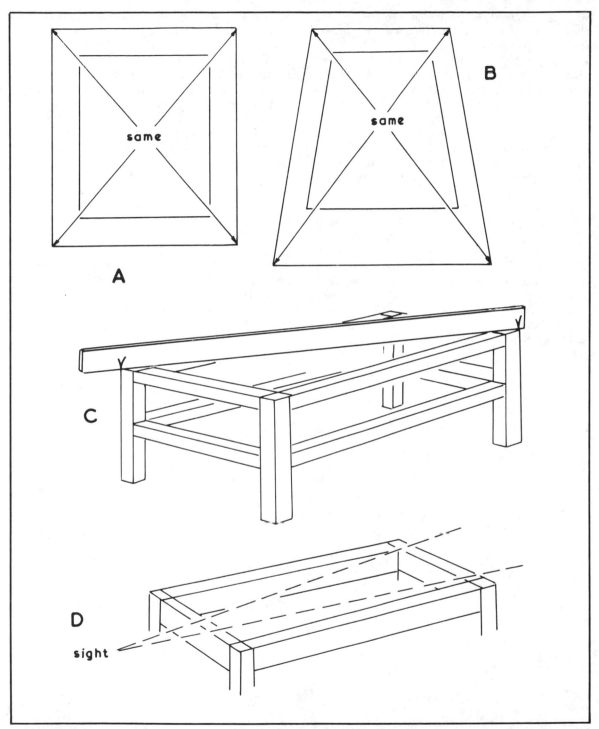

Fig. 3-11. Squareness or symmetry can be checked by comparing diagonals (A, B, and C). Twisting or winding can be checked by sighting across.

will be the same. This also applies to a symmetrical shape. It is true about its centerline when diagonals are the same (Fig. 3-11B).

You can measure diagonally with an expanding rule or tape measure, but it is safer to mark a board. Make *peck marks* on the edge (Fig. 3-11C) and compare the two directions. In this way, you avoid the possible error of misreading rule divisions or confusing them.

In many assemblies, there are opposite parts that have to match, usually as a pair. Normally, it is best to make one part and check its accuracy. Then true the other part by putting it over it in the correct relative position (inside to inside). When you have an assembly to make up, it is nearly always best to take two opposite sides with more parts than the other way. Get them together and matching before bringing in the parts the other way.

As you progress with assembly, check diagonals as often as the opportunity occurs. For instance, you make up two end leg assemblies for a table and then you have to add a top built up of strips. Check the diagonals of the top assembly as it is added. Then check that the legs are perpendicular to the top by measuring from their feet diagonally to the corners of the top at each side. You will probably be adding bracing to hold the legs, but do not secure any brace until you have checked the squareness of whatever it is to hold.

For a chair, you can make up opposite sides with arms and seat rails. You know that they match, but as you join them with crosswise parts, check diagonals across the back legs and the front legs. Finally, check squareness as viewed from above. Usually this can be done by measuring diagonals across the seat. Even then, stand back and look for twists that are not apparent when squaring.

Twists can usually be seen by viewing the assembly from a distance and in several directions. It does help to view across things that should be parallel. If you sight one thing across its partner opposite (Fig. 3-11D), any variation will be obvious. This also applies when looking through a table or chair to see if the legs match. If the assembly is glued, do all this checking before the glue has started to set. Then you can usually pull the parts true. If they still try to spring to the incorrect positions, you put a weight on top or clamp diagonally in the direction that will pull the shape right. You will have to overcorrect slightly to allow for springing back.

Chapter 4

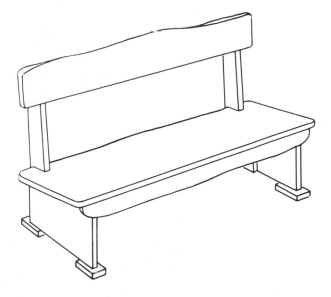

Simple Seats

S OMETHING TO SIT ON IS THE MOST NEEDED TYPE of outdoor furniture. It does not necessarily have to be anything elaborate. There are places and circumstances where a top firmly supported at the right height is all that is needed. This is particularly so in the natural surroundings of trees, bushes, and paths where there is a need for an occasional place to rest. The sort of chair or lounger that would be right on a patio or in a formal garden would not look right and particularly so if it had brightly colored cushions.

There are other situations where simple seating is all that is required. Examples are in a play area or where the seats are likely to get rough use or suffer from neglect. You can leave a simple bench or stool out in all types of weather. Something more elaborate and valuable would have to be put under cover or taken indoors when out of use.

From the practical point of view, simple seating is easier to make. The structures are rather basic. The joints are simple. Usually there does not have to be much regard for precision. Many simple seats can be made with only a few simple tools.

Many simple seats can be made with wood that might not be suitable for anything more advanced nor for making indoor furniture. There is much wood that is sound and durable, but it is normally discarded when converting lumber to standard-size boards. This can be obtained inexpensively or for free. Some of it has the waney edges of the outside of the tree where it has been cut right through the log. This can be regarded as a design feature for a seat to be positioned among natural surroundings.

RUSTIC BENCH

A free-standing bench seat can be made in a size to suit its surroundings and the available materials. It uses wood in as near its natural state as needs permit. The bench can be positioned in a field or woodland where it will match surroundings. Almost any wood can be used, but for the strongest and longest-lasting seat it should be a hardwood free from large knots. If softwood is used, sections should be thicker and a very long life should not be expected. Treating the wood with a preservative will lengthen life. If the wood has been recently felled, sap should be allowed to dry before preservative is applied.

When a log is prepared for cutting into boards, it is

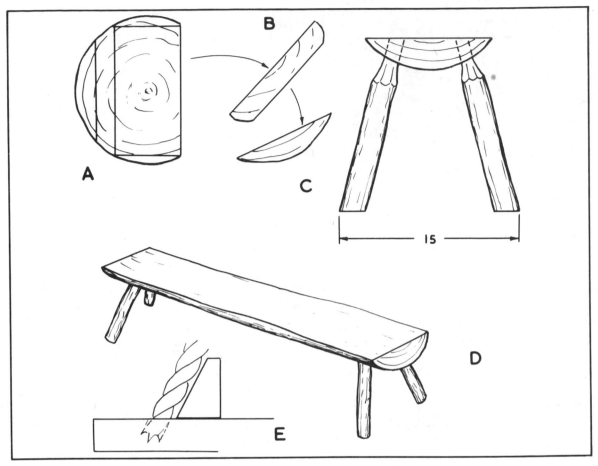

Fig. 4-1. Parts of logs and branches can be made into stools and benches.

first cut to approximately square section (Fig. 4-1A). The curved pieces removed are usually discarded, but many of them are suitable for seat tops. This will apply to the first board cut as well if it has a wandering waney edge. This would make it uneconomical to convert to a parallel board (Fig. 4-1B). Both of these offcuts can be suitable as bench tops.

Remove any bark that remains. The traditional tool for doing this is called a *spud*. It was a long-handled tool—something like a broad chisel—with a thin, but not sharp, cutting edge. You can manage with an ax or a large chisel. If bark is left, it harbors insects and it will trap water that might introduce rot. It could also mark clothing. Except for removing bark, the waney edge should be left. Sharp edges or exceptionally projecting parts should be leveled.

The top surface should be made reasonably flat, but the perfection of surface required for indoor furniture is unnecessary. A coarsely set plane, used diagonally to the grain, will usually level unseasoned wood. Remove any sharpness around the edges, but otherwise leave the natural appearance.

The legs are also natural pieces of wood that are cut from poles. Their size depends on the overall sizes of the bench, but a diameter of about 2 inches should suit most constructions. Remove any bark. The knots left by small branches can be leveled, but do not use pieces with large knots. Have the legs too long at this stage, and bring them to matching lengths after assembly.

The legs fit into holes in the top. The size of holes will depend on available equipment, but they should be at least 1 inch and preferably up to 1½ inches. How you arrange the holes depends on the shape of the board section. If it is a parallel thickness, you can mark out a regular arrangement. If you are dealing with an irregular shape, such as the outside curved section, the holes do not have to be arranged squarely or in line. Aim to spread the feet at least as wide as the board. If it is narrower, let them be about 15 inches apart on the ground (Fig. 4-1C) when you have cut them to the correct height. At the ends of the bench, the feet should not be very far in from the end of the seat. Otherwise someone sitting on the end could tip the bench (Fig. 4-1D).

Drill from the top diagonally outward. You might be able to estimate the angle—particularly as each leg can slope differently on an odd-shaped piece—or you could cut a scrap-wood template as a guide (Fig. 4-1E). If the grain breaks out as the drill goes through the underside, that should not matter.

Taper the end of each leg to drive into its hole (Fig. 4-2A). It will be stronger if you do this gradually on a long slope than if you have a more abrupt change of section. The traditional way of doing this is to use a draw knife (Fig. 4-2B), while the wood is held diagonally in a vise, but you can get a similar effect with a broad chisel used with its bevel downward. It will help to draw a circle of the right size on the end. Have a piece of scrap wood with a hole of the right size drilled in it to slide over the end so that you can see that it is down to size for a sufficient length to go through the seat. There is no need for absolute precision, but aim to get a reasonable drive fit.

Make a saw cut in the end to take a wedge. Assemble the joint with the cut across the seat grain. Let the leg end project slightly. Then drive in the wedge (Fig. 4-2C). You will have to decide if you want to use glue. If you do use glue, it must be a waterproof type (preferably a boat-building grade). If you know the wood is still green or only partly seasoned, it is best to assemble each joint dry. Wedging will tighten it and the shrinkage that occurs as the wood dries should further tighten it. Wood that is still

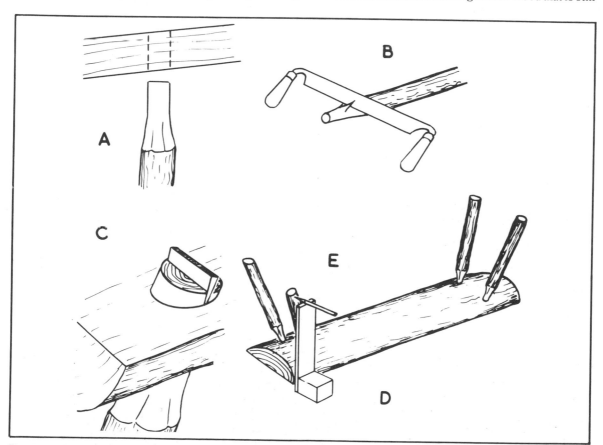

Fig. 4-2. Tapered ends can be driven into holes and wedged, then legs cut to length.

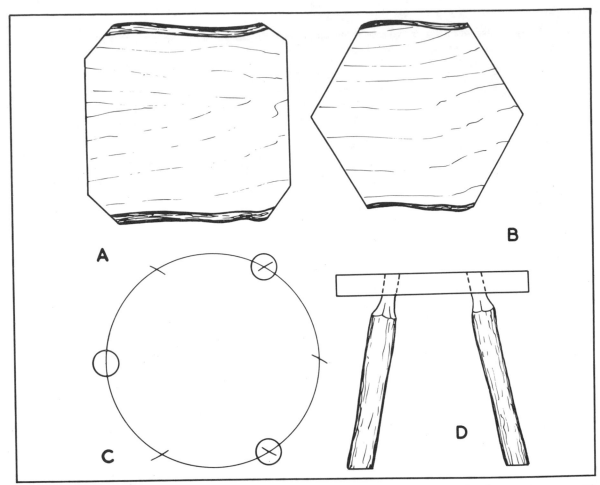

Fig. 4-3. Waney-edged wood can have its ends shaped to make a stool. Three legs stand better than four on uneven ground. Legs should be splayed at least to the limits of the top.

wet with sap does not bond well with any glue.

With all four legs in place and their tops planed level, invert the bench so you can mark the leg lengths. Make a simple gauge with a strip of the right height attached to a base block (Fig. 4-2D). Use this with a pencil on the end to mark as far round each leg as you can (Fig. 4-2E) as a guide to sawing off. Take off any raggedness from the end and bevel all around so the risk of splitting, if the bench is dragged over concrete or stones, is reduced. That completes the bench.

RUSTIC STOOL

A long bench will find its own level when standing on four feet, but if you bring the legs closer together it gets increasingly difficult to make them stand level if the ground is uneven. Because of this stools and small seats were once made with three legs. A tripod arrangement will stand without wobbling on any surface. In the old days of earth floors in the home, and particularly in the milking shed, three-legged stools were standard. Stools made in this way will produce individual seats to match the rustic bench.

The top can be a piece of waney edged wood that is cut to about the same length as its width and with the corners trimmed off (Fig. 4-3A). You could cut the ends at two angles so that the final shape is approximately hexagonal (Fig. 4-3B). This would match the three-legged arrangement.

The arrangement of holes for the legs does not have to be equally spaced, but they should not be too far out.

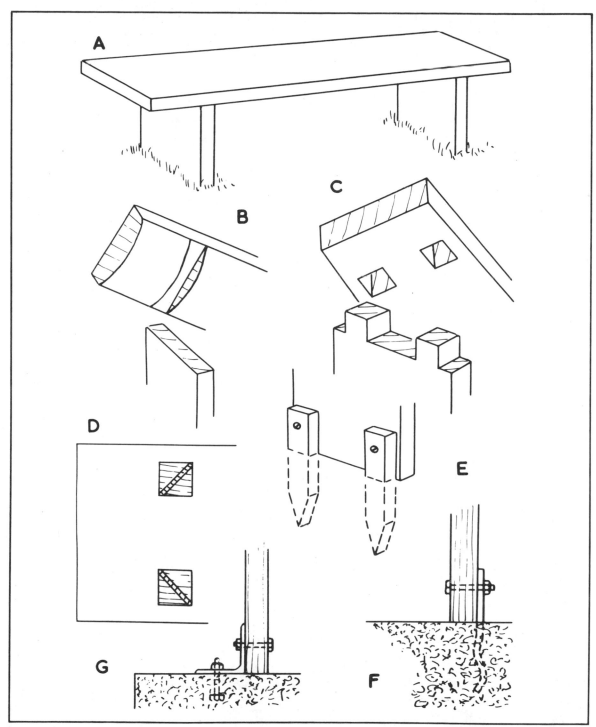

Fig. 4-4. Bench ends can enter the ground (A). Their tops can be notched (B) or tenoned (C and D). Feet can be pegged or bolted down (E, F, and G).

What is more important is reasonably equal spacing on the ground. If you are dealing with an awkwardly shaped top, you might have to alter the angle of a leg to fit it into the top shape, yet bring it to part of a regular pattern at the floor. A top in its natural form will be more interesting than a piece of wood that fits into a symmetrical shape.

The way to get even spacing is to draw a circle and step off the radius around the circumference. It will go six times so legs come at alternate marks (Fig. 4-3C). Fit and level the legs in the same way as for the bench. Try to finish with the top level and the bottoms of the legs fairly close to the area covered by the top (Fig. 4-3D) for reasonable stability if the user leans or tries to tilt his seat.

FIXED BENCH

Alongside woodland paths there might be a need for simple seats that are secured to the ground. A simple bench top can have vertical end legs that are held down in some way (Fig. 4-4A). The top should be hardwood about 2 inches thick. It can have waney edges or can be trimmed parallel. Its top should be level and reasonably smooth, but if the underside is rough that does not matter. It needs no special preparation except for the removal of sharp edges all round.

One way of making the bench is to let the legs into the ground—by digging holes and compacting the soil firmly—then the tops of the legs are cut level and the seat is nailed on. A firmer support can be obtained from using concrete instead of compacted soil around the legs. There is a snag to either arrangement. Buried wood will rot and sometimes quite rapidly. Some woods, such as oak, will withstand burial longer, and you can soak the wood in preservative first, but it is better to keep the wood above ground.

To do that, the bench is made as an above-ground assembly and held down in some way. The simplest assembly is nailed. If the underside of the top is uneven, make a groove across parallel with the top surface for the leg to fit into (Fig. 4-4B). Usually the leg is the same thickness as the top, but if you have thicker wood it can be used as it is. Drill the top for the nails to reduce the risk of splitting. The hole should be the same size as its nail or only very slightly smaller. Because you will be driving into end grain in the legs, they need not be drilled. Ideally, use nails protected by galvanizing or other means. Plain iron nails should provide a reasonable life.

A better way is to tenon the legs into the top (Fig. 4-4C). Two square tenons should be enough unless it is a very wide seat. Remove the waste from the mortises by drilling and chopping out with a chisel. Make the tenons slightly too long. Cut them for wedges that can come across the grain or might be arranged diagonally (Fig. 4-4D). As with the rustic bench, the joints can be assembled dry. This is particularly so if you are working with green wood. Or you can use a waterproof glue.

There are many ways of attaching the legs to the ground. If the ground is level and suitable for driving pegs into it, use oak or other hardwood pieces driven in as far as possible. Then screw or bolt through (Fig. 4-4E). If these rot after several years, you can replace them. You will still have the bench intact.

It might be better to put down a concrete base. You might want to concrete over the area where users' feet will come. It might be sufficient to just have concrete blocks under the bench legs.

Strips of metal can be let into the concrete with holes for screws into the wood (Fig. 4-4F). Bend the metal or chop teeth into it with a cold chisel to help it hold in the concrete. Alternatively, put pieces of angle iron on top. These are held down with the special bolts intended for concrete work or with ordinary bolts buried in the concrete (Fig. 4-4G). In both cases, have holes ready for screws driven into the bench legs.

If the bench is made of hardwood, it will probably look best if untreated and left to weather to a natural appearance. The bench could be made of softwood, but then it would be better to treat it with preservative and paint it. Dark green is the usual paint color for a natural environment. Periodic repainting would be necessary to protect the wood.

SLAB BENCH

A free-standing seat made from quite thick wood will be fairly heavy, but that could be an advantage if it is to spend most of the summer outside standing on concrete, wood, or level ground. The weight makes for steadiness and discourages users from tipping the seat or moving it from the place you prefer to leave it.

For stability, it is better to let the legs slope out slightly to give a broad base (Fig. 4-5A) with the minimum risk of tipping. If the wood is at least 2 inches thick, mortise and tenon joints between the parts should give all the strength needed—without additional bracing.

Set out one end, showing the angle the leg is to come (Fig. 4-5B), and arrange its foot almost as far as the overhanging top. Set an adjustable bevel to the angle and use it for marking out the joint and the foot of each leg (Fig. 4-5C). Mark out the outline of each leg, but cut the joints before cutting the outsides to shape. The tenons

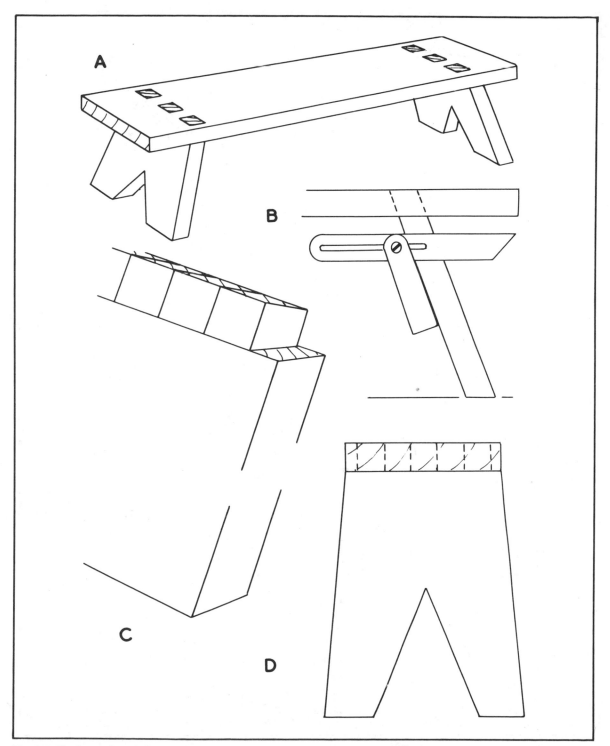

Fig. 4-5. Sloping and cut legs provide stability.

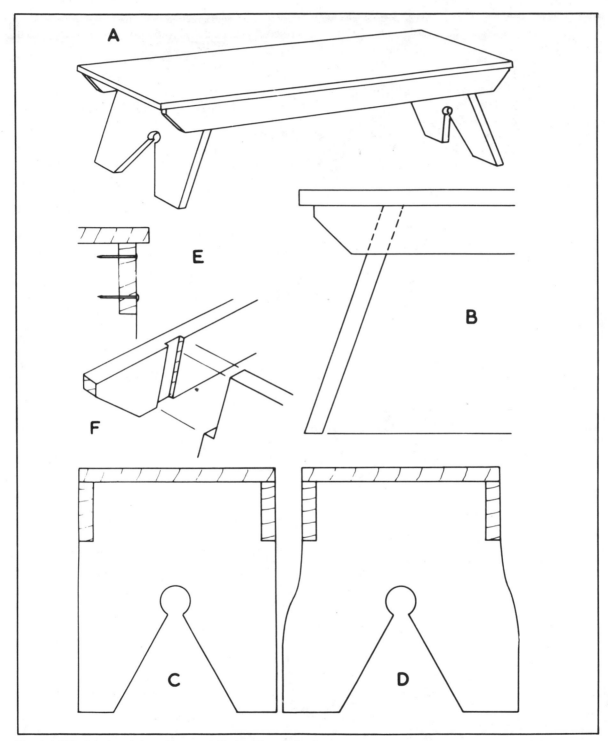

Fig. 4-6. This light bench has sides to strengthen the sloping legs.

and the spaces between them should be about the same, but you will have to adjust this according to the width of wood you are using.

Keep the tenons and mortises on both sides of the wood. Watch the lines on both sides when cutting the tenons. Drill out some of the waste from the mortises, but chop to the outlines from both sides with a chisel. Use the adjustable bevel as a guide to the angle you hold the chisel and saw.

Cut the tapers on the sides of the legs and the V out of the bottom (Fig. 4-5D). Remove sharpness before assembly. Wedge the tenons in the usual way. Check how the bench stands on a level surface. Almost certainly you will have to plane the feet to remove wobble, but try moving the bench and turning it round before being satisfied that you have it right.

LIGHT BENCH

If you want a bench seat that is not too heavy for moving about, the wood will have to be thinner than in the slab bench. That means you will have to use additional bracing because joints between the top and legs alone cannot be trusted. This bench is intended to be made of ¾-inch or ⅞-inch prepared wood. If well made and given a varnished or painted finish, it will have uses indoors as well as outside.

Length and width should be according to your needs (Fig. 4-6A), but 9 inches is about the minimum satisfactory width. The bench can be as short as 18 inches for a one-person stool or up to perhaps 84 inches or even longer with thicker wood. Height should be between 15 inches and 18 inches.

Draw an end to show the angle (Fig. 4-6B). The legs could be parallel (Fig. 4-6C) or broadened to increase stability (Fig. 4-6D), particularly if the top is narrow.

The rails under the top are notched into the legs. In the simplest construction, the joints there are directly nailed (Fig. 4-6E). But it would be better to notch the rails slightly (Fig. 4-6F) and use glue and screws. Do not cut more than ¼ of an inch out of the rail and trim the leg edge accordingly.

The legs have holes drilled for the saw to cut into. Do all the work you have to on the legs, including removing sharp edges, before assembly. Prepare the rails similarly, including well-rounding the lower edges, where the hands will grip to move the bench. Assemble

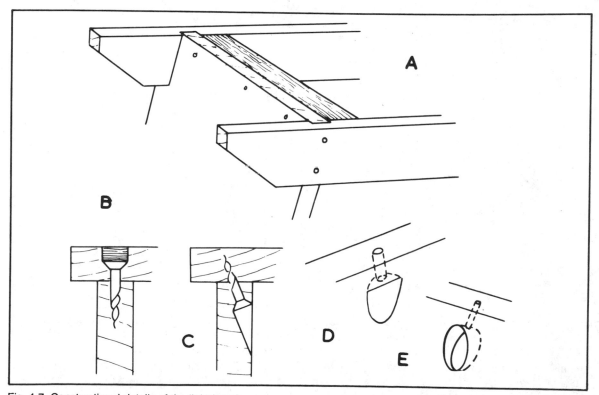

Fig. 4-7. Constructional details of the light bench.

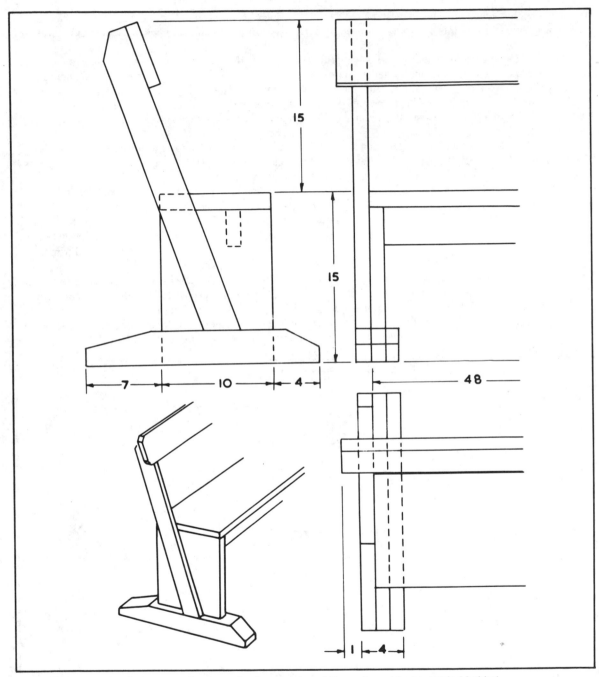

Fig. 4-8. A bench of nailed construction has a back supported at the ends and feet extended behind.

the rails to the legs with glue and screws. Bevel strips to go between the rails inside the leg tops (Fig. 4-7A). Glue and screw them in place.

Prepare the seat by rounding its top and bottom edges all round. The simplest way to fit it is with nails driven downward all round. For the simplest construction of a bench that is not regarded as very important, that would be satisfactory.

A better way is to screw downward. The screw heads could finish level with the surface, but it would be better to counterbore the screws and fill the holes with wood plugs (Fig. 4-7B). If you do not want screws or plugs to be visible on top, it is possible to do all screwing from below. At the legs, there can be several screws up through the crosswise strips. Along the rails, there can be pocket screws driven from inside the rails (Fig. 4-7C).

Chop the recesses with a chisel and drill so that the holes come about on the center of the top edge (Fig. 4-7D). Another way of making a recess is to drill diagonally with a large bit (Fig. 4-7E). Be careful that its point does not go through. Besides screwing, by whatever method, use waterproof glue in all joints.

NAILED BENCH WITH BACK

If a plain bench is to have a back, the simplest way to arrange it is to have the bench ends and top level so that the back support can go directly on the end without any need for notching or other shaping.

The bench shown in Fig. 4-8 is intended to be made from wood that finishes about 1¼ inches thick. Some of it could be waney edged. The top or both edges of the back could retain their natural shape. So could the edges of the ends and the underside of the seat rail. The front edge of the seat should be straight and rounded-in section.

The sizes shown suit a seat for two or three. See Table 4-1. The ends could be attached to the ground (as described for earlier benches). As shown here, the seat is intended to be free-standing with a broad enough base to keep it steady in normal use. It would be possible to make the bench with cut and glued joints, but here it is shown nailed. This seems more appropriate to a seat that is to have a natural look without a high finish.

Nails 3 inches long should suit most parts if made in hardwood, but you will need longer nails if you are using soft wood or driving into end grain. Drill holes in the top piece of wood almost as large as the nail diameter in order to reduce the risk of splitting. In most places the nail can

Table 4-1. Materials List for Nailed Bench with Back.

1 seat	10	× 48	× 1¼
1 seat rail	3	× 48	× 1¼
2 ends	10	× 15	× 1¼
4 feet	3	× 22	× 1¼
4 feet fillers	3	× 8	× 1¼
1 back	6	× 54	× 1¼
2 back supports	3	× 30	× 1¼

force its way into the bottom piece. Near an edge it is wise to drill an undersize hole at least part of the distance the nail will go.

Prepare the seat and its rail (Fig. 4-9A). Nail them together with the seat overhanging the rail enough to fit on the ends. Cut the ends squarely and nail on the seat (Fig. 4-9B). This gives the basic form to which other parts are added.

The feet (Fig. 4-9C) could be added before or after joining the ends to the seat. Make one long piece and use it as a pattern for marking the other feet parts. The projecting parts are tapered to half depth. Then matching filling pieces (Fig. 4-9D) go between to make up the thickness. The basic bench is shown with the bottom flat, but if it is to stand on uneven ground it would be better cut back to the width of the end so as to form feet (Fig. 4-9E). Use waterproof glue and nails driven from both sides in the assembly of the feet. Trim the ends and bottom edges after the glue has set.

The slope of the back is probably best found by experiment. You can then find what angle of the back board seems most comfortable on the particular seat. As shown in Fig. 4-8, the bottom of a back support is about central over the foot and it slopes to come almost completely on the end of the seat. A support does not have to go right down an end, but it looks neater if it is cut to go against its foot.

Attach the back supports to the ends (Fig. 4-9E), then nail on the back to overhang equally each end (Fig. 4-9F). Check squareness during assembly. The precision required for indoor furniture is unnecessary, but great variations from squareness will spoil appearance. Your final chance of pulling the seat square comes when attaching the back.

There is usually no need to sink nails and cover them with stopping in this sort of construction. You must be careful that there are no projecting heads on which clothing could be snagged. If you are using wood that has not been fully seasoned, allow for it to shrink in thickness as it dries out. Punch the nail heads slightly below the surface so that they will not be left above the surface if the wood gets thinner. If it is possible to visit the bench in six months time, go over it with a hammer and punch to tighten all nails. Unseasoned wood is best left untreated. Paint or varnish on it would tend to peel and come away. Store the wood up to one year if you eventually want to paint it.

SLAB BENCH WITH BACK

In a rural setting, a bench made from slabs cut across the

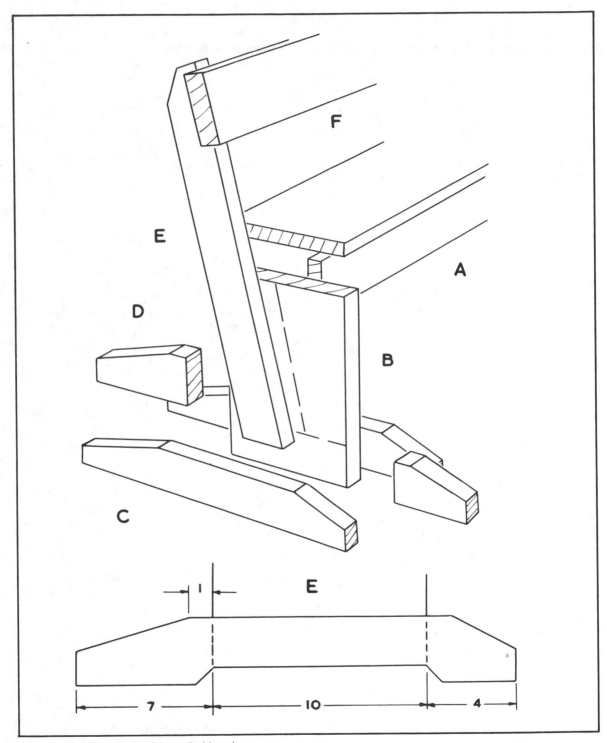

Fig. 4-9. Assembly details of the nailed bench.

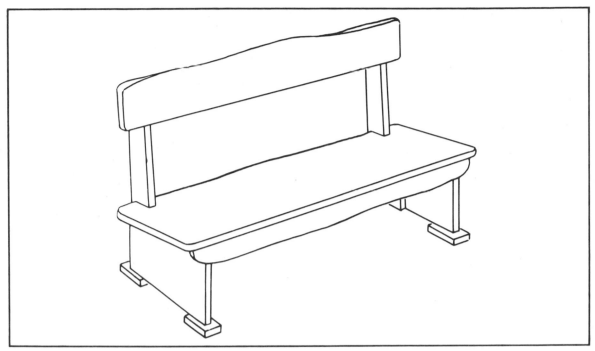

Fig. 4-10. A bench made from slabs with waney edges.

log to leave waney edges will often look better than one made from parallel plain boards. There have to be straight edges in some places, but elsewhere the natural curving edge helps the bench to match its surroundings.

Comfort comes from sloping the seat backward with the back angled to match. The slope also makes the seat shed rainwater easily. The suggested design is shown (Fig. 4-10). The sizes shown in Table 4-2 are for a bench 48 inches long (Fig. 4-11), but other lengths are possible. In any case, construction might have to be adapted to suit available wood.

For strength, the seat supports are made with the grain across. The back supports have their grain crossing them so they provide mutual support and resistance to splitting. The seat notches round the back supports and is kept straight by two rails underneath.

It will help if you draw an end view full size (Fig. 4-12) taking into account the available materials. Get the slope of the seat on a pattern of 2-inch squares and draw in the other parts to match it.

Make the seat supports (Fig. 4-13A) with their grain across and nail on strips to the front edges after notching them to take the front rail (Fig. 4-13B). The front rail will have a waney edge downward so that the notches at each end will not be the same. At this stage, you can cut the

notches only part way down the front. Trim them during assembly when you are putting in the rail.

The back supports (Fig. 4-13C) are cut to match the seat slope and overlap the seat supports. Rear edges finish about 1 inch behind the bottoms of the seat supports. At the top, notch the edges to take the back (Fig. 4-13D). Although the back can have an upward waney edge, its lower edge should be straight so the notches can be cut completely. Variations in back width will be upward.

Assemble the ends with the back supports inside the seat supports. Be careful to make a pair of them. You

Table 4-2. Materials List for Slab Bench with Back.

2 ends	14	× 15	× 1¼
2 end fronts	1	× 15	× 1¼
2 back supports	7	× 30	× 1¼
4 feet	2½ ×	5	× 1¼
1 rail	4	× 42	× 1¼
1 rail	4	× 49	× 1¼
1 seat	16	× 49	× 1¼
1 back	6	× 49	× 1¼

(No allowance for waney edges)

53

could screw through from opposite sides or use large nails driven through and clenched. The strongest joints will be bolted. Attaching four ¼-inch bolts through each overlap should be enough. Have washers under the nuts. If the wood shrinks as it dries out, you will be able to tighten the nuts. Coach bolts are a good choice. If you use ordinary bolts, put washers under the heads as well. It helps to have oversize washers to reduce the tendency to pull into the wood.

The feet (Fig. 4-13E) are simple blocks nailed or screwed underneath. Let them extend about 1 inch back and front. If the bench is likely to be dragged about, take

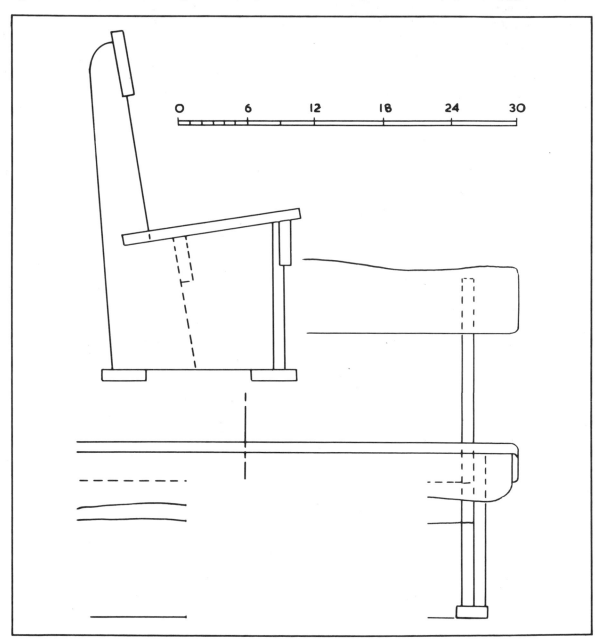

Fig. 4-11. Suggested sizes for a slab bench.

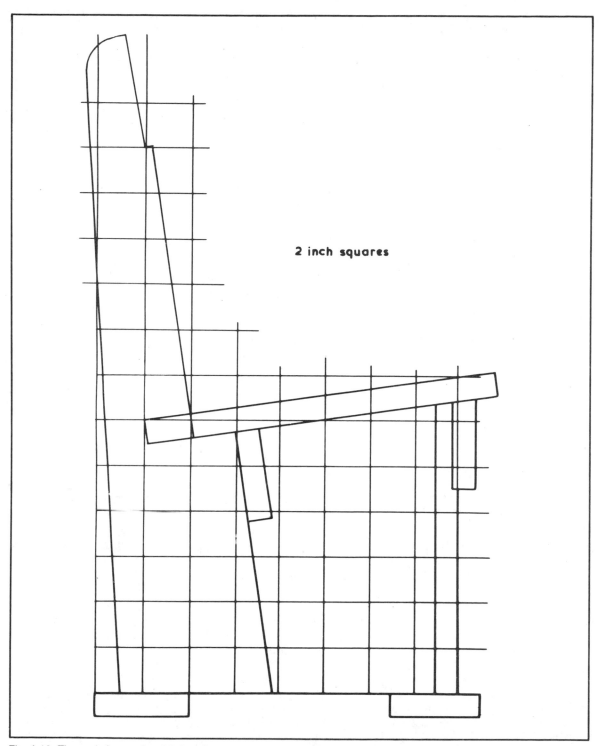

2 inch squares

Fig. 4-12. The end shape of a slab bench.

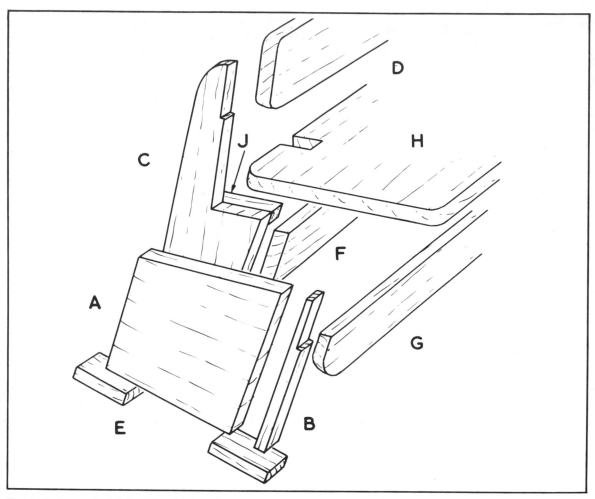

Fig. 4-13. Assembly details of the slab bench.

the sharpness off edges and corners to prevent splintering on stony ground.

The inner seat rail (Fig. 4-13F) needs a straight top edge and square ends. It is this rail that decides the bench length and settles its squareness. Its lower edge can be waney or straight. Nail or screw it to the inner edges of the back supports. While you are doing this, check that the two ends stand upright when on a level floor.

Make the front rail so that it projects about 3 inches past each end (Fig. 4-13G). Its top edge needs to be straight, but it must be beveled to suit the seat angle. Round the extending ends and take off any sharpness of the waney edge so that a hand put under the bench will not get scratched. Trim the notches to suit and nail or screw on the rail.

The seat (Fig. 4-13H) should have a straight front edge, but it does not matter if the rear edge is straight or waney. Mark its length to be slightly more than the front rail. Hold the seat against the assembly to mark the positions of the notches around the back supports. Cut them to make a close fit. When you assemble the piece, put small strips (Fig. 4-13J) inside the angles to give support to the overlaps. Round the front edge and outer corners of the seat before the final fitting.

You could nail or screw the seat on, with the heads level, but it is better to counterbore screws and glue plugs over them to give a neat top finish. Hold the seat down with screws at about 2 inch intervals across the ends. They can be spread to about 6 inches spacing along the rails.

The back can be the width you like, but it looks best if the waney top edge is higher near the center. Make it the same length as the seat. Round ends and exposed edges. Attach it to its supports the same way as the seat.

This type of bench can be made more attractive by having something carved at the center of the back. It might just be the date cut in with a knife. There could be a motif formed from the initials of the maker or owner. It might be the badge of an organization. Whatever is done should be simple and bold. Natural wood, probably not fully seasoned at the time of carving, does not accept fine detail carving without the risk of breaking out.

Chapter 5

Chairs

A GREAT VARIETY OF CHAIRS CAN BE MADE FOR outdoor use. Some simple chairs are described in Chapter 4 and seats for more than one person are described in other chapters. The rougher and more rustic seats are usually large enough for two or more people. Building chairs includes rather more advanced woodworking techniques using cut and glued joints instead of simple nailed construction. Most chairs for outdoor use in the garden or yard are made from planed and seasoned wood with mortise and tenon joints in many, if not all, meeting places between parts.

Chairs are often made to match tables, using generally similar layouts and construction, so there is a balanced appearance when several chairs are grouped round a table. Some seats for more than one person can be made to match as well. It is worthwhile assessing probable needs and keeping in mind a general pattern even if you are only making one chair at first.

If chairs are made from prepared wood, stock sizes of sections can be less than specified due to the quoted size being before machine planing. You will find that 2 × 2 inches quoted is actually not much more than 1¾ inches finished. That does not matter providing you allow for it

when marking out. Where joints have to be cut, it is always advisable to mark from the actual pieces of wood, rather than rely on measurements for widths of cuts.

In better quality chairs, any nails ought to be galvanized or otherwise protected from corrosion. Iron screws should also be protected and they can be counterbored, where the wood is thick enough, so that plugs can be glued over their heads. Modern waterproof glue, particularly the type intended for boatbuilding, will help to make strong weatherproof chairs.

SIDE CHAIR

The outdoor side chair has a normal sitting height (Figs. 5-1 and 5-2) for use with a table outside. With cushions it provides a certain amount of relaxation, but not as much as those chairs shaped for lounging. It is more for working at a table or for having outdoor meals.

The seat is made of slats (Fig. 5-2A) and the back is similar (Fig. 5-2B). Firm attachments of the slats gives stiffness to the chair. The other parts have mortise and tenon joints (Fig. 5-3A). There is no need to take the tenons right through. They will be strong enough if they

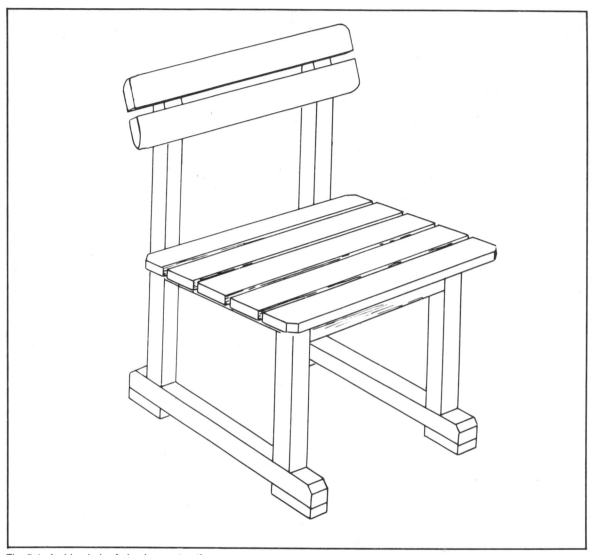

Fig. 5-1. A side chair of simple construction.

go in about two-thirds of the thickness and are one-third of the thickness in width.

Make a full-size drawing of a side view (Fig. 5-3B) to get the sizes of parts. Mark out the pairs of legs together. The bottoms of the legs tenon into the bottom rails. The back of the seat is 1 inch lower than the front. Set an adjustable bevel to this angle and use it for marking out the joints made by the seat rails.

Cut the tops of the rear legs to give the back slats a slope (Fig. 5-3C). Some corners are shown cut off. For neatness they should all be marked the same (Fig. 5-3D).

The chair might stand directly on the bottom rails, but any unevenness in the ground would cause it to wobble. To reduce this risk, feet can be put underneath (Fig. 5-2C). Assemble the two chair sides over the full-size drawing and check that they match each other. Clean off surplus glue and level the surfaces, if necessary, before going on to complete assembly.

Clamp the front rail tight and check its squareness with the legs. At the same time, nail or screw on the seat slats checking that the sides are kept parallel. Space the slats evenly and cut off the front corners (Fig. 5-2D).

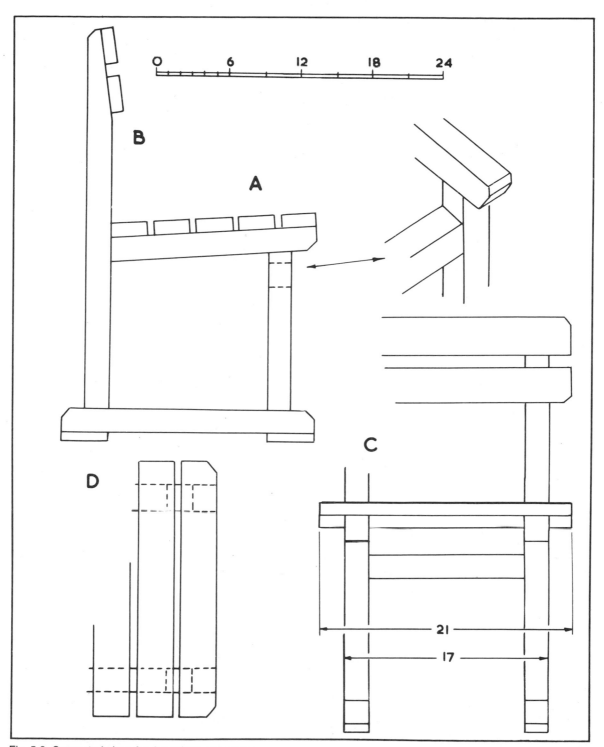

Fig. 5-2. Suggested sizes for the simple side chair.

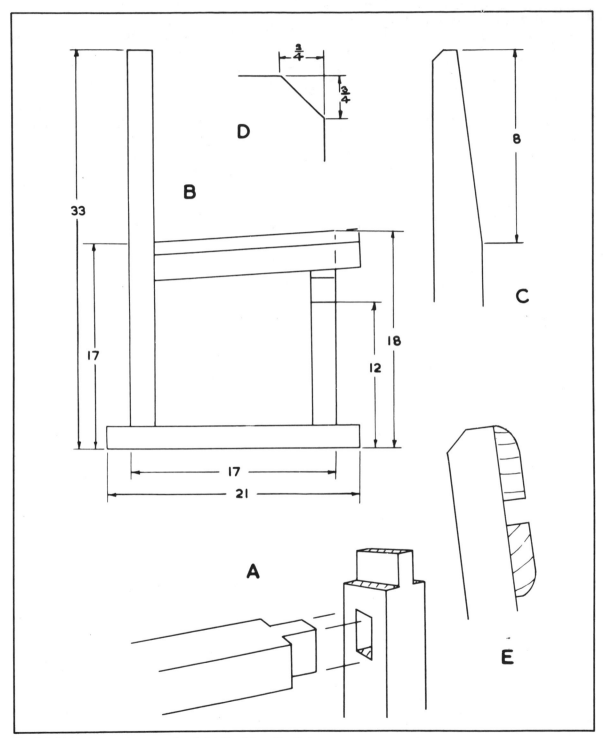

Fig. 5-3. Main sizes and constructional details of the side chair.

The back slats can be made more comfortable if they are given a rounded cross section (Fig. 5-3E) above and below. Take off their outer corners at the standard angle. That completes assembly, but make sure there is no roughness or raggedness before finishing with paint or varnish. See Table 5-1.

Table 5-1. Materials List for Side Chair.

2 front legs	2 × 18 × 2
2 rear legs	2 × 33 × 2
2 bottom rails	2 × 22 × 2
4 feet	2 × 5 × ⅞
2 seat rails	2 × 22 × 2
1 front rail	2 × 17 × 2
7 slats	3 × 22 × ⅞

SCREWED ARMCHAIR

Some armchairs are made with mortise and tenon joints. They are pieces of furniture to admire and be proud of and they are the better quality end of the range of outdoor seats. There are situations that do not justify high-grade construction. Perhaps the maker has doubts about his skill to make that type of seat. Then there is a case for relying on nails or screws. The armchair shown in Fig. 5-4 is made almost entirely by putting pieces of wood over each other and screwing. Providing the screws are driven correctly, are of adequate length and there are enough of them, the chair should have a reasonable life. Nearly all of the wood is 3 inches wide and ¾ of an inch thick. This will simplify ordering. See Table 5-2.

For most of the joints where ¾-inch wood has to be

Fig. 5-4. An armchair with simple screwed joints.

Table 5-2. Materials List for Screwed Armchair.

4 legs	3 × 30 × 1¼
2 arms	3 × 28 × ¾
2 arm supports	3 × 9 × ¾
2 seat sides	3 × 26 × ¾
1 seat front	3 × 24 × ¾
1 seat back	3 × 24 × ¾
5 seat slats	4 × 23 × ¾
5 seat slats	3 × 30 × ¾
1 back bar	3 × 27 × ¾
1 back tie	3 × 20 × ¾
1 back cover	1½ × 20 × ¾

screwed, use 1½-inch or 1¼-inch-by-8-gauge screws. Where the lower piece is end grain, increase the screw length to 2 inches. Glue can be used in the joints as well.

The chair has legs that slope as part of a triangle, in side view, but they are upright when viewed from the front (Fig. 5-5A). The seat and back are made of slats with gaps between to shed rain water. The chair will often be used with cushions that have securing tapes so the cushions do not move in use. The cushions can be taken indoors when not needed.

Get the shape of the side view by drawing it to full size. The principle lines are the legs and arm (Fig. 5-5B). Then the seat is drawn square with the front legs (Fig. 5-5C). At this stage, you can decide on the angle of the back. As shown, it slopes back at only slightly more than 90 degrees to the seat. That gives good support for reading, knitting, or being occupied in some other way. If the chair is expected to be used more for just relaxing, the back could slope more. Some chairs have adjustable backs, but in this simple construction it does not move.

The legs (Fig. 5-6A) are tapered and all the same. Make the arm supports (Fig. 5-6B). At the front, taper to the extended arms. At the rear, allow enough length for supporting the back. To take the thrust of a person leaning hard, arrange blocks to come behind the back bar (Fig. 5-6C).

The seat is made up as a boxlike unit. Let the side pieces overlap the back and front. The front is square, but the rear slopes to suit the back slats (Fig. 5-6D). The seat slats are spaced evenly across the framework with the front one on the edge and rounded (Fig. 5-6E). Slope the edge of the rear slat.

Screw the arm supports to the legs. Make sure the opposite pairs match. Mark where the seat assembly comes on the front legs and then screw it to the legs. Make sure the chair will stand level and the front edge of the seat is parallel with the floor. Put the back bar between the arm supports.

Make the back slats and the back tie that goes across

their tops. Space the slats evenly on it and on the rear of the seat (Fig. 5-6F). Screw in place. Make a cover piece to go on top of the back and well round its edges to improve appearance (Fig. 5-6G).

The arms (Fig. 5-6H) are parallel, but they could be tapered slightly to the rear and should be well rounded at the front and on the top edges. For the neatest finish, counterbore the screws in the arms so they can be plugged. When sanded level they would be inconspicuous under varnish.

TENONED ARMCHAIR

The armchair described in this section is comparable to the previous one in size and general appearance, but it is more substantial and most of the parts are joined with mortises and tenons. It should have a long life and not suffer much if left outside for most of the year. Wood sections (Table 5-3) suggested can be softwood providing it is well protected with paint. A rot-resistant hardwood would be better and it could be painted or varnished, or it might be left untreated and allowed to weather to blend in with its surroundings. In that case, the joints should be secured with a boatbuilding-quality waterproof glue and have dowels driven across the tenons of the main structure.

The chair shown in Fig. 5-7 is at a size that could be used as it is or with cushions. The ends could also be used to make a longer bench seat. The sections of lengthwise wood suggested should also be satisfactory for a bench up to about 5 feet long to seat two or even three people close together.

The important shapes are the ends (Fig. 5-8A). In front view, the legs are upright, but from the side both lower parts flare out a little. Then the slope of the back is cut into the extension of the back legs. The arms slope slightly because they are higher at the front. The seat also slopes at about the same angle and it is given a slight hollow in the top so that the slats across make a little concession to body shape. The ends are made up as identical units and the other parts fit between them, with the bottom rail jointed. Otherwise the parts screw on.

Draw the main lines of the end shape to full size (Fig. 5-8B). The arm is square to the front leg (Fig. 5-8C) and the rake of the back is about the same angle as the front leg. Allow for the slope of the seat, but the bottom rail (Fig. 5-8D) comes parallel with the floor.

Taper the widths of the front legs (Fig. 5-9A). The front edge of the rear leg is in straight lines, but the change of shape at the back can follow a curve (Fig. 5-9B). Do not go too thin near the center of each leg. It is

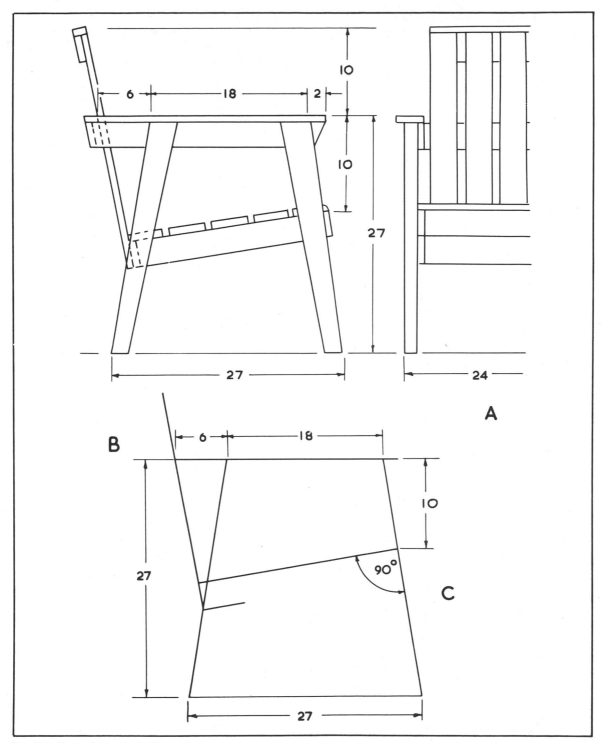

Fig. 5-5. Sizes of the screwed arm chair.

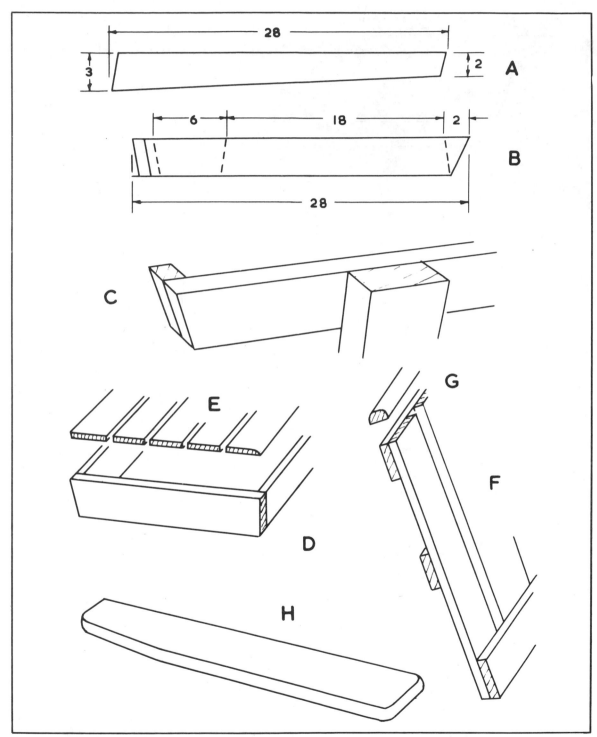

Fig. 5-6. Details of parts of the screwed arm chair.

Table 5-3. Materials List for Tenoned Armchair.

2 front legs	3 × 23 × 2	
2 rear legs	5 × 37 × 2	
2 seat rails	3 × 21 × 2	
2 arm rails	2 × 18 × 2	
2 lower rails	2 × 23 × 2	
1 stretcher	2 × 24 × 2	
1 front rail	3 × 24 × 2	
1 backrail	3 × 25 × 1	
5 seat slats	3 × 28 × 1	
4 back slats	4 × 28 × 1	
2 arms	5 × 24 × 1	

worthwhile examining the grain formation of the wood. Grain is not usually straight along the wood. If you can mark out the wood so that a curve in the grain follows the shape of a leg, it would be stronger than if your cuts go across grain lines.

Mark where the other parts come on the legs. Prepare the pieces that will come under the arms and the lower rails (Fig. 5-9C). Cut the pieces for the seat rails (Fig. 5-9D). The ends for the tenons will be straight, but hollow the top edges so the pair match. Do not weaken the wood by going too thin at the center.

All of the parts are the same thickness. Mark out with the face sides outward and make the tenons ⅝ of an

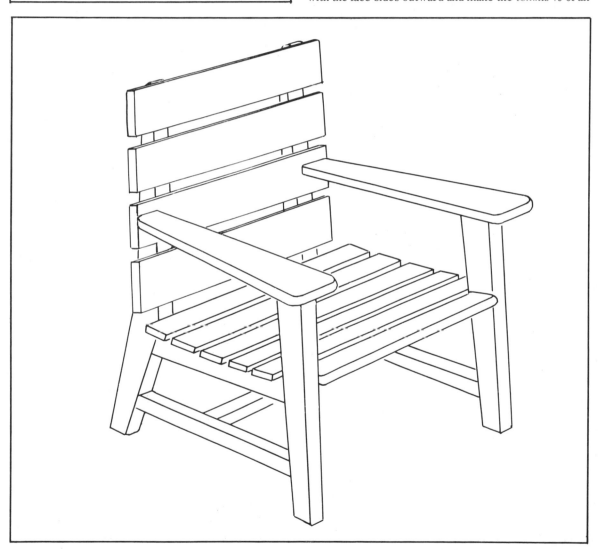

Fig. 5-7. An armchair with mortise and tenon joints.

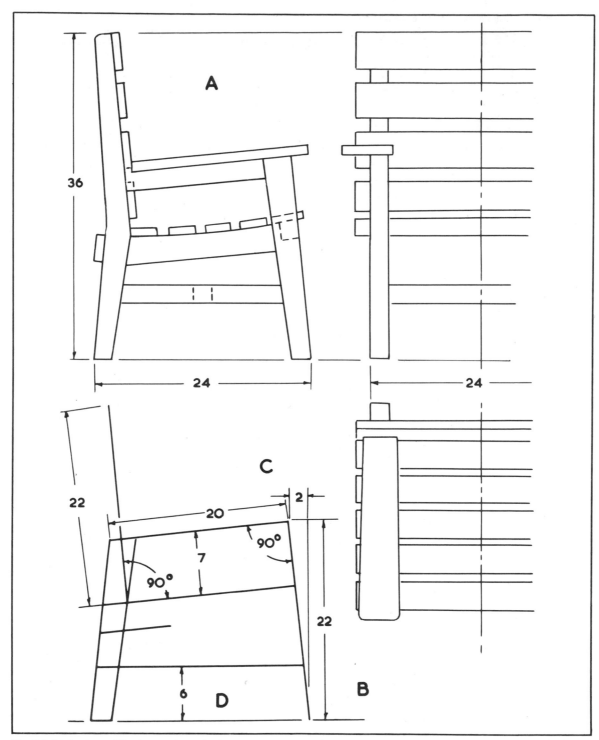

Fig. 5-8. Main sizes of the tenoned armchair.

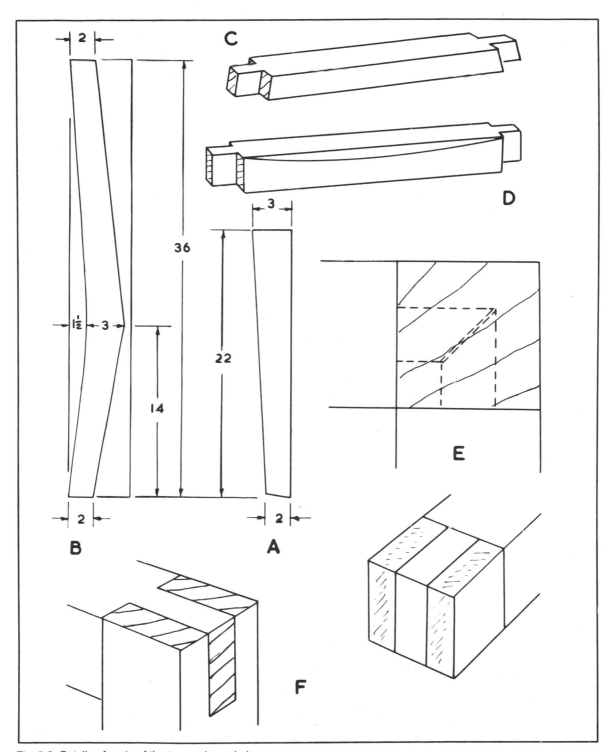

Fig. 5-9. Details of parts of the tenoned armchair.

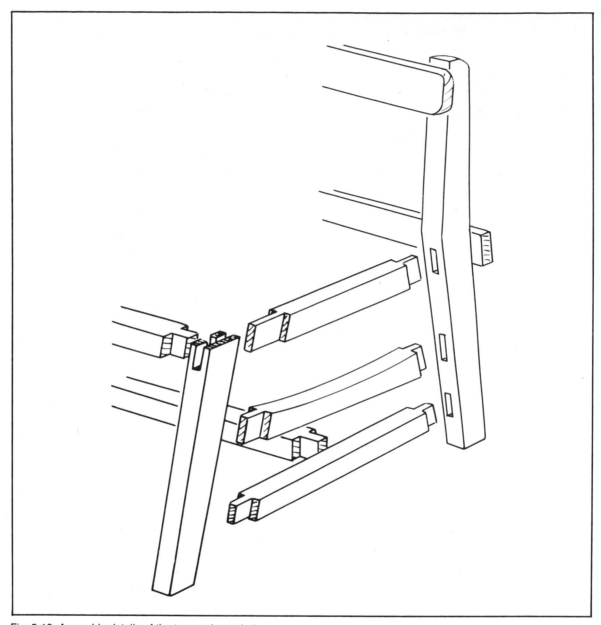

Fig. 5-10. Assembly details of the tenoned armchair.

inch or ¾ of an inch wide. They should go about 1½ inches into the legs (Fig. 5-9E). The exploded view of an end shows the joint arrangement (Fig. 5-10). The top front joints will be covered by the arms. It will be simplest to use open through mortise and tenon joints there (Fig. 5-9F). At this stage, the two ends are the same except for the mortises in the lower rails—which must face inward.

Pull the joints tight with clamps, if possible, and then drill and fit dowels across them. See that each end frame remains flat. Check the second frame over the first to see that it matches.

Make the bottom lengthwise rail or stretcher (Fig. 5-11A) and the front rail. These have to be pulled tight at the ends so they determine the lengths of other parts.

Make the back rail that screws to the back legs (Fig. 5-11B). This and the stretcher and front rail will hold the ends in the correct relative positions for the slats to be added. Check squareness and that the assembly is without twist before adding the slats.

The back slats are wider than the seat slats. Make the seat slats, with rounded top edges and well-rounded ends that overlap the supports by 1½ inches,. An exception is that the front slat comes between the front legs and is supported by the front rail (Fig. 5-11C). Space the slats

evenly round the curved supports and screw them down. For the neatest finish, counterbore and plug over the screw heads.

Prepare the back slats in the same way as the seat slats and to the same lengths. The space between the bottom back slat and the rear seat slat should be about the same as the spaces between the back slats. The lower back slat will have to be notched round the arm rail (Fig. 5-11D).

The arms mount on top of the side frames and are

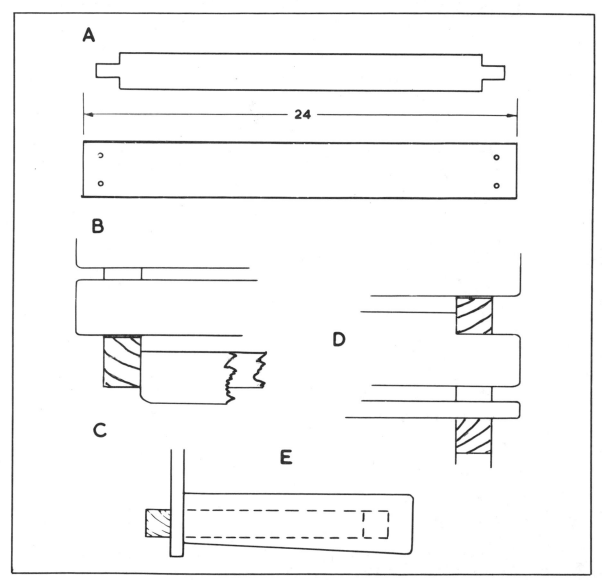

Fig. 5-11. Slat and arm details of the tenoned armchair.

best held with counterbored and plugged screws. The forward ends should be rounded. The arms look best if kept parallel on the inner faces, but tapered outside toward the rear (Fig. 5-11E). Well round all the upper surfaces. Take the sharpness off all exposed edges of other parts before painting or varnishing.

SAWBUCK LOUNGE CHAIR

The chair shown in Fig. 5-12 is intended to fill the need for a light comfortable small chair with a lounging angle. Its shaping allows it to be used without padding (although cushions could be added). It can be carried easily so several of these chairs could be provided for guests to

Fig. 5-12. Sawbuck lounge chair.

move around as they gather into groups. If made of good quality wood and given a suitable finish, the chair could also be used indoors.

The main structure consists of two crossing frames, joined with a few crossbars, then the seat and back are curved plywood. The wood should be hardwood and the crossing pieces should have reasonably straight grain without knots. You might be able to select pieces with the grain following the curve of each piece. The plywood should be exterior or marine grade. If you use veneers, they must be bonded with waterproof glue.

The sizes shown in Table 5-4 and Fig. 5-13 give a

Table 5-4. Materials List for Sawbuck Lounge Chair.

2 inner legs	5 × 34 × 1
2 outer legs	4 × 34 × 1
4 rails	2 × 20 × 1
1 seat	18 × 21 × ¼
1 back	8 × 21 × ¼

chair of relaxing proportions to suit an adult. A slightly smaller version could be made for a child. In particular, the front edge could be lowered to suit shorter legs. In that case, the seat would also have to be reduced back to front.

A full-size drawing is essential and it can be drawn on a pattern of squares (Fig. 5-14A). Strength has to come where the parts cross; do not reduce sizes there. Mark the locations of the two supporting pieces under the seat and the single one at the back. There is also a rail between the rear legs. The surfaces toward the sitter are straight, but the other surfaces can be curved (except where the parts cross each other).

Where the pieces cross, notch them into each other, but do not use full halving joints to bring the parts to the same level. That would remove too much wood from each piece. Instead, cut not more than ¼ inch from each piece (Fig. 5-14B) so that the back legs come outside the seat legs.

The seat and back have similar curves. A simple way of forming them is to use two thicknesses of ⅛-inch or 3mm plywood. Cut this with the grain of the outside veneers the straight way of the parts—the short direction—two for each part slightly too large at this stage.

Have two stiff boards that will not deflect when clamping over them and four strips longer than the width of the pieces being shaped. Take off sharpness of the edges that will come against the plywood. Put the plywood between the strips and boards; then squeeze with clamps (Fig. 5-14C). The exact amount of deflection is not important, but aim to push in about a 1-inch curve. If that dry trial is satisfactory, open up and coat the meeting surfaces with waterproof glue. Then clamp again. If the plywood is rather stubborn, dry clamp and leave the assembly overnight. Preferably you should curve it a little more than you will eventually want so that the plywood becomes accustomed to curving. Then when you make the glued assembly, the seat or back will hold its shape.

An alternative is to make your own curved plywood from veneers. If possible, get veneers at least as thick as

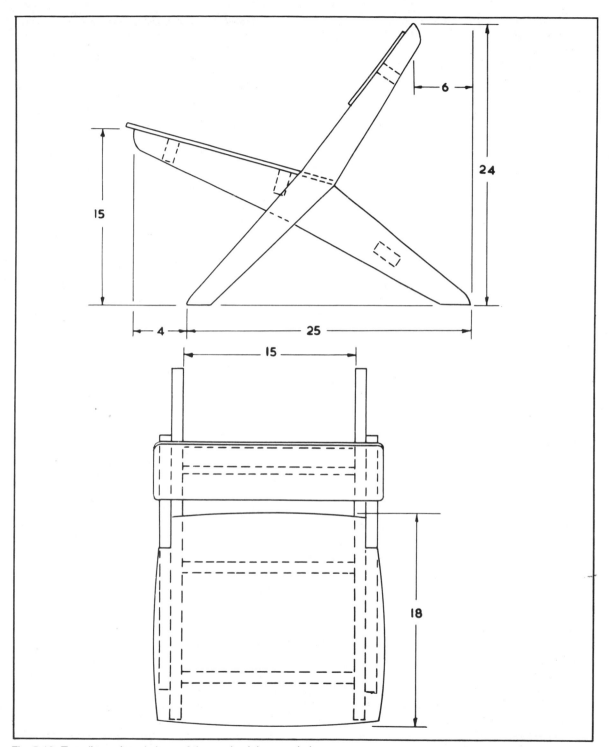

Fig. 5-13. Two dimensioned views of the sawbuck lounge chair.

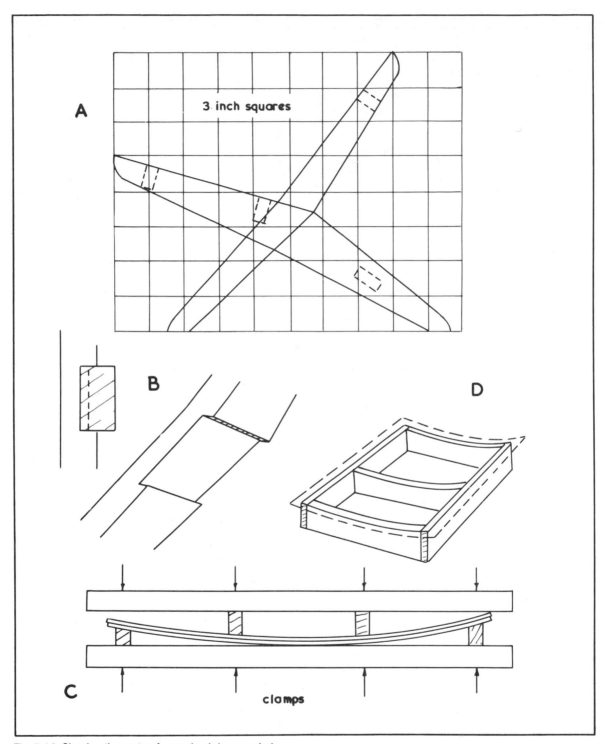

A

3 inch squares

B

D

C clamps

Fig. 5-14. Shaping the parts of a sawbuck lounge chair.

74

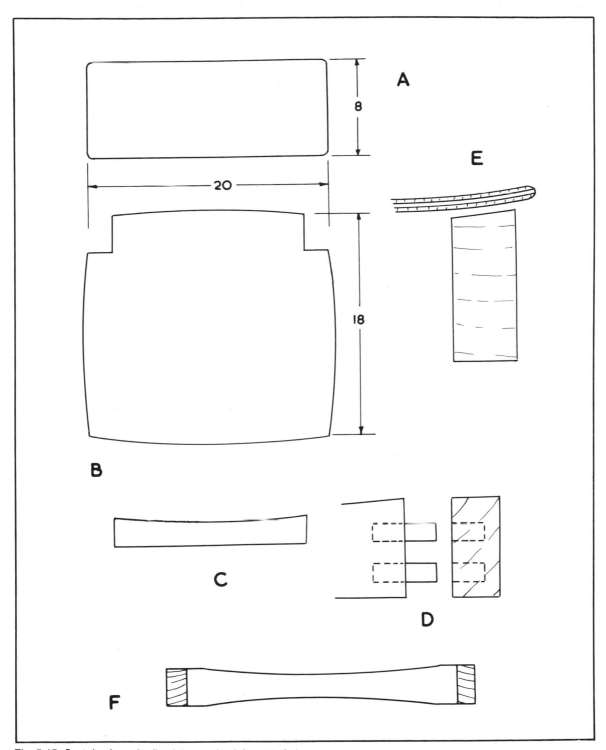

Fig. 5-15. Seat, back, and rails of the sawbuck lounge chair.

those used in plywood (which are between 1mm and 2mm, or 1/16 inch upward. The thinner veneers used in cabinetwork would require too many thicknesses to be glued. To get a smooth, curved shape you have to make a jig or former. It can be a frame with thin plywood sprung to shape on it (Fig. 5-14D). There will probably have to be at least one intermediate crossbar to keep the plywood to a regular curve. Have another piece of flexible plywood ready for applying pressure.

Prepare enough pieces of veneer to make up nearly a ¼-inch total thickness, but make it an odd number so that both outside veneers have their grain the short way. Put newspaper over the former so the veneers will not become attached with any surplus glue. Apply glue to the veneers and bring them together. Put the loose plywood over the top, with newspaper underneath, and then put on pressure with strips of wood and C-clamps. Leave it until you are certain the glue is hard. Some glues appear to be hard in a few hours, but they need a day or more to build up their full strength.

Whichever method of shaping is used, trim the back piece parallel and to a length that will overhang the supports slightly. Round the outer corners (Fig. 5-15A). The seat also overhangs, but it looks better if the edges are cut to curves. At the rear, you have to shape the seat to fit between the outer legs (Fig. 5-15B). Round all edges.

Use the back as a template for marking the hollows in the supporting pieces. All three are the same curve (Fig. 5-15C). They could be tenoned into the legs, but dowels are suggested (Fig. 5-15D). Cut the ends squarely to fit inside the legs. Make the one behind the back longer than those under the seat and between the inner legs.

The curved parts have to bear against their supports. The slope of the meeting surfaces is not much and you might screw through without shaping. But it would be better to bevel the edges (Fig. 5-15E).

The lower rail between the rear legs is a simple piece doweled at its ends or tenoned into the legs. Round its edges. If you want to follow on the curved theme of the seat edges, it could be given a hollow in its width (Fig. 5-15F).

Round all ends of the side assemblies and take the sharpness off exposed edges. The tops project above the back so they should be well rounded. Glue the crossed legs. Waterproof glue only should be sufficient. If you think reinforcement is necessary, drive two screws into each joint from inside—where the heads will not show. Check to make sure that opposite sides match.

Join these parts with the crosswise members (pulling together wtih clamps). Check squareness at seat level and see that the chair stands upright. The plywood parts will hold the chair in shape. If you think it is necessary, triangular blocks can be glued in the corners of the framing under the seat.

Leave this assembly for the glue to set before adding the plywood parts. They can be glued down. If you can get close fits, glue alone might be all that is needed. Then there will be nothing to mar the surfaces. Glue does not hold well if the joints are less than perfect and you will probably need to use fine nails with small heads. They can be punched below the surface and covered with stopping. If you prefer to use screws, be careful to get them level with the surface for a neat effect. You might even get their slots all in the same direction across the chair.

For outside use, finish with varnish or paint. If the chair will also be taken indoors, you might want to stain it to match existing furniture and finish it with varnish.

STRIP ARMCHAIR

A simple robust armchair can be made of hard or soft wood. The soft wood must be well protected with preservative and paint or varnish. All of the parts (Table 5-5) are

Table 5-5. Materials List for Strip Armchair.

2 rear legs	3 × 32 × 1
2 front legs	3 × 23 × 1
4 side rails	3 × 20 × 1
2 arms	3 × 21 × 1
5 cross pieces	3 × 20 × 1
2 cross pieces	3 × 21 × 1

made of wood of the same section. In the simplest form, it is possible to make all the joints with screws using just two 10-gauge-by-2½-inch, flat-head screws at most crossings. If several chairs are to be made, it is possible to prefabricate the parts for all of them to standard sizes—with edges rounded and holes drilled—before doing any assembly work.

The chair (Fig. 5-16) has a squared shape with some rounding of the arms and a slope to the back. The sizes shown in Fig. 5-17 give a reasonable proportion for most purposes, but they could be modified slightly. Do not use the design extended to make a bench for more than one person without introducing additional lengthwise members to give rigidity to the extended shape.

Make all four legs (Fig. 5-18A and 5-18B). Make the side rails (Fig. 5-18C) with screw holes arranged diagonally. Make the arms to match (Fig. 5-18D). At the rear,

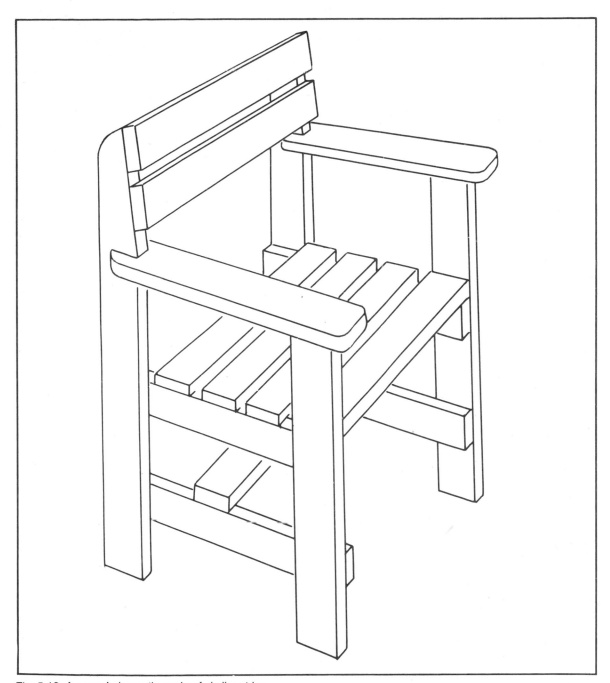

Fig. 5-16. An armchair mostly made of similar strips.

the slot should make a close fit on the leg and be drilled for two screws (entered at opposite sides to miss each other). Round the edges and corners of the arms. Assemble the sides with the crossbars inward. Check that they are square and match each other. If you prefer, use glue as well as screws.

Prepare the five pieces that make the seat and lower rail (Fig. 5-14E). Round the top edges of the seat. Have

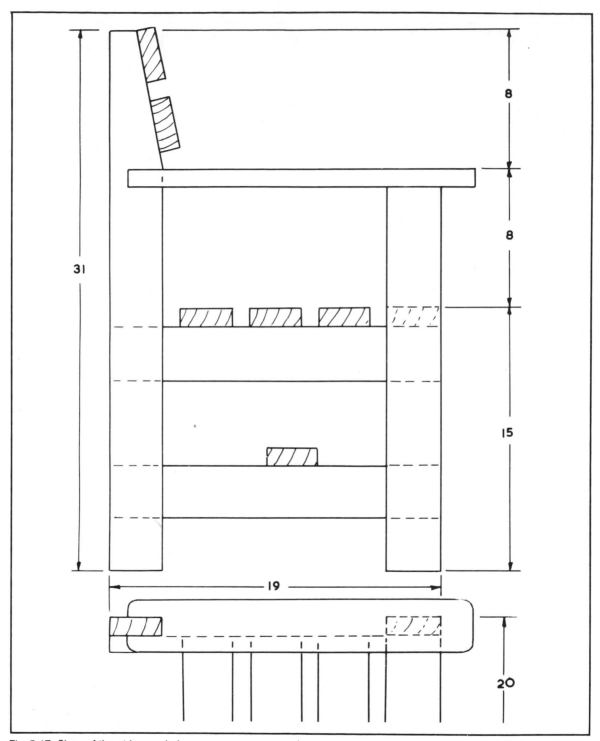

Fig. 5-17. Sizes of the strip armchair.

78

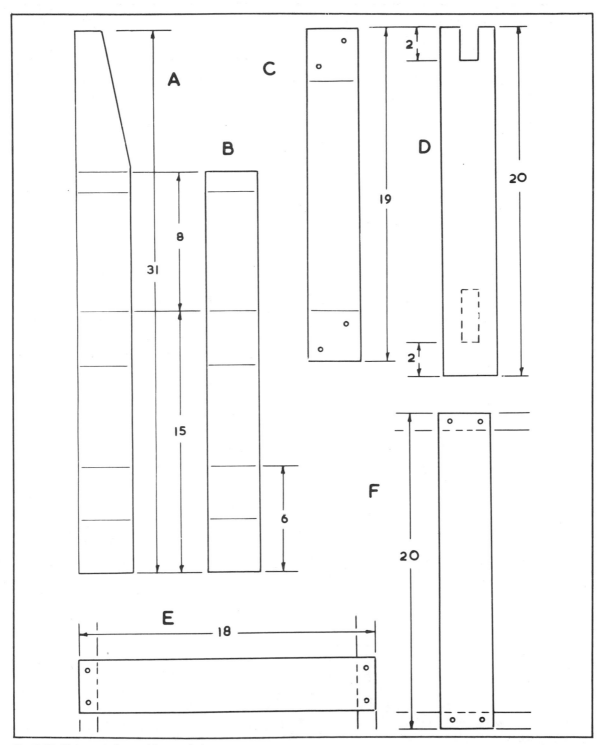

Fig. 5-18. Main parts for a strip armchair.

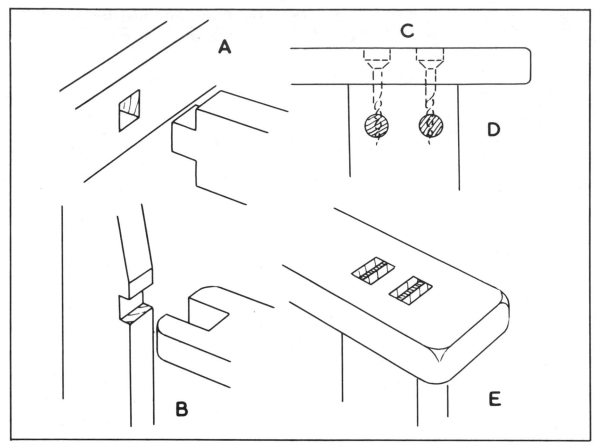

Fig. 5-19. Constructional methods for the strip armchair.

the front rails level with the legs and space the others evenly. The back rails (Fig. 5-18F) are longer, but check the final length on the chair before cutting and fitting in place. The lower rail is screwed to the side rails.

A simple arrangement of lap and screws at each crossing might be adequate, but anyone wanting a more craftsmanlike construction will prefer to include some fitted joints.

The lower rail would be better arranged upright and tenoned (Fig. 5-19A). Tenons taken through and wedged would be strongest.

If the joint between each arm and its rear leg is altered to include a shallow notch in the leg (Fig. 5-19B), the arm is positively located and the screws are relieved of downward strain.

The screws through the arm into the front leg should be counterbored (Fig. 5-19C), but they go into end grain and that might not provide a good grip on the screw

threads. One way of making such a screwed joint tighter is to put dowels across so that the screw threads pull into them across their grain (Fig. 5-19D). It would be better to use mortise and tenon joints instead of screws between the arms and the front legs. Take the tenons through and wedge them (Fig. 5-19E). You could make stub tenons if you do not want their ends to show.

SLAB ARMCHAIR

Wide boards, cut straight across a log, are often available from a saw mill. The chair shown in Fig. 5-20 is intended to make use of these slabs (which can be 1½ inches thick or more). The finished chair is intended to be kept outdoors almost indefinitely. Its sawn surface will weather to blend in with its surroundings. Some woods will benefit from treating with preservative, but oak and other durable hardwoods can be left untreated. The chair is

Fig. 5-20. An armchair, made from slabs, with tusk tenons for the main joints.

Table 5-6. Materials List for Slab Armchair (Approximate Only).

2 sides	20 × 38 × 1½
1 seat	15 × 31 × 1½
1 back	12 × 31 × 1½
2 arms	3 × 13 × 1½
4 wedges	2 × 5 × 2

shown free-standing. It can be moved about, but if its position is settled it could have the legs extended to go into the ground or it might be held down by pegs into the ground or brackets to a concrete base.

Sizes are not crucial and they can be adapted to suit available wood. See Table 5-6. It is possible to make use of waney edges as decorative features. There is certainly no need to plane straight edges where they would match surroundings better if left to the natural curves. Only the joints and the bottom edges need accurate cutting. The sizes shown in Fig. 5-21 give a seat of comfortable proportions. If you vary them to suit your wood, keep the seat about the same area and height. Have the back at a moderate slope and a position to come below the shoulder blades.

Examine the wood for flaws. Knots that are obviously well bonded to the surrounding wood will not mat-

ter if they come in the body of a part, but they would be weak if they have to be cut to make joints. Look for shakes. These are the natural lengthwise cracks that sometimes occur in a growing tree. If the wood has not yet fully seasoned, they are liable to open as the wood dries further. A shake that goes through to the end of the wood will not matter, but it would be an unacceptable weakness in a short part such as the front of the seat or toward the edge of the back piece.

With wood of uneven width, the vital setting out includes the positions and angles of the seat, back, and arms in relation to the floor (Fig. 5-22A). This can be set on a side that has its bottom edge cut straight. Make sure there is enough wood round the marked positions to provide strength. If you have to alter sizes to suit the wood, give the seat a slight tilt (5 degrees to horizontal is shown) and slope the back rather more (10 degrees to vertical is shown), but keep the arms horizontal.

Mark the full widths and then the mortises. Both are 6 inches wide, but the ones for the seat are offset in its width. Prepare the seat and back and mark the chair width across both pieces the same so that they fit evenly between the sides. Then mark the tenons, centrally on the back pieces (Fig. 5-22B) and toward the back on the seat (Fig. 5-22C)).

Remove the waste from the wide mortise carefully. Drill out as much as possible. Then trim with chisels from both sides toward the center of the thickness so as not to break out the grain fibers. The holes should be a reasonably tight fit on the tenons. Deal with each joint independently and mark them so the same parts go together during assembly. This is particularly important if the wood varies in thickness—as newly sawn wood often does.

Prepare the four wedges (Fig. 5-22D). Give them a slight taper (¼ inch in 4 inches is about right) and bevel the top, which will be hit during assembly. Cut the tapered holes to match the wedges, but have the inner edges slightly inside the thickness of the mortised part (Fig. 5-22E) so the tightening wedge pulls the tenon into the mortise without itself coming against the inner edge of the hole in the tenon.

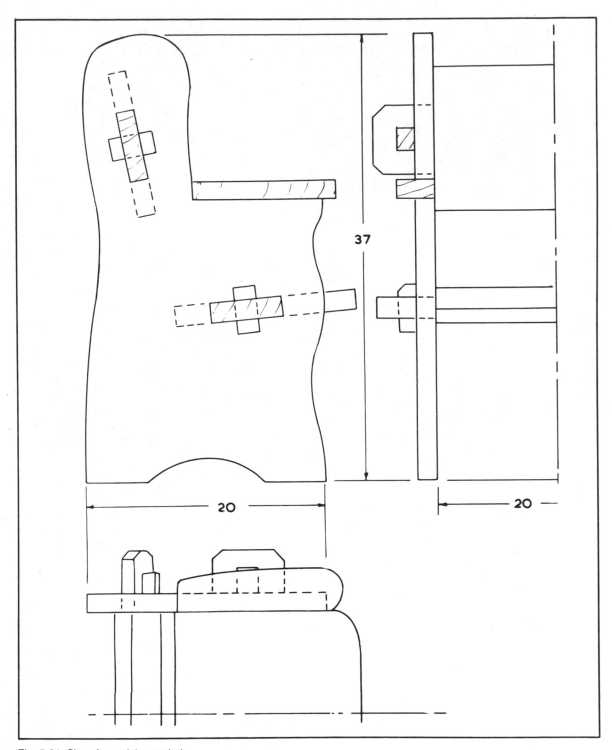

Fig. 5-21. Sizes for a slab armchair.

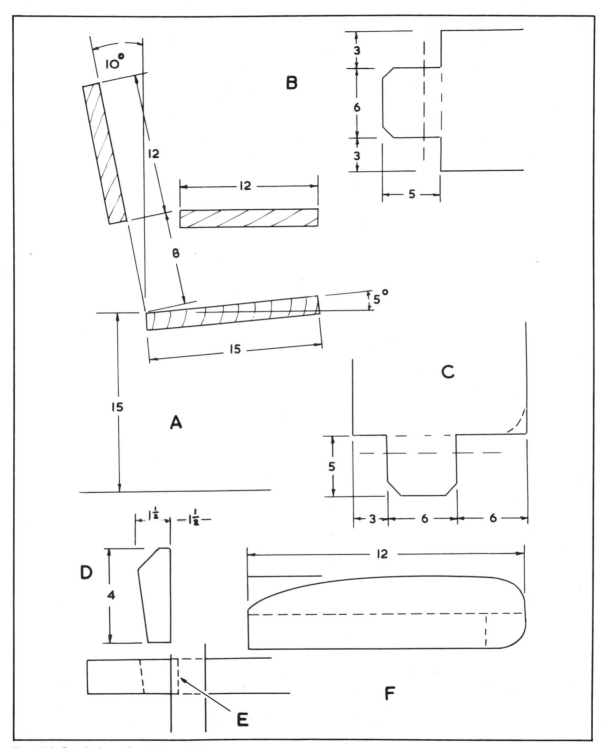

Fig. 5-22. Detail sizes of a slab armchair.

83

Some parts of the wood can be left with waney edges, but those edges that will come into contact with a user should have any sharpness removed. You could use a waney edge at the fronts of the chair sides, but otherwise you can bandsaw to a curve (Fig. 5-21). Round the front corners of the seat and remove any sharpness along its front edge.

The arms (Fig. 5-22F) are nailed or screwed on to the sides with their inner edges level. Make their widths about twice the thickness of the wood. Round the fronts and outer edges and take off any sharpness around the sides. Although a natural and rather rustic appearance is a feature of the other parts of the chair, the chair arms should be shaped and cleaned up so they are comfortable for bare human arms.

CHAIR WITH ADJUSTABLE BACK

Being able to alter the angle of the back of a chair allows it to be used in its more upright position for reading or knitting while the tilted positions allow for relaxing. The armchair shown in Fig. 5-23 has roomy proportions. It can be used with or without cushions and it can have its back moved to three different angles.

The seat is exterior-grade plywood sprung to a curve across; this is supported between two pedestals under the arms. The back is hinged behind the seat and its angle is controlled by a bar that drops into slots in the arms (Fig. 5-24). The sections given in Table 5-7 are intended to suit softwoods. Nevertheless, the back stop and the arms would be better in hardwood if the chair is to be left outside in all types of weather and given much use. Softwood for these parts might wear excessively at the slots used to adjust the back.

Start by setting out the main lines of a side full size (Fig. 5-25A). Front and rear legs have the same slopes so lay out each side of a centerline. The seat line drawn is the top edge of the seat sides. Draw the tapers of the legs from 3 inches at the top to 2 inches at the bottom. The legs can be marked out and the tapers planed, but leave cutting the ends until later. This gives you the angles and sizes of the seat sides. They could be screwed and glued to the insides of the legs, but they are better notched in a little. It need not be much and certainly there is no need to make full halving joints; ¼-inch notches in both parts will do (Fig. 5-25B). The rear end of each side goes past the edges of the legs so that it can take a crossbar. The

Fig. 5-23. An armchair with an adjustable back.

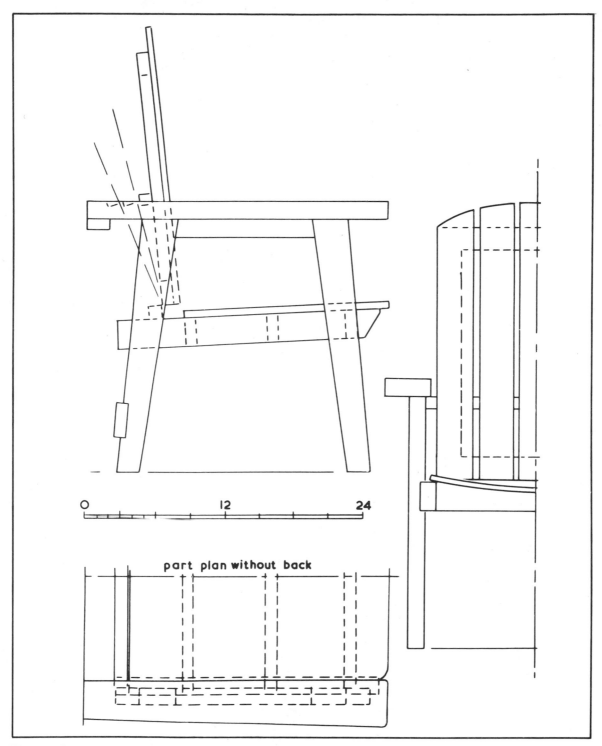

part plan without back

Fig. 5-24. Sizes of an armchair with an adjustable back.

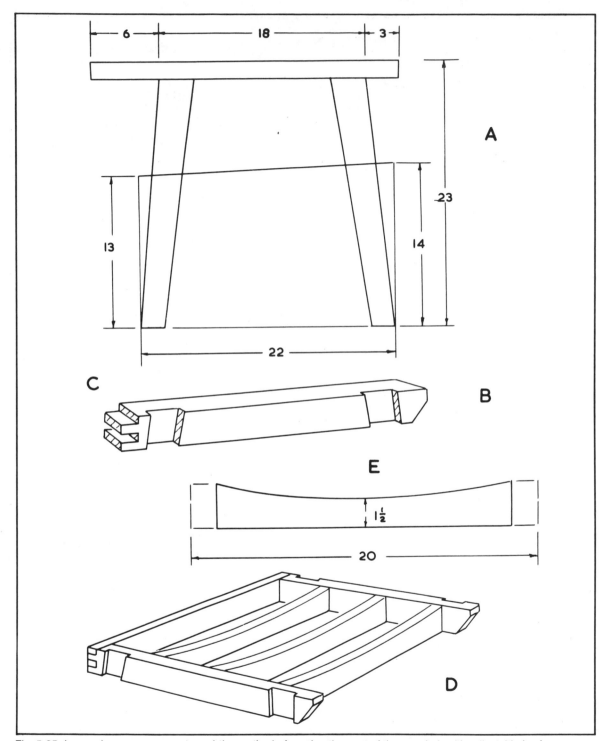

Fig. 5-25. Leg and arm arrangements and the method of curving the seat of the armchair with adjustable back.

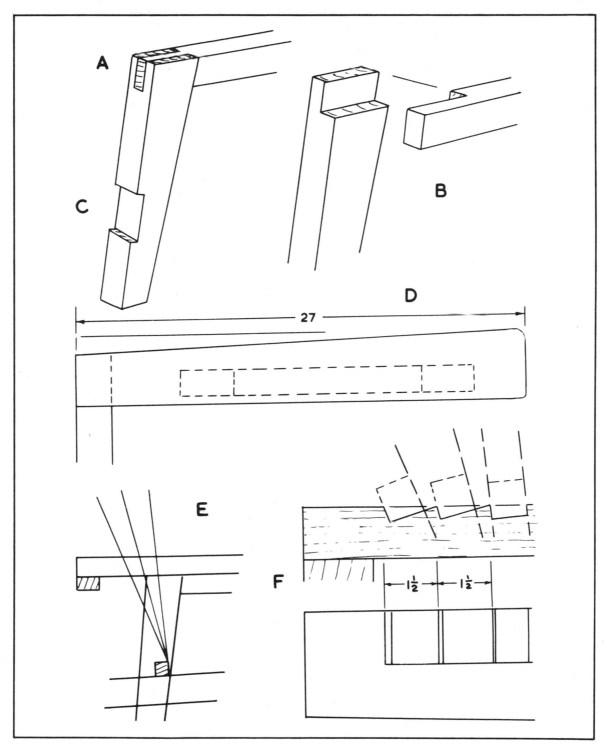

Fig. 5-26. Joint details and adjustment notches for the back.

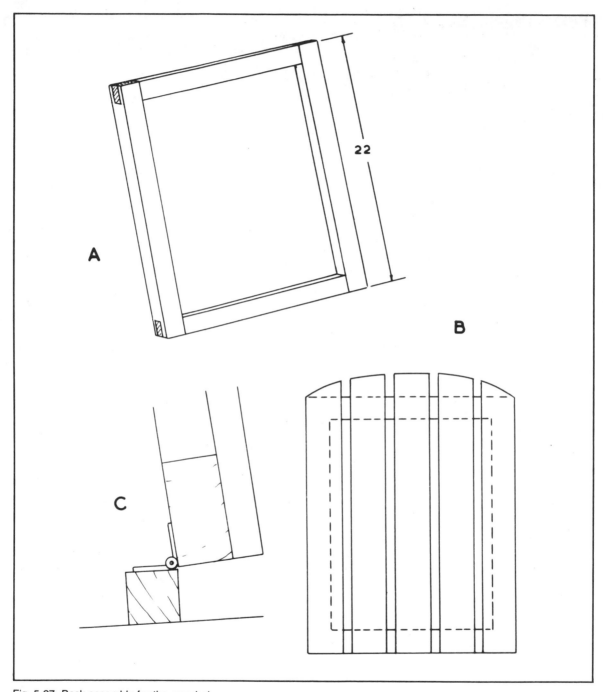

Fig. 5-27. Back assembly for the armchair.

Table 5-7. Materials List for Chair with Adjustable Back.

4 legs	3 × 24 × 1½	
2 arms	4 × 28 × 1½	
2 arm supports	1½ × 18 × 1½	
2 seat sides	2½ × 24 × 1½	
4 seat crossbars	2½ × 22 × 1	
1 back rail	3 × 24 × 1	
1 hinge bar	1 × 24 × 1	
1 seat	18 × 22 × ½ plywood	
2 back sides	2 × 24 × 1	
2 back crossbars	2 × 18 × 1	
5 back slats	3 × 24 × ⅝	
1 back stop	1 × 24 × 1	
1 back retainer	2 × 27 × 1	

crossbar can be screwed on, you can allow for cutting a comb joint there (Fig. 5-25C), or the parts could be dovetailed.

The curve of the seat across is held by three crossbars (Fig. 5-25D) between the sides. If the 2½-inch pieces curve down to 1½ inches at the center, that will be enough curve (Fig. 5-25E). You can draw a curve around a thin batten sprung to shape through the end corners and a mark at the greatest depth. Make sure all three pieces match. Their ends could be tenoned into the sides or screwed. Join these pieces to the sides and bring in the back rail so that you get a squared assembly (which can be used to mark the plywood seat).

Plywood will probably bend to this moderate curve with its outer grain either way, but it will be easier if you arrange the grain of the outside veneers back to front. The seat plywood comes level with the rear curved crossbar, but at the front it extends a little and has rounded corners. At the sides, cut it to clear the notches at the legs. Fit the plywood with glue and plenty of small nails. It will help to have some stout pieces of wood that can be laid back to front over the plywood and held down with clamps on their ends while the glue sets. Be careful not to distort the seat. Have the framework resting on a flat surface during assembly.

At the tops of the legs, the arm supports can be tenoned into the legs (Fig. 5-26A) or halved to them (Fig. 5-26B) and screwed from inside as well as glued. Join them at the same time as you join the legs to the seat assembly.

Check squareness and see that the assembly stands upright. Besides the crossbar at the back of the seat, another rail goes across the legs. It could be screwed on without letting in, but a shallow notch improves rigidity (Fig. 5-26C). A hinge bar goes across the seat sides between the rear legs.

The arms are shown with a slight taper from back to front on the outer edges (Fig. 5-26D). Keep the insides parallel with each other. At the back, there have to be notches for the back stop. This is square sectioned and ought to be a reasonably accurate fit in its notches. The notches have to be at different angles in each position. To get these shapes, draw a side view of the parts concerned. Intended sizes are shown, but check your own chair in case there are slight variations (Fig. 5-26E).

The notches do not have to go the full width of an arm (Fig. 5-26F). Cut them carefully. You could leave final paring to size with a chisel until assembly is complete. Then you will have the back swinging and the actual bar to fit.

Well round the exposed edges and corners of the arms, but leave the edge square where the notches come and below at the back where there will be a crosswise retainer. Fit the arms by screwing downward into the supports and legs (preferably counterboring and plugging). Be certain to get the inner surfaces parallel and square to the chair. Screw the retainer strip under the rear ends of the arms. It is there to prevent the back going right down if the back stop is omitted or improperly fitted. It could act as a fourth position for the back if an even more reclined position is needed.

The back is a separate frame made up of 1-×-2 inch strips. Preferably the corners will be joined with open mortise and tenon or bridle joints (Fig. 5-27A). Make the width an easy fit between the chair arms; there can be ½ inch clearance at each side. The back slats are level with the frame at the bottom, but they are extended at the top so they can be curved. Make them too long and then put them temporarily in position and spring a lath to a curve for the top (Fig. 5-27B). Take off all sharpness on the slats before nailing or screwing them to the frame.

Almost any available hinges can be used between the back and its bar on the seat. If you have to get them specially, two 2-inch hinges should be suitable (Fig. 5-27C).

Fit the back stop. Keep its ends square, but it can be rounded elsewhere. Try the back in each position and trim the notches where necessary.

Chapter 6

Other Seating

THERE IS NO CLEAR LINE BETWEEN WHAT ARE simple seats and what are more complicated seats. It is also difficult to draw a line between chairs and other seats. If a chair is made longer, it is no longer a chair, but the constructional work will be the same. Seats described in this chapter mostly require rather more advance techniques than those in Chapter 4, but the work is still not very difficult.

Most seats in this group are larger than chairs (they can seat two or more people), but they have backs and they can have arms like chairs. The general form can be like some of the simple seats with these additions.

The provision of seating is one of the main requirements of outdoor furniture. If a seat can be made to serve more than one person, it will be more economical of space and will usually mean less work for the craftsman than if he made individual seats.

SAWBUCK BENCH

The cross-legged arrangement, like a sawing trestle or sawbuck, allows for providing back support with the extension of a leg at each end. This is not quite as simple as might be expected because the usual symmetrical ar-

rangement of the crossed legs would bring the back support some way behind the seat and legs would not go far enough to the rear to prevent the risk of tipping.

Instead there has to be an asymmetrical arrangement so that the back is more upright and the rear leg extends far enough (Figs. 6-1 and 6-2). The important parts are the pair of end structures. The lengthwise parts can be any reasonable length; 60 inches would make a seat for two or three. See Table 6-1.

The first step is a full-size setting out of an end (Fig. 6-3). Draw a floor line and the seat with its support (Fig. 6-3A). The lower edge of the rear leg slopes from the bottom of the seat support to 14 inches back from the front (Fig. 6-3B). The other leg starts vertically under the front of the seat (Fig. 6-3C) and slopes to 6 inches behind it (Fig. 6-3D). The back rail notches into it to come nearer upright (Fig. 6-3E).

Lay out the legs and make halving joints where they cross (Fig. 6-4A). Do this in pairs so that the long part comes inside. Cut the notches at the tops and round the backs. You might prefer to leave cutting the lower ends of the legs until after assembly. Then you can check to see that the cuts come level across the two legs.

Fig. 6-1. A bench with sawbuck legs.

Attach the seat supports to the ends with glue and nails or screws from inside. Strengthen and stiffen the halving joint with another strip on its inside (Fig. 6-4B). Cut it to come close to the seat support.

The seat is made of three pieces of 2-×-4 inch wood that should be of good quality because later warping or twisting would affect the comfort of the seat. The front two pieces overlap the ends by 2 inches, but the other piece stops between them. Choose the best piece of wood for the front and well round its exposed edges and ends. Make the next piece the same length, but cut it away to fit around the leg extension (Fig. 6-4C). Cut the third piece to the notched length of the second one.

Fit the seat parts to their supports. Nailing can be sufficient, but for the best quality finish counterbore for screws that can be covered with glued plugs. For a length up to about 60 inches, the seat boards will have enough stiffness in themselves. If the seat is to be longer, there can be a strip under the front board notched into the supports (Fig. 6-4D) and screwed at intervals to the seat.

Make the back the same length as the seat, but well round its edges and ends so there is no roughness whatever way it is handled. Screw it to its supports. Check squareness during assembly; use diagonals across the rear of the bench. The seat might have to stand on uneven ground, but it should first be checked on a level surface and the bottoms of the legs should be trimmed where necessary. Bevel around the bottoms of the legs to reduce the risk of splintering if the bench is dragged along rough ground. When painting or varnishing, make sure plenty is applied to the end grain of the bottoms to prevent water absorption.

TUSK TENONED BENCH

Much medieval furniture was held together with what are

92

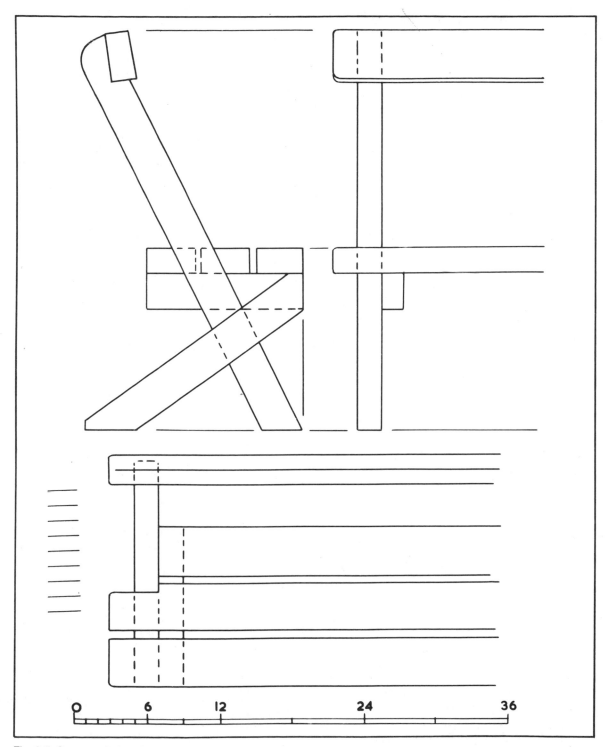

Fig. 6-2. Suggested sizes for a bench with sawbuck legs.

Table 6-1. Materials List for Sawbuck Bench.

2 legs	3 × 36 × 2
2 legs	3 × 24 × 2
2 leg stiffeners	3 × 22 × 2
2 seat supports	3 × 14 × 2
3 seats	4 × 60 × 2 (or as required)
1 back	4 × 60 × 2 (or as required)

now called *tusk tenons*. Such a tenon goes right through a mortise and is held tight with a wedge. This was a satisfactory way of putting together furniture when proper seasoning was not understood. Joints could be tightened easily if the wood shrank. It also allowed furniture to be taken apart. When a feudal lord traveled, he took much of his furniture with him and his staff put it together at any of his stopping places.

It is possible to make a bench where the lengthwise parts are all tusk tenoned into the ends. It can be made of parallel planed pieces of wood, but the example shown in Fig. 6-5 is made of slabs of waney-edged wood.

Sizes depend on available wood, but suggestions give a reasonable proportion using wood about 1½ inches thick (see Table 6-2 and Fig. 6-6A). Although edges may come as they will you have to establish straight lines where the joints come, to get proper fits. Wide boards with the grain vertical make up the ends (Fig. 6-6B). If there is no straightedge to work to, draw a line through the slope of the back to act as a datum from which other parts can be measured. The back should be between 10 inches and 15 inches wide (Fig. 6-6C), with its tenon about half that width. The seat is shown as two boards dipping in a shallow V to give an approximation of a curved seat (Fig. 6-6D). The tenons should be about half the width of each board.

With the general arrangement marked on one end, its mortises can be cut. If you are using parallel planed wood, the shapes can be continued over each of the edges to the other side. Then cutting can be done a little from each side. For rougher wood, it should be satisfactory to do most of the cutting from the one marked side. A small amount of breaking out on the far side will not matter. Drill through near the corners of each mortise. Then more holes can be drilled inside the lines (Fig. 6-7A). In that way, only a small amount of chopping with a chisel will be needed to remove the waste center. Square the edges by further chopping with chisels. The mortises do not have to be close fits on the tenons, but it might be as well to leave finishing the mortises until you have the tenons ready to try in them. Bring the second end to the

same stage as the first.

Lay out the back and seat boards so you can draw parallel lines across to mark what will be the insides of the ends (Fig. 6-7B). The meeting edges of the seat boards should be fairly straight. A slight waneyness of the seat front edge will not matter, but if it is very uneven it would be better to straighten and round its section.

The tenons must go through far enough to take the wedges and have enough wood beyond to avoid grain breaking out when a wedge is driven. Allow for the wedges being fairly thick and about the same distance of solid wood on the tenon beyond them (Fig. 6-7C). Cut the wedge slots to match their slope. So that the wedge will tighten against the bench end, cut the slot back so some of it remains within the end mortise. If the wedge ever hits that surface, it will cease to tighten.

Leave some excess wood on the tenons; they can all be trimmed to matching lengths later. Similarly, make the wedges overlong at first. Then they can be trimmed to about the same length and penetration after assembly. Otherwise you can get one wedge much further in than another. This might not matter except for a uniform appearance.

Make a trial assembly. Mark the cuts on the tenons and wedges. Then dismantle and cut off these parts. Take off the sharpness of the corners and edges (Fig. 6-7D).

Arms on the ends can prevent warping and provide comfort (Fig. 6-7E). Nail or screw the arms in place. Carrying them back to the rear mortise, providing it does not interfere with wedging, will increase stiffness.

If the bench is to be held down with stakes or other attachments to the ground, the bottoms can be left flat. If it will be moved about, it will be more likely to stand level on uneven ground if the bottoms are cut away to make feet (Fig. 6-6E). The three boards making the back and seat should provide enough stiffness, but if you feel that more is required you could add a stretcher underneath (Fig. 6-6F). This is held at the ends with tusk tenons and wedges the same as the other parts.

Even if the bench is to remain in one place, the wedged tenons can be regarded as a design feature. They

Table 6-2. Materials List for Tusk Tenoned Bench.

2 ends	22 × 36 × 1½
1 back	12 × 57 × 1½
2 seats	9 × 57 × 1½
1 stretcher (optional)	6 × 57 × 1½
2 arms	4 × 22 × 1½

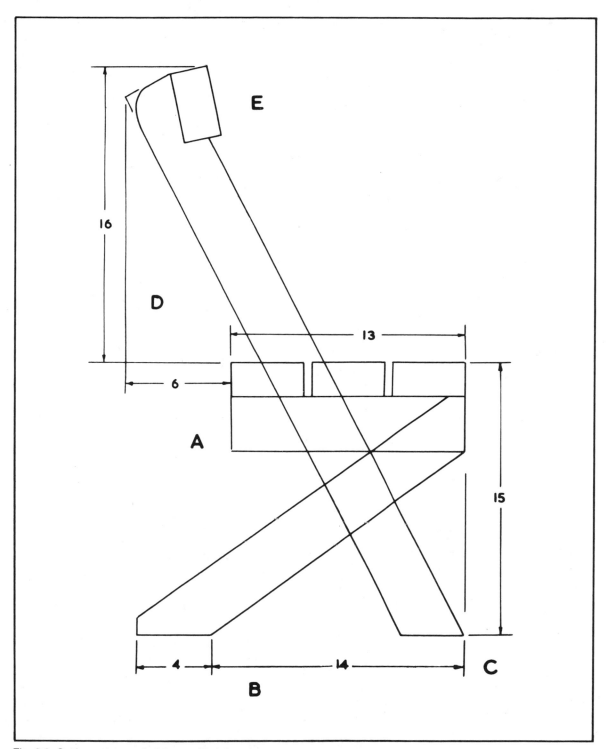

Fig. 6-3. Setting out an end of the sawbuck bench.

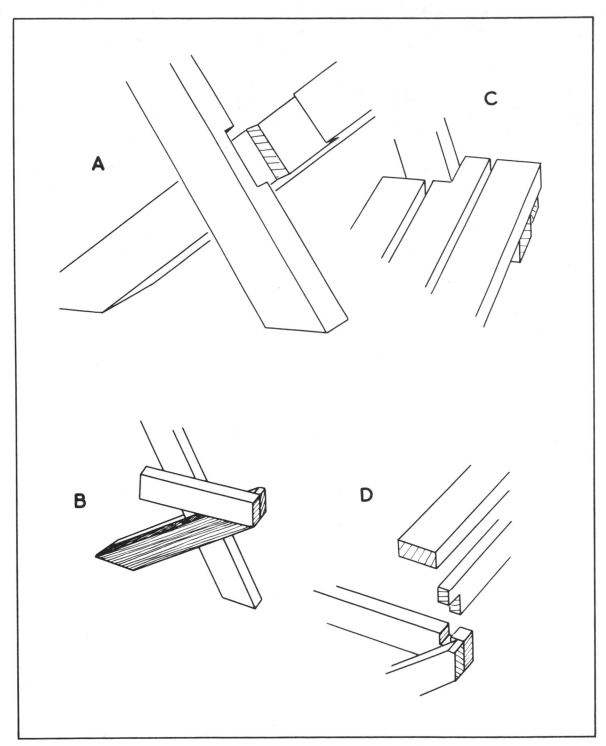

Fig. 6-4. Constructional details of the sawbuck bench.

Fig. 6-5. This bench was designed to suit available waney-edged boards.

also allow you to tighten the structure by driving the wedges further, if the seat becomes shaky.

If you ever want to store the bench away, knocking out the wedges allows you to separate it into its component parts. If that is your intention, take care to get the slots and wedges sufficiently alike for them to reassemble in any place satisfactorily. Otherwise you will have to mark the wedges and tenons so they are brought back to the same places.

BENCH WITHOUT ARMS

This is a simple seat that could be made any length. See Table 6-3. It is shown 48 inches long, but it could be short enough to be a single chair. It could also be lengthened to seat more people. If it is very much longer the wood should be thickened to prevent the seat and back springing too much. If the seat wood seems too flexible, the boards could be linked with one or more battens underneath. For a very long seat, there could be another upright arrangement at the middle.

The ends are shown sloping inward (Fig. 6-8A). This gives a greater spread of the feet with good resistance to

tipping endwise. Nevertheless, with the small amount of overhang there is little risk of tipping and the ends can be made upright if you prefer. Fitting the ends at a slope means cutting bevels instead of square edges at some places. Otherwise there is no difference. The slope is not enough to alter sizes for practical purposes.

Because the ends are 24 inches wide, it is unlikely that single boards can be obtained so two or more pieces will have to be joined. This also avoids cutting out a large waste piece. Arrange the joints so that they avoid the mortise for the stretcher and preferably do not come directly under where the back extends upward. The shape (Fig. 6-9A) will allow you to plan the joints economically.

Table 6-3. Materials List for Bench without Arms.

2 ends	24 × 34 × 1	(from narrow boards)
1 back	9 × 49 × 1	
2 seats	8 × 49 × 1	
1 stretcher	3 × 40 × 1	

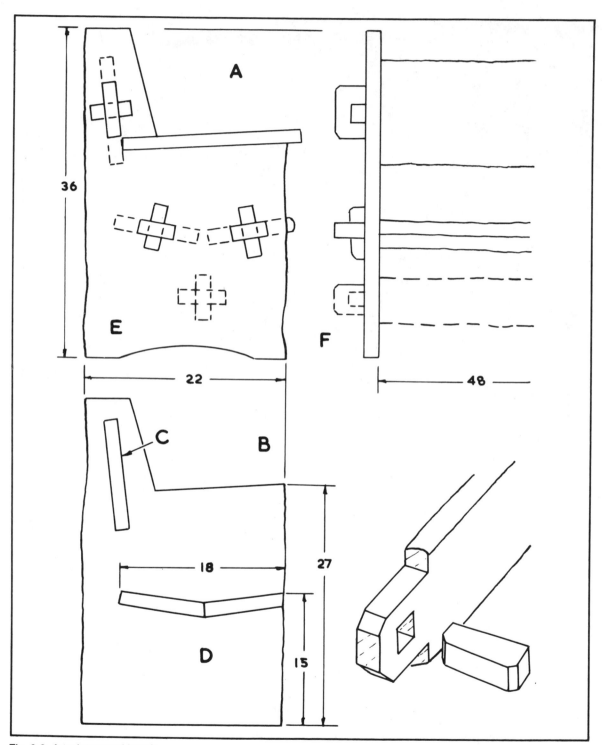

Fig. 6-6. A tusk-tenoned bench.

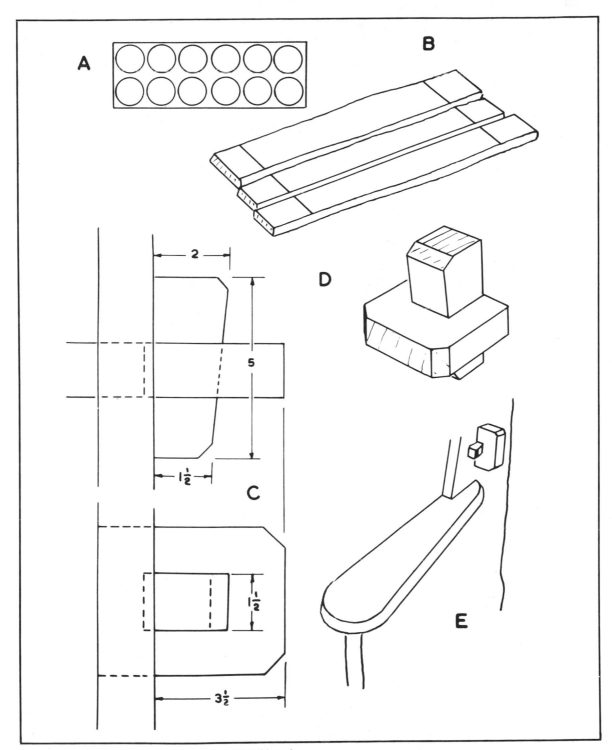

Fig. 6-7. Constructional details of the tusk-tenoned bench.

It can be sufficient to join the boards with simple glued joints, using a fully waterproof glue. If you are doubtful about the dryness of the wood, it would be advisable to reinforce the joints. Putting battens across would be unsatisfactory as swelling and shrinking of the wide boards later might cause cracking. You could put dowels between the board edges (Fig. 6-10A); ⅜ inch dowels taken about 1 inch into each board should be sufficient. Use a jig when drilling or mark out the edges carefully (Fig. 6-10B).

Another interesting and effective way of joining is to use secret slot screwing. This pulls and secures the joint with screws that are hidden. Use two or three screws in each joint. Mark the meeting edges together with extra marks on one piece ½ inch from the first marks (Fig. 6-10C). Use flat-headed steel screws. For 1-inch boards, they could be 10 gauge by 1 inch. Drill at the single marks for the screws and drive them until the threaded part is buried and not more than ¼ of an inch projects (Fig. 6-10D). On the other board, drill holes at the second marks large enough to clear the screw heads (Fig. 6-10E). Go deep enough to let the head enter.

At the other marks, drill holes that will clear the necks of the screws. Remove the waste between the holes by drilling and chiseling out to make a slot (Fig. 6-10F). Bring the boards together so that the screws go into the opposite holes. Then drive one board along the other until the screw heads have cut their way along the bottoms of the grooves to the other ends (Fig. 6-10G). If that assembly of the joint is satisfactory, drive the boards back again until the screws will lift out. Give each screw a quarter tightening turn. Apply glue to the surfaces and drive the joint together again. The screws act as clamps as well as reinforcements.

The shape shown (Fig. 6-9A) allows for a tilted seat and a back that slopes at about 100 degrees to it. The outer edges could be straight, but they look better with curves. Do not cut in too much at the back because that could weaken it. The curve at the bottom helps in providing feet that stand a better chance of coming level on uneven ground than a broad straight base. Note the small curve between the edge under the seat and the upright part. A curved inside corner is always stronger than an angular cut because there is less risk of a split developing.

If the ends are to slope, set out the angle (Fig. 6-8B) and use an adjustable bevel when cutting joints. The seat boards could be nailed or screwed down, but for the best quality work they are tenoned. Two tenons at each place should be sufficient. Allow the tenons through with

diagonal saw cuts for wedges. Then trim level (Fig. 6-9B).

The stretcher will have to be cut at an angle on each end with tenons through, kept the full thickness of the wood, and tightened with double wedges (Fig. 6-9C). Take sharpness of the edges before assembly.

The back is a single board. It could be screwed directly to its supports, but it is a better fit if they are notched (Fig. 6-9D). Counterbore and plug the holes for the best appearance.

In its basic form, the bench has parallel lengthwise parts (with the sharpness taken off their edges and corners). The seat boards could have their edges fully rounded and the corners given a good curve (Fig. 6-11A). The back would be treated to match in the same way.

The back provides an opportunity for decoration. Edges could be curved (Fig. 6-11B) or the top edge shaped (Fig. 6-11C). Do not use elaborate decoration that has angular corners. They may be uncomfortable against shoulders. You could cut out the center of the back (Fig. 6-11D) or it could be carved (Fig. 6-11E). Use a fairly bold treatment of a leaf or something similar. This is not the place for very detailed or deep carving. You could use incised lettering with a name or initials or just the date you made the bench (Fig. 6-11F).

The stretcher tenon could be carried through and rounded (Fig. 6-11G). It could have a tusk extending far enough for a wedge to be driven across, but that would just be for decoration because the furniture could not be disassembled.

A problem with end grain resting on the ground is the absorption of moisture; that would eventually lead to rot. Absorption into side grain is much less. One method of protection is to paint the end grain with waterproof glue, but that does not penetrate very far and could get rubbed through if the bench is dragged on stony ground. It is better to screw on feet with their grain across and the screws far enough below the surface to be clear of the ground (Fig. 6-11H). When these get worn, they can be replaced.

PARK BENCH

A strong bench similar to the types often used in public parks, is equally suitable for a garden or yard. If made of teak or another wood that withstands any weather, it can be untreated and left in place all during the year. If made of other wood, it should be treated with preservative and paint. It is not too heavy for two people to carry so it can be moved under cover in bad weather. The shape is intended to provide reasonable comfort without cushions

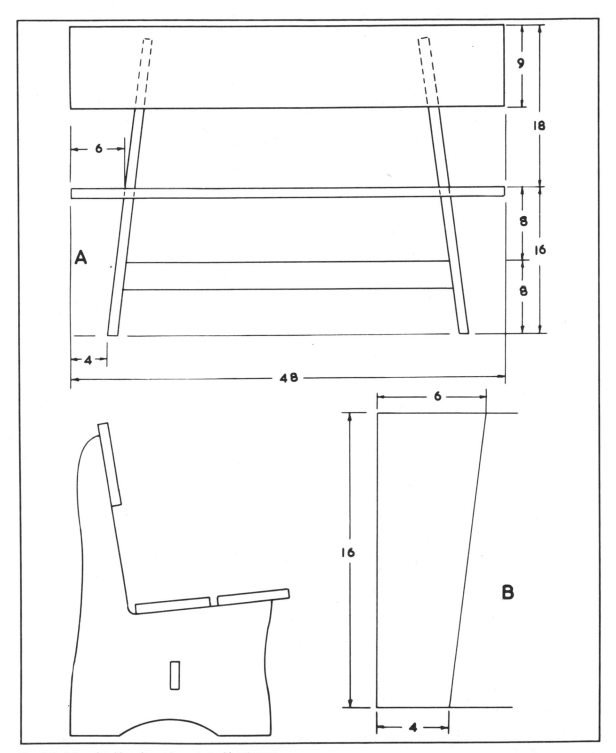

Fig. 6-8. A bench with splayed legs, but without arms.

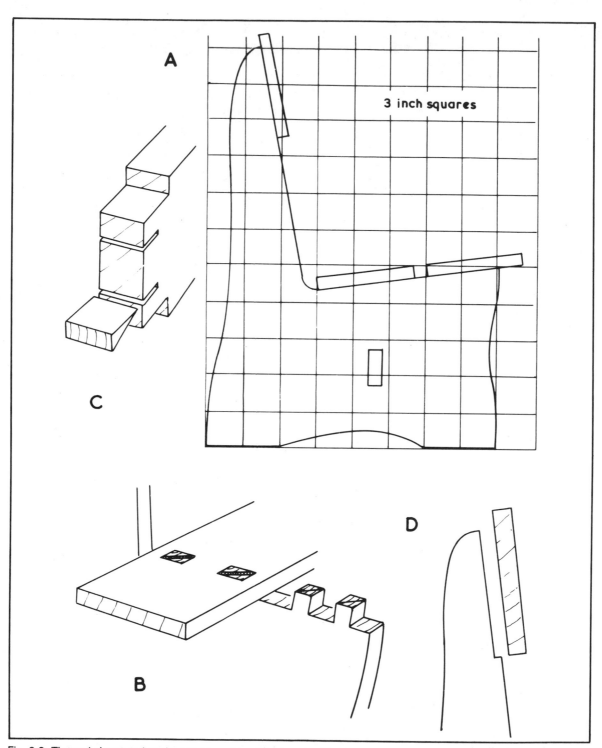

Fig. 6-9. The end shape and method of assembly of the bench without arms.

or other padding (Fig. 6-12). Padding can be added for longer use.

Sizes are for a 60-inch bench designed to seat three people (see Table 6-4 and Fig. 6-13). The seat is made of slats arranged on a curve and the back is inclined to give a restful position.

The front legs are 1¾ inches square (Fig. 6-14A) and the back legs are cut to that bent section from a wider piece (Fig. 6-14B), to provide the slope of the upper part. Note that the bend comes just above seat level and the change of direction should be curved—not an abrupt angle. Mark the legs together to get the seat and bottom rail joints level. Mark the two rear legs together to get the back rail positions the same. Note that they must be in the same plane to match the back slats.

Nearly all joints are with stub tenons and they should

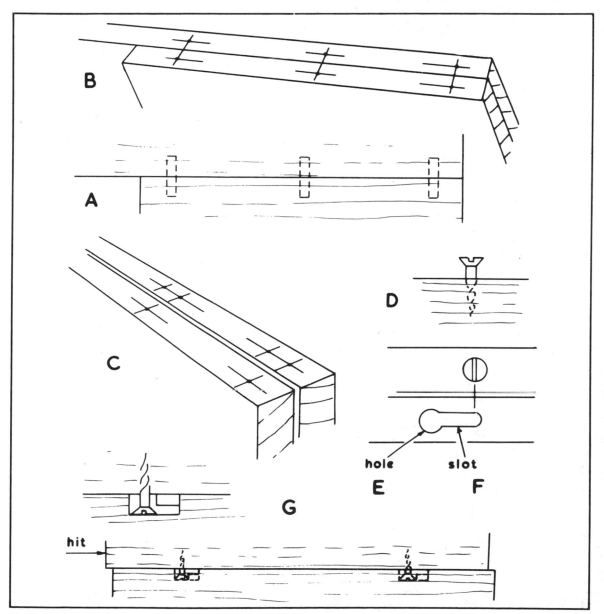

Fig. 6-10. How to join boards with dowels or secret-slot screwing.

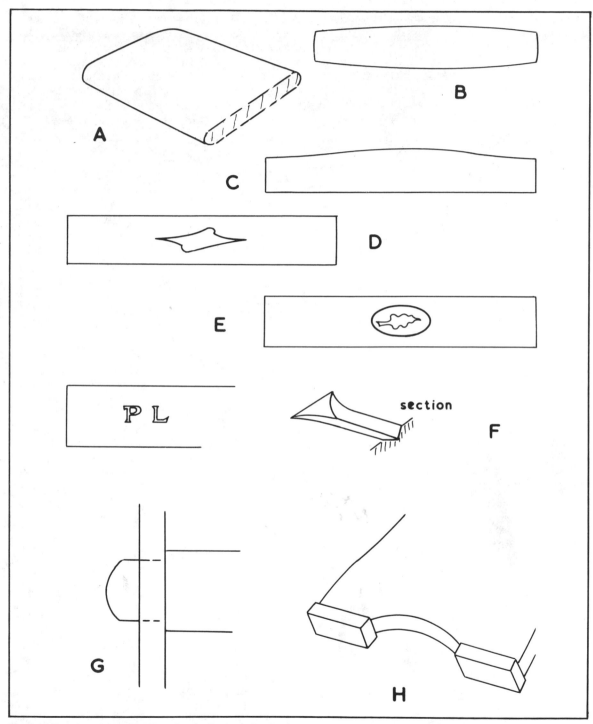

Fig. 6-11. Bench parts can be shaped or the back can be decorated with a cutout or carving. Tenons can project and feet can be added.

Fig. 6-12. A park bench of a popular type.

go about 1¼ inches into the 1¾ inch legs (Fig. 6-14C). For most parts, the tenons can be ½ inch thick.

Mark the seat and lower rails together (Fig. 6-14D). The top of the seat rails dip to 2 inches thick with a fair curve. The two intermediate seat supports must have the same curves. Mark them at this stage, but do not cut them to length yet. Cut the mortises and tenons for the bottom and seat rails at each end.

Make the arm rests (Fig. 6-14E). They are parallel, except for tapering to the rear legs, where they tenon in. At the front, there is not much depth for tenons. You might prefer to screw downward into the tops of the legs. If tenons are to be used, it is best to use twin ones to get enough glue area (Fig. 6-14F).

Prepare the lengths. Get all the distances between shoulders the same (Fig. 6-15A). The seat front rail comes almost level with the front of the legs and can be given a barefaced tenon. This allows for curving the front edges adequately (Fig. 6-15B). The seat back rail also comes near the front of the rear legs, but it does not need rounding. Its purpose is to take the ends of the inter- mediate seat supports.

Top and bottom back rails are the same with tenons into the legs and a number of light slats arranged ladder- like along them (Fig. 6-15C). Because they are thin, mortises could be cut to take the full thickness or they could be shouldered on one side only (Fig. 6-15D). The back assembly can be made up, but be careful that it is square. Get diagonal measurements the same. It is the squareness of this assembly that controls the squareness lengthwise of the rest of the seat.

Make up the pair of ends. Check squareness and

Table 6-4. Materials List for Park Bench.

2 front legs	1¾	×	23	×	1¾
2 rear legs	3½	×	34	×	1¾
2 bottom rails	1¾	×	20	×	⅝
4 seat rails	3	×	20	×	⅞
2 arms	3½	×	23	×	⅞
2 seat rails	3	×	60	×	1⅛
2 bottom rails	1¾	×	60	×	⅞
2 back rails	3	×	60	×	⅞
11 back slats	2	×	13	×	½
5 seat slats	2	×	61	×	⅝

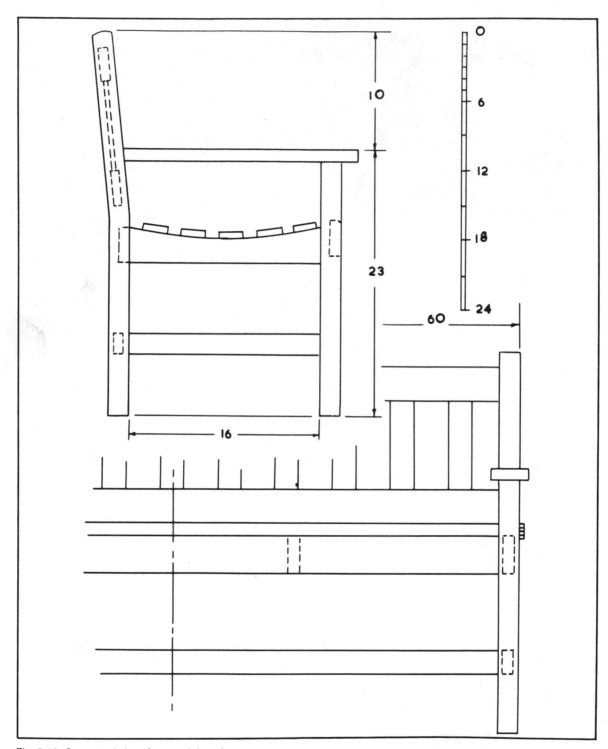

Fig. 6-13. Suggested sizes for a park bench.

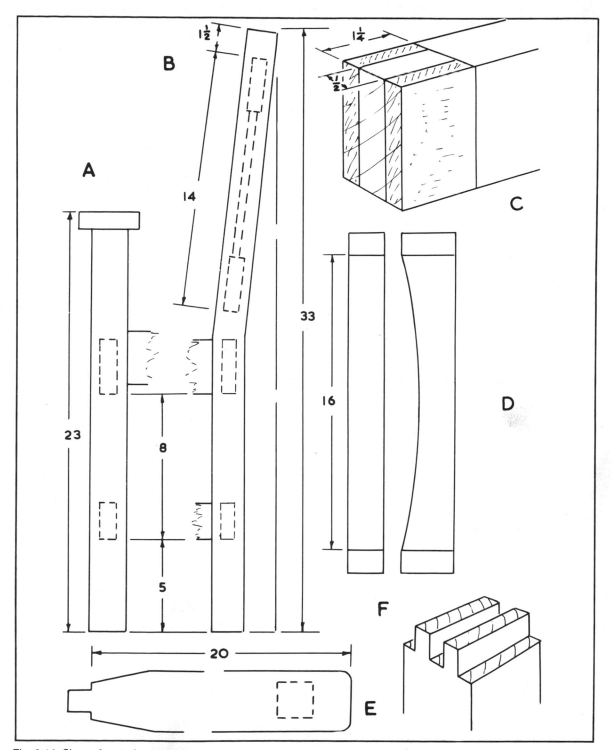

Fig. 6-14. Sizes of parts for a park bench.

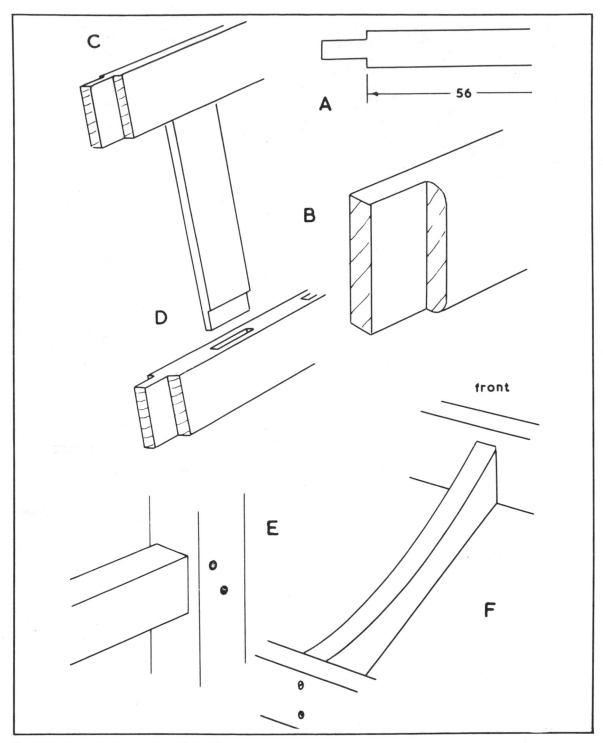

Fig. 6-15. Assembly details of a park bench.

check that opposite ends match. The arms and seat are parallel with the floor; they should be square to the legs. Let the glue set on the end and back assemblies before going further. So far as possible, pull joints together with clamps. If you prefer, dowels could be put through the main joints; two ¼-inch dowels set diagonally would be right (Fig. 6-15E).

Join the ends with the lengthwise parts while the ends are standing on a level surface. Check squareness as viewed from above, as well as in other directions, before the glue sets.

The seat slats will go past the ends a short distance and will need intermediate supports. Make the supports to fit between the seat rails where they can be screwed (Fig. 6-15F). They could be tenoned or doweled, but screws should be sufficient. Use a long, straight piece of wood between the end seat rails as a guide when fitting the intermediate supports so that you can get the curved tops in line.

Make the seat slats with rounded tops and ends. Attach them with a central screw at each crossing. Space them evenly. So far as possible, have the gap behind the front seat rail the same as the gaps between the slats (For the sake of a uniform appearance).

Take the sharpness off exposed edges, but except for the tops of the rear legs there is no need for much rounding. If it is a wood that will suffer from water absorption, treat the bottoms of the legs with waterproof glue.

NAILED LONG BENCH

There is sometimes a need for a bench that will seat several people and offer somewhere to rest without the need to provide comfort for a long period. A simple board on supports, like a long stool, is the absolute basic provision, but anyone wanting to relax briefly on a long walk will appreciate a back as well as a seat. This seat is intended to be made to any reasonable length and it can be quickly and easily put together. See Table 6-5. Ease of construction is a nice feature if there is an urgent need or if several similar seats are required. The bench shown in Fig. 6-16 could be made short enough to be a single seat. It is shown 8 feet long. It could be made any length to suit available space or the intended number of sitters. Supports are the same as the ends and should be spaced equally. Do not exceed 30 inches between them, particularly for softwoods. Much depends on the stiffness of the chosen wood.

The frames must be all the same. Make one and use it as a pattern when assembling the others (Fig. 6-17A).

Table 6-5. Materials List for Nailed Long Bench.

5 legs	3 × 31 × 1
5 legs	3 × 16 × 1
10 rails	3 × 19 × 1
4 seat slats	3 × 97 × 1
3 back slats	3 × 97 × 1
1 top slat	3 × 99 × 1
1 front slat	3 × 99 × 1
2 ends	3 × 27 × 1

Use nails long enough to go right through. Leave enough projecting for the points to be clenched; three or four nails at each crossing should be enough. With most woods, it will be advisable to drill slightly undersize for each nail. Besides preventing splitting, this will keep the nail straight and make driving easier. Put scrap wood underneath, for the point to enter, so that it does not become buckled on a hard surface or damage a bench top. Check squareness carefully as any flaw in that will be repeated in the others.

Frames at opposite ends of the bench must be a pair, with the uprights on the outside (Fig. 6-17B), but it does not matter which way around the intermediate frames are assembled. The lengthwise parts for the seat and the back all extend to the outside surfaces of the legs (with the seat ones overhanging their supports by that much). Prepare all these pieces. They should be straight if uneven gaps are not to spoil appearance, but for some situations precision will not be important. Round the upper surfaces and ends, except for the front seat edge, which will meet the front slat.

Mark the spacings of the intermediate frames on the upper back and front seat slats (and on the others if you prefer). Nail the upper and front slats to the end frames and check their squareness. Bring in the intermediate frames and nail the slats to them. Check that this assembly stands level and then add the other slats, equally spaced. At the front, nail the front slat to the front legs and to the front seat slat (Fig. 6-17C). Two 2½-inch or 3-inch nails at each crossing and at about 10-inch intervals along the front should make a strong assembly.

The seat should be stiff enough to resist lengthwise loads. If you think it is necessary, you could add another lengthwise strip nailed to the back legs (Fig. 6-17D) or to the bottom rails.

There is no provision for arms in the basic design. Nevertheless, it would not be difficult to extend the front end legs upward, nail on strips (Fig. 6-17E), and then put flat pieces on top (Fig. 6-17F). Add a little shaping to provide comfort.

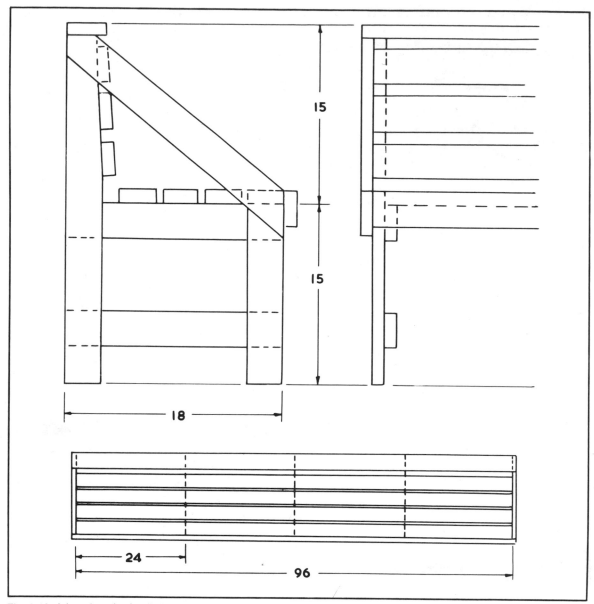

Fig. 6-16. A long bench of nailed construction.

Alternative to arms are sloping pieces (Fig. 6-17G) nailed outside the legs. They are not much use as arms, but they prevent anyone sliding off the end of the seat. If this is done, continue the top slat to overlap them.

ISLAND SEATING

If seating is required in an open situation for more people than can be accommodated on one bench, there could be several benches. It would, however, be more economical and compact to arrange all-round seating on one unit. If the seating is there so people can admire the view, they only want to face that way and single benches are the answer. If all that is required is somewhere to rest and the outlook is much the same all around, seats can be back to back.

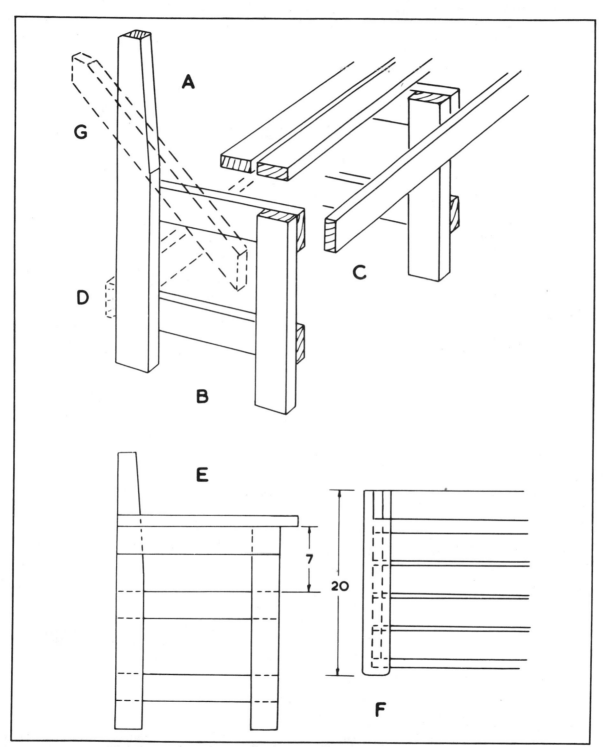

Fig. 6-17. Assembly details of nailed bench and alternative arm construction.

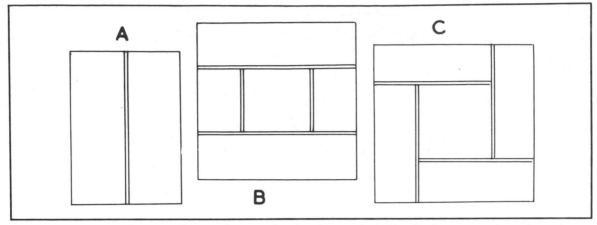

Fig. 6-18. If seats are to have uses in more than one direction, they can be back to back or arranged round a center.

A simple arrangement is a pair of benches with a common back between them (Fig. 6-18A). You have then provided twice the capacity in the same length. Rather more seating can be provided by using a square layout (Fig. 6-18B). The backs of the long seats enclose the ends of the short ones. A variation on this has the seats staggered (Fig. 6-18C). Of course, the layout does not have to be square. It can be longer one way if that suits the situation.

With back-to-back seats, there is mutual support so there is no risk of tipping backward and you do not have the problem of arranging rear legs to resist the effect of sitters' pressure on the seat back. You can slope the rear legs to give a comfortable back without compensating by raking the legs backward.

BACK-TO-BACK BENCH

This layout bench can be nailed or screwed (Fig. 6-19). The sizes given are suggestions (see Table 6-6 and Fig. 6-20) and the method can be used for seats of many other sizes. For very long seats, there must be intermediate supports that can be repeats of the end frames. Even when the seat is short enough for only two or three each side, the seat and back slats should be linked with pieces across.

The shapes of the end frames can be laid out from the general drawing (Fig. 6-20). The sloping center pieces taper to a total 3 inch width at the top. Assemble the parts by nailing or screwing (Fig. 6-21A). Nail the beveled center pieces together. Make sure the opposite ends match with their cross members inward.

Make the front rails (Fig. 6-21B). They finish the same length as the seats, but the end frames join them 3

inches back from their ends. Bevel the under surfaces at the ends. The capping over the backs is the same length (Fig. 6-21C). Join the end frame with these parts and make a central piece to go between the seat rails. It could be doweled or tenoned into them, but it should be satisfactorily nailed (Fig. 6-21D).

There are four struts that provide resistance to sideways loads and it is easiest to fit them at this stage. They each go from the lower rails of the end frames to the central piece between the seat rails (Fig. 6-22A). Arrange their positions so they will come under seat slats. Although they could be kept in line, it is easier to make strong nailed joints if they are staggered slightly (Fig. 6-22B).

Before making and fitting the struts, have the assembly standing level. Once the struts are added the shape will be held. Sight along to see that one end is not twisted in relation to the other. Measure diagonals at seat level.

Cut the struts to size to fit closely in place. They should all be the same and it is advisable to make a template from scrap wood (so as to get the lengths and angles correct). Attach with nails through the meeting surfaces.

Table 6-6. Materials List for Back-To-Back Bench.

4 backs	3	× 32	× 1
5 cross rails	3	× 36	× 1
2 front rails	3	× 76	× 1
7 back slats	3	× 76	× 1
2 back braces	3	× 12	× 1
6 seat slats	4	× 76	× 1
4 struts	3	× 36	× 1

112

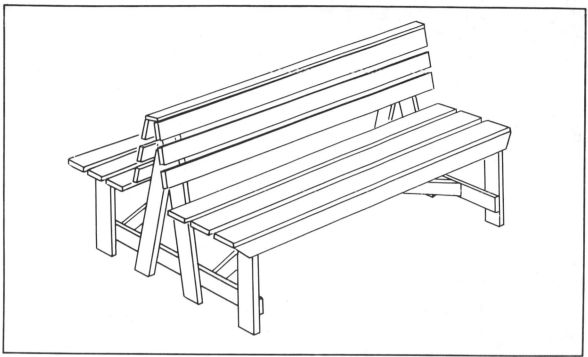

Fig. 6-19. A back-to-back bench.

Round the exposed ends and edges of the back slats. They will be spaced with 1-inch gaps between them. The braces that held them in place at the centers cannot be fitted after nailing to the end frames. Therefore, position them with nails from the back before attaching them to the end frames (Fig. 6-22C). Finally, have the seat slats rounded and nail them to the end frames and the central rail. Nail the front slat along the seat rail each side as well.

SQUARE SEAT

A seat that faces in four directions is basically a pair of ordinary benches linked by matching members that form seats fitted between the backs of the long ones. There will be an open square at the center and its area will depend on the total size. See Table 6-7. Only a certain width is needed to sit on whatever the overall sizes may be. The open center could enclose a tree or bush or it would be possible to fit it with a tray to take pot plants or other decorations.

The example shown in Fig. 6-23 has outer benches large enough to seat four people each. The inner benches will take two each (making for a total of 12 people). The method of construction shown (Fig. 6-24) uses nails or screws with slats for seats and backs, but this serves to indicate the technique that could be adapted to use some of the more advanced constructions described for benches and chairs.

The best approach is to consider the two long benches and to make them first (with the extensions described to take in the other parts). The key part that settles many other sizes is the main back leg (Fig. 6-25A)—of which there are four. For the inner seats, there are four pieces that match the upper parts of the legs, but finish below the rail at seat level (Fig. 6-25B). Notch the legs to take the rails, where shown, using the actual pieces of wood as a guide to sizes. There is no need to notch the smaller pieces for the backs of the inner seats.

Table 6-7. Materials List for Square Seat.

4 legs	4 × 31 × 1
4 legs	3 × 16 × 1
4 inner backs	4 × 20 × 1
10 rails	3 × 75 × 1
2 cappings	3 × 75 × 1
2 cappings	3 × 38 × 1
6 seat slats	4 × 75 × 1
2 seat supports	3 × 19 × 1
6 back slats	3 × 75 × 1
6 seat slats	4 × 40 × 1
6 back slats	3 × 40 × 1

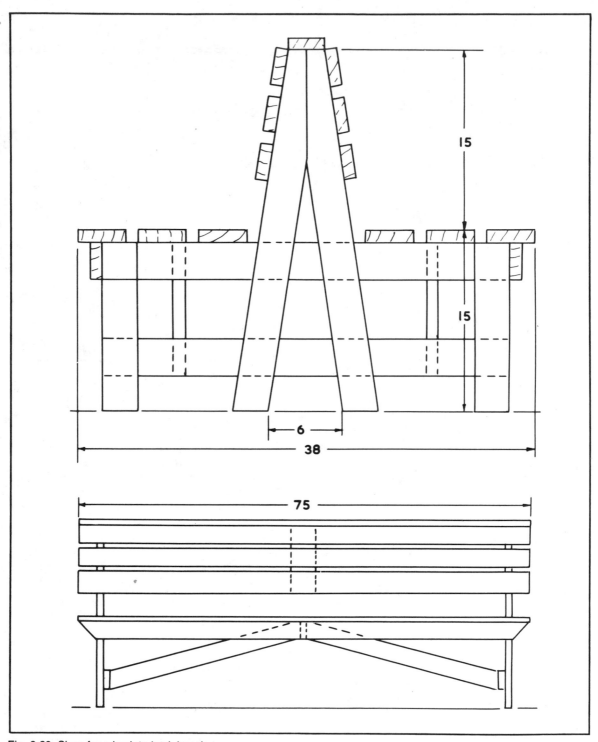

Fig. 6-20. Sizes for a back-to-back bench.

114

The front legs are simple pieces (Fig. 6-25C). They are only needed at the outer corners and would have no use in the inner seats.

Prepare the pieces that go between the legs. Make up ends first. The legs are linked across with a seat rail on the outsides of the legs (Fig. 6-25D) and a lower rail across on the insides (Fig. 6-25E). This will give you two matching opposite frames.

Link these opposite assemblies with the rails that fit in the seat back notches (Fig. 6-25F) and the front seat rails (Fig. 6-25G). Check squareness of the whole as-sembly by measuring diagonals. If necessary, put on a temporary diagonal brace to hold the parts square.

The seat slats on the long side need at least one intermediate support. Providing the slats are reasonably stiff, one at the center between rails should be enough (Fig. 6-25H). Nail it between front and back rails. If the long seat slats are fitted at this stage, they will hold the assembly true. Round the ends and edges. Then nail to the end frames and the front seat rail. They can finish level with the end frames or be carried over a short distance each end.

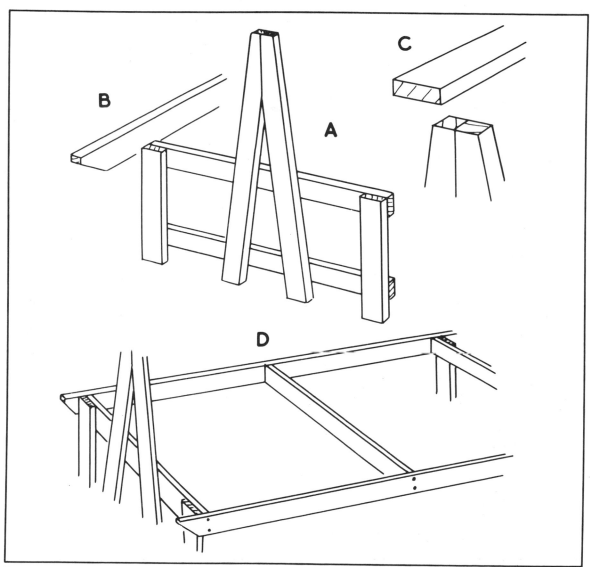

Fig. 6-21. Constructional details of a back-to-back bench.

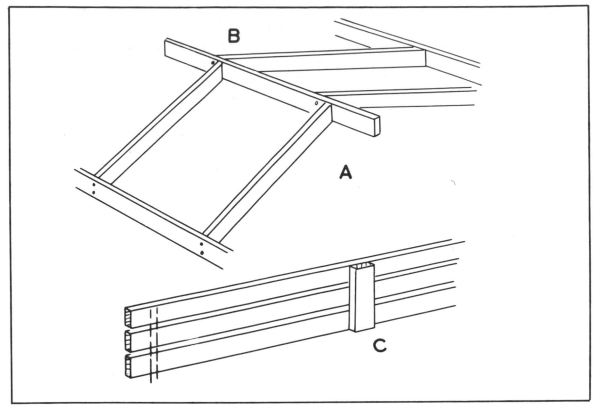

Fig. 6-22. Details of the bracing and set of a back-to-back bench.

The linking rails at seat level serve as seat rails for the inner seats. Measure from these to locate the short back pieces. These should be screwed to the rails across the long seats (Fig. 6-26A). Secure screwing there will be better than nailing because these parts must not move in use. There would usually be no need for any rails between these back pieces. If you think they are advisable, nail strips to the backs of them.

The seat slats for the inner benches are nailed to the rails across the backs of the long benches (Fig. 6-26B) and to the rail crossing the front. Get their spacing the same as on the long benches so that the design looks uniform.

Put on the back slats in a similar way all round. It will be easiest to deal with the short ones first. If the long seat slats overhang at the ends, treat the back slats in a similar way. The long slats will require a linking piece at the center similar to those of the previous seat.

Make a capping to go over the tops of the seat backs. The long ones nail to the top rail and the uprights. The short ones go on in a similar way, but where they come

against the others, notch them in (Fig. 6-26C).

If the seat is not to be near a natural feature, you could make a lift-off top to fit over the space. That would serve as a shelf on which to put a piece of sculpture, a floral display, or some pot plants. The cover should not be made permanent because that would make access to the center difficult.

A simple cover can be made of boards cut large enough to rest on the capping. Attach framing underneath to hold them together and keep them central on the seat (Fig. 6-26D).

STAGGERED SQUARE SEAT

The four sides of a square seat need not be arranged as in the last example, but they can fit into each other in a staggered plan so that each of the four sides is the same (Fig. 6-27A). Constructionally, the work is not as difficult as you might think because the identical parts fit into each other.

Using the general design of the last example, ends

116

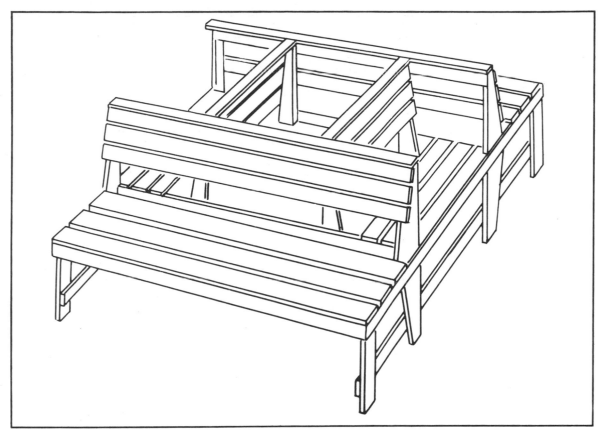

Fig. 6-23. A square seat with long and short sections.

are made in the same way. Notches are used for length-wise pieces cut in the backs and allowance is made for rails that go right through. Instead of the rails forming seats sandwiched between long benches, they go on to form seats to the next corner.

Make each end with rails long enough to reach the corner behind it (Fig. 6-27B). Keep both rails on the outsides of the legs. The rails can then be joined to the next end to form a square (Fig. 6-27C). The top and seat level rails have to join to each other. This can be done with mortise and tenon joints (Fig. 6-27D) or you could put wood blocks on the corners (Fig. 6-27E) and screw through. Metal shelf brackets would be neater.

Attach the sloping pieces to take the back slats in the way described for the last example. This gives you the main parts linked and something to build on to complete the seat. The seat slats rest on the frames and on the rails at seat level on the back of the next section. The back slats go against the top of a back leg and the tapered piece behind the next seat. Link the slats with cross pieces if

they seem too flexible without them. Cappings go on the tops of the backs and are notched into each other on the inner corners.

The materials suggested are the same sections as for the U-shaped square assembly except that the slats and inner rails are all shorter than the long benches by the width of a seat—about 56 inches long. The size of the seat as a whole is easily modified by altering the lengths of these parts. For use in a confined space, the backs could be brought so close together that the square in the middle is only a few inches across, producing four single chairs, each facing square to its neighbor. If the seat is much enlarged, there would have to be more intermediate supports, (made similar to the end frames).

This makes an interesting and unusual seat form, and particularly if it is arranged round a tree or shrub. If there is nothing at the center, it will usually be worthwhile to make a lift-off cover for the space to support a floral display and to prevent unauthorized use of this vacant space.

117

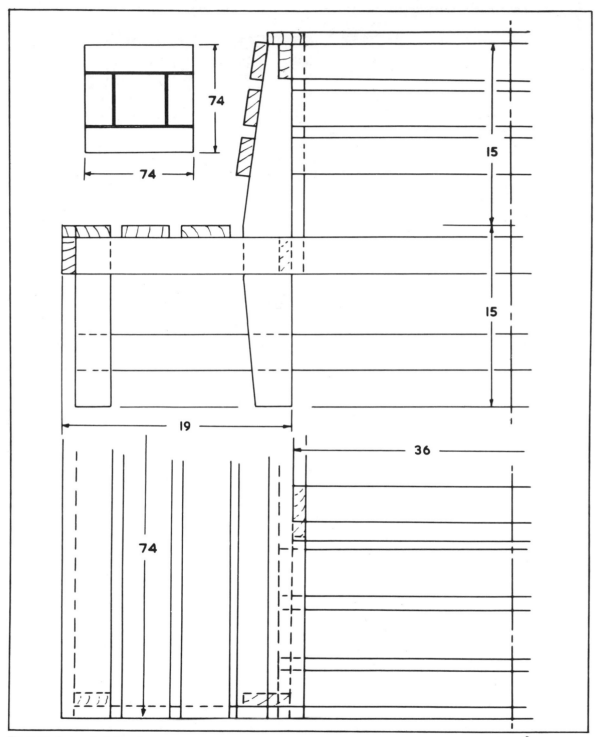

Fig. 6-24. Suggested sizes for a square seat.

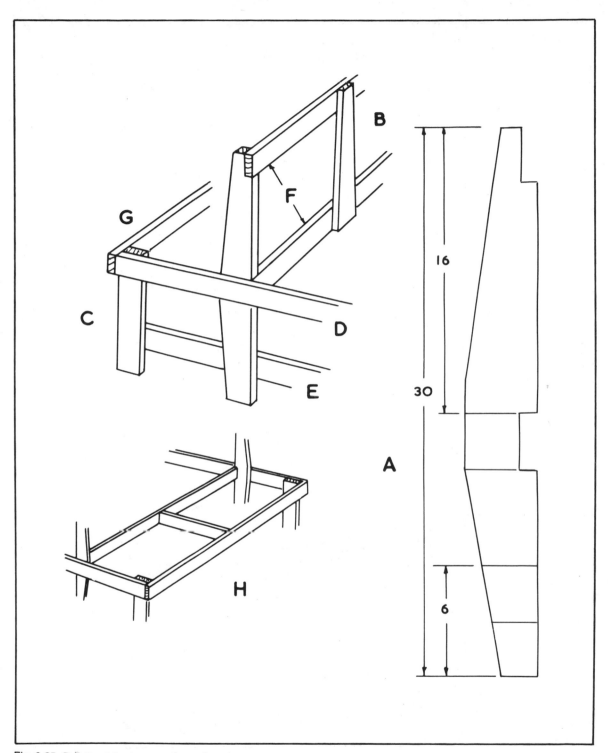

Fig. 6-25. Details of the long sections of seat.

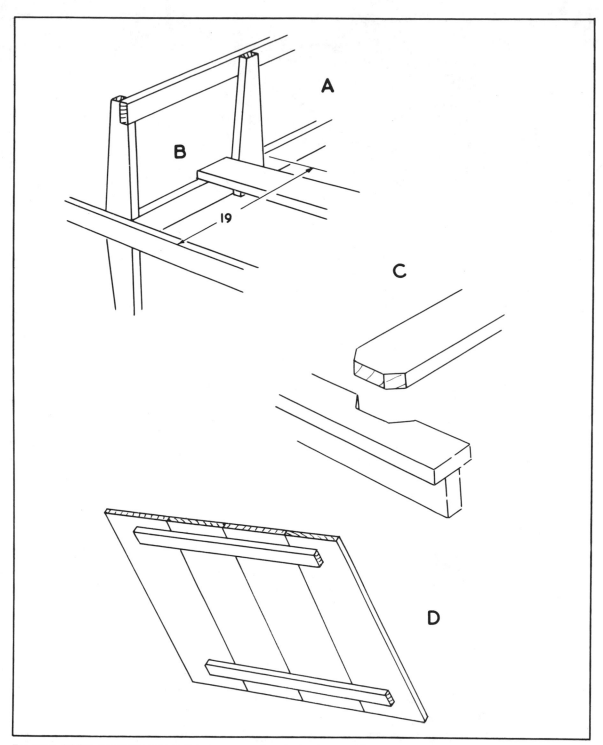

Fig. 6-26. Adding the short sections to a square seat and a top to cover the center.

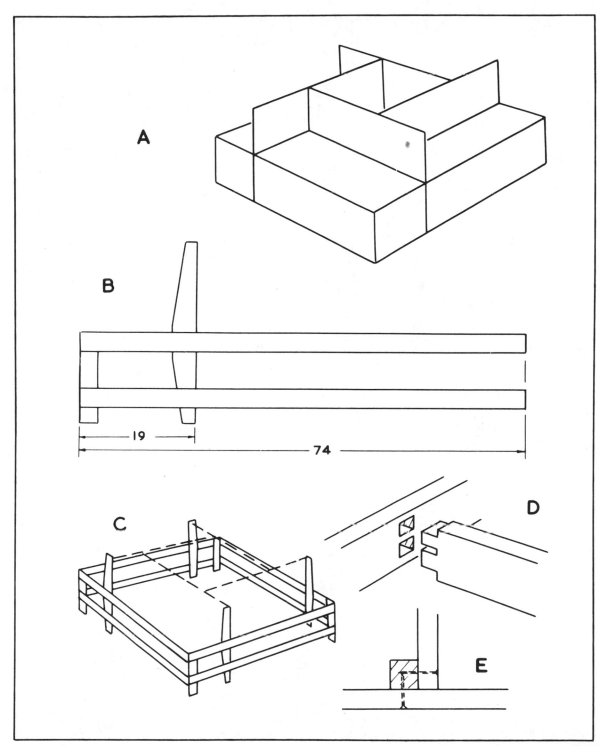

Fig. 6-27. Design details for a staggered square seat.

Fig. 6-28. A bench made using boards mostly in their natural shape, with arms added.

SLAB BENCH

The availability of pieces of wood cut straight across a log can suggest a seat design. Quite often, the design can be planned around the sizes of wood available. This bench makes use of similar wide boards for the ends with the seat, back, and rail made of waney-edged boards. Only enough of the natural edges are eased off to ensure comfort. The bench could be completed with open ends without affecting strength or stability, but the example shown in Fig. 6-28 has been given arms supported on posts independent of the bench ends.

The sizes suggested in Table 6-8 and Fig. 6-29 should be used as a guide, but there is scope for variations to suit the available wood. Examine wood for flaws. Sound knots in the body of a piece of wood will not matter, but keep knots clear of edges or joints. Look for natural splits that occur in a growing tree. Providing they run to

an end that is supported, most shakes will not matter except for appearance.

The vital parts are the seat and back. Arrange for the seat to be level or slightly tilted back. Then make the back rather more than 90 degrees to it; up to 10 degrees would be suitable (Fig. 6-30A). Mark out the seat height from ground level and the back in relation to it, add the lower rail, then scheme the shape of an end around it. Make the best use of the wood. The back and the lower rail each have tusk tenons through the ends, but the seat rests on the end with a slight notch into the upright part of it (Fig. 6-30B).

The tusk tenons and their matching mortises should be about 6 inches wide (Fig. 6-30C). Arrange the tenons to go through far enough to take the wedges. Have enough end grain outside to take the thrust when a wedge is driven, (without risk of splitting).

Make the back and the rail with the same distance between shoulders (Fig. 6-30D). Make the wedges (Fig. 6-30E) and cut the holes for them so that they will drive in and tighten the joints without themselves touching the bottoms of the holes in the tenons (Fig. 6-30F). Draw the ends together temporarily with the wedged joints so that you can mark out the seat. Be careful that the bench is standing level while you are doing this.

Make the seat to overhang the ends by an inch or so and round the extending corners (Fig. 6-31A). It could be nailed to the ends, but it is better to use screws that are counterbored and plugged. Do not attach the seat permanently if you intend to add arms.

The arms and their posts can be made of 2-inch wood with tenoned joints used between them and the other parts. The posts are square and have tenons through the seat or at least 1 inch deep if it is very thick (Fig. 6-31B). At the top, the strongest joint has double-stub tenons (Fig. 6-31C). In the simplest construction, the posts are upright, but they could slope forward. That would mean cutting the joints at an angle in that direction. It would be possible to let the posts slope outward as well. This would make an interesting piece of joint layout to deal

Table 6-8. Materials List for Slab Bench.

2 ends	18	× 35	×	1½
1 seat	13	× 56	×	1½
1 rail	8	× 60	×	1½
1 back	12	× 60	×	1½
4 wedges	2	× 5	×	2
2 arms	4	× 16	×	2
2 posts	2	× 12	×	2

122

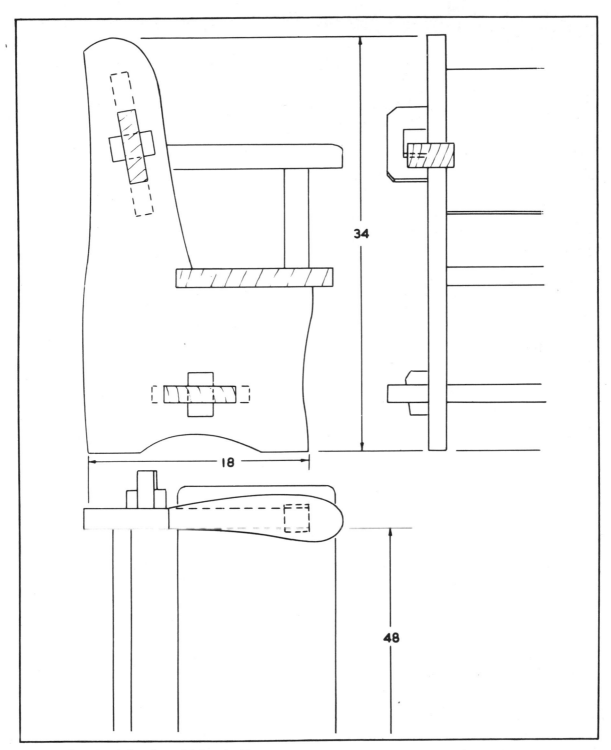

Fig. 6-29. Suggested sizes for a slab bench with arms.

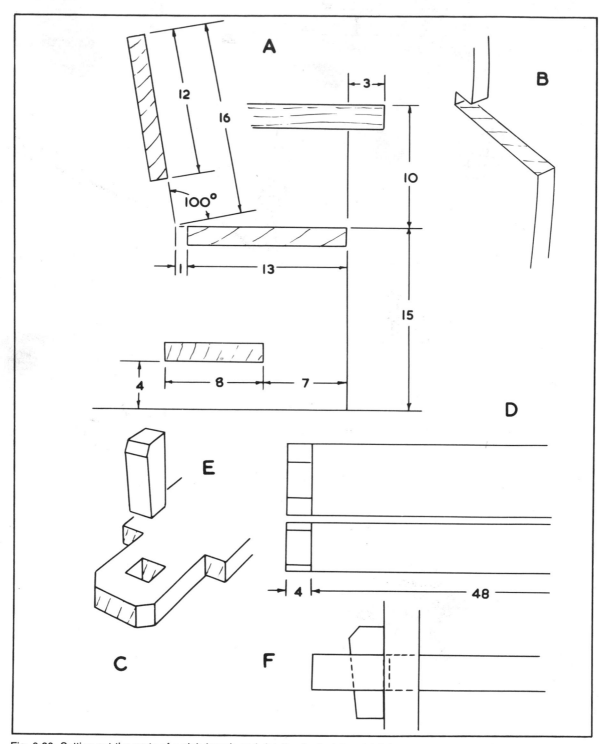

Fig. 6-30. Setting out the parts of a slab bench and details of a tusk tenon joint.

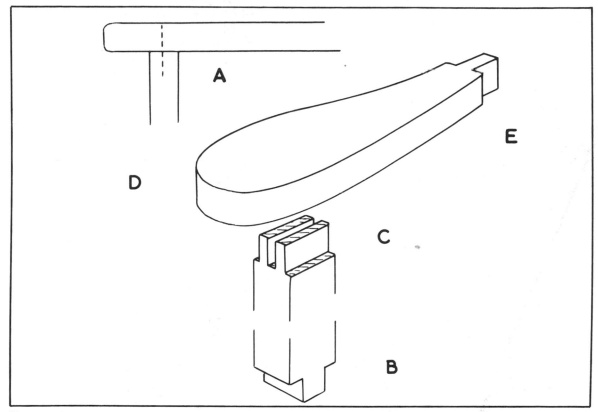

Fig. 6-31. An arm and its post.

with the compound angles, but that would hardly be justified for such a rustic piece of outdoor furniture (unless you want to display your skill at carpentry).

The arms can be curved in any way you prefer (Fig. 6-31D), but allow for a tenon into the upright part of the end (Fig. 6-31E).

Assemble the back and rail to the ends with their wedges driven tightly. Screw down the seat and glue in plugs. Glue the posts into the seat mortises. You can get maximum tightness with foxtail wedges in stub tenons. If the mortises go right through, join the posts to the seat before that is screwed down so you can wedge the tenon ends from below. There can also be foxtail wedges in the tenons upward into the arms and between the arms and the uprights. Always arrange the saw cuts for the wedges at right-angles to the grain of the mortised part. There tightening will be best and the risk of splitting minimal.

This type of bench is best left in its natural state except for treating with preservative if it is a type of wood requiring it. Wood is often supplied before it has fully dried out. Go back after the seat has been in use for a month or so and drive the wedges tighter.

BATTEN BENCH

This is a light bench seat that is made entirely from wood of 1-×-3 inch section. A total of 48 feet will make 48 inches long. See Table 6-9. Although construction is light (Fig. 6-32) and the bench is easily moved, it is rigidly braced and able to stand up to plenty of use.

The general drawing (Fig. 6-33A) gives details of a bench proportioned to finish 48 inches long. It could be made slightly longer, but sections of wood should be increased for anything over 60 inches.

The end frames (Fig. 6-34A) are made as a pair with the cross members inside. If the laps are glued, three screws about 10 gauge by 1¾ inches long should at each joint be strong enough. That size screw could be used throughout. The tapered pieces that provide a slope at the back are cut diagonally through a 3-inch width (Fig. 6-34B). Nail them to the back legs. Assemble the ends squarely and check that the pair match.

Prepare the wood for the seat and back battens.

Table 6-9. Materials List for Battened Bench.

2 back legs	3 × 34 × 1
2 front legs	3 × 24 × 1
2 seat rails	3 × 22 × 1
1 seat brace	3 × 18 × 1
2 arms	3 × 23 × 1
2 backs from one	3 × 13 × 1
2 braces	3 × 28 × 1

Round all exposed edges and corners. Drill for two screws at each end. Cut the pieces for the seat first and make the back pieces longer—to reach the back legs. With the ends upright, screw on the seat battens; keep their spacing even and the assembly parallel. Fit the back top two battens, but leave the bottom one until the arms are being fitted.

The arms go on top of the front legs (arranged centrally). Let them extend forward of the legs and cut away round the rear legs (Fig. 6-34C). Mark the back legs where the arms are to come and fit the remaining back batten immediately below this.

The arms could be screwed downward into the front legs and that should be satisfactory. These are the points of greatest twisting loads and some strengthening might be advisable. There could be blocks of wood glued in the angles (Fig. 6-34D). Dowels in place of screws would be stronger (Fig. 6-34E). Tenons through make an alternative (Fig. 6-34F). Glue and screw the other end of each arm to its rear leg.

Underneath, the struts go from the lower rails at the ends to a strip brace beneath the seat battens (Fig. 6-33B). Notch the lower ends over the rails and notch the tops at the brace. Stagger them so they overlap (Fig. 6-34G). You can then screw them to each other as well as to the brace. The two struts should be the same. Try standing the bench level and upright. You might have to manipulate it slightly to get the lengths of the struts the same. If you put the bench together with the struts differing by more than minimal amounts, you will be securing it in a position that is not symmetrical in some way.

Fig. 6-32. A simple bench seat made from standard strips.

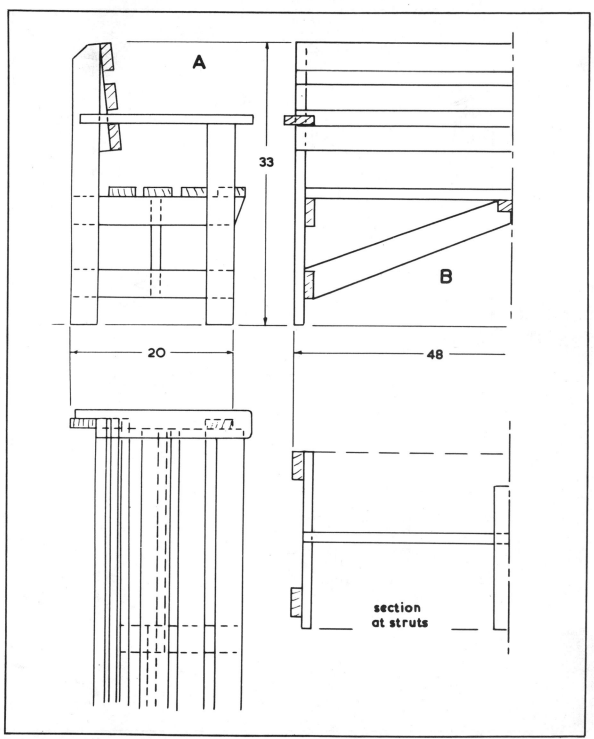

A

33

20

B

48

section
at struts

Fig. 6-33. Sizes for a light strip bench with arms.

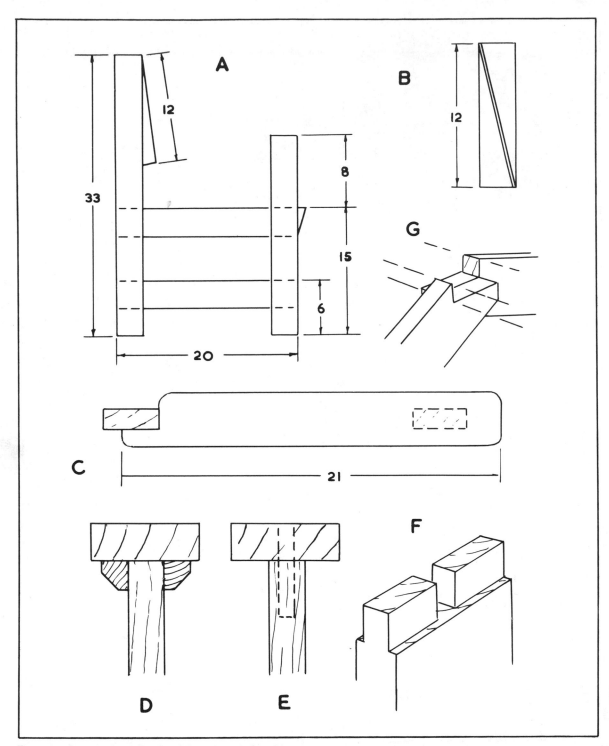

Fig. 6-34. Constructional details of the light strip bench.

Chapter 7

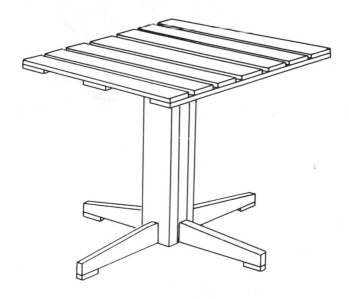

Tables

T HE NEED FOR TABLES COMES ONLY SECOND TO the need for seats in outdoor furniture. They will vary from permanent structures attached to the ground and of sufficient size for many people to enjoy meals, to smaller tables that can be moved, to others that may be folded and stowed away. Folding tables are described in Chapter 9. Within the other categories, there are a vast number of designs. The primary need is a flat top at a suitable height from the floor. It is in the means of support that designs vary.

Tabletops for use indoors are always without gaps. If boards have to make up a width, they are joined tightly edge-to-edge. Sometimes such a closed top is needed outdoors, but in many cases the top is made of many boards with gaps between. One advantage of this is in shedding rain water more easily. The gaps should not be too wide or there will be difficulty when a cloth is spread over and cutlery and other small items press the cloth into the gaps. For normal use, the gaps should not exceed ½ inch (although there are many tables in use with wider spaces).

A table should stand firmly. The ideal arrangement for stability is three legs that will not wobble no matter how uneven the ground. For most tables, it is preferable to have four legs to give support near each corner. The spread of legs on the floor is greater than the spread of most chair legs. This aids in finding a level stand. If the supports are not individual legs, but there are broad surfaces at the bottom, it is always advisable to thicken at the corners to provide feet (as in the first example).

Be careful to brace against diagonal or sideways loads, as well as those pressing directly downward. There must be enough stiffness in the joints. If the top and any shelf are firmly attached, they also serve as stiffeners. Lower rails act as stiffeners, but if it is a table where someone will be sitting on a chair with their legs underneath, the rails have to be kept out of their way. In the first example, the end rails support a shelf of slats far enough in not to interfere with a sitter's legs at the sides.

LIGHT TABLE

Figures 7-1 and 7-2 show a rigid, small table with a shelf below. It is a height suitable for meals using a chair with seat height of 16 inches to 19 inches. The design is intended to match the chair shown in Fig. 5-1. Its construction is basically similar so it will be advisable to

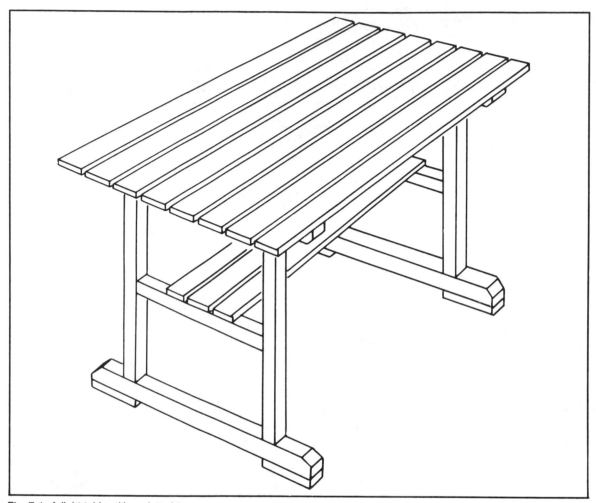

Fig. 7-1. A light table with a slatted top.

refer to the instructions for the chair for some details. Table 7-1 specifies material for a table 36 inches long and 27 inches wide, but these sizes could be modified within reasonable limits. For a much longer table, the supports ought to be made of thicker wood.

It is not essential to make a full-size drawing, but it might help to lay out an end view—either complete or to one side of its centerline. This will help in spacing the slats and show the sizes of other parts.

Mark out the legs together (Fig. 7-3A). The mortise and tenon joints do not go through and are arranged similar to those on the chair (Fig. 5-3A). The top and bottom rails (Fig. 7-3C) are the same. Mark them together and cut the mortises. Bevel all the ends. Make and attach feet (Fig. 7-3D) under the bottom rails. Be careful

to get the center rails (Fig. 7-3E) the same length between the mortises on the top and bottom rails. This way the joints will pull tight. Assemble both end frames. Measure diagonals to see that they are square. Check that they match each other.

It is important that all the top slats are flat and straight. Variations will be very apparent in differences of level or uneven gaps. If you have to use slats that are not quite perfect, keep them for the shelf. There they will not be so obvious. Take sharpness of the edges and ends of the slats, but otherwise concentrate on keeping them straight and parallel in width and thickness. The outer slats can have their corners cut off, but otherwise leave the ends square.

Attach the outside slats to the cross rails and mea-

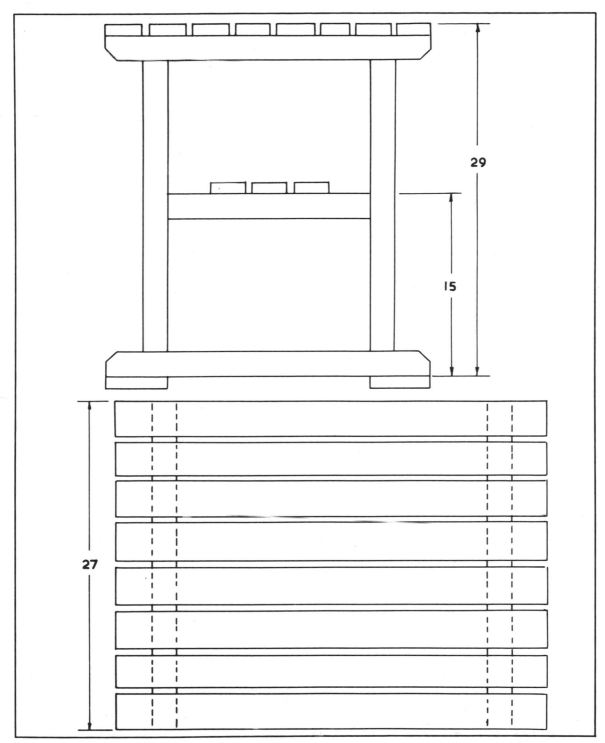

Fig. 7-2. Sizes for a light table with a slatted top.

Table 7-1. Materials List for Light Table.

4 legs	2 × 29 × 2
4 rails	2 × 28 × 2
2 rails	2 × 22 × 2
4 feet	2 × 6 × 7/8
8 slats	3 × 37 × 7/8
3 slats	3 × 31 × 7/8

sure the top for squareness. Lay the other top slats in place and adjust them to get even spacing (before attaching them). Use a straight piece of wood across an end to get all pieces level.

Check that the legs are square to the top. If there is any difficulty in making the table stand true, nail on temporary diagonal braces while you fit the shelf slats (Fig. 7-3F). Arrange them centrally. They could carry through to the same lengths as the top ones, but they are shown cut off at the rails. The outer edges of the outside slats could be rounded in case they are knocked by bare legs.

The table should be rigid enough. If you think extra stiffness is needed, metal angle or shelf brackets can be put between the tops of the legs and the adjoining top slats (where they will be inconspicuous).

SCREWED SLATTED TABLE

A light table will make a suitable companion to some of the arm chairs described in Chapter 5. It is of simple construction, with all of the joints nailed or screwed, without the need to cut and fit any piece into another. Most of the wood is all of the same section. See Table 7-2.

The slatted top is enclosed (Fig. 7-4) to make a neat surround and give an impression of a more stout construction than would be obvious without the border. The legs are splayed and steadied by struts that also brace the top without getting in the way of a sitter's legs. The sizes give a reasonable table for at least four people to use (Fig. 7-5A).

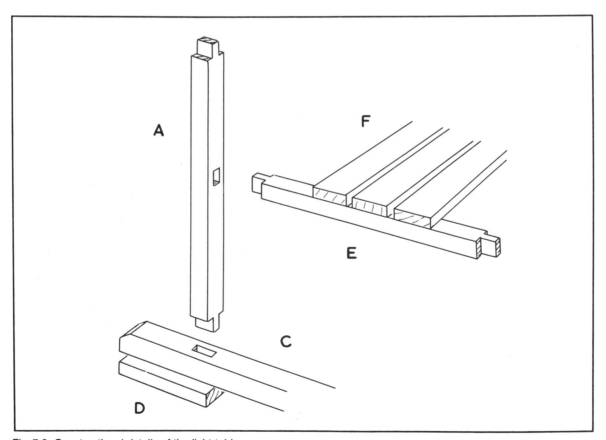

Fig. 7-3. Constructional details of the light table.

8 top slats	3	×	60	×	¾
4 crossbars	3	×	32	×	¾
2 boarders	1½	×	61	×	¾
2 borders	1½	×	33	×	¾
4 legs	3	×	28	×	1½
4 leg rails	3	×	32	×	¾
2 struts	3	×	38	×	¾

If the top slats are not a full 3-inch width, it will be advisable to lay them out so as not to have excessive gap ɔ. Then make the overall width of the table to suit the re ult you get. Spaces should be ⅜ of an inch or ½ an inch. Wider gaps might interfere with things put on the table or cause a table cloth to sag between.

Make up the top by screwing the slats to crossbars at the ends (Fig. 7-5B) and others that will also take the bracing struts (Fig. 7-5C). For neatness you could screw upward so that the top surface remains smooth. Fit the outside slats and check that the assembly is square by measuring diagonals before adding the other slats. Level the ends and then frame around with strips (Fig. 7-5D and 7-6A).

Make the crossbars at the tops of the legs (Fig. 7-6B) to fit into the frame and against the end crossbars. Bevel the ends to the frame, but do not fit into the frame yet.

To get the slope of the legs, draw a half section of an end (Fig. 7-5E). The legs taper from 3 inches at the top to 2 inches at the bottom. Make them all the same and cut the ends to the angles obtained from the half section drawing. Mark where the lower rails will cross.

Assemble the legs to the top crossbars and to the rails. Note that these pieces cross on opposite sides of the legs. Make sure the assemblies are symmetrical by checking diagonals and see that opposite ends match. Screw the leg assemblies inside the end crossbars (Fig. 7-6C).

The two struts cross and have to be notched around the leg rails and crossbars under the top. It is important that they hold the legs upright when viewed from the side. Have the table inverted. If necessary, nail on temporary pieces of scrap wood at the sides to hold the leg assemblies square to the top. It is advisable to get the shapes of the struts with scrap wood to use as templates for marking the final pieces of wood. Screw the notched ends and the crossing of the struts (Fig. 7-6D).

Fig. 7-4. A screwed, slatted table with a bordered top.

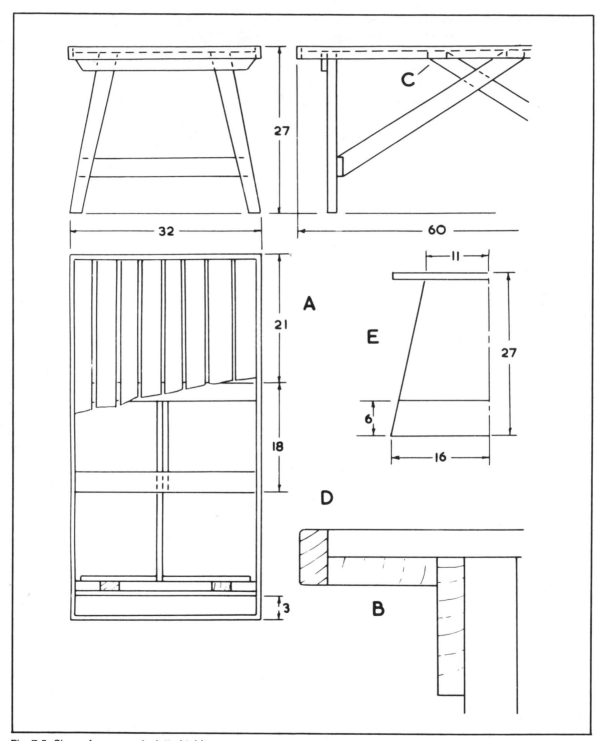

Fig. 7-5. Sizes of a screwed, slatted table.

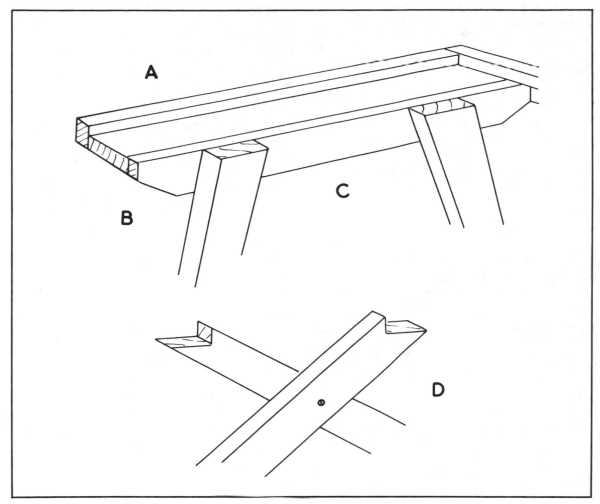

Fig. 7-6. Leg and strut arrangements for the screwed table.

See that the table stands level. Round the edges and corners of the top before finishing with paint.

ROUND PATIO TABLE

A round tabletop can be supported with three or four legs. The table shown in Fig. 7-7 has four legs and is intended to stand on a deck or patio where the surface is reasonably flat. It would, of course, be suitable for any level ground. It could be used as a table only, but there is a shelf below and a hole through the center of this as well as through the top which would take the upright of an umbrella. The distance between the top and the shelf is enough to support the umbrella without it wobbling.

The top is made of several boards, with gaps between, and held to shape with strips across underneath.

These also serve as attachments to the under framing (which is made up as a straightforward square table). The sizes shown in Fig. 7-8 and Table 7-3 should suit most purposes. If the table is altered, arrange the top to an odd number of boards so that the central hole comes at the center of one and not at a gap.

The framework is best tenoned together, but it would also be possible to use dowels. The legs (Fig. 7-9A) are all the same. Top rails (Fig. 7-9B) and bottom rails (Fig. 7-9C) are also in matching sets. The joints are on the same level. Allow for the tenons being mitered in the legs (Fig. 7-9D). The lower rail tenons can be the full depth of the rails, but at the top cut down a little and divide the tenons (Fig. 7-9E).

Make up two opposite sides first by carefully squaring and checking that the pair match. Pull the joints tight with clamps. If you do not have enough clamps, you can pull a joint tight and drive a nail from the inner surface of the leg through the tenon at each side to hold the parts while the glue sets. Then you can move the clamp on to another position. Join the opposite assemblies with the other rails and be certain that the table stands upright and squarely.

The top is best dealt with in two stages. First cut the boards close to their final sizes. Final curving of the edges is not done until after assembly.

Lay out the boards for the top and mark the center of the middle one. Improvise a compass of 18 inches radius (Fig. 7-10A) so you can draw a circle of the right size. It might help to put temporary spacing pieces between the boards. They need not be full length; they can be short strips positioned near where the circumference of the circle will come. Cut fairly closely to the line, but leave a little for trimming after assembly.

One stiffening piece goes across centrally and the other two have to be positioned so that they will come over the top rails of the framework (Fig. 7-10B). Let all these pieces be too long and then glue and screw them on from below. After assembly, cut the ends to the curve, trim the circle finally to shape, and bevel the cross pieces underneath (Fig. 7-10C).

Make and fit the shelf before attaching the top. It is made as a regular octagon screwed to the lower rails (Fig. 7-10D). To get a regular shape, mark out the plywood to a square that matches the rails. Draw two diagonals and measure half the length of one (Fig. 7-10E). Use this distance to measure along each edge of the square from each corner in each direction (Fig. 7-10F). Join these marks. If you have laid it out accurately, you will have eight equal sides (Fig. 7-10G).

If the table is to support an umbrella or shade, drill centrally for the upright in the shelf, before screwing it to the rails. The hole does not have to be a close fit on the

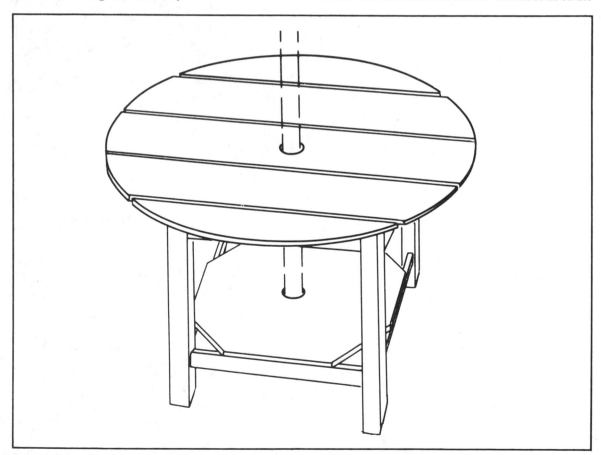

Fig. 7-7. A round patio table on four legs.

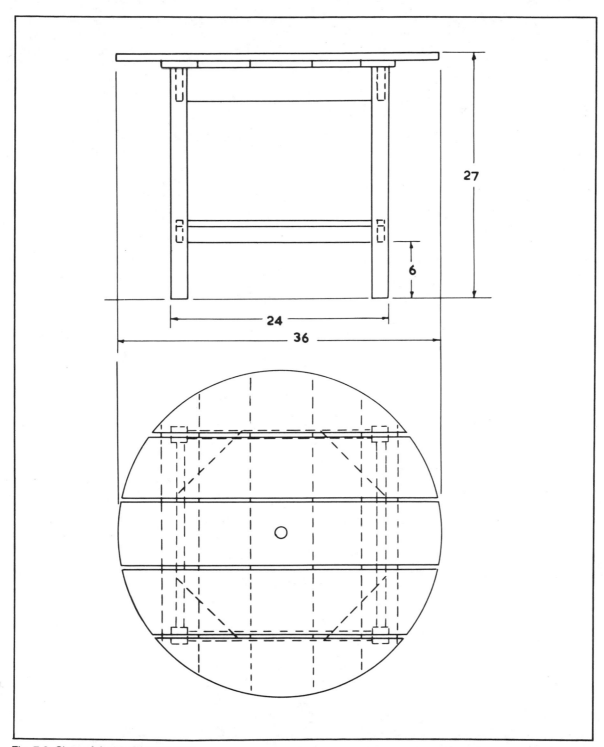

Fig. 7-8. Sizes of the round patio table.

Table 7-3. Materials List for Round Patio Table.

4 legs	1¾ × 27 × 1¾	
6 tops	6¾ × 37 × ⅞	
2 tops	3¾ × 33 × ⅞	
4 top rails	3¾ × 24 × ⅞	
4 bottom rails	3¾ × 24 × ⅞	
1 shelf	24 × 24 × ½ plywood	

upright because that should go in and out easily. As much as ¼ of an inch clearance would be acceptable. Drill a matching hole at the center of the top. Most umbrella uprights are intended to go through to the floor, but if you have one that needs a stop you can put another piece of wood under the hole in the shelf.

Be careful as you position the top on the framing. The two holes must line up to hold the umbrella upright. Where the two crossbars come over the top rails, screw downward, in the gaps between top boards, into the rails and into the tops of the legs (Fig. 7-10H). Those four screws at each position might be enough, but you can put one or two more downward into the other rails where the central crossbar comes. There is plenty of thickness. Counterbore and plug over the screw heads.

As with most outdoor furniture, hardwood would be the best choice for this table. This would be particularly true if it is expected to be left outside in wet conditions. It would be lighter and easier to move if made of softwood, but it would then have to be stored under cover. If it is well protected with paint, however, an occasional wetting would not matter. In any case, the plywood shelf should be exterior- or marine-grade plywood.

TRIPOD TABLE

A table that wobbles can be quite a nuisance. This is particularly true if drinks are spilled. To get over the

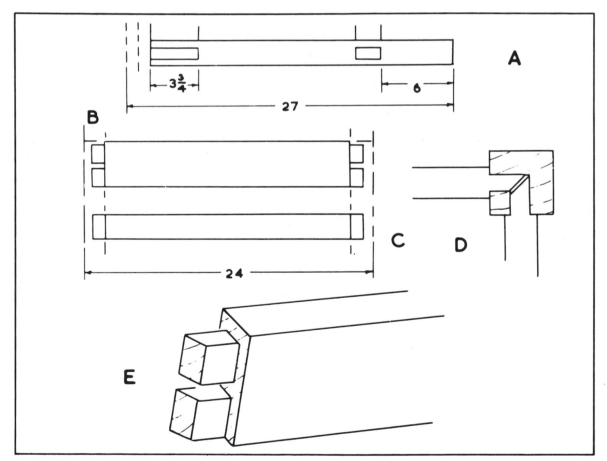

Fig. 7-9. Parts of the supports for a round patio table.

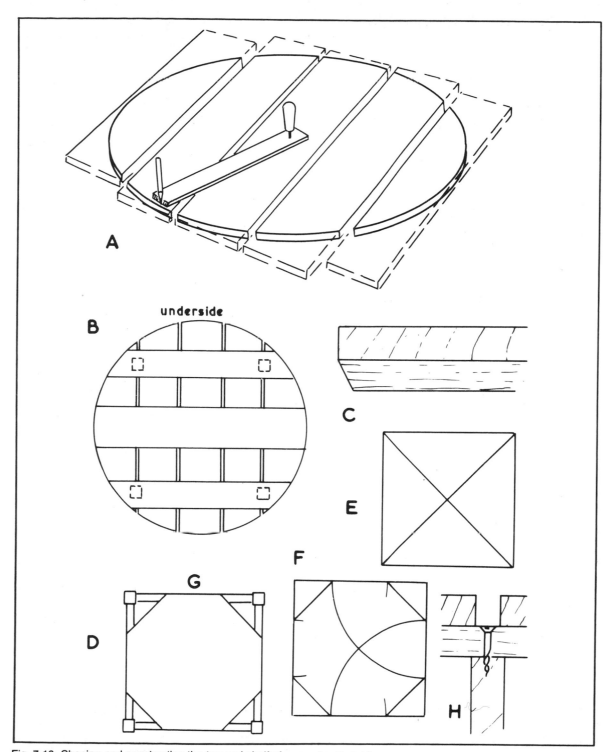

Fig. 7-10. Shaping and constructing the top and shelf of a round patio table.

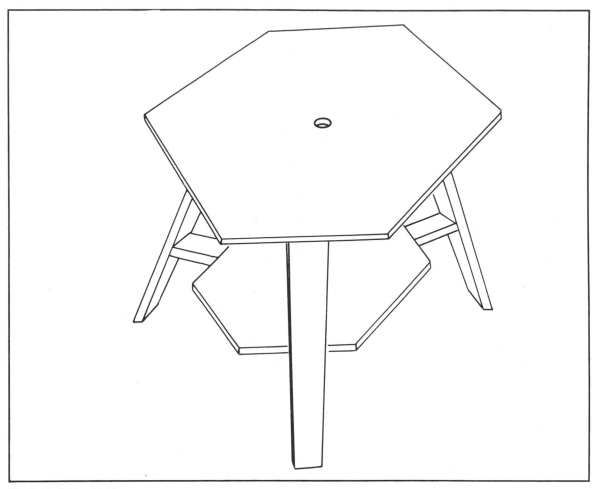

Fig. 7-11. A tripod table.

difficulty of a finding a level base for four legs, the table can be made with three legs. A problem with having three table legs is making a matching top. The usual square or rectangle does not match the configuration of the legs. It is better to either have a round top or one with sides that are a multiple of three. There are tables with triangular tops, but they have long points that are liable to be knocked. There are tops with 12 sides. These are not very different from round, but the more common top has six sides (Fig. 7-11).

This table shown in Fig. 7-12 has a top and shelf made from plywood (which must be exterior or marine grade). The legs slope outward from strips attached below the plywood at both levels. There are alternative methods of jointing.

Draw a full-size view square to one leg (Fig. 7-13A).

This will give you the angle and size of a leg and the same information on the two levels of rails. Set an adjustable bevel to the angle and keep it at this setting when marking out all the parts. Before marking and cutting any wood, decide on the joints to be used. The legs can be nailed or screwed to the rails at both levels (Fig. 7-13B). At the top, there can be a notched joint (Fig. 7-13C) and a tenon at the shelf level (Fig. 7-13D). A slightly stronger notch at the top can be dovetailed (Fig. 7-13E). When cutting the parts, allow for the chosen joints.

Give the legs a taper (Fig. 7-14A). Cut the tops and bottoms to the angle of slope and prepare their joints. Do the same with the rails (Fig. 7-14B and 7-14C). The rails come close at the center, but they do not have to meet. There is no need to carefully fit them against each other and they can be cut slightly short.

140

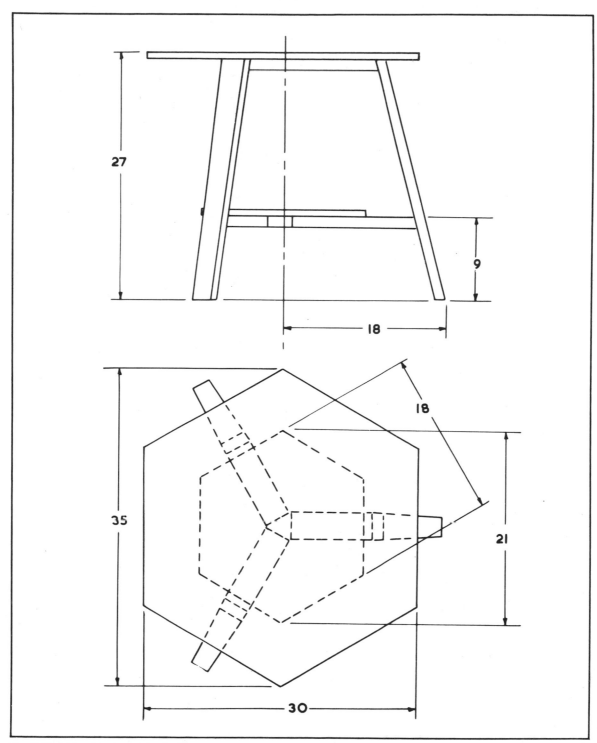

Fig. 7-12. Main sizes for a tripod table.

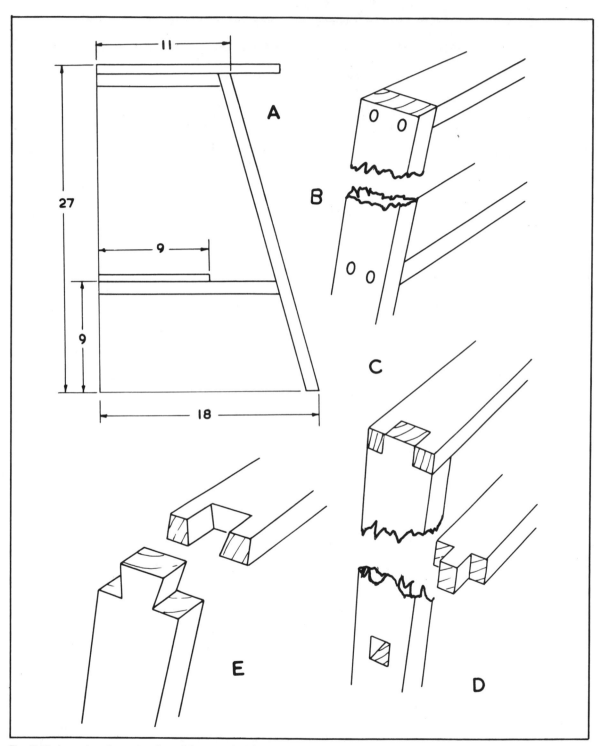

Fig. 7-13. Layout and construction of the tripod table.

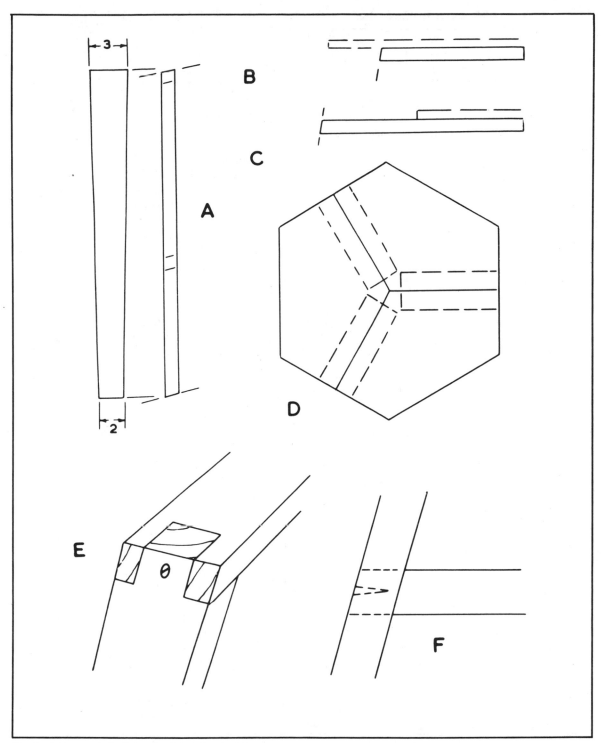

Fig. 7-14. Leg and shelf details of the tripod table.

Table 7-4. Materials List for Tripod Table.

1 top	30 × 39 × ½ or ¾ plywood
1 shelf	18 × 22 × ½ plywood
3 legs	3 × 30 × 1
3 top rails	3 × 12 × 1
3 shelf rails	3 × 17 × 1

Make the top and shelf to the sizes given in Fig. 7-12 and Table 7-4. Take care to finish with regular hexagons. Check that all edges are the same length all round. The simplest way to get the shape is to draw a circle and step off the radius around the circumference—which it will do six times—and then you join the points. An improvised compass, with a spike through a strip of wood and a pencil at the end, will draw circles. Mark the centers on the undersides of both pieces and draw lines radiating to the centers of alternate sides. Mark the widths of the rails on these lines (Fig. 7-14D).

Attach the rails under the plywood with glue and screws driven upward. If the table is to support an umbrella, drill the centers of the plywood and make sure the rails are clear of the holes. During assembly, put the shelf over the inverted tabletop to check that the radiating rails at each level match their partners. Anything more than a minor error will cause a leg to be out of true and this would spoil appearance.

With the table inverted, assemble the legs to the other parts. If there are screws or nails only, drive them all partway. Then check the symmetry of the assembly by measuring that the shelf is parallel with the top and the legs are at the same slope (before tightening all of them). It is difficult to clamp the top joints if they are notched or dovetailed. Drill each for a screw to pull and hold the joint while the glue sets (Fig. 7-14E). If the lower joints are tenoned, let the tenon go through so that it can be tightened by wedging (Fig. 7-14F).

Try the table on a level surface and check by measuring all round that the top is level. If it is not, trim a leg to bring it level. Bevel around the bottoms of the legs to reduce the risk of splitting (particularly if you have used softwood). Even if you do not use preservative all over, it is worthwhile standing each leg in preservative for a day. It will soak into the end grain and reduce the risk of rot due to water absorption.

STRIP-WOOD TABLE

A very simple table can be made of strips of wood and with nearly all the joints screwed (Fig. 7-15). It is possi-

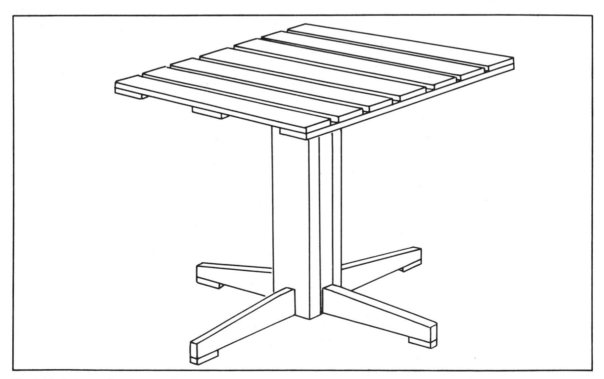

Fig. 7-15. Strip-wood pedestal table.

Table 7-5. Materials List for Strip-Wood Table.

7 tops	3	×	31	×	1	
3 tops	4	×	31	×	1	
2 feet	3	×	27	×	1¼	
4 feet	1	×	4	×	1¼	
2 posts	4	×	27	×	1	
2 posts	1½	×	27	×	1¼	or to suit umbrella
2 cleats	1	×	5	×	1	

ble to prefabricate all the parts (Table 7-5) for later assembly. This design is suitable for offering as a kit for a customer to assemble or as a subject for quantity production of a large number.

The top pieces have gaps between and crosspieces below. The central pillar is hollow and the upright of an umbrella can pass through it. The feet are formed by two crossed pieces (Fig. 7-16).

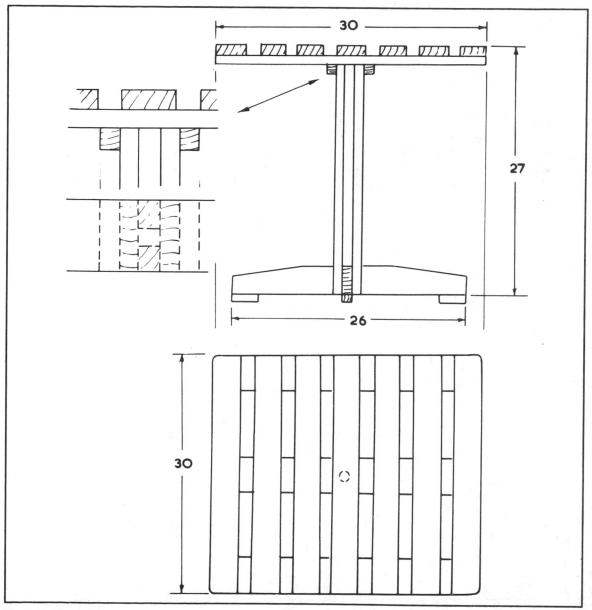

Fig. 7-16. Sizes of a strip-wood pedestal table.

145

If you have the umbrella or shade that will be used, check the diameter of its shaft and make the thickness of the spacers in the column to suit.

Prepare the feet (Fig. 7-17A); they are halved where they cross. Add the pieces under the ends (Fig. 7-17B) and glue the crossing. Hold it square with weights or other means (while the glue sets).

Make the parts for the column (Fig. 7-17C). Notch the 4-inch pieces to suit the feet. In the other direction, notch the filler pieces if they are thick enough (Fig. 7-17D). If you have not needed to thicken them to suit an umbrella, they can be cut short and packings can be used on each side of the feet, if necessary (Fig. 7-17E). At the top, check that the parts are cut squarely because this will

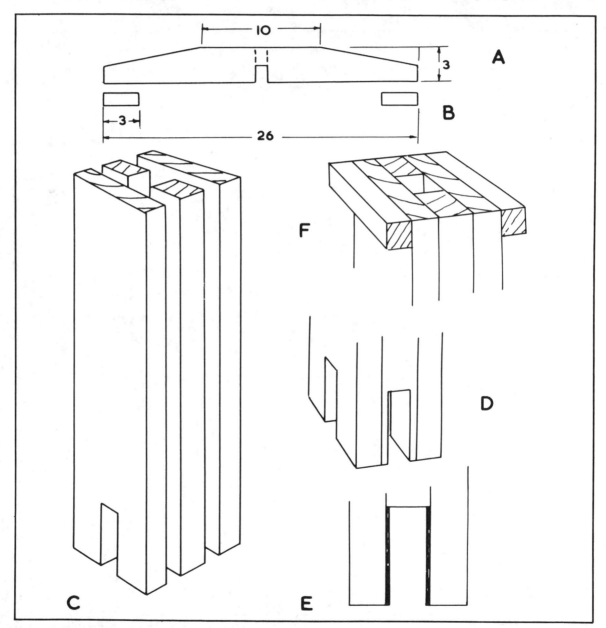

Fig. 7-17. Construction of the pedestal and feet.

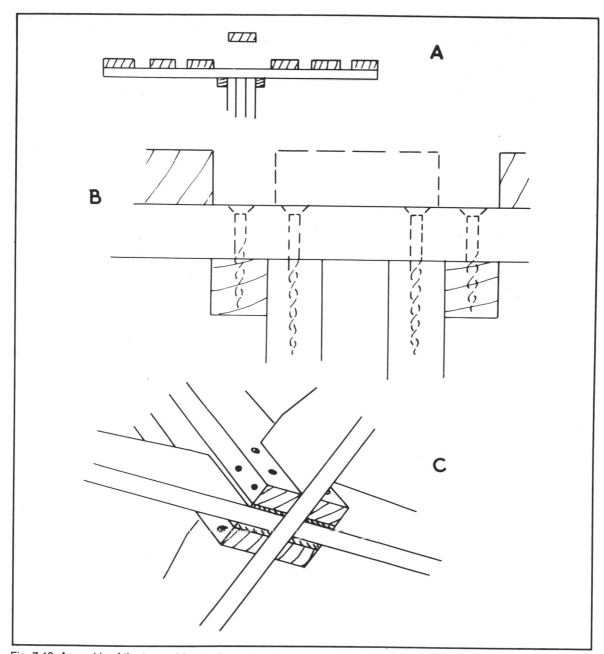

Fig. 7-18. Assembly of the top and feet to the pedestal.

affect the level of the tabletop. Assemble the column parts with glue and screws. Add cleats on the 4-inch pieces (Fig. 7-17F) and make sure the whole top surface is flat as well as square to the sides.

Assemble the tabletop after cutting or marking all pieces to length. Screws can be driven upward so that the exposed surface is not marked by screw heads. At this stage, leave out the center top piece (Fig. 7-18A), but have it ready. Screw and glue the parts together. Then level edges and round the outer edges and corners.

Mark where the column comes under the top on the central cross member. Drill for screws downward into the column. Use 3-inch screws into the end grain and 2-inch screws into the cleats (Fig. 7-18B). Add the central top strip and then drill downward through the center to suit the umbrella.

Invert the table and check that the pillar is perpendicular to the top. Bring the crossed feet into their slots. Check their fit. If that is satisfactory, drill for screws each way (Fig. 7-18C) and then glue and screw in the feet. While doing this, measure from the underside of the top to the ends of the feet to see that these parts are parallel and the table will stand level. Try it the right way up and leave for the glue to set. Finish with preservative and varnish or paint.

SIMPLE SLAB TABLE

Boards cut right across a large log suggests a simple table construction. Cut any roughness off the waney edges. Otherwise leave the natural shape. End supports can be made of similar material. Some lengthwise bracing completes a table. There is a limit to the size that should be made this way. It depends on the widths and thicknesses

available, for 2-inch boards a top about 24 inches by 48 inches is reasonable.

The table shown in Fig. 7-19 uses the wood as it comes from the saw mill. You might have to do some planing of the top surface to make it acceptable and flat. All of the parts are nailed or screwed. Construction is basic (Fig. 7-20A).

Although the long edges can be far from straight, the ends should be square to a mean line along an edge if the top is to look right. Draw a centerline and mark the ends square to that (Fig. 7-20B). At the same time, mark where the supports will come underneath. The sharp corners of waney-edged boards are easily broken so you should either bevel or round them.

Make the leg tops and bottoms parallel in the same way as the tabletop and cut into the bottoms to make feet for steadier standing than the full width would provide. Two lengthwise rails are needed for stiffness. Get their lengths the same. Make a straightedge on the top one (Fig. 7-20C). The deeper this rail is the more stiffness it will provide. The bottom rail can be narrow and can either be parallel or have waney edges.

Assembly is with nails or screws. As they have to

Fig. 7-19. A simple slab table of screwed construction.

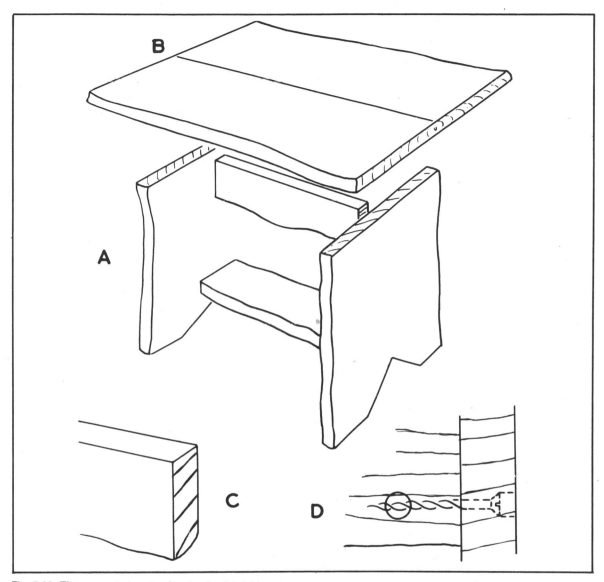

Fig. 7-20. The separated parts of a simple slab table.

grip in end grain, they should be fairly long. As a rough guide, with 2-inch wood, let the fastening go about 4 inches into the lower part.

In most woods, it is advisable to drill undersize holes for the nails. This helps to keep long nails straight and makes driving easier. It also reduces the risk of splitting. For screws, drill clearance holes in the top piece and undersize holes for most of the length of the screw in the lower piece. You can leave the screw and nail heads level on the surface, but it would be better to sink them a little and cover with stopping. Screws are better counterbored and plugged. It will help to strengthen screwed joints if you drive dowels across the wood. Then the screw threads will bite into the cross grain of the dowel for increased hold compared with that of end grain (Fig. 7-20D).

TENONED-SLAB TABLE

The tenoned-slab table can be made larger than the simple slab table. The construction is more suited to large

149

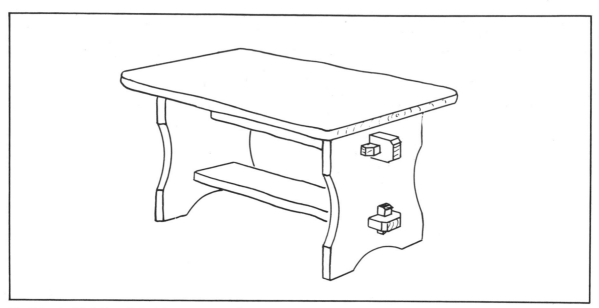

Fig. 7-21. A slab table with tusk tenon construction.

Fig. 7-22. A plain table made with the minimum of shaping of slabs cut across a tree.

150

sizes. It uses wedged tusk tenons through the ends to make joints that should be stronger than nailed or screwed ones. It also gives a more attractive appearance (Figs. 7-21 and 7-22). The construction is shown with a single top rail (Fig. 7-23), but for a very large top there could be two top rails, spaced about 12 inches apart, for additional stiffening.

The size of the available board for the top will determine the table sizes. Make the height about 30 inches, but relate other sizes to the proportions of the top. You could increase the size of the top by joining two boards, keeping their outer waney edges, but straightening their meeting surfaces (Fig. 7-24A). If the wood has been fully seasoned, you could glue this joint, preferably with dow-

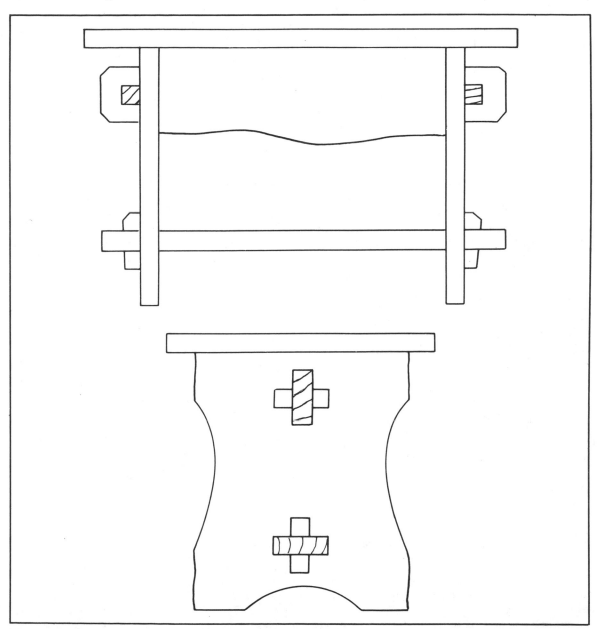

Fig. 7-23. General arrangements of a slab table with tusk tenons.

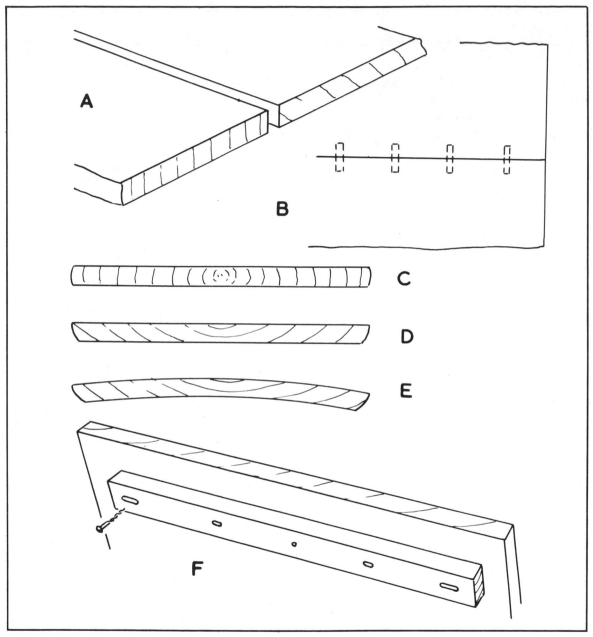

Fig. 7-24. Building up a table top (A and B). Effects of grain on warping (C, D, and E). Stiffening with a slot-screwed batten or cleat (F).

els (Fig. 7-24B). For many tables, made from moist wood, it will be necessary to depend on battens underneath.

Battens will also resist the tendency of the top to twist or warp. You can tell if there is much risk of warping by looking at the end grain. A board cut across the center of the tree might shrink in its thickness, but it should remain flat. The further from the center the board is cut, the greater the risk of warping. If the end shows the center of the annual rings (Fig. 7-24C), it should remain flat. If the annual rings show the board has come further out (Fig. 7-23D), it can be expected to warp in the direction that tries to straighten the annual rings (Fig. 7-24E).

Battens can be underneath inside where the legs will come and intermediately according to the length. A spacing of 24 inches is reasonable. Besides the tendency to warp, the wood will shrink as it dries and expand again if it takes up water. That should be allowed for in the battens. Use a round screw hole at the center, but further out cut slots for the screws (Fig. 7-24F) so the screws can slide in them if the tabletop gets wider or narrower.

Make the top first, with its ends squared and corners rounded, as for the previous table. The ends can keep the waney edges as they are or you can cut into the sides as well as the bottom (Fig. 7-25A).

Make sure the two rails are the same length between shoulders. The tusk tenons on the bottom rail will be central, but at the top keep the tenons far enough down to avoid weakening the short grain in the legs above the mortises (Fig. 7-25B). The widths of tenons will depend on the boards, but if your wedges are made from 2-inch square wood, the tenons should be at least three times this width (Fig. 7-25C).

Make them extend beyond the wedge hole rather more than the thickness of the wedge so that there is enough end grain there to resist any tendency to break out (Fig. 7-25D). Give the wedges a moderate taper; ¼ inch in 5 inches would do. Taper the holes to match and cut back the hole below the surface of the leg so the tightening wedge does not close against it. The joints will almost certainly slacken after a time. Give the wedges a blow with a mallet periodically until the joints settle down. This will probably be after several months if you start with partially seasoned wood.

With the underframing assembled on a flat surface and battens under the top, center the top over the legs

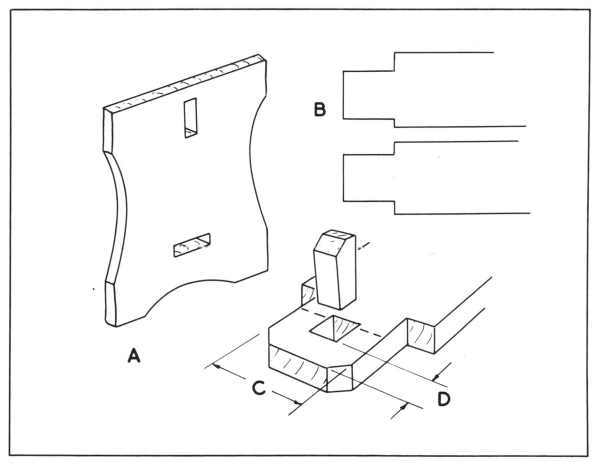

Fig. 7-25. The design of a tusk tenon and its wedge.

Fig. 7-26. A table with an oval top made from three boards.

and mark around them underneath as a guide for drilling pilot holes for screws or nails. Fasten the top down by one of the methods suggested for the previous table.

OVAL TABLETOP

The tabletop that provides the most space within its size is rectangular. If you increase the number of sides or round the corners, within the same overall sizes, you must reduce the area. Shaping is often done for the sake of appearance. It can also be done to remove sharp corners. An attractive shape is an ellipse. This is often called an "oval," but that really means egg shaped, with one end larger than the other.

An elliptical top could be substituted for one of another shape on the underframings already described. The example has shaped slab ends and a tenoned rail (Fig. 7-26). An elliptical top could be made from one wide board or several joined together. If boards are of different widths, avoid having narrow ones at the sides. Not much would be left when the curves are cut.

The special problem is drawing the ellipse. There is

no easy way comparable to drawing a circle with a compass. There are geometric ways of finding a large number of points, on the circumference, that have to be joined. It is possible to use compass curves with two smaller radii at the ends joining two larger ones at the sides. This gives an approximation, but to the practiced eye it is not as good as a true ellipse.

One practical way, particularly applicable to the large ellipse needed for a tabletop, use a pencil, a loop of string, and two awls or nails. You will have to arrive at the arrangement by trial and error, but to start draw a lengthwise centerline, with another the other way (Fig. 7-27A). Measure half of the minor axis along half the major axis and divide the difference by two (Fig. 7-27B). That gives you a probable position for the awls. This is called the *foci* (plural of focus).

Push the awls or nails into these points and tie a loop of string around them long enough to reach the end of the long line (Fig. 7-27C). Put a pencil in the loop and pull it around; keep the string taut all the time (Fig. 7-27D). That will draw an ellipse. If you find the ellipse is finishing too narrow, bring the awls slightly closer together

154

and adjust the size of the loop to reach the end again. If the ellipse is too wide, move the awls a little further apart. This can be done directly on the tabletop.

If you prefer to work from a template, you can use a scrap piece of plywood or hardboard that is half the width of the top and experiment to get the curve you want. Then cut it and mark round it on the tabletop. If you turn the template over on a marked line, you can check the accuracy of the setting out. You might have to make slight adjustments.

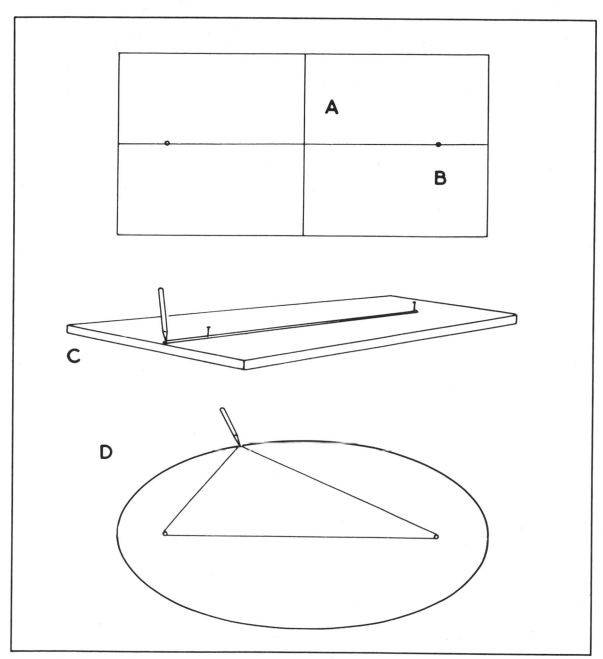

Fig. 7-27. Drawing an ellipse using nails, string, and a pencil.

USING EXISTING SUPPORTS

A table might not have to be made completely if you can find some other support of the right height. A sawn-off tree stump can be given a tabletop even if there has to be some packing to get it level. It might be possible to use a rocky outcrop that will hold one end of the table while you provide legs only for the other end.

There are some interesting bygones that are no longer required for their original uses. Some farm equipment had cast-iron supports. Old mangles or wringers had cast-iron stands. Much older equipment was operated at table height so it is often possible to take off the upper parts and bolt on your tabletop.

An example is shown in Fig. 7-28 where a tabletop has been put on a treadle sewing machine stand. In this case, the treadle is still there and it will turn the flywheel. Amusement is provided for children and their parents!

If you use old ironwork, first check it for rust. The protective treatment for some old machines was surprisingly weatherproof. Do not remove it if it is still sound. If there is rust, wire brush it and treat it with rust-inhibiting fluid. Leave it for the time specified by the manufacturer and then paint over it. Dark paintwork under a wood top finished with varnish or oil in its natural color can be very effective.

Fig. 7-28. A table built on a sewing machine treadle.

Chapter 8

Combination Furniture

T HERE ARE SOME SITUATIONS WHERE IT MAY BE better to have furniture performing two or more functions than to have separate items. Usually the combined piece is more compact, but the parts cannot be moved in relation to each other. There is also the value of mutual support. It is possible to design a combined item with fewer and lighter parts than two separate items, yet have adequate stability and strength. Each part will support the other. If a table and a seat, for instance, are combined you need have little fear of the table being inadvertently pushed over or a seat being tipped.

It is advisable not to devise some piece of furniture with multiple functions. You could arrive at something that is inconvenient to use and is not fully functional. There are some ingenious folding combination items that will soon break or fail to function. Always consider fitness for its purpose. The combination item should do all that the separate items would do and, if possible, do them better.

The picnic table is probably the best-known example of a very functional combination piece of outdoor furniture. It is better for its purpose in most situations than separate benches and a table. It stands up to exposure and

neglect well, it is very steady, and its construction is simple and sturdy.

PICNIC TABLE

The basic picnic table with attached benches is found in use all over the world on campgrounds, rest areas, and anywhere that people want to eat outdoors. It can be used in your yard or on a patio or deck. You will probably want to give it a rather better finish than if it is to go into more rural surroundings.

The tabletop has to be level and of sufficient area and the seats must come in a convenient relation to it. Several methods have been used in the structure to hold these parts correctly, but a common and successful way uses splayed legs under the tabletop. Crossbars are used to support the seats. The construction described here follows the most common form. As shown in (Fig. 8-1), all of the assembly is made of 2-×-4 inch wood. If it is machine-planed, the sizes may be about ¼ inch less. That must be allowed for when laying out the work. See Table 8-1.

The sizes shown in Fig. 8-2 are for a table that will seat up to eight people. The seats are longer than the

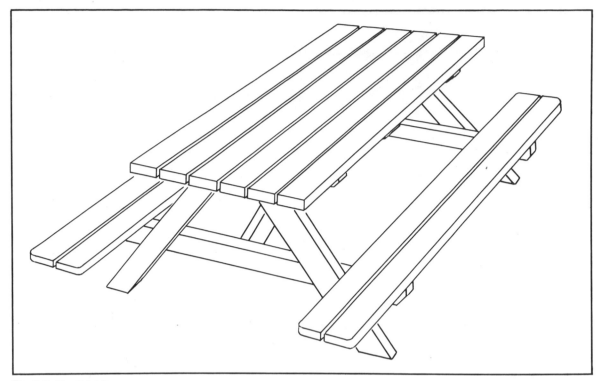

Fig. 8-1. Picnic table.

tabletop so the best use can be made of its ends. If the table is to be made much larger, the wood sections should be increased. In any case, the top could be made of fewer wider boards and the seats could be single wide pieces (if they are available). The materials list would have to be altered accordingly.

The important setting out is the splay of the ends. Draw a half view of the main lines of an end (Fig. 8-3A), preferably fullsize. That will give you the angles of crossing parts. Nearly all of the construction can be nailed, screwed, or bolted with the pieces merely resting against each other. The joints that get the most load are where the seat supports cross the legs. It would be better to notch these parts together. There is no need to go very deeply into each piece; ½ inch should be enough (Fig. 8-3B).

Although the tips of the legs go out to a 48-inch spread in setting out, cut back squarely about 1 inch to remove the risk of the fine angle splitting (Fig. 8-2A). Nail or bolt the cross rails to the tops of the legs (Fig. 8-3C) and check one assembly over the other.

Prepare the boards for the table top. They should be level and parallel so that they go together with straight and equal gaps. Bevel or round the outer corners. Mark the positions of the legs on the top pieces and then assemble squarely with equal spaces. Watch that the parts go together squarely both across and between the top and the upright directions of the legs. For the best finish, counterbore screws so that they can be plugged to give a smooth surface without metal showing.

Have the table inverted and nail or screw on the central crosspiece under the top. Make the diagonal struts (Figs. 8-2B and 8-3D). They are notched at both ends over the cross members and have to be cut so that they finish holding the legs perpendicular to the top. It will probably be advisable to first cut a piece of scrap wood. Then note any errors on it to be put right when you

Table 8-1. Materials List for Picnic Table.

6 tops	4 × 61 × 2
4 seats	4 × 73 × 2
2 seat rails	4 × 49 × 2
3 top rails	4 × 26 × 2
4 legs	4 × 60 × 2
2 struts	4 × 33 × 2

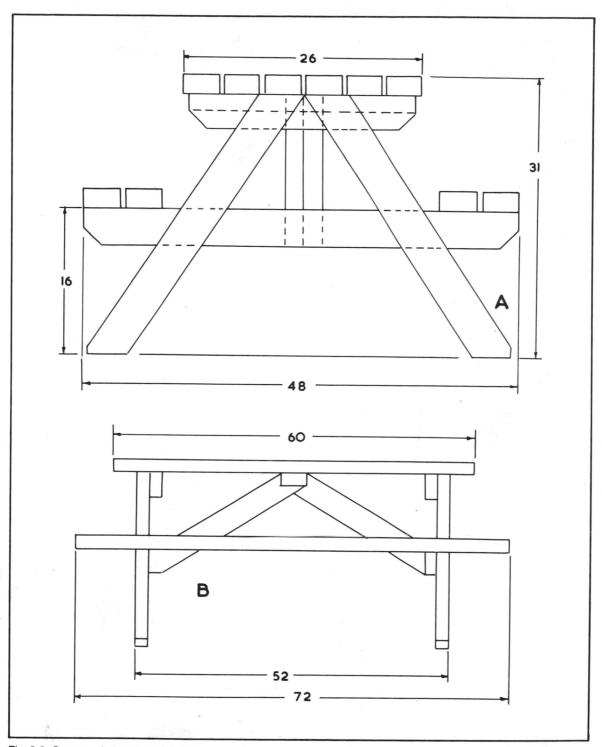

Fig. 8-2. Suggested sizes for a picnic table.

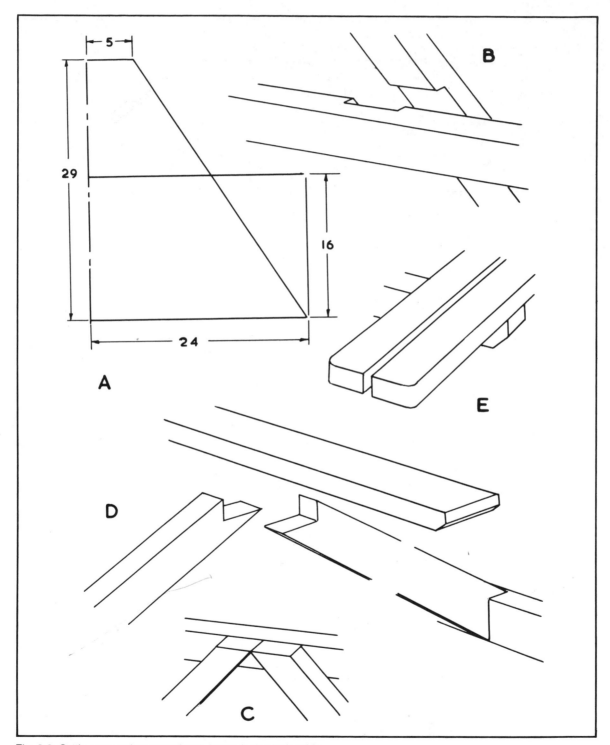

Fig. 8-3. Setting out and constructional details for a picnic table.

cut the actual struts. When you assemble, the struts come against each other on the table rail so that their meeting surfaces will be central. Fit the struts with nails or screws.

Bring the table the right way up and check how it stands on a level surface. The top and the seat rails should be parallel with the floor and the legs should stand without wobbling. If you have to trim one or more leg ends, do that at this stage.

Attach the seats (Fig. 8-3E). Allow the same projection on each end and round the exposed corners.

Some woods can be left untreated, but this is the sort of furniture that will be left outdoors almost permanently so most woods should be treated with preservative. Then they can be painted.

LIGHT PICNIC TABLE

The first picnic table described in this chapter is the strong and heavy type that is not going to be moved at all or very rarely. If it is possible that the table will have to be moved more often, if only to allow the grass to be cut, a lighter version is worth making. Obviously, it will not be so well able to stand up to neglect and rough use, but it can be plenty strong enough.

This table (Figs. 8-4 and 8-5) is made entirely of wood 1 inch by 3 inch section. See Table 8-2. For the minimum weight, it could be a straight-grained softwood. Preferably, it should be one of the resinous types that has a good resistance to water penetration and rot. Because the sections are thin, the wood should be seasoned before use so that there is little risk of warping later. Wood planed all around is advisable, but at least have the top surfaces planed.

Some of the laying out and constructional work is very similar to that of the first table. Refer to those instructions as well as those following. The tabletop and seats are at about similar spacings to the first table. Top and seats are shown the same length. It would be unwise to incase the overhang of the seat ends in this thinner wood unless some more stiffening is provided.

The legs slope at 45 degrees, but it is advisable to set out a full-size end view to get the relative sizes and cuts. The legs have to cross at the same level so that they can be enclosed by the seat rails. There should be full halving joints (Fig. 8-6A) between them. You can use waterproof glue in the joints, but there can also be a bolt through centrally. At the top, the rails are 22 inches long and cut to match the legs (Fig. 8-5A). The joints each

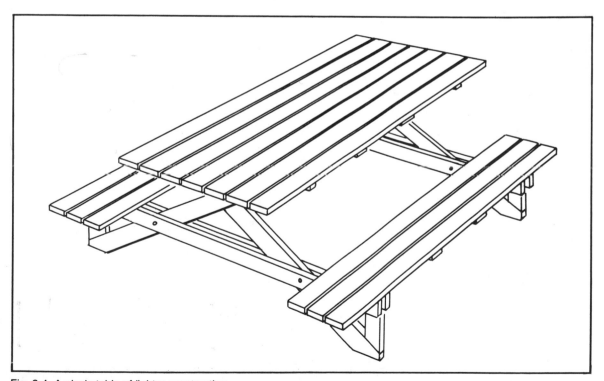

Fig. 8-4. A picnic table of lighter construction.

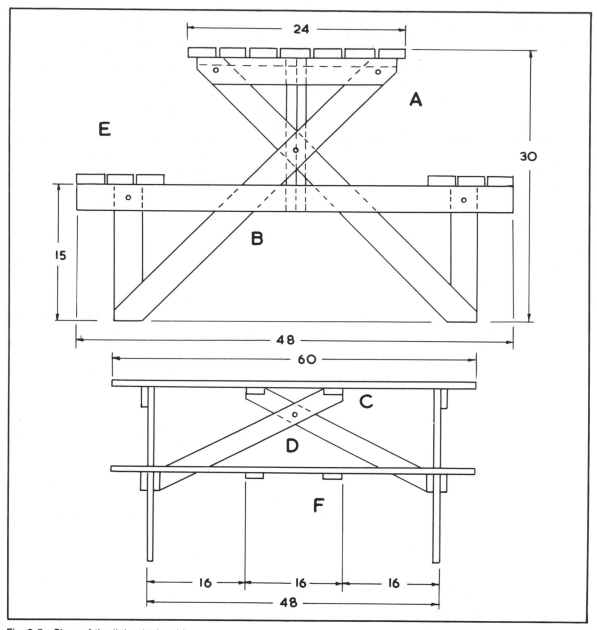

Fig. 8-5 . Sizes of the light picnic table.

have a central bolt. All the bolts in this table can be ⅜ of an inch in diameter and preferably galvanized or otherwise protected against corrosion.

Mark the seat rail positions on the legs and attach them with glue and bolts (Fig. 8-5B). Near their extremities, also enclose the posts (Fig. 8-6B) that are

necessary in this light construction to take the weights of the seat in use.

Those joints are simply bolted through. At the bottoms of the posts, the leg and post are in the same plane so there has to be a different joint (of which there are several possibilities). The most craftsmanlike joint is a

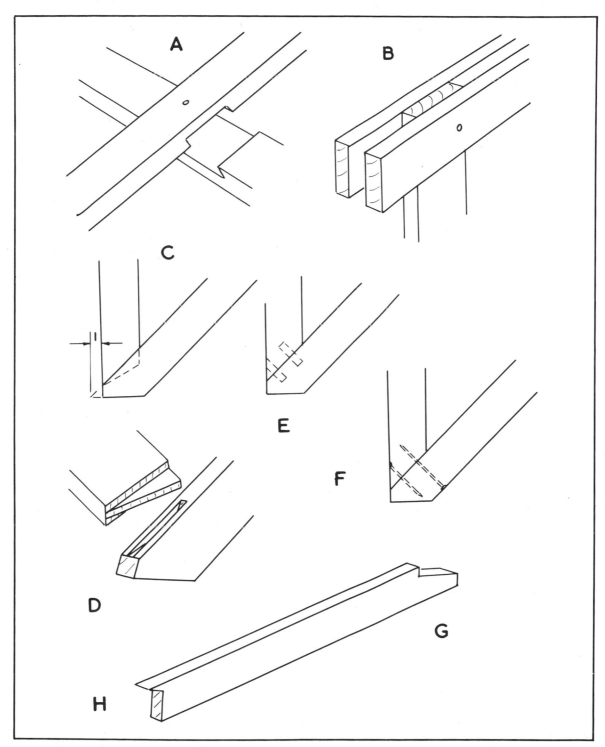

Fig. 8-6. Constructional details of a light picnic table.

Table 8-2. Materials List for Light Picnic Table.

7 tops	3 × 61 × 1
6 seats	3 × 61 × 1
4 seat rails	3 × 49 × 1
4 seat posts	3 × 15 × 1
4 top rails	3 × 24 × 1
4 seat rails	3 × 10 × 1
2 braces	3 × 36 × 1

special type of mortise and tenon (Figs. 8-6C and 8-6D). The post comes 1 inch in from the leg end, but the leg should not be cut off until after the post has been glued in. A tenon tapering to 1 inch deep should be sufficient, but you can go deeper if you prefer.

An alternative is to cut the post to bear against the leg and put two ½-inch dowels through (Fig. 8-6E). One can go right through the tapered end of the post, but the other must be shorter. The simplest joint is with long nails into holes drilled slightly undersize—with one each way (Fig. 8-6F). Be careful positioning the posts so they finish upright or they will look unsatisfactory.

Have all the tabletop strips prepared. Round the outer edges and corners, but there is no need to do anything to the inner angles. Space the strips evenly across the top rails. The outer strips can come 1 inch outside the ends of the rails. Check squareness as you put on the top. Attach the outer pieces first and measure diagonals before adding the other strips. Counterbored and plugged screws are the best attachments, but you could use screws with their heads on the surface or nail the parts together.

Invert the table and put on the intermediate rails (Fig. 8-5C), screwing from below. They are needed to give stiffness to the thin top. The two braces are similar to those of the first table, but they cross to opposite rails. There is a similar problem in getting their lengths and angles of cuts. A scrap piece cut to make a template is advisable. At the top end, the notch fits up to the tabletop and surplus is cut level with the rail (Fig. 8-6G). At the lower end, the strut goes over the rail (Fig. 8-6H). Nail or screw the end joints and put a bolt through the overlap (Fig. 8-5D). During this assembly, check that the legs are perpendicular to the top.

Turn the table the right way up. Prepare the seat strips in a similar way to those for the top (with the outer edges and corners rounded). Screw them to the rails with similar spaces to those of the top (Fig. 8-5E). They should be linked together intermediately to provide mutual stiffness. Central crosspieces can be sufficient,

but two pieces are shown each side (Fig. 8-5F) at the same spacing as the top rails. Screw them from below.

If the table is to be used on concrete, there can be thin strips under the ends of the legs to act as feet and take the wear during dragging. These can be replaced when damaged instead of the legs becoming worn. They would also prevent water absorption on damp ground. In any case, finish the table by painting.

DOUBLE GARDEN SEAT

A combination of two chairs and a table and shelf gives both users places beside them for refreshments, things they are using, and storage below. The whole thing is a unit that can have a permanent place or be mounted on wheels or casters for moving about.

The two chairs are very similar to individual seats, but each has only two legs to the ground. If all eight legs reached the ground, there might be difficulty in leveling them all. To give rigidity to the structure, the seat rail at the back and the lower rail at the front are deep and go through from end to end. The seats are shown flat with slats, but they could be hollowed. The table and shelf are shown as made of exterior grade plywood, but they could also be slats.

Much of the construction can be doweled, but the design is shown with mortise and tenon joints, where appropriate, and simple notches or screwed joints elsewhere. See Table 8-3. The general appearance (Fig. 8-7) shows that it is easiest to understand if you consider the unit as two chairs with some parts extended to provide the links.

In front view (Fig. 8-8A), the bottom rail goes across. The seat rails and the table rails fit between the legs. The shelf rests on the long bottom rail. The important view for sizes is one end (Fig. 8-8B). It will help in your marking out if you make a full-size copy of this. There is no shaping, you can work from measurements only. The back view (Fig. 8-9) shows the seat rail going across in one piece, but there is another rail to support the tabletop and a lighter lower rail going across takes the shelf and inner legs. In both views, the chair backs can be seen as vertical slats between horizontal pieces. The chair arms are level with the insides of the legs and extend outside the seats.

Mark out the back legs (Fig. 8-10A). The inner ones are similar, but stop at the bottom rail with stub tenons (Fig. 8-10B). The front outer legs reach the floor (Fig. 8-10C), but the inner ones join the long rail with stub tenons (Fig. 8-10D). The tapers on the back legs start above and below the seat slats and rails. The long seat rail

Table 8-3. Materials List for Double Garden Seat.

Legs

2 rear	3 × 32 × 2
2 rear	3 × 28 × 2
2 front	2 × 25 × 2
2 front	2 × 21 × 2

Long rails

1 seat	3 × 72 × 2
1 front	3 × 72 × 2
1 rear	2 × 72 × 2

Chair parts

6 rails	2½ × 24 × 2
4 rails	2 × 22 × 2
4 back rails	2 × 24 × 1
8 back slats	3 × 15 × ½
4 arms	4 × 25 × 1
8 seat slats	4 × 25 × 1

Table and shelf

6 rails	2 × 24 × 2
2 trays	23 × 26 × ½ plywood

notches into the legs, but cut more from the legs than the rail so as not to weaken the rail (Fig. 8-10E). The ends of the rail can be tenoned into the outer legs (Fig. 8-10F).

The long front rail can also be tenoned into the outer legs, but at the inner legs make the stub mortises and tenons no more than 1 inch deep. During assembly, you can put a dowel through each joint (Fig. 8-10G).

Other rails that come within the individual seat construction are mortise and tenoned into the legs in the usual way (Fig. 8-11A). All surfaces finish flush, but at the seat level add small cleats to support the ends of the front seat slats (Fig. 8-11B). The lower side rails have to be cut at an angle where they join the tapered rear legs.

The horizontal chair back rails can be joined to the legs with bareface tenons (Fig. 8-11C) or dowels. The slats can also have barefaced tenons into the rails. Space them so the gaps between them are the same as the gaps next to the legs (for a uniform appearance). Round the edges of the rails and slats before assembly.

The arms are 4 inches maximum width, but you can taper them or curve them as you prefer (Fig. 8-11D). The best joint at the front is a stub tenon or a pair of them (Fig.

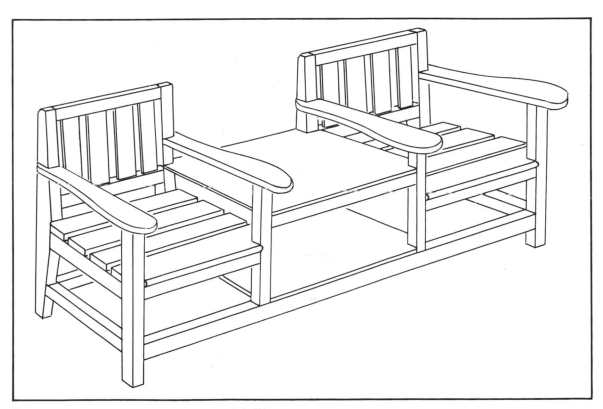

Fig. 8-7. A double garden chair with table and shelf between.

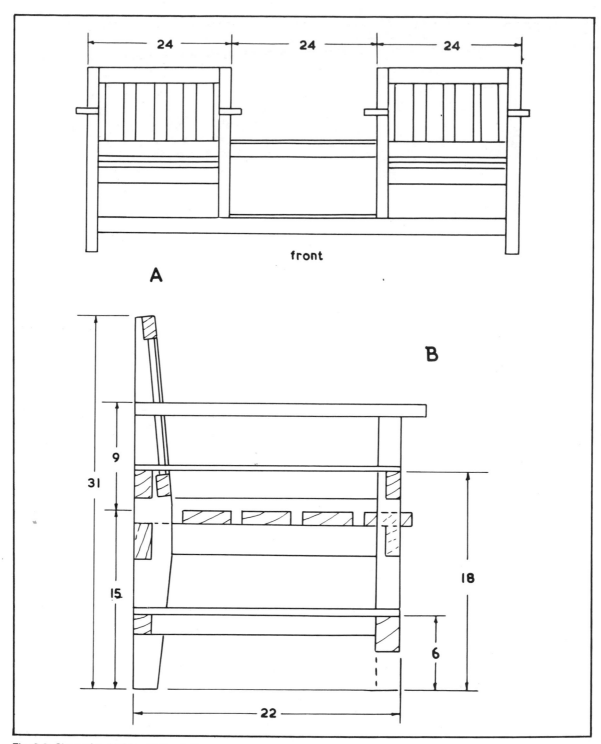

Fig. 8-8. Sizes of a double garden chair.

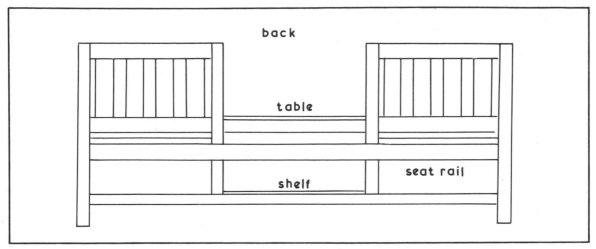

Fig. 8-9. Back view of the double garden chair.

8-11E). Use foxtail wedging if you think that is necessary. At the rear legs, the arms can notch to the legs, to take the load, and then be screwed from outside (Fig. 8-11F).

To support the shelf, there are two long rails running through. Rails back to front can be tenoned into them a short distance from the legs (Fig. 8-12A). That will be stronger than cutting the joint into the leg where there is already a joint between a leg and a long rail. The shelf need not be cut until the framework is assembled. Then you can make a close fit of it. Glue and screw it downward into the rails. It is probably satisfactory as a plain surface that is easily wiped off. You can put strips around with gaps for removing dirt (Fig. 8-12B).

The tabletop has rails tenoned into the chair legs (Fig. 8-12C). You could tenon rails the other way into the legs as well, but it is convenient to arrange them similar to those under the shelf, into the front and back rails (Fig. 8-12D). The tabletop is plywood made and fitted like the shelf. Strips at the sides prevent things falling into the chairs (Fig. 8-12E). A similar strip at the back will stop things falling there, but the front can be left open or with partial strips—leaving a gap for cleaning.

Unlike most chairs, do not make the end assemblies first. Instead get the front and back assemblies together as far as they will go. Use the lengthwise pieces to unite the uprights, check for squareness, and try one assembly over the other. Pull the joints tight and put dowels through tenons for extra strength. The back assemblies of rails and slats should hold the parts squarely.

Next join in the rails that go back to front. Start with the lower rails and work up through the seat and table

rails. When these are tight, bring in the arms. If any adjustment has to be made, that is most easily done at the arms. Assemble on a level surface and check squareness of the assembly without table, shelf, and seat slats. The plywood table and shelf should go in squarely and lock the assembly to shape. The seat slats are made in the usual way with rounded top edges and screws downward into their supports. Let the front slats project slightly and well round its outer edges.

If wheels are to be used, choose casters with wheels about 3 inches in diameter on the stem fittings intended to push into holes in the legs. Be careful of making the seats too high. You will have to shorten the lower parts of the legs, if you are using wheels, to keep the seats about 15 inches from the ground. In any case, if cushions are to be used, allow for their thickness. It is the compressed thickness that counts and that is not usually very much.

If the seat is to be painted, it will probably be given the same color all over. It could be made distinctive by painting seat slats, the tabletop, and the shelf a different color than the rest of the woodwork.

Some modifications are possible. There could be shelves at table level extending outside the chairs. Build in supporting rails between the back and front legs and make wooden brackets to come under the plywood shelves (which will serve as additional table space).

The space between the tabletop and the shelf can be enclosed to make a compartment for game materials or for anything that needs protection from animals. Sides and back can be made of plywood and a pair of doors can be made to meet at the center. You could hinge doors at the bottom to drop as a flap.

167

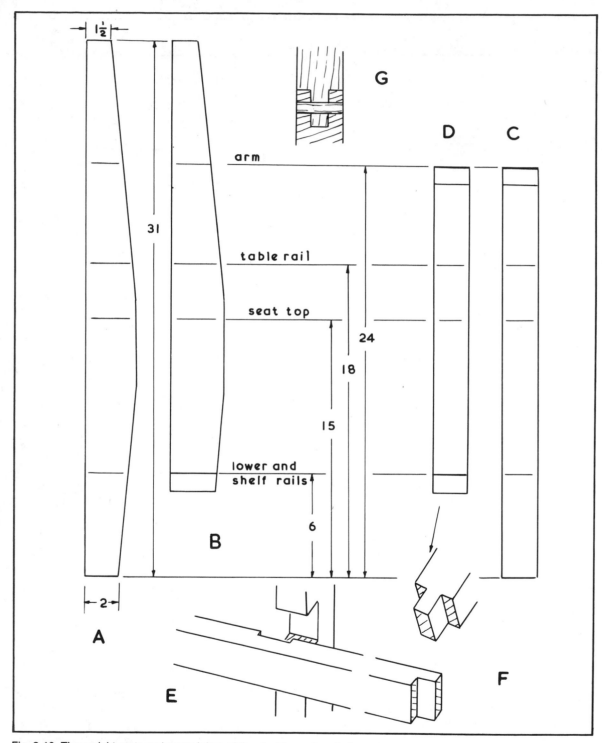

Fig. 8-10. The upright parts and some joints of the double garden chair.

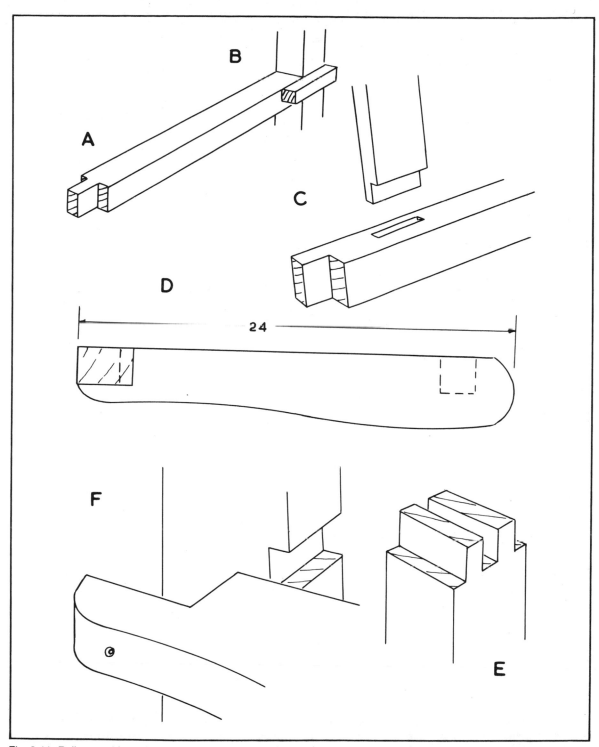

Fig. 8-11. Rail assembly and an arm for the double garden chair.

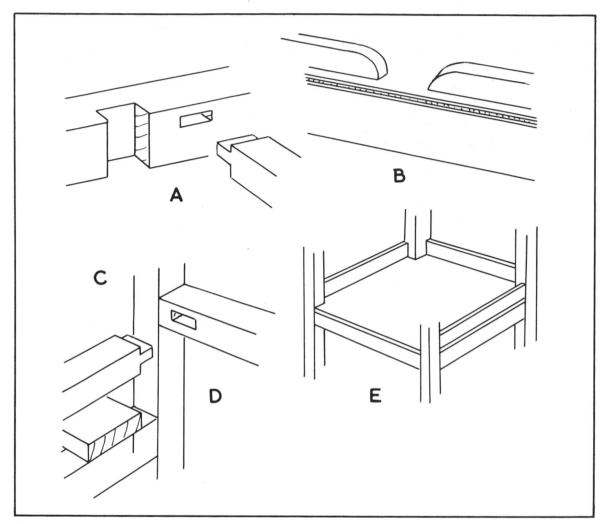

Fig. 8-12. Tray and table details for the double garden chair.

SEAT/BED/LOUNGER

Something that can be used as a seat, adapted to be a lounger and then assembled flat as a bed, has obvious attractions. This is particularly true when it can be reduced in size for storage. Figure 8-13 shows a three-part piece of furniture of very simple construction. It can be used without padding, but could become very comfortable with cushions linked together (as described for use with a lounger). The size is sufficient for use as a bed, indoors as well as outside, if fitted with the linked cushions or a separate mattress. See Table 8-4. Construction is substantial and the assembly should not suffer if left outdoors for long periods.

There is a main central part 30 inches long and two similar end pieces 24 inches long. All of these parts are 24 inches wide. If you want a total length greater than 78 inches, the end parts could be made longer. The height is controlled by the capability of the legs in the central part to fold into it. If you want a greater height, the length of 30 inches must be increased. You can gain another inch of height for every extra 2 inches of length.

The parts are hinged together. The head end will fold on to the center section with their slats coming together. The foot end is hinged underneath, so that it folds under, with slats outward (Fig. 8-13A). The central part has two pairs of legs. The end parts have single sets

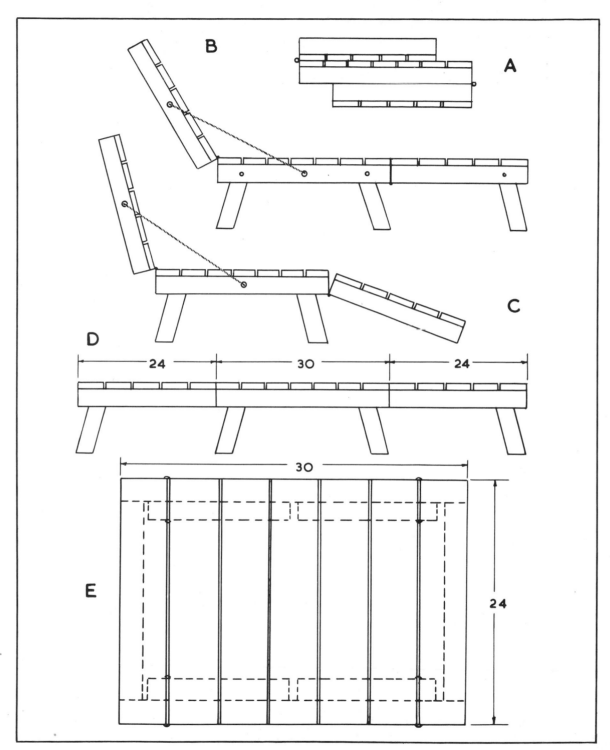

Fig. 8-13. Several layouts are possible with this seat/bed/lounger.

Table 8-4. Materials List for Seat/Bed/Lounger.

Center section	
2 sides	3 × 31 × 2
2 ends	3 × 21 × 2
7 slats	4 × 25 × 1
4 legs	3 × 13 × 2
Two end sections	
4 sides	3 × 25 × 2
2 ends	3 × 21 × 2
10 slats	4 × 25 × 1
4 legs	3 × 13 × 2
2 struts (optional)	2 × 30 × 1
4 leg rails (optional)	4 × 21 × 1

at their ends. In all cases, the legs fold inside the framing (when not needed). When lowered, the legs rest against the ends of the framing.

As a lounger, the foot end is kept level and the head end raised (Fig. 8-13B). As a seat, the foot end lowers (Fig. 8-13C). As a bed, all the legs are lowered to bring the assembly level (Fig. 8-13D).

Construction could all be by screws or nails. The corner joints of the framing could be tenoned. Make the central part first (Fig. 8-13E).

Get the frame square and nail on the slats so that they are evenly spaced. Two or three nails at each end should be sufficient. Plane the slat ends level with the framing. Make the two frames in the same way (except they are 24 inches long).

The legs are all the same and you will need eight of them. They have to fold into the framework without projecting so make sure that they are the same width as the frame sides or plane them slightly narrower. Bolt holes come centrally and 4 inches from the corners of the frames (Fig. 8-14A). It is the size of the central frame that controls the lengths of the legs because they must fold to almost touch (Fig. 8-14B). Drill for ⅜-inch or ½-inch bolts and round the tops of the legs so that they will turn on their bolts without fouling the undersides of the slats. Leave some surplus wood at the bottom until you can try a set of legs in place. Open the legs on the center section and use a straightedge parallel with the top to mark across the leg ends. If you are working to the sizes given, the longest legs you can allow for will lift the section 12 inches above the ground (Fig. 8-14C).

The best hinges to use are the strap type with arms extending about 6 inches each way. They can be mounted near the edges of the sections so that screws go into the sides of the frames. At the head end they come on top. At the other end they are underneath. If you want to use ordinary butt hinges, three 4-inch ones arranged across the joints should be satisfactory.

The head end will have to be held up in some way for a seat or lounger. Ropes could be used; ⅜-inch diameter synthetic rope would' do. Drill holes to take the rope at the center of each part on both sides (Fig. 8-14D). On the center section, the knot must not project inside. There it could interfere with the legs folding. Counterbore with a larger drill to sink the knot into the wood (Fig. 8-14E). It might be advisable to do the same on the head section, but if you locate the hole where it misses the folded leg the knot will come inside. That will be a help if you want to adjust the angle of the two parts.

The rope can stay in place when the parts are folded and need not be disturbed unless you want to alter the angle of the head or make a bed. If you prefer a more rigid support, there can be wooden struts.

A strut can go from the centers of the parts. Arrange its length to suit the most upright position you expect to want the head to be (Fig. 8-14F). Use bolts with countersunk heads inside and extending enough outside to take washers and butterfly nuts. Do not cut the ends of the struts too short outside the holes because the short grain may break under load. Leaving about 2 inches is better (Fig. 8-14G).

That setting holds the head end in position for upright seating. If you drill more holes in its sides lower, the head will slope back more if the bolts are moved at each side. Small differences are enough. Try coming down in two 1½-inch steps. They should give enough alternative angles.

For temporary folding, the struts can be left attached at one end, but they will project past the end of the package. For compact out-of-season storage, they should be removed.

The legs are shown as individuals. At the lengths suggested, they should hold without wobbling. If they seem loose or a larger and taller piece of furniture is being made, there should be a rail between each pair of legs. It cannot be put on the surface because that would interfere with folding. It must be notched into the edges or tenoned centrally to the legs. A section of 1 × 4 inches should be satisfactory for the rail.

PICNIC TABLE WITH CANOPY

The common picnic table is a utilitarian piece of outdoor furniture, but it is more of a bench that does its job than a piece of decorative or personalized furniture for your

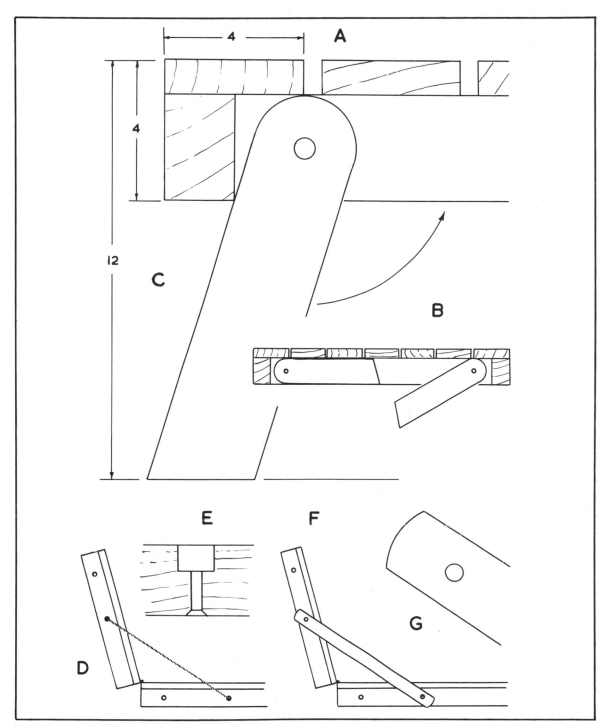

Fig. 8-14. Leg and back arrangements for the seat/bed/lounger.

Table 8-5. Materials List for Picnic Table with Canopy.

4 legs	4	×	84	×	2
2 seat rails	3	×	68	×	2
2 table rails	3	×	38	×	2
2 canopy rails	3	×	80	×	2
4 gussets	6	×	10	×	1
8 canopy rafters	2	×	98	×	2
1 ridge	4	×	102	×	2
2 canopy rails	2	×	98	×	2
4 table tops	9	×	96	×	2
1 table rail	4	×	38	×	2
2 table struts	3	×	54	×	2
6 seat tops	4	×	102	×	2
8 seat cleats	2	×	13	×	2
1 ridge	4	×	102	×	2
4 seat ends	4	×	13	×	1
with seat backs:					
Increase seat rails to	3	×	88	×	2
4 back supports	3	×	34	×	2
4 bottom rails	3	×	28	×	2
4 back rails	4	×	102	×	2

yard or garden. It serves a valuable purpose in many public places. If you want something different on your own property, one way of enhancing its appearance and usefulness is to build it with a canopy and possibly with backs to the seats. See Table 8-5.

This combination table/seats/canopy is first described without backs to the seats (Fig. 8-15), but seat backs are described later. Sizes suit an overall length of 96 inches, but the ends can be used with tables and seats of other lengths. The wood sections are intended for softwood and could be reduced slightly for hardwood.

The sizes (Fig. 8-16) allow for eating at a convenient height. The canopy gives ample clearance as you stoop to sit. The canopy overhang is not much, but there has to be a limit. Its width could be increased if you prefer.

If possible, set out an end, or half of it, full size on the floor to get the angles and sizes of the legs. Otherwise, it is possible to lay down a pair of legs and move them into the correct relative positions and mark angles and the positions of other parts on them. The ridge goes between the tops of the legs so that they are notched to suit, but cut them back enough to clear the slope of the canvas

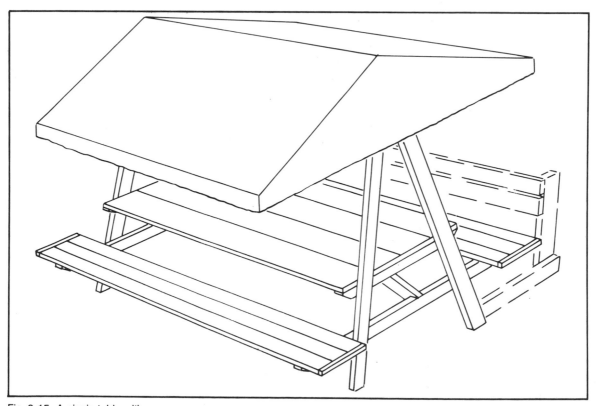

Fig. 8-15. A picnic table with a canopy.

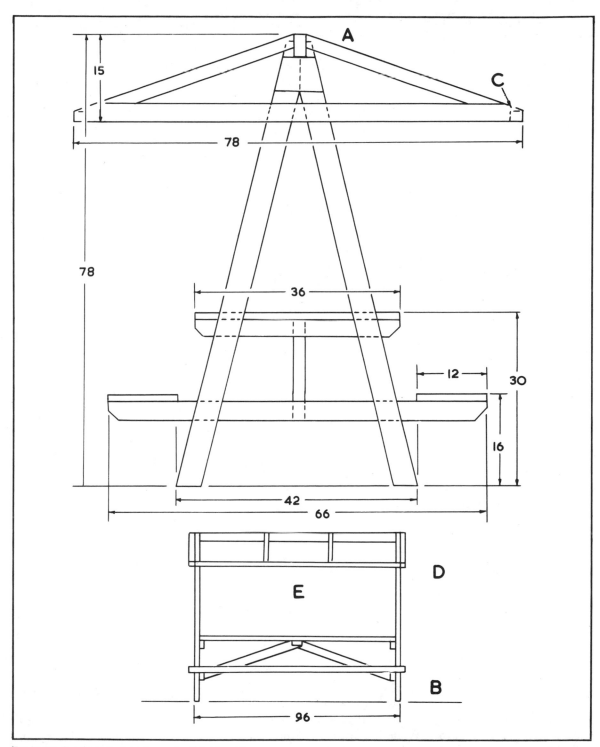

Fig. 8-16. Suggested sizes for a picnic table with canopy.

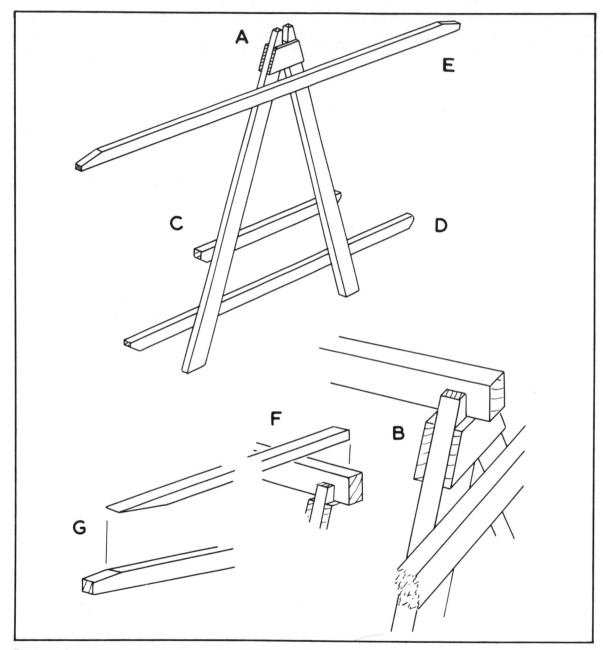

Fig. 8-17. Construction of the end frames of a picnic table with canopy.

canopy (Figs. 8-16A and 8-17A). Join the legs under the ridge with gussets both sides (Fig. 8-17B). The table rail (Fig. 8-17C) and the seat rail (Fig. 8-17D) have their ends beveled underneath and they go across the legs symmetrically and parallel with the floor. Measure carefully.

Errors might not be obvious until assembly is complete. Then it will be too late for correction.

For strength, it will be best to bolt through these joints; two ⅜ inch bolts at each position are suitable (Fig. 8-18A). If you prefer to use screws, it is advisable to cut shallow notches for the rails in the legs to resist any tendency for the rails to slide down (Fig. 8-18B). You could bolt through the gussets at the top, but screws should be strong enough there.

The seat and table rails are on the inside of the legs, but the canopy rail goes on the outside. That should also be bolted to the legs. Make sure it is parallel with the other rails (Fig. 8-17E). A pair of rafters go from the ridge to its ends. They do not have to provide much strength. They can be nailed in place. Cut them to fit against the ridge (Fig. 8-17F). At the other end, bevel them and the ends of the rail, down to 2 inches deep (Fig. 8-17G), so that there is a smooth slope on the roof angle.

The table and its struts brace the whole assembly. It

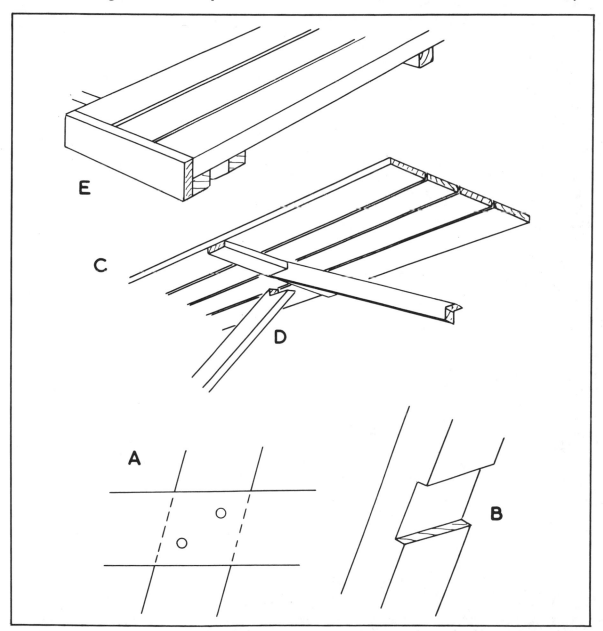

Fig. 8-18. Seat and table details of the picnic table with canopy.

is suggested that four pieces, 9 inches wide, make up the top. Other widths available could be used. They need not all be the same. Allowing for planing to width, there will be gaps of ¼ inch or so between boards. Nail the top boards to their rails on the ends. Under their centers put a rail across. It can be cut a little short and its lower edge beveled so that it is inconspicuous and does not interfere with users.

The two struts go from the seat rails to the rail (Figs. 8-16B and 8-18C). Notch them over the seat rails and cut the center notches so that each strut goes across the full width of the rail and its full depth is against the top boards (Fig. 8-18D). Let the struts overlap each other on this rail so that they can be nailed to the rail and to each other. While doing this, check that the table and legs are square to each other. Measure diagonals from top and bottom corners of opposite legs. It will help to have the ridge piece in position, but not finally nailed until you are satisfied that the parts are square. Because getting the strut ends correct is important, it will help to cut a thin piece of scrap wood to size first. Allow for corrections to it (if necessary) as you use it as a template for the actual struts.

The seats are shown made of three pieces, but you could use other widths. Like the tabletop, they are assembled with narrow gaps. The ends could be open, but they look neater closed (Fig. 8-18E). Put cleats across the ends and two others spaced evenly between to brace the boards to each other. Then close the ends with strips that should have their outer edges and corners well rounded. Nail the seats to their rails.

Check the rigidity of the assembly at this stage. It should not flex lengthwise. If you consider it necessary, put metal brackets between the ridge piece and the inner gussets to the legs.

To give shape and support to the canvas canopy, put lengthwise rails between the end rails (Figs. 8-16C and 8-16D). Join them to the ridge with intermediate rafters (Fig. 8-16E) to keep the shape and prevent the canvas from sagging. Sight along from the ends as you fit these rafters to check that you are keeping the slopes the same.

You could get a canvas cover made from paper templates, but light canvas can be sewn on a domestic sewing machine. That gives you an opportunity to get an exact fit. Assemble the panels inside out over the framework and pin them together on the lines that have to be sewn. Allow for the edges hanging down about 6 inches. Those edges could be turned under in a straight line or made scalloped. While sewing the seams, include pieces of tape at intervals long enough to tie round the framework at about 24-inch spacing.

Comfort is increased if the seats are given backs (Fig. 8-19). Construction is the same, as already described, except the seat rails should be made about 20 inches longer. The back angle will be about 10 degrees from vertical, or a little more, but make sure all four

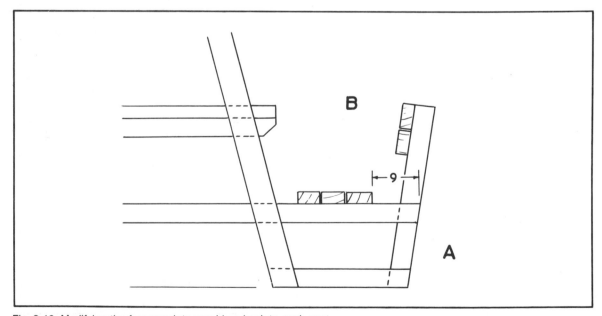

Fig. 8-19. Modifying the framework to provide a back to each seat.

supports are the same. During the assembly of the ends, put the short bottom rails across the insides of the legs and arrange the supports inside them and the seat rails (Fig. 8-19A). If you want to fasten the table to the ground, it would be better to take these bottom pieces across in single lengths. Then brackets or pegs to the ground can be attached to them.

The backs are shown at the same height as the table, but they could be a few inches higher or lower if you prefer. Two rails similar to those of the seat are shown in Fig. 8-19B. They should be stiff enough without intermediate supports. You could brace them to each other by putting short packings between them at one or two places. If the seat needs stiffening, you can add struts similar to those under the table. Place them from the bottom rails to other rails put across under the seat.

Chapter 9

Folding Furniture

MOST OUTDOOR FURNITURE IS USED ONLY OCCA-sionally. In some cases it will be convenient for the furniture to be rigid and permanently in shape, but for many things it is better if its size can be reduced. If furniture can be folded or disassembled, parts will occupy much less storage space. Care is needed with disassembled parts so that you do not lose any of them. This is particularly true for nuts, bolts, and washers. Most folding furniture does not require loose parts, so there is nothing to lose, but the folded item will not reduce to quite as small a package as some disassembled table, chair, or other item.

Besides the convenience of reducing bulk for storage of furniture used in the vicinity of the home, folding furniture is useful for camping and other trips where you need to stow everything as compactly as possible if you are to get it all into the vehicle.

It is important that a folding piece of furniture be strong enough during use and when folded. Some things are satisfactory when assembled, but a comparatively fragile part will be exposed to damage when folded. Of course, it is important to guard against inadvertent folding when the item is in use. There must be a definite lock in some way. There must be no risk, for instance, of a chair collapsing under a normal load.

Some folding furniture is designed most ingeniously and usually with rather complicated mechanisms. This type is more suitable for factory production because there are special parts that most individual craftsman cannot make. In any case, a simple action is preferable to a complicated one. It is easier to make and it is less likely to go wrong.

Folding furniture manufactured in quantity is mostly metal formed by machine. This technique is unsuitable for the home shop. Wood is the preferred material, but some simple metalwork is needed. This involves sawing, filing, drilling, and some simple bending. All of this can be done with hand tools, if necessary.

For the sake of lightness, wooden folding outdoor furniture is normally made with sections no thicker than necessary. Because of this, it is advisable to select straight-grained hardwood that is free from knots. Softwood would not normally be used. If it is, sections should be increased and joints would have to be reinforced in many places with metal brackets or plywood gussets.

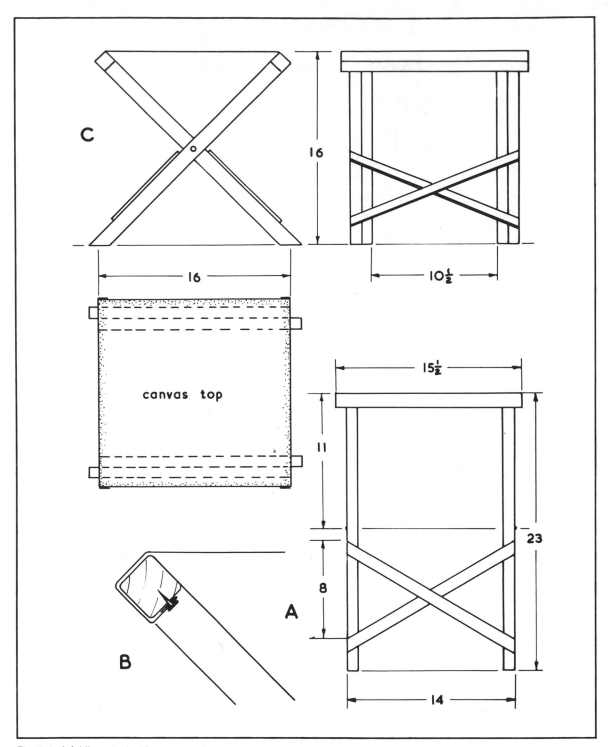

Fig. 9-1. A folding stool with a canvas top.

Table 9-1. Materials List for Folding Stool.

2 tops	$1\frac{1}{8} \times 16 \times 1\frac{1}{8}$
4 legs	$1\frac{1}{8} \times 24 \times \frac{7}{8}$
4 braces	$\frac{7}{8} \times 18 \times \frac{1}{4}$

Folding furniture should be painted or varnished to prevent the wood from absorbing moisture as well as for the sake of appearance. A boat varnish gives good protection and allows the grain to show through resulting in a lighter appearance than a painted surface. Pay particular attention to any end grain that will rest on the ground because it is particularly prone to soak up moisture.

FOLDING STOOL

This is a basic type of seat with a canvas top that is comfortable to use. It packs to under 3 inches thick. It is suitable for camping and fishing as well as in your yard. The parts are made as two frames pivoted near their centers (Fig. 9-1) with canvas across the top bars. The frames are the same except that one is narrow enough to fit inside the other. See Table 9-1.

Mark out the two top bars (Fig. 9-2A), but do not round the edges until after the joints are cut. Mark out all four legs (Fig. 9-2B). Leave the cutting of the bottom angled ends until after assembly. The joints are simple mortise and tenons (Fig. 9-2C). They should be strong enough, but if you have any doubts you can add strip metal brackets inside each (Fig. 9-2D). Check that the legs of the narrower assembly fit inside the other ones.

The braces on the outer pair of legs should come below the pivot points (Fig. 9-1A). Otherwise they will interfere with the action by hitting the inner legs when the stool is opened. This would not happen with the inner legs if the braces were higher, but it is standard to put both sets at the same height. As shown in Fig. 9-2E, the braces are put on through the marked positions on the legs and held at each place with one screw—then cut level. Where the braces cross they are sprung over each other. It would weaken them too much to cut halving joints there. Have the legs fitted into each other when you put on the braces so that you see that they will be able to move.

The pivots can be coach bolts. Let the square neck pull into the outer leg, include a thin rivet between the legs, and then have a washer and nut inside (Fig. 9-2F). Cut off the bolt end fairly close to the nut and hammer over its edges all round while the head is supported on an iron block (Fig. 9-2G) so the nut cannot work loose. Instead of a bolt you could use a rivet if you prefer.

The seat can be a plastic-coated material or plain-proofed canvas about 15 ounce per square yard grade. The width needed is 15 inches. If you are able to get this stock width, it will have a *selvage* where the thread turned back during weaving (this will not fray). If you have to cut wider canvas, allow enough for turning under. This is advisable in any case because a *tabled* edge will provide strength where it is needed.

If you cut the canvas with *pinking shears*, you can machine sew a single line of stitches without turning the canvas in (Fig. 9-3A) because the edge will not fray. If you cut straight, it will be better to fold the edge in and stitch through it (Fig. 9-3B). Rub down the folds with the handle of a knife, or something similar, before stitching.

Where the canvas is attached to the top pieces, allow folding under so that you can drive tacks there (Fig. 9-1B). Bringing the canvas round three edges of the wood relieves the tacks of strain. Fold the canvas around the tops of the legs and arrange tacks or large-headed nails closely; 1 inch apart will probably be close enough.

As you fit the canvas, check the amount of opening and the height of the stool (Fig. 9 1C). Allow for the canvas stretching a little. When you have finished attaching the canvas, open the stool fully so that you can mark and cut the bottoms of the legs parallel with the top.

FOLDING CHAIR

The stool just described has many uses, but if you want more comfort there has to be a back; attaching arms would be even better. A type of folding chair, that is built around a folding stool, is a well-tried design for wood construction. As shown in Fig. 9-4, the chair has ample size for comfort when opened and it stands rigidly. It packs to only a few inches thick. Its side view is the same size whether opened or closed. See Table 9-2.

The framework, including the arms, is made of wood, but the seat and back are canvas. This will conform to body shape and provide comfort. There are some simple metal links and spacers to be made. The most attractive finish would be boat varnish, with the metal parts painted. You can paint the wood as well if you prefer. It would be unwise to leave the wood bare because it would absorb moisture.

The general drawing (Fig. 9-5) shows that the seat is a stool. There is a pair of sides linked to the stool and joined with canvas to form the back. You can make the stool first and fit the sides to it, but it is probably easier to get an accurate assembly if you start with the pair of sides. Then adjust the spacings of the stool sides and legs to suit.

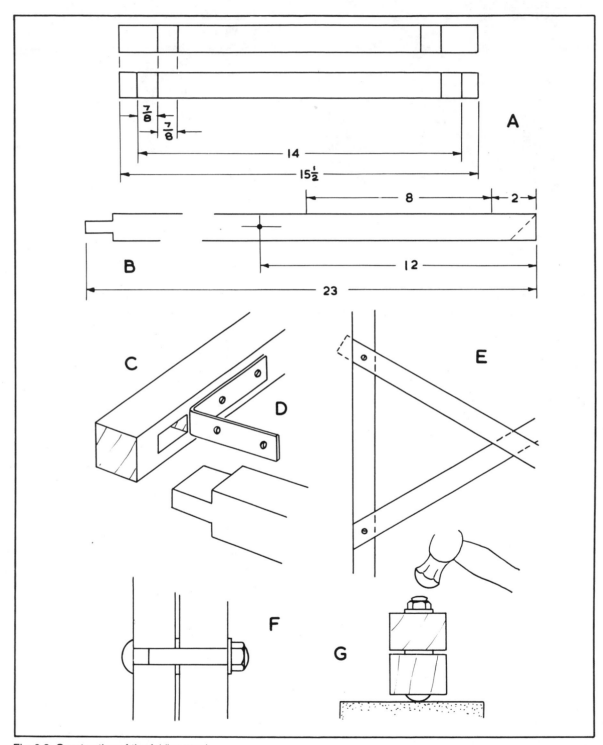

Fig. 9-2. Construction of the folding stool.

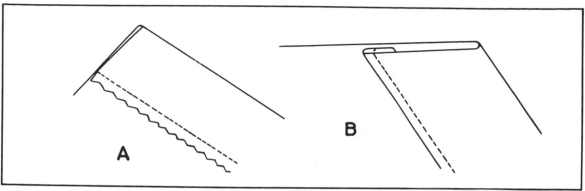

Fig. 9-3. Sewing details of a canvas stool top.

Set out the chair side full size (Fig. 9-5A). Make the parts with square edges. After cutting the joints and doing general shaping, all edges that will be exposed are better rounded (Fig. 9-6A). Most joints can be doweled. You could use mortise and tenons if you prefer.

Mark out the four upright legs together (Fig. 9-6B). Drill ¼-inch holes for bolts, 1 inch up from the bottom, to form stool pivots. The side rails dowel into the marked positions on the legs (Fig. 9-6C). The tops of the legs have dowels into the arms (Fig. 9-6D).

The arms are parallel except for rounding at the front and a taper at the back. The side slats are too thin for

dowels and it will be better to slot them into the arm and rail (Fig. 9-6E).

The back piece and the arm that attaches to it should be marked and cut to match. The back (Fig. 9-5B) has its bottom cut to an angle against the leg, but it would weaken it to go to a feather edge. Well round the top. The joint between the end of the arm and the back has to resist the thrust of a person sitting and leaning back. A joint that cuts too much out of the back can cause it to break there under pressure. So that there is enough wood left in the back, join the arm with a single ⅝-inch dowel. Drive a wedge from behind (Fig. 9-6F). There should never be

Fig. 9-4. A folding armchair.

Table 9-2. Materials List for Folding Chair.

4 stool legs	1¼ × 26 × ⅝
2 stool crossbars	1¼ × 18 × 1¼
2 stool rods	⅝ × 18 round rods
4 side legs	1¾ × 26 × ⅞
2 side rails	3 × 18 × ⅞
2 side slats	4 × 15 × ½
2 arms	3 × 22 × ⅞
2 backs	1¾ × 26 × ⅞

much load on the joint at the bottom of the back because thrust at the top tends to push that joint together. Use glue and one or two screws there. After you have prepared all parts and rounded where advisable, assemble to make a matching pair.

The stool is made up of two crossbars to take the canvas, with four crossed sides, held below the pivot with lengths of dowel rod (Fig. 9-7A). The sizes of the sides shown (Fig. 9-5C) will give a satisfactory spread when opened.

As you set out the stool, the crossbars are as long as the widths of the sides, but the joints between them and their legs have to be spaced to suit the spacing of the chair side legs. One pair of the stool legs, that come outside the others, has to fit between the chair side legs with just enough clearance for thin washers. Then the inside stool legs must fit between them with similar clearance.

The legs might be joined to the crossbars with dowels, but it would be better to use tenons, either right through (as in the stool first described) or with stub tenons (Fig. 9-7B). Round the top edges of the crossbars (Fig. 9-7C). Drill for ¼-inch pivot bolts 1 inch from the rounded bottoms of the stool legs and again at the pivot points.

Drill for the dowel rods that brace the lower parts of the stool legs. When you assemble, the rods can go right through and be held with glue and nails driven across.

The central pivot of the stool is a ¼-inch bolt or rivet taken through washers. The pivot of the outside stool legs to the bottom of the side rigid legs is the same (Fig. 9-7D). Coach bolts, as described for the first stool, could be used (but rivets are shown). When you do the final assembly, have the prepared rivet head outside and hammer over on the washer on the inside.

At the other side, there is a gap to be filled between the stool leg and the side rigid leg. Use short pieces of tube on the rivets. Make the length to take up the thickness of the outer stool leg (Fig. 9-7E). You can make a

trial assembly with the rivets or bolts loose, but do not tighten them until you have the canvas on and the metal links ready.

The links that join the stool to the sides and permit folding are pieces of strip metal about ⅝ of an inch wide and under ⅛-inch thick; 3/32 inch would be ideal, but any strip about this section could be used. Iron is the obvious choice, but that is liable to rust. Painting iron before assembly will give ample protection. Brass would resist corrosion and stainless steel would be a good choice. Some of it, however, is difficult to bend and drill.

The straight links that join the outside stool legs to the rigid side legs (Fig. 9-7F) are simple, straight pieces. Mark the centers of the holes with a centerpunch and use these dots as centers for drawing the end curves before drilling.

At the other side of the chair, the links should have the same distance between the holes, when finished, but the links have to be cranked to allow for the legs being in a different plane (Fig. 9-7G). Bending can be done while the strip projects above the vise jaws. Drill holes to suit the screws used; 10-gauge screws are suitable. Countersink the holes so the heads will not project and interfere with folding.

The best positions for the links are found by a trial assembly. Have the rivets or bolts put in loosely and open the chair to the sitting position. Attach the links temporarily to the rear stool legs only, about 3 inches down from the crossbar. Put screws into the side legs when the links are about horizontal. Try the folding action. Then alter the screw positions until the action is correct. Mark and drill similar positions for screws at the front. Measure across the top of the stool in the open position as a guide to the length of canvas to fit.

Do any finishing to the woodwork before attaching the canvas—including the parts that will be covered by canvas—for the sake of protection. The seat canvas is dealt with in the same way as described for the stool. A width of 15 inches or 16 inches would be suitable. Roll the canvas over the crossbars and tack closely underneath. In the first fitting of the seat canvas, aim to have it finish taut in the open position to allow for some stretching. When the seat canvas has been fitted, you can assemble the pivot rivets or bolts together with the links. You should then have the seat standing with its sides upright.

The back strip of canvas should be 7 inches or 8 inches wide. Deal with the edges in the same way as the edges of the seat. Do not stretch it as tightly as the seat; it can start with a little slackness. Wrap the ends round the wood and tack inside in the same way as the seat.

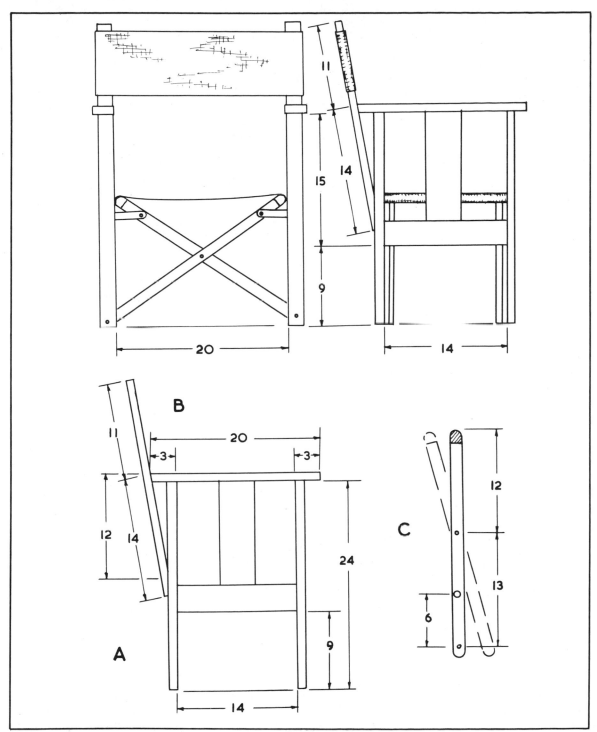

Fig. 9-5. Sizes of a folding armchair.

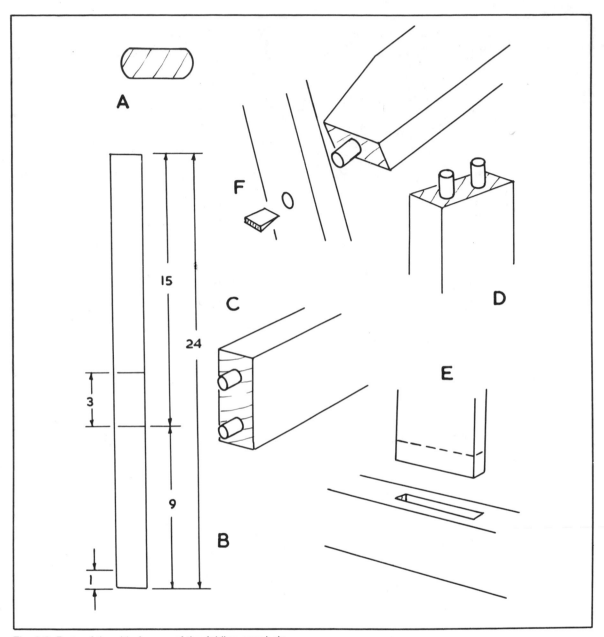

Fig. 9-6. Parts of the side frames of the folding armchair.

CHAIR WITH FOLDING BACK

A seat without a back support does not provide as much comfort as a chair. It is possible to make a chair that is a development of the first stool, yet it packs to almost the same size. It is a folding stool with the crossed legs supporting a canvas top, but on one pair of legs there are

pivoted the uprights of a back that will swing down when the legs are folded (Fig. 9-8). When a stool without a back is used, the sitter usually has his legs toward a free canvas side. If there is a back, one of the bars has to come to the front.

In the general drawing (Fig. 9-9), you can see that

the back pivots on the outer legs and their crossbar is extended for it to press against (Fig. 9-9A). See Table 9-3. At the top, there is a plywood back support (Fig. 9-9B). The parts have to be arranged to give clearance when the back uprights fold down. The inner legs have a crossbar that does not extend to the width of the outer legs and the canvas inside that (Fig. 9-9C).

The four legs are the same except for the pivot holes for the back in the outer ones (Fig. 9-10A). Leave the cutting of the angled bottoms until after assembly. The joints to the crossbars will be the same as in the first stool (Fig. 9-2C) and you can include metal brackets (Fig. 9-2D) if you prefer.

Make the back uprights (Fig. 9-10B). The simplest

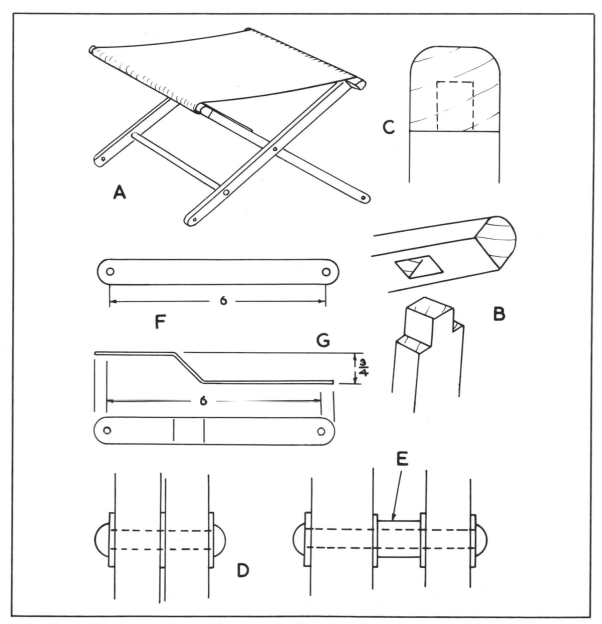

Fig. 9-7. Details of the folding seat part of the armchair.

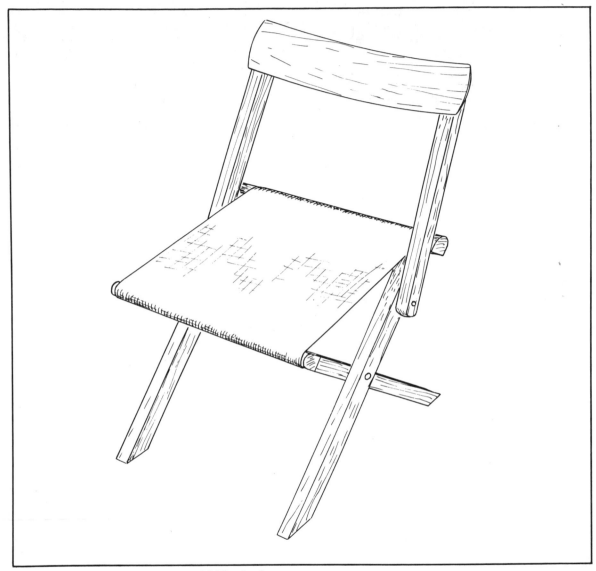

Fig. 9-8. A chair with a canvas seat and folding back.

back is a flat piece of plywood ¼ inch or ⅜ inch thick glued and screwed to the side pieces. A more comfortable back is curved. The amount of curve is not crucial, but about 1½ inches in the width is enough.

A curved back can be made with two pieces of ⅛-inch plywood, cut to width, but with some excess length at this stage. Prepare two stiff boards and three packings that will go across the plywood. Round their edges. Put glue on the meeting surfaces of the plywood and squeeze in a vise or with clamps to a suitable curve (Fig. 9-10C).

Table 9-3. Materials List for Chair with Folding Back.

4 legs	1⅛	×	24	×	1⅛		
2 backs	1⅛	×	21	×	1⅛		
1 crossbar	1⅛	×	19	×	1⅛		
1 crossbar	1⅛	×	16	×	1⅛		
4 braces	⅞	×	18	×	¼		
1 back	3	×	18	×	¼	plywood	
or 2 backs	3	×	18	×	⅛	plywood	

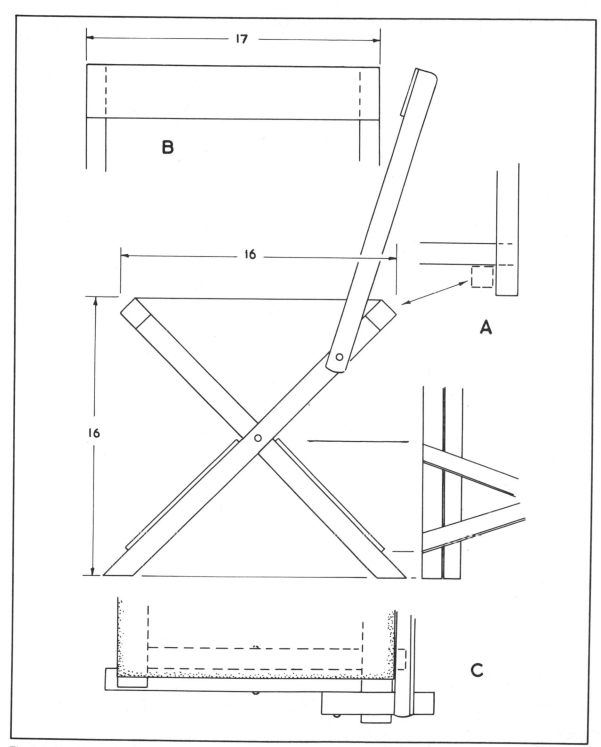

Fig. 9-9. Sizes for a chair with a folding back.

When the glue has set, trim the wood to size. Allow for slightly curved ends (Fig. 9-11A) and round the back edges in section whether you make it flat or hollowed. For the hollowed back, notch the uprights to suit the slope on each side so they remain parallel when the back is glued and screwed on.

The distances between the back uprights and the two sets of legs have to be made to match each other. Work to the actual wood. This might be slightly thicker or thinner than drawn. Put the back parts together with the outside edges 17 inches apart (Fig. 9-11B). Make the back crossbar long enough to extend ½ inch past the back uprights and make the joints for the outer pair of legs so that they will come inside the back uprights (Fig. 9-11C). Allow for thin washers between them.

Make the length of the front crossbar so that it does not quite reach the outside edges of the outer pair of legs, and position the joints for its legs to come inside the outer legs (Fig. 9-11D). Round the edges and ends of the crossbars and then assemble the legs to them. Also attach the braces (Fig. 9-11E) in a similar way to those of the first stool. Spring them over each other where they cross. Keep them below the pivot position so that they do not obstruct the legs when opening.

Make the central pivots between the legs with bolts or rivets as described for the first stool or the chair. The back pivots are made in a similar way, but there must not be any projections on the insides of the outer legs. Otherwise that might interfere with folding (Fig. 9-12). Use bolts or rivets with countersunk heads on the inside (Fig. 9-10D).

Varnish or paint all the woodwork before assembling

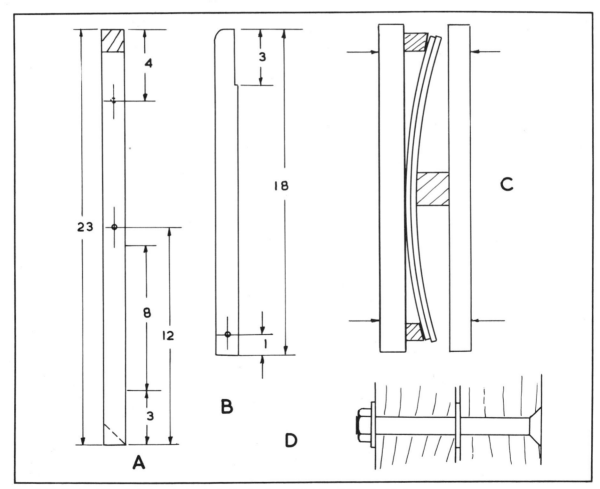

Fig. 9-10. Parts of the chair, how to laminate the back, and details of the pivot bolt.

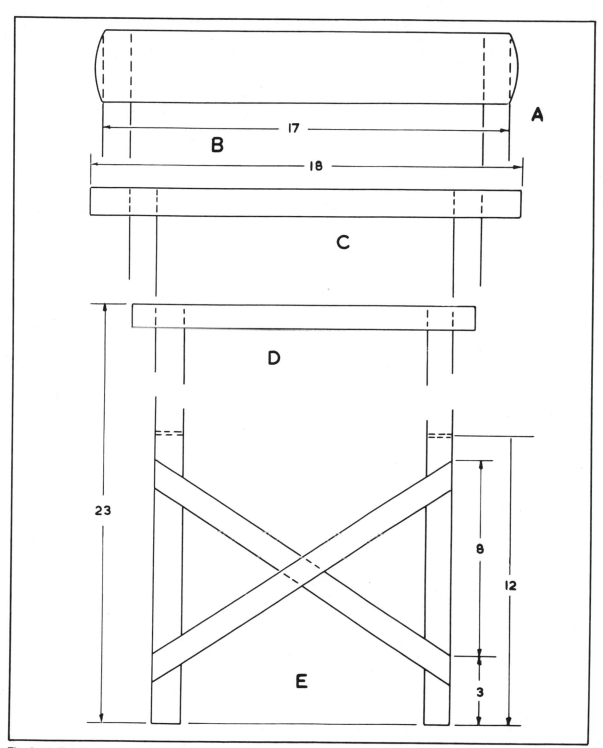

Fig. 9-11. Relative sizes of the chair parts.

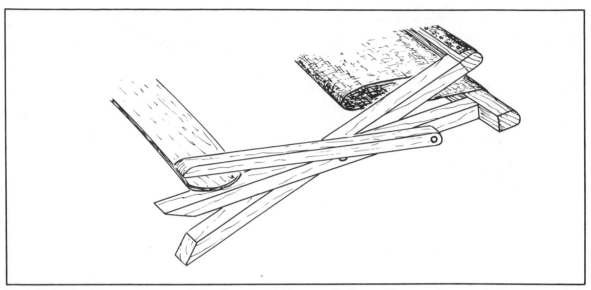

Fig. 9-12. Widths of the assemblies must allow the parts to fold over each other and there must be no projecting bolts or nuts to interfere.

the parts. Then fit canvas as described for the first stool. Its width must be kept a small amount in from the ends of the front crossbar so that the chair will fold without the back being obstructed.

DECK CHAIR

The fold-flat deck chair is common in many forms in most parts of the world. There are versions with leg rests, canopies, arms, and other additions, but the basic pattern is the most common form. It serves as a simple and comfortable adjustable seat that can be stored in a minimum of space. The example shown in Fig. 9-13 is of straightforward construction with no extras. The sizes given will make a chair of average size. If other sizes are used, remember that the inner assembly has to fold inside the outer one and that the strut part must swing over the top of the outer frame for folding. If the canvas is flat and moderately taut when the chair is folded, it will curve into a comfortable shape when the chair is set up.

There are two frames pivoted together. A strut assembly allows the chair to be at any of three angles (Fig. 9-14A). When the frame is folded, the two four-sided parts close into line and the strut part rests on them (Fig. 9-14B). This brings the assembly down to less than 4 inches thick.

All of the parts are 1-×-2 inch section and should be of straight-grained hardwood free from flaws. A heavy person using the chair puts considerable strain on some

parts. The width shown is intended to take canvas 18 inches wide, but that can be adjusted if only canvas of another width is available. See Table 9-4.

Mark out the long sides (Fig. 9-15A). All of the ends with crossmembers tenoned in are made the same (Fig. 9-15B). The ends are rounded using the edge of the crossmember as the center for the compass. Mark out the

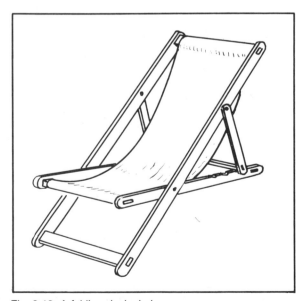

Fig. 9-13. A folding deck chair.

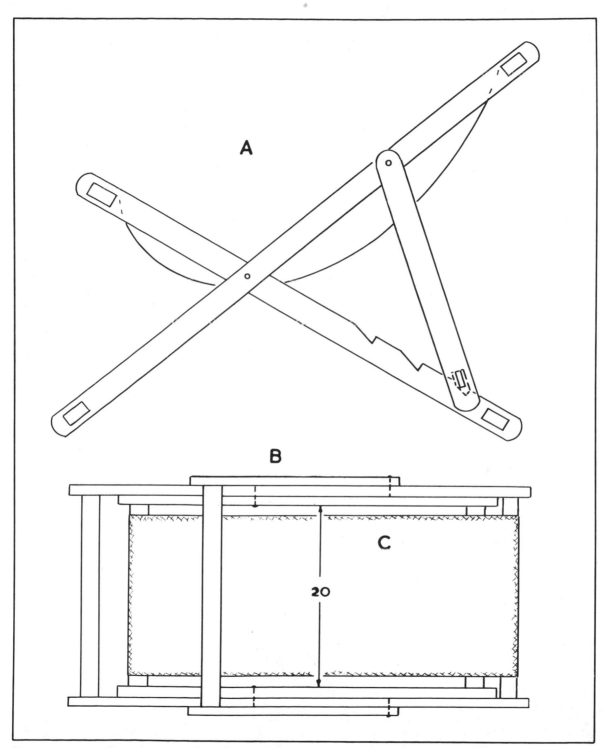

Fig. 9-14. The general arrangements of a folding deck chair.

Table 9-4. Materials List for Deck Chair.

2 sides	2 × 52 × 1
2 sides	2 × 43 × 1
2 struts	2 × 24 × 1
5 crossbars	2 × 27 × 1

shorter sides (Fig. 9-15C). The notches for the strut are cut into a ⅜-inch hole (Fig. 9-15D). It is possible to make all the notches the same and have the strut crossmember an average shape. Because the angle it meets the side is different in each position, the best fit is obtained by making the furthest notch as shown and having the strut crossmember match it. Alter the other positions to suit during a trial assembly. All of the notches will be cut into ⅜-inch holes, but the angles into them will be slightly different at the inner two positions.

Make the strut sides (Fig. 9-15E). The bottom joint is similar to the others except that the tenon is cut back to allow the bevels on the crossmember (Fig. 9-15F). The top is cut semicircular and drilled for the bolt (Fig. 9-15G).

The joints are all tenons about ½ inch wide (Fig. 9-16A). Round the edges of the crossmembers of the four-sided frames (Fig. 9-16B). Cut the tenons slightly too long and put saw cuts across them so that the joints can be tightened with wedges (Fig. 9-16C). They are planed level after the glue has set. Make sure assemblies are square and the inner frame should fit inside the other with just enough clearance for a washer on each side.

Pivots can be ¼ inch or 5/16 inch coach bolts. For the main pivots, have the heads outside. Have them inside for the strut pivots. Include washers between the parts and under the nuts (Fig. 9-16D). After the final assembly, cut off any surplus threaded end of each bolt and rivet the remainder by hammering on to the nut to lock it. If the notches for the strut are to be individually fitted, do that during a temporary assembly.

Take off the sharpness from the edges of the main parts. This is particularly important for anyone sitting in the chair. But do not reduce the cross-section much. Varnish the wood before final assembly so that you can get at the parts that would otherwise be difficult to reach.

If the canvas is bought already the right width, its selvages can be used as they are because they will not fray. If you have to cut wider canvas, turn in the edges (as described for the folding chair).

Have the frames folded so that they are in line. The canvas has to go from the front rail of the inner frame to the top rail of the outer frame (Fig. 9-14C). Allow enough

to wrap round the rails and turn in to be tacked. You can tack to the edges of the rails (Fig. 9-16E), but for the strongest joint the canvas should go round to the flat part (Fig. 9-16F). Tacking in this way is easy enough for the first end, but you can get enough slackness in the canvas to swing a hammer at the other end by folding the frames the wrong way (after you have settled on the canvas length). If fastened in that way, the canvas under load helps to keep the tacks in place.

SLAT-TOP STOOL

A canvas-topped stool can provide more comfort, but it could suffer if left out in all types of weather. An all-wood stool will have better weather resistance. This stool (Fig. 9-17) has a top made of narrow strips so that it does not trap water on crossed legs that fold flat with the top alongside. The sizes shown in Fig. 9-18 and Table 9-5 are for a stool of minimum size that can be stowed compactly. It is just big enough to act as a reasonable seat. The top can be softened with a cushion and possibly provided with tapes for lashing on.

The wood is all of fairly thin section so the design is unsuitable for most softwoods and the best choice will be one of the lighter straight-grained hardwoods. Sizes quoted are the finished ones and some parts would not be strong enough if sawn sizes were used and planed thinner.

There is no need to make a full-size drawing unless the sizes are to be altered. As shown, the ledged end of the outer leg assembly swings down to close in line with the other leg and the top drops between them.

Start with the top. Take the sharpness of the slats. Mark out and cut the supports (Fig. 9-19A), but do not cut the notch yet. Its exact size and angle will be determined later in a temporary assembly with the legs. Attach the slats to the supports (Fig. 9-18A). The distance the supports are in from the ends of the slats must be the same thickness of two legs with a washer between. It would not matter if the distance is up to ⅛ of an inch further in than that, but do not allow too much.

Make the four legs (Fig. 9-18B). The tops are semicircles about the centers of the holes in the inner legs. Although the tops of the outer legs are the same shape, they do not require holes. The final angles of the bottoms are best marked with a straightedge across during a temporary assembly.

The pivots can be rivets or bolts ¼ of an inch in diameter, but there has to be clearance at their heads where parts cross when folded. That only happens at one side in each place. You can use countersunk rivets or bolt

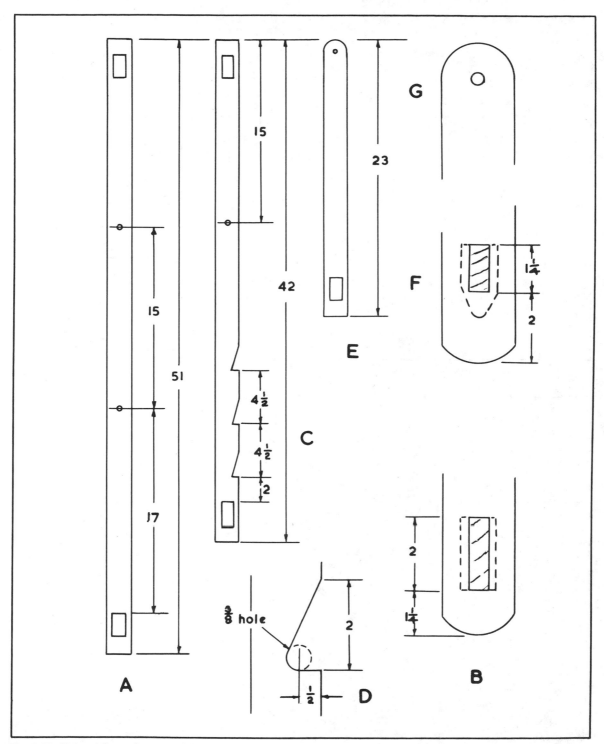

Fig. 9-15. Sizes of the main parts of the deck chair.

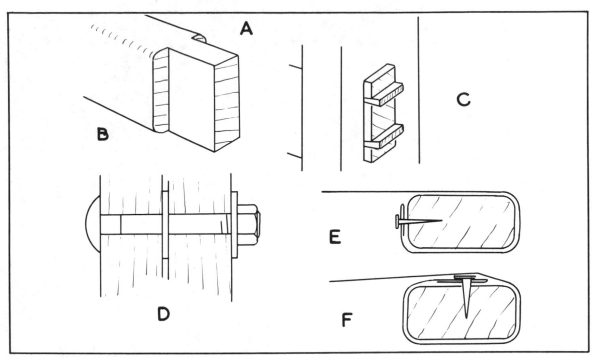

Fig. 9-16. Assembling, pivoting, and canvasing the deck chair.

Fig. 9-17. A slat-topped folding stool.

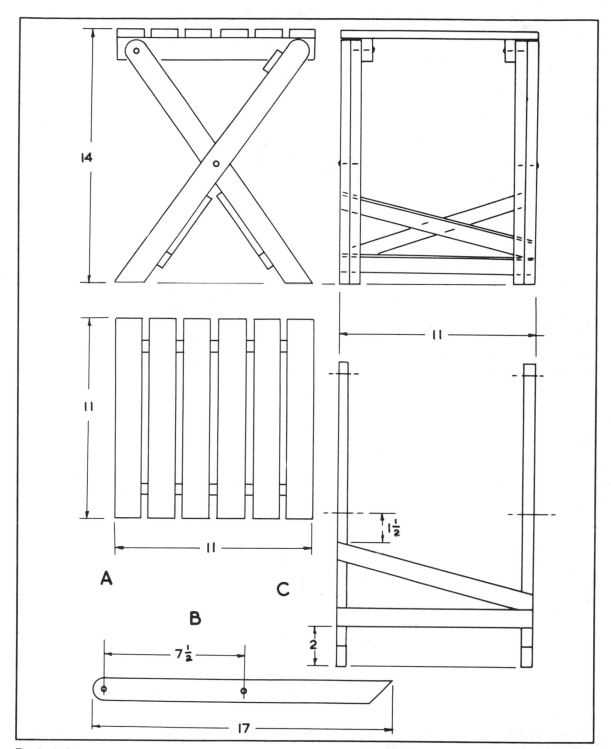

A

B

C

Fig. 9-18. Sizes for a light, slat-topped folding stool.

Table 9-5. Materials List for Slat-Top Stool.

6 tops	1½ × 12 × ⅜
6 top supports	1¼ × 12 × ⅝
4 legs	1¼ × 18 × ⅝
2 braces	1 × 12 × ⅜
2 braces	1 × 13 × ⅜
1 ledge	1½ × 12 × ⅜

heads (Fig. 9-19B). The nut or other rivet head can project at the other side. If you have to use a snap head, counterbore enough to get it below the surface (Fig. 9-19C).

The leg assemblies must be square and parallel if folding is to be smooth. You can use the top you have assembled for squaring. Join the legs with their central pivots temporarily. Then attach the inner legs with their pivots to the top. The pivots can then be folded between them. That will give you the distances the legs have to be apart.

When you put braces on, they have to come on the undersides of the leg when the stool is in use and the tops of the diagonals must be kept low enough to clear the opposite legs when the legs are spread. Put the straight braces across (Fig. 9-18C). Then arrange the diagonals close to them (Fig. 9-19D). Glue and a single screw at each position should be sufficient.

Adjust the stool to its position for use. See that the top is parallel with the floor. Hold the ledge strip against the legs so that you can mark the shape of the slot each side by penciling along the edge of the leg and marking the thickness of the ledge. Cut the slot to about half the thickness of the top support (Fig. 9-19E). Make this an easy fit on the ledge. Move the ledge up to the position to go into the slots and mark where it goes on the legs. Open the stool and attach the ledge to the legs.

When you are satisfied with the action, separate the parts for varnishing or painting. Then bolt or rivet together.

SLAT-TOP CHAIR

A stool provides a simple and compact seat. If it is to be used for long, there will be a need for a seat back. The stool just described would not be satisfactory if it was made into a chair by extending one of its legs. That would give the back too much slope and extend it so that it would be unstable if the user leaned back. The arrangement of legs has to be altered to bring the back more upright and extend the rear legs to give support (Fig. 9-20).

General construction is very similar to the stool. The shape and sizes given (Fig. 9-21 and Table 9-6) show how the chair form is obtained. A full-size drawing is not essential. Angles can be marked during assembly. A full-size side view will help in understanding the layout.

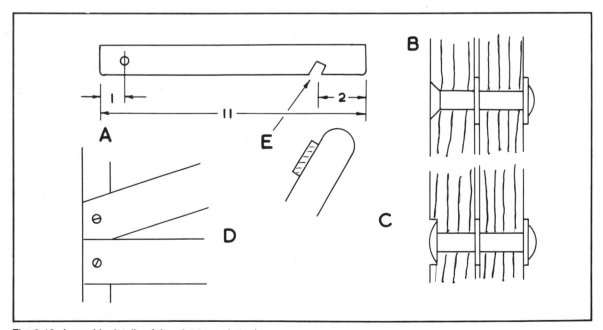

Fig. 9-19. Assembly details of the slat-topped stool.

Fig. 9-20. A slat-topped folding chair.

To fold the chair, the legs are brought into line while the seat slides up the back to also finish in line. If sizes are altered, there must be enough space allowed in the back for the seat to accommodate below the back slats.

Make the long legs (Fig. 9-22A) and the short legs (Fig. 9-22B). Get the angles of the ends from your full-size drawing or leave marking and cutting them until you make a trial assembly. The pivots can be as suggested for the stool, either rivets or bolts (Fig. 9-19B and C), with the same need of clearance where parts come together when folded. Drill for the pivots.

Make the seat supports (Fig. 9-22C) and drill for the

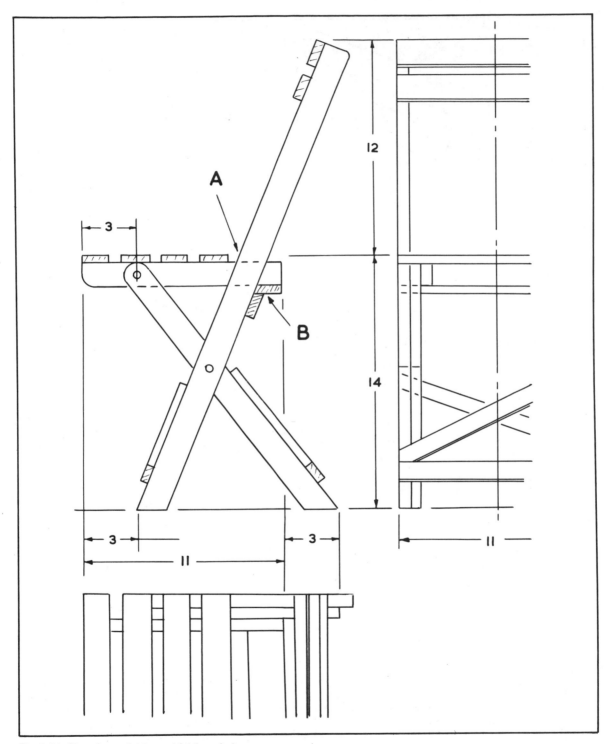

Fig. 9-21. Sizes for a slat-topped folding chair.

Table 9-6. Materials List for Slat-Top Chair.

4 seats	1½	×	12	×	⅜
2 seat supports	1¼	×	12	×	⅝
1 seat crossbar	1¼	×	12	×	⅝
2 legs	1¼	×	21	×	⅝
2 legs	1¼	×	30	×	⅝
3 back slats	1½	×	12	×	⅜
2 braces	1	×	12	×	⅜
2 braces	1	×	15	×	⅜

pivots. Round the lower front corner. The slats have to be arranged to take the seat as far back as possible, but the rear one must have enough clearance on the long legs to allow it to fold (Fig. 9-21A). The crossbar below (Fig. 9-22D) extends to the outer legs and is beveled to fit against them. The ledge across the long legs should have a matching bevel (Fig. 9-21B). These parts come together and take much of the chair's load. They should be securely glued, screwed, and accurately fitted.

Stiffening of the leg assemblies is similar to the stool, but the braces come on the outsides of the legs because of the different method of folding. Make up the seat except for the crossbar underneath and temporarily pivot the legs to it and to each other. That will allow you to swing the parts into their folded position and attach the braces (Fig. 9-22E) and the back slats (Fig. 9-22F) to keep the legs at the correct widths.

Try the action of the chair—opened and closed. Check that the seat is level. Trim the angles at the bottoms of the legs, if necessary. Separate the parts for sanding and follow with varnish or paint. Close the pivots finally and attach the crossbar below the seat.

SLAT-TOP TABLE

A table with a slat top is an obvious companion to the slat-top stool and chair. This one is lightweight and arranged to fold in a very similar way. Its general appearance is like a larger version of the stool (Fig. 9-17). It does not have to carry as much weight as a stool or chair—so sections of wood do not have to be proportionately greater—but the increased size means that there is more tendency to push out of shape if it is not adequately braced.

Construction is the same as for the stool (except for the differences given below). See Table 9-7. The table shown assembles to 22 inches each way. It folds by the legs with the ledge swinging down; then the top closes against them.

The top is made of slats on two supports (Fig.

9-23A). Arrange them to overhang enough to cover the legs (Fig. 9-23B). Because of the size, there is a risk of the top going out of shape. To prevent this, put strips across the inside and level with the outer edges of the third slat in from each end. You could tenon these parts together, but it should be satisfactory to nail them. Inside the pieces glue and screw triangular blocks on stiffeners (Fig. 9-23C).

The legs (Fig. 9-23D) are made like those of the stool. There are pivot holes where they cross and other pivot holes at the top of one pair of legs only. To give greater rigidity there are two diagonal braces on each pair of legs (Fig. 9-23E). They can spring over each other where they cross. There is no need to cut a joint there; halving joint would weaken the wood too much. Let the braces come as high as they can on the legs (providing they do not foul each other or the opened legs). Set the widths of the leg assemblies with the tabletop as a guide.

As with the stool, make a trial assembly so that you can mark the slot for the ledge and its position on the legs. When that works satisfactorily and the tabletop finishes level, take the assemblies apart for painting or varnishing. Then tighten the rivets or bolts.

LONG TRESTLE TABLE

It is often useful to have one or more fairly light tables that can be folded flat when not needed. It is even more useful to have a folding arrangement that does not involve any special action or loose pieces.

The table shown in Fig. 9-24 has a framed plywood top and legs. The legs are held upright by struts, that are held in place by gravity; when folded upward toward the center, the legs come close to the top and the total thickness is only a few inches. It is the folding of the legs that control the length of the table. It would not be impossible to let the leg ends overlap, but that would increase the folded thickness. Otherwise the length must be enough to keep the legs clear of each other. If the table is to stand 30 inches high, the length of the top cannot be less than about 65 inches. The example shown is 72 inches. The main parts are shown 1¼ inches thick for rigidity. They could be increased to 1½ inches, but it would be unwise to reduce them much unless lightness is the most important requirement. Width can be anything you want to make it, but it is shown as 27 inches. The leg assemblies and the top are the same width. See Table 9-8.

The plywood supports the top framing, and there is little need for joints between the top parts. Corners could be mitered or the flat pieces could be halved. Use glue

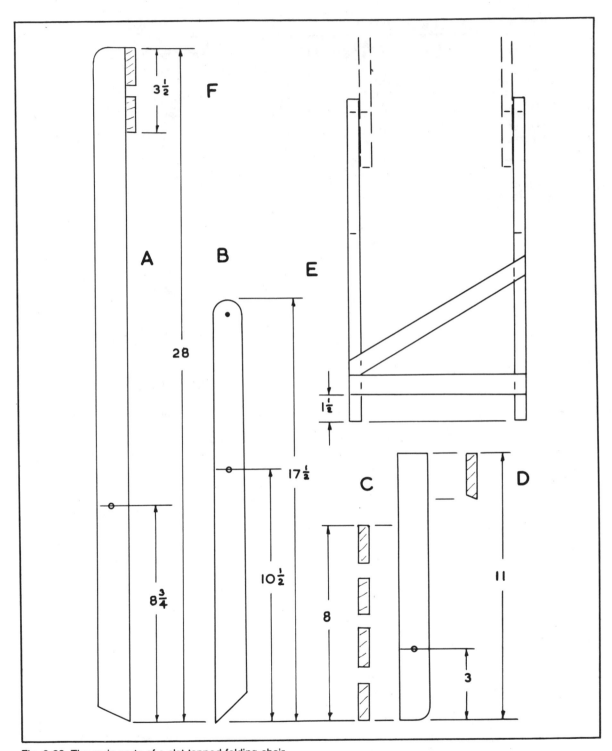

Fig. 9-22. The main parts of a slat-topped folding chair.

Table 9-7. Materials List for Slat-Top Table.

9 tops	2	×	23	×	½
2 top supports	1¼	×	23	×	⅝
2 top supports	1¼	×	20	×	⅝
4 legs	1¼	×	30	×	⅝
4 braces	1	×	27	×	⅜

and plenty of nails through the plywood. Make up the top with the strips framing the plywood, but do not attach the other cross pieces yet.

Make up two leg assemblies (Fig. 9-24A). At the top, the rail is best tenoned into the legs (Fig. 9-25A). For a simpler construction, it could be screwed to their inner surfaces. The lower rail comes 6 inches from the

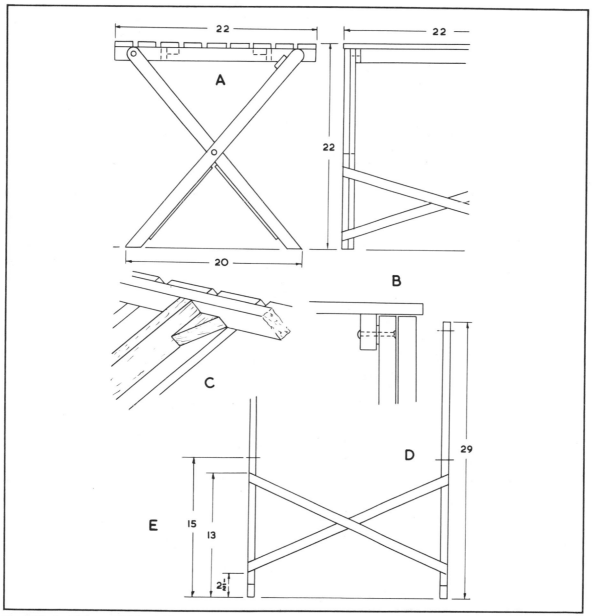

Fig. 9-23. A slat-topped folding table.

205

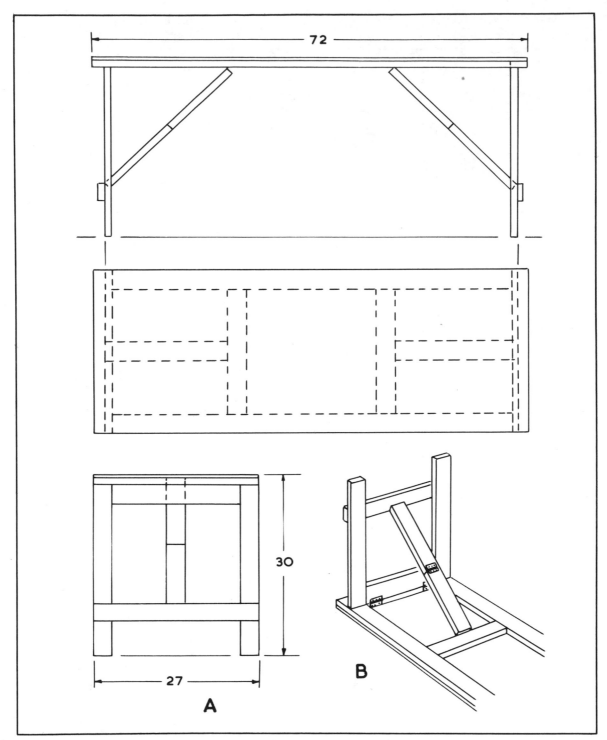

Fig. 9-24. A long table with legs to fold under.

Table 9-8. Materials List for Long Trestle Table.

1 top	27	× 72	×	½ plywood
2 top frames	3	× 74	× 1¼	
4 top frames	3	× 28	× 1¼	
4 legs	3	× 30	× 1¼	
4 leg rails	3	× 27	× 1¼	
4 struts	3	× 16	× 1	

ground and is screwed and glued to the outer surfaces of the legs (Fig. 9-25B). Except for seeing that the parts are square and match each other, assembly is simple.

So the table can be made to let the legs fold neatly, it is necessary to get certain distances correct. From the center of the hinge between the legs and table (Fig. 9-25C) to the center of the hinge at the top of the strut (Fig. 9-25D), must be the same as the distance from the first hinge to the hinge on the lower leg rail (Fig. 9-25E).

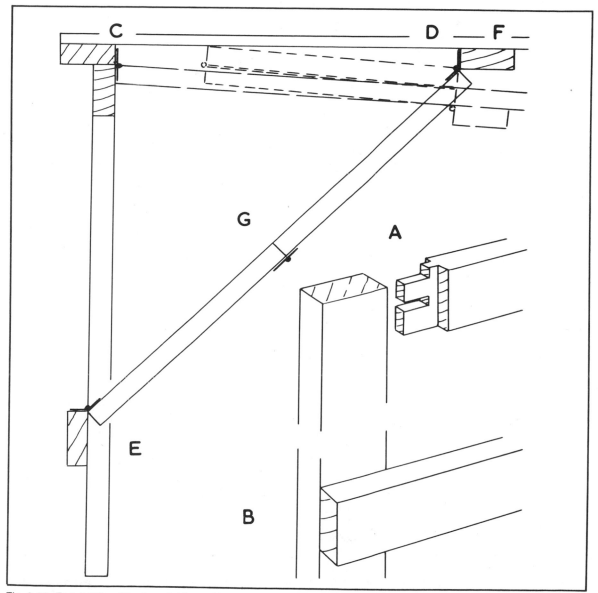

Fig. 9-25. End details of the long folding table.

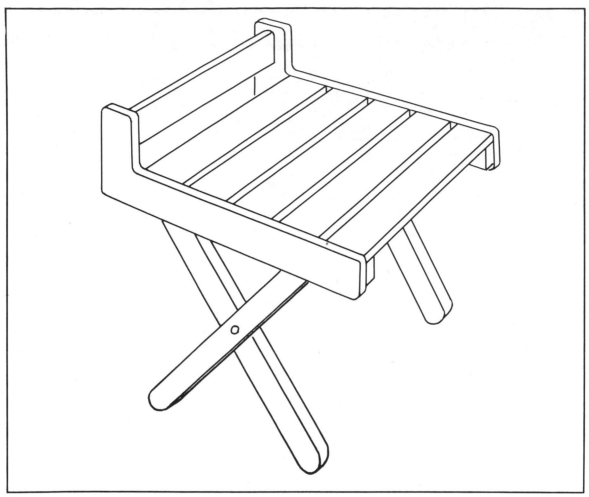

Fig. 9-26. A footrest to use with a chair.

With a leg in place, measure the distance between the hinges when the leg is square to the top. Then measure the same distance along the top and that is where you put another piece across (Fig. 9-25F). Put another one across the same distance from the other end.

Measure the overall length of a strut when the leg assembly is square to the top. Make each strut divided into two equal parts (Fig. 9-25G).

All of the parts can be joined with 3-inch hinges. Hinge the tops of the leg assemblies to the ends of the top framing (Fig. 9-24B). Hinge the ends of each pair of struts together so that they meet closely when laid out straight. Any space between the ends will cause the struts to sag in use. Join the struts to the rails with hinges on top, leave the central hinges underneath. When the table is standing

the right way up, the struts should stay in place. To fold, push them toward the top and lay the legs against the top.

This plain table can have a cloth over it for outdoor use. The edges can be framed round with thin wood to cover the plywood edges. The top can have Formica or a similar laminated plastic on it. If you prefer a solid top, several boards can be used, with battens across underneath used for hinging the legs.

FOOTREST

If you are sitting in a chair and want to put your feet up, a stool can be used. For greater comfort it is better to have a support with a cushion at the same height as the front of the chair seat. The support shown in Fig. 9-26 looks like a

208

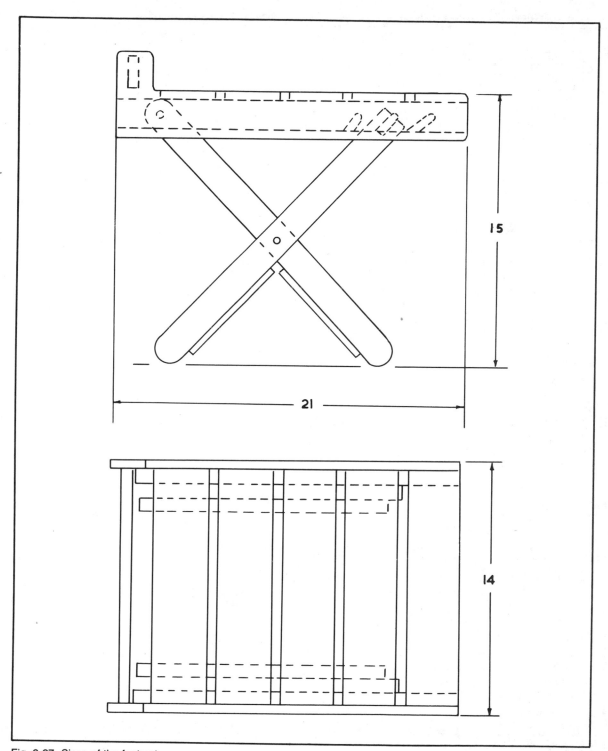

Fig. 9-27. Sizes of the footrest.

Table 9-9. Materials List for Footrest.

4 legs	1½ × 20 × ¾
2 top rails	1½ × 21 × ¾
2 top cover rails	5½ × 21 × ½ plywood
5 slats	3 × 15 × ½
1 slat	2 × 15 × ½
2 leg braces	1 × 20 × ⅜
1 leg crossbar	1½ × 14 × ½

stool, but it is not really intended for that (although it could make a temporary seat). It is meant to come against a chair where it can be adjusted to bring its cushion close to the height of the chair. There is a rail at one end to keep the cushion from being pushed off when the user changes the position of his feet.

The footrest can have the legs adjusted to give three different heights. The average height is 15 inches to the

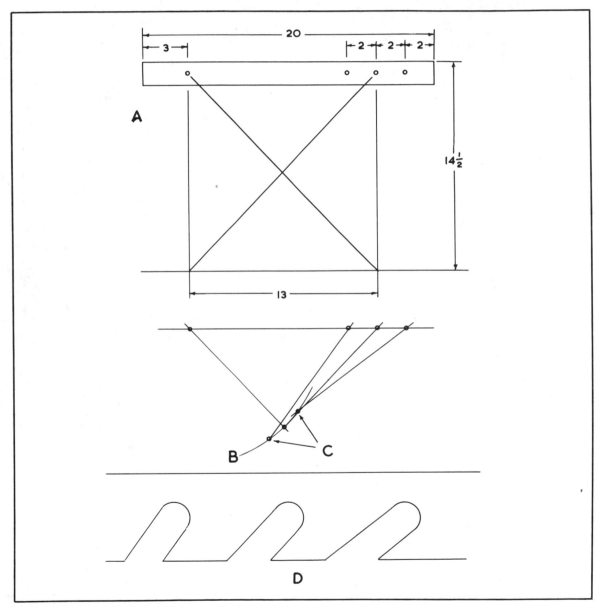

Fig. 9-28. Set-out of the footrest to allow adjustment.

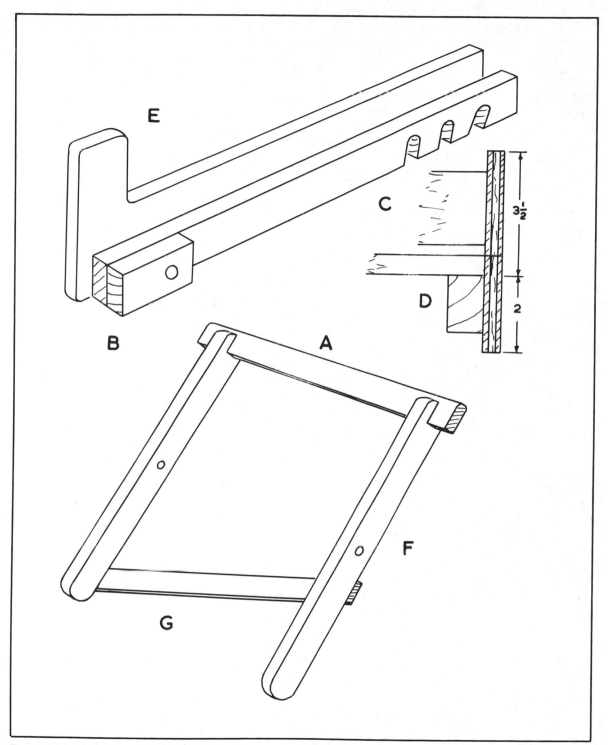

Fig. 9-29. A side and leg of the adjustable footrest.

top of the slats (Fig. 9-27). If another height would suit your needs, the leg length can be altered. The sizes of wood suggested suit a close-grained hardwood. For softwood they should be increased slightly. See Table 9-9.

The legs cross as in a folding stool. One pair have a crossbar (Fig. 9-29A) that engages with slots in the top rails. Changing slots alters the footrest height. The other pair of legs cross between them and are pivoted to the other end of the top rail. There is a packing (Fig. 9-29B) to allow for the thickness of each outer leg. The footrest can be folded to reduce thickness, but it is not intended to go flat.

It is the top rail and its slots that control other sizes (Fig. 9-28A and 29C). To get the shapes and angles of the slots, set out a side view of the rail—with its centerline and the centerlines of the legs—using the middle slot position (Fig. 9-28A). With the pivot point as a center, draw an arc through the leg crossing (Fig. 9-28B). That shows the path the crossing takes when the leg swings to other positions. With the same radius and the other slot locations as centers, mark on the arc two other center positions (Fig. 9-28C). Through those points draw new centerlines of the leg and its crossbar. With those lines as guides, you can draw the shapes of the slots (Fig. 9-28D). Drill holes first to suit the thickness of the crossbar and cut the sides of the slots into them. Round the entrances to the slot for easy adjustment.

If you do not want to go to that trouble, mark the shape of the center slot from the layout and draw the approximate shapes of the other two slots by estimation. You can trim them to their final shapes during assembly by trying the fit of the crossbar. In any case, a tight fit is not wanted.

Make the pair of top rails (Fig. 9-29C) and join them with the top slats. Space them evenly and with their ends cut level with the outsides of the rails (Fig. 9-29D). Make the outside pieces of plywood that will cover these ends (Fig. 9-29E). These go ½ inch below the rails, come level with the tops of the slats, and have ends projecting upward to take another rail that retains the cushion. Have these pieces ready, but do not fit them yet.

Make the four legs (Fig. 9-29F). One pair have their tops rounded and drilled for pivot bolts. The other pair are cut back with slots to take the crossbar. This projects enough to fit into the slots in the top rails. Allow for ⅜-inch bolts. To brace the legs, put diagonals across. One on each pair of legs should be enough (Fig. 9-29G). Arrange them at opposite angles.

The top pivot bolts through the rails must have their heads let in flush at the outside so that the cover pieces can be fitted. If you use countersunk bolts, that is easy, but with other heads you will have to counterbore to let them in. Fit these bolts and attach the plywood cover rails. Make the end rail and fit it with screws through the plywood into its ends. If you prefer, you can cut mortises through the plywood and tenon the rail ends. Screws should be strong enough.

Assemble the footrest and test its adjustments. Then disassemble and get ready for painting.

Chapter 10

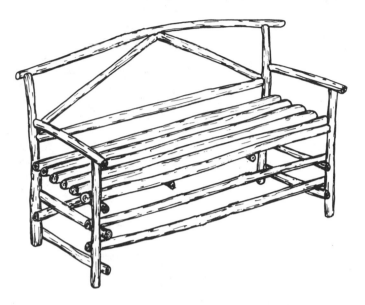

Rustic Furniture

S OME OUTDOOR FURNITURE CAN BE MADE FROM natural poles and logs just as it is cut in the forests. Even if you cannot cut the wood yourself, you might be able to get suitable material where trees are being felled or undergrowth is being cleared. Poles in the sizes you want usually are burned and those doing the work probably will be glad to have you take the wood away. What is needed are poles up to 3 inches in diameter. Although you need straight pieces for many projects, they do not have to be very long. What is curved or twisted over a long length could yield the 3 feet or so that you want straight. In any case, much of the attractiveness of this type of furniture is in the natural shaping of the wood. The curve can be included as a feature or a slight variation from the precision of planed wood and it can be regarded as characteristic of the material.

Obviously, poles recently felled will contain sap, but in the sizes you will be using, drying out will be unlikely to affect the wood enough to matter. Lengthwise shakes could open up, but they do not usually affect strength. Whether to leave the bark on or not is something you have to decide according to the wood. If the bark is firmly attached, as it is with some of the smooth-barked hardwoods, you can leave it. But if the bark can be lifted,

the final furniture will be better if the bark is peeled off before use. Otherwise it might come away of its own accord after the furniture has been made. This could leave a patchy and unsatisfactory appearance.

Cut off branches and twigs, but be careful not to tear along the grain of the pole. If you use a hatchet, cut from the under side (Fig. 10-1A). It is better to use a saw and then plane the remaining knots level (Fig. 10-1B). A useful alternative to a plane is a Surform tool or a rasp. Both of these can follow the curve easily. One problem with some rustic furniture is the roughness that can be uncomfortable or snag clothing. Level off knots and other extending pieces before building the wood into furniture. Do not go so far as to plane the smooth parts of the wood. It should still look as natural as possible.

Sort your spars into sizes. Cut off parts that are obviously of no use to you. Do not throw a piece away because of its shape. It might fit into a construction or give you ideas for using it as decoration. If the wood tapers much, it is not usually worthwhile using anything under 2 inches diameter in furniture. For legs and other load-bearing parts, 3 inches is the diameter to choose. Cut away ends that are undersize. You might have to cut away part of the thick end of a pole. In felling, that end

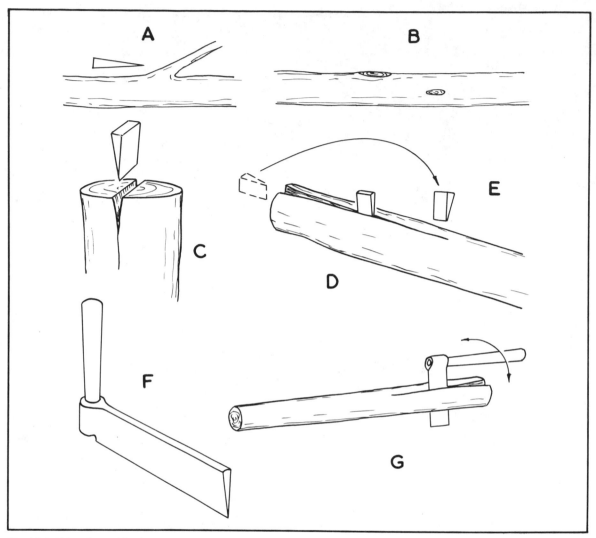

Fig. 10-1. Natural wood for furniture should be cut cleanly and cleft inside of sawn—if possible.

could have been bent and split if all the worker was doing was clearing quickly and expecting the wood to be burned.

Most of the wood will be used in the full, round section. You might want to have flat surfaces that you can get by cutting a log or a pole along its center. With a suitable circular saw available, you can cut the log that way, but it is possible to cleave a log with hand tools. One way is to start a split with an ax or by driving in a steel wedge (Fig. 10-1C). If the wood still has plenty of sap in it, it will cleave easily and you can watch the split progress. Drive a wedge in the side (Fig. 10-1D). That will

release the end wedge and force the slit further. Use the wedge from the end to drive in further along (Fig. 10-1E), to lengthen the split and release the first wedge, to be entered in the split again, and so on in turn along the log.

The wood must have a reasonably straight grain and you cannot continue a split through knots. The split will follow the grain. Bumps will have to be leveled, but free-flowing, large undulations will not matter and can be considered a feature of rustic furniture.

A traditional tool for cleaving poles of moderate size is a *froe* (Fig. 10-1F). A new froe might be difficult to find, but if you can find one, it is first hit into the log. Then you widen the split by wobbling the handle from side to side (Fig. 10-1G). It is possible to direct the split more one way than the other, within limited amounts, by using uneven levering strokes.

JOINTS

Rustic furniture can be described derogatorily as "hammer and nail" carpentry. Much assembly is done with nails, but in better work the nails are usually supplementing fitting joints. Nails should be protected by galvanizing or other means. This is particularly true for unseasoned wood where the moisture in the wood will attack steel. You can get away with driving a nail without a preliminary hole in many places, but near an end or where the direction the nail takes is important. It helps to have a pilot hole, drilled undersize for most of the depth the nail has to go, or right through if it is to be clenched. Clenching is advisable in many assemblies. The nail point need not project much, but you should be able to turn back enough to give a rivet effect to the fastening.

Cleft wood can be joined face to face with clenched nails—possibly one from each side arranged diagonally—so as to come in different lines of grain (Fig. 10-2A). Sometimes round pieces crossing have to be nailed in the same way, but it is better to put some flats on the meeting surfaces. You can scoop hollows (Fig. 10-2B) or saw more like halving joints (Fig. 10-2C).

Unless the parts have to cross in the same plane, there is no need to cut very deeply. Another way of getting a good bearing surface in that sort of crossing is to hollow one piece to match the curve of the other (Fig. 10-2D). There you only have space to drive one central nail (if it is to be effective).

If two parts make a T-joint, one may be cut out and the round end driven in, possibly with a nail from the far side (Fig. 10-2E). A closer fit will come from thinning the piece that goes into the slot (Fig. 10-2F). If the meeting is diagonal, you can do something similar with a V cut (Fig. 10-2G). Let the full round of the other piece fit in. A nail comes through from the far side. You get a neater effect by trimming the end to fit the V cut (Fig. 10-2H). The two circumferences then more nearly match each other. There can be a nail through, but in some situations it is better across the inserted end (Fig. 10-2J).

If you are working with dry wood, you can use glue and nails in these joints, but nearly all waterproof adhesives are ineffective between damp surfaces. If the wood has not been fully seasoned, you must rely on nails only. The nail is there to keep one part in another and the load is taken by the way the parts are fitted together.

A different, interesting construction uses an auger or a large bit in a brace, and a draw knife (see Chapter 2). The work of the draw knife can be done with a broad chisel and a mallet or a hatchet. The basic joint is then very similar to doweling. The dowel is formed like a round tenon on one piece (Fig. 10-3A). A hole for testing can be drilled in a thin piece of wood that can be slipped over the end being tapered to test that it is to size as far back as needed. With a little practice, you will find you can get the end round and accurate by estimation and very little testing. It is important that you shape the end so that it goes far enough into the hole to provide a good bearing surface.

In some things, the peg can go right through. That might be tight enough in itself, but it helps if you spread the end of the peg. Make a saw cut across it before driving it. Arrange that so it comes across the direction of the grain of the other part (Fig. 10-3B). Then drive a wedge into the cut. Even if the parts are softwood, use a hardwood for the wedge. This should be plenty long enough to be trimmed after driving as far as possible.

If it is a hole that does not go through, you can still wedge the end by *fox wedging,* as is sometimes done with stub tenons. Have a saw cut in the end. Then make a short wedge to fit. Estimate how much it can be expected to go into the cut. When it hits the bottom of the hole, it will spread the wood (Fig. 10-3C).

It is possible to use nuts and bolts instead of nails and particularly in large assemblies or where several thicknesses are involved. Wood screws have fewer applications in rustic work. If they are used, they should be of a noncorroding metal or steel screws should be galvanized. With bolts, it is preferable to use those with square or hexagonal heads. This way a wrench can be used. The square neck of a coach bolt does not grip well in unseasoned wood. This is even less so if it is only in bark. Tightening fully will be difficult and loosening a rusted nut will be next to impossible.

LADDER

Although not strictly a piece of furniture, a small ladder is useful and it illustrates the use of pegged ends in holes. At one time, ladders of all sizes were made in this way (and some still are). This example is long enough for many jobs (Fig. 10-4A), but the same method could be used for any length. Much depends on the pole that is cleaved to make the sides. It has to be reasonably straight. For the small ladder it is about 3 inches diameter. If there is a taper, keep the thicker end at the bottom. Make the distance to the top of the first rung the same as

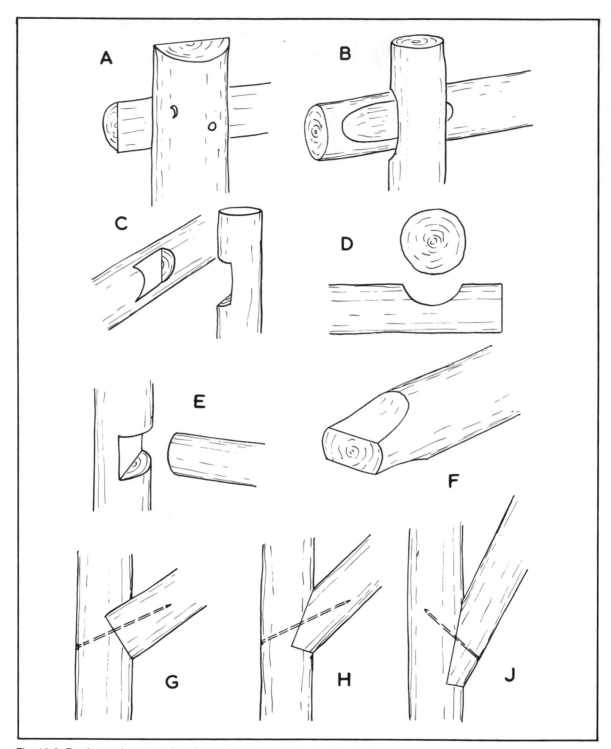

Fig. 10-2. Rustic wood can be joined by nailing and notching in various ways.

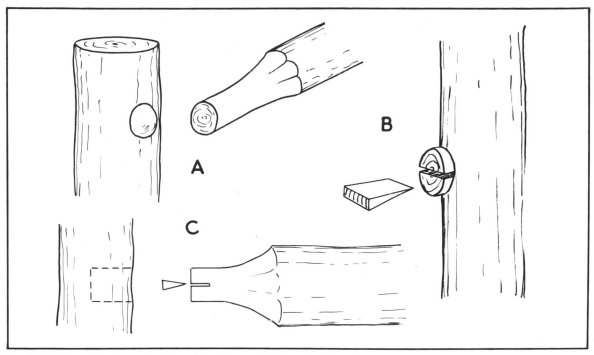

Fig. 10-3. Tapered ends can be driven into holes and tightened with wedges.

the distance between rungs (Fig. 10-4B). This is usually 10 inches.

Cleave the pole as accurately as you can. It could, of course, be run through with a circular saw or a chain saw equipped with a jig for doing this work. Traditional ladder makers argued that cleaving did not break through the fibers of the grain and therefore left the wood stronger, even if not quite as flat. If necessary, level the inner faces of the ladder sides. Then put them together and mark across the positions of the rungs (Fig. 10-4C). Drill these centrally right through. It might have been thought that the holes could be drilled across before dividing the pole in two, but that might result in some holes not being accurately centered on a cleft face.

A long ladder is made with a taper, but this short ladder could be tapered or parallel. A taper of about 2 inches in 5 feet is enough. Allow for this when cutting and fitting the rungs. The ladder sides are most easily cleaved from forest-grown spruce or other softwood that does not have knots from branches and it will split straight. The rungs are better made of hardwood—such as oak, ash or hickory—for strength. For occasional use in your yard, almost any wood can be used. Hardwood should be about 1½ inches in diameter. Taper the ends of the rungs to fit the holes that should be about ⅞ of an inch

in diameter, and long enough to go through. Allow for the ladder taper in cutting the rungs to length, but they will go through and can be finally adjusted then. Put saw cuts for wedges in all ends.

Drive the rungs into one side and then add the other side. Engage a rung at one end and fit the side on to the others in turn. Drive the side on with a board resting on it to spread the hammer blows. Work along the ladder, changing sides if necessary, until all the rungs are through the holes, with a little projecting in each place. Drive the wedges in turn. You might want to go back and tighten further as the work progresses. Do not cut off the ends of the rungs and the wedges until you are satisfied that the whole ladder is assembled as you want it.

Make sure the ends of the sides are level at their ends. Measure from the end rungs. Bevel all around the ends to prevent the grain from breaking out. If the wood is dry, you can paint the ladder. It is common to only paint the sides and about 2 inches on to each rung. The parts you step on are bare.

TABLE FRAME

A complete table could be left outdoors in all weather, but it is convenient to be able to remove the top to a sheltered

217

place when it is not in use. The table shown in Fig. 10-5A has a pair of end supports driven into the ground and a lift-off top of planed boards.

When you drive posts into the ground, the actual amount of penetration is always doubtful. Have the upright poles too long and cut them to the same height after driving. If the ground is so hard that a hole has to be dug, you are able to settle the amount of penetration. Compact the soil around the leg or even case it in concrete.

Do not sharpen to a fine point (which will crumble). A square end with at least ½ inch left flat (Fig. 10-5B) is better able to stand driving. Each leg should go about 12 inches into soft ground or a little less into hard soil. Put a mark a known distance from the point so that you will be able to judge how much is below ground. If possible, soak the wood in a bucket of preservative for a day so that rot is delayed. Carry the preservative above ground level. It is at the surface that rot is often worst.

Have an assistant watch the pole as it is driven so that the pole is kept as near upright as possible. Mark where each post is to come, but you can adjust the top to fit whatever spacing results. Cut the tops of the posts level. It is better to use a level on a straight board (Fig.

10-5C) than to rely on measuring from the ground that might not be level.

Make the crossbars. Cut notches to go over the posts (Fig. 10-5D) and nail downward into them. Check the state of the tops of the crossbars. Remove high spots with a hatchet, knife, or plane.

The top could be several loose boards laid alongside each other, but it would be better to make up a top with battens below. These can be spaced so they will stop the top sliding on the supporting crossbars (Fig. 10-5E).

PORTABLE TABLE

This is a rustic table that is not attached to the ground. It can be moved even though it is not intended to be a lightweight assembly. There is a frame at each end with the parts notched together. Lengthwise parts are pegged into holes and the top is made from cleaved wood or sawn boards (Fig. 10-6A).

Choose four similar posts for the legs and four pieces that match for the crossbars. If thicknesses vary, the lower rails can be thinner. You can join the crossbars and legs with notches cut in each or you can make rounded hollows in the legs for the rails (Fig. 10-2). Mark the legs

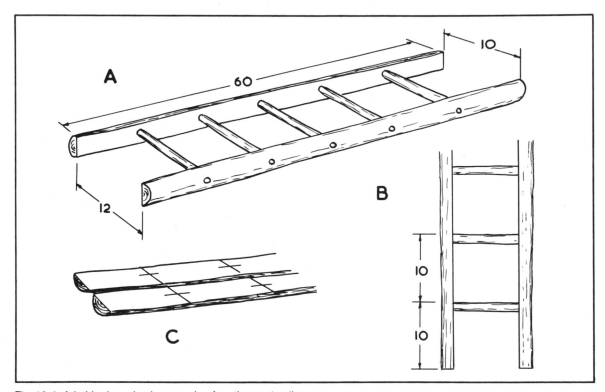

Fig. 10-4. A ladder is a simple example of rustic construction.

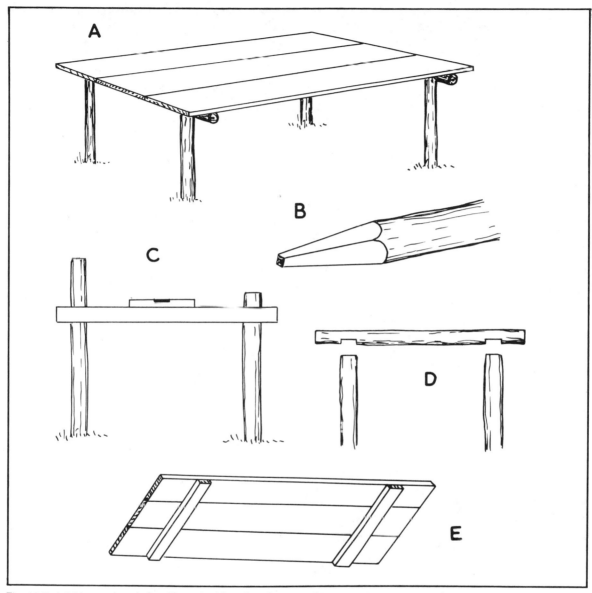

Fig. 10-5. A table can be made with posts driven into the ground to support a top on crossbars.

together. It does not matter if the crossbars are too long at this stage. Nail these joints (Fig. 10-6B). Square the assemblies and see that they match in a similar way to that for tables made of planed wood. The horizontal parts come on the outsides of the legs.

There are two lengthwise rails into the legs and a central stretcher into the lower end rails. The most convenient joints in those positions are pegged ends into holes. The ends could go right through, but part way with

fox wedges will do (Fig. 10-6C).

If boards are to be used for the top, space them parallel with narrow gaps and nail into the end crossbars. Use an iron block or another hammer under the rail to support it while hammering (Fig. 10-6D). If you use cleft pieces, trim adjoining edges so the gaps are approximately parallel. At the ends, scoop away the rounded undersides so the pieces will bed down level (Fig. 10-6E). Then nail in place.

PEGGED STOOL

This stool is entirely pegged (Fig. 18-7A). The size should suit the materials; about 15 inches in each direction would be a good choice. Use straight pieces about 2½ inches diameter for the legs. The other parts can be just under 2 inches. Taper the tops of the legs to fit holes in the top crossbars and measure down the same distance on each for the lower rails. Assemble these parts (Fig. 18-7B) and check them against each other. Use glue on dry wood as well as nails.

The rails that link the ends are paired. Mark the ends together to get the hole spacing the same. Taper the rails

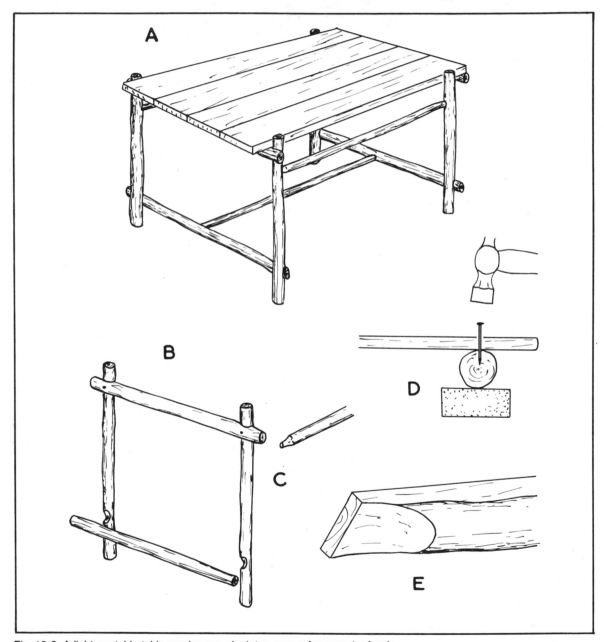

Fig. 10-6. A light, portable table can have a plank top over a framework of rods.

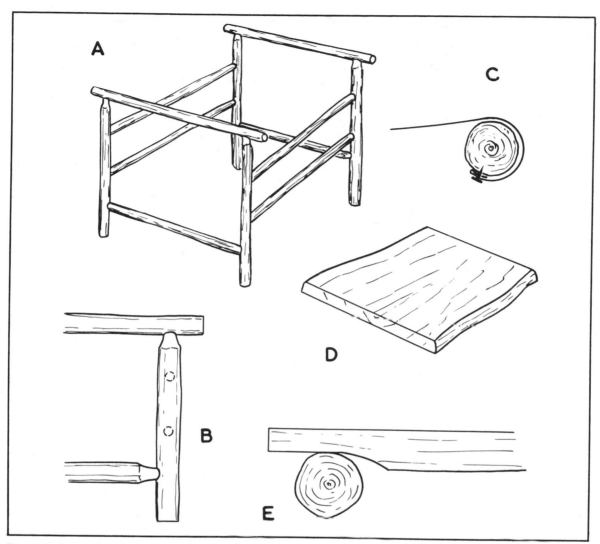

Fig. 10-7. Suggestions for the construction of a framework and top.

and join them with fox wedges. Pull the joints tight with clamps, if possible, and check squareness by standing back and looking at the stool from several directions.

Several tops are possible. There could be a piece of canvas stretched across and tacked underneath (Fig. 10-7C). A sawn board with waney edges can be nailed on (Fig. 10-7D). There can be two or more cleft poles fitted in the same way as suggested for the tabletop, with close edges and pared ends (Fig. 10-7E).

A piece of exterior plywood or some boards held together with battens can be used, but they would not really fit in with the rustic effect.

MILKING STOOL

You might not want to milk a cow or goat, but this stool can have many other purposes. Its top is a piece cut across a log and there are three legs let in (Fig. 10-8A). Three legs will stand firm on any surface no matter how uneven it is.

Sizes are governed by the wood used for the top. This should be about 12 inches across. A smaller piece would still be useful. The legs have to be evenly spaced and slope outward at the same angle. Extreme precision will not be needed, but it is best if the legs are not too far from geometric accuracy.

Draw a pitch circle for the leg holes and then step off the radius round it. The holes will come on alternate marks (Fig. 10-8B). Decide on the angle you want the legs to slope outward. Their feet should come just outside the area covered by the top. The exact angle is not important, but all three legs should have the same slope. Cut a piece of scrap wood to the angle to serve as a guide (Fig. 10-8C). The size hole depends on the size of the stool, but it will be between ¾ of an inch and 1 inch. Drill from the top downward. Have a piece of scrap wood below for the drill to run into as it goes through, but as you are drilling into end grain there is little fear of breaking out.

Have the legs slightly too long. Taper the tops to go into the holes. Drive them through and wedge them (Fig. 10-8D). Invert the stool and measure the lengths of the legs by using a rule straight up from the table surface to the same height on each leg. Then cut them across to match. Remove the sharp edges around the feet once you have tried the stool for level the right way up.

CHAIR

A full chair made entirely of round poles does not offer the comfort of one made from planed wood, but you could always add cushions. It would be improved by making the seat and back with cleaved wood having its flat sides to the body (Fig. 10-9A).

The general layout is very similar to arm chairs

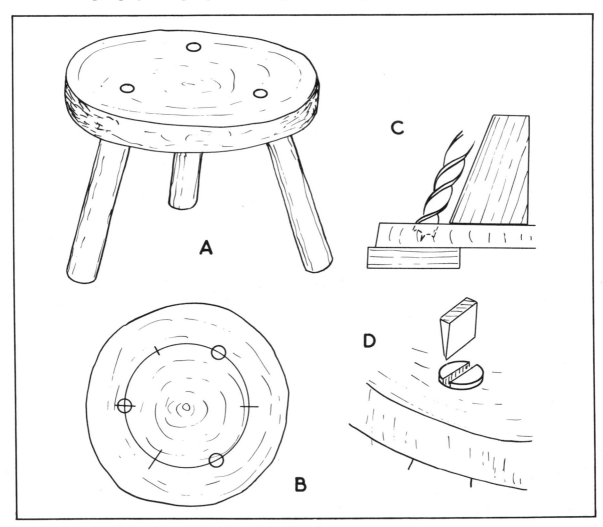

Fig. 10-8. A stool can be made with a section of log and three legs.

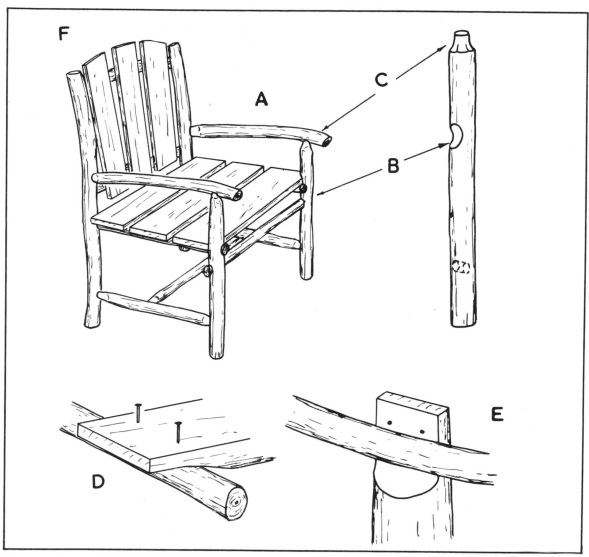

Fig. 10-9. The parts of a rustic armchair are notched and plugged together.

made from squared wood. There are two long back legs and two front ones that go above the seat to hold the arms. If you have any bent poles, a pair will make the back with some slope. Notch the rails that support the seat into the legs on the inner surfaces. The bottom rails could be notched similarly or be pegged into holes (Fig. 10-9B). The arm will peg into the back legs and notch or peg over the front legs (Fig. 10-9C). Make up the two ends as pairs, with matching pieces of wood, as far as possible.

The back has upright pieces on curved rails. The sizes are governed by available pieces of wood. The rails

need not have much curve, but that should be about the same in the two rails. Cut pegged joints into the legs. Before assembling them, use their sizes as a guide to the lengths of the other rails going across. The front rail will be notched into the legs below the seat rails and the bottom rails peg into the side rails. Assemble all these parts and check that the whole thing is reasonably square.

The seat is made of cleaved, 3-inch poles notched over the seat rails (Fig. 10-9D) and nailed in place. Round the front edge, but otherwise the pieces can be as they come (except remove any lumps that would prevent a close fit or a level top). Make the back pieces in a similar way (Fig. 10-9E). Cut their tops to a curve after assembly (Fig. 10-9F). Use a Surform tool to remove any sharpness that will come toward a sitter, but otherwise retain the natural rustic appearance of the wood.

BENCH

A bench is made like a long chair, but there has to be some stiffening lengthwise to keep it in shape (Fig. 10-10A). The suggestion is for a bench about 60 inches long, with a seat 15 inches high and wide.

The two ends are very similar to those for the chair (Fig. 10-10B). An extra rail goes across the ends. Back and front lengthwise stretchers are joined to the legs and not the bottom rails. This allows notched joints to the legs instead of pegs to the rails. A similar rail goes above the seat level between the back legs and the top of the back notches over the legs (Fig. 10-10C). The top rail could have a curve up to its center.

For lengthwise stiffness, arrange two diagonals in the back (Fig. 10-10D), going into notches in the rails. Besides stiffness, they help to fill the back as something to lean against. Notch the rails, but leave final cutting of

the diagonals until after assembly. Then you can square up the seat frame and fit the diagonals to hold it in shape.

The seat is made up of round poles. Notch over the rails in the end frames, but arrange two crossbars under the poles—equally spaced intermediately—to link them together (Fig. 10-10E). Rigidity of the seat depends on close fitting joints and tight nailing.

ARCH

An arch provides a decorative feature in itself, and allows climbing flowers and plants to interweave and make an attractive effect—usually over a path. Sizes and construction can vary, but this one uses diagonally braced ladderlike sides and a trussed top with diagonal braces (Fig. 10-11A).

The uprights will usually go into the ground. Allow for pointed ends to enter about 12 inches (Fig. 10-11B). The height should be enough to walk under. That means about 84 inches if you allow for trailing and hanging fronds. Poles need to be up to 100 inches. All of the parts can be notched on the surfaces of the poles (Fig. 10-11C) or they can all come in the same plane (Fig. 10-11D). In any case, square up the opposite assemblies and securely

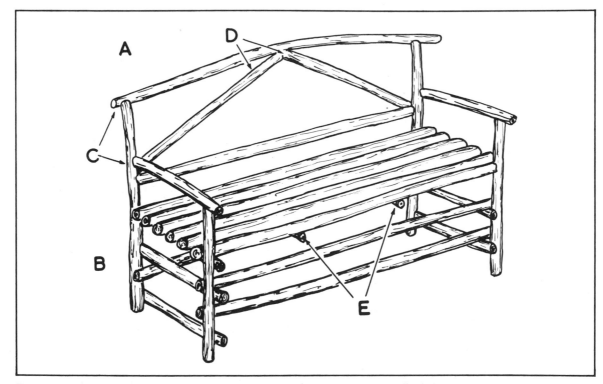

Fig. 10-10. The construction of a bench is a development of the previously described chairs and tables.

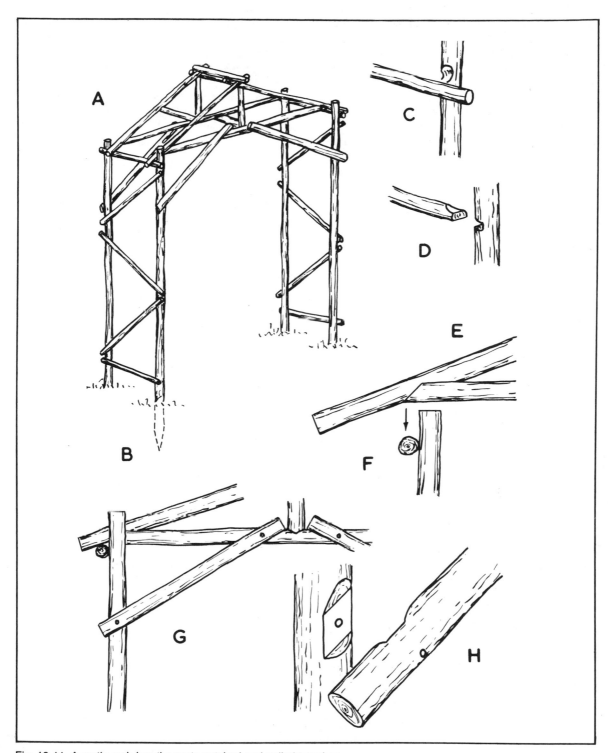

Fig. 10-11. A rustic arch has the parts notched and nailed together.

nail them. At the top, the rails act as ledgers to support the trussed top.

Make up a pair of trusses (Fig. 10-11E), with the horizontal pieces notched into the sloping ones, which will come over the ledgers and be nailed to them. Arrange pieces across the sloping parts to hold the trusses at a suitable distance for them to fit between the upright posts (Fig. 10-11F).

The posts will get some rigidity from being driven into the ground, but the whole structure has to be braced to keep its shape, with diagonal struts. So far as possible, keep them high enough not to get in the way of persons walking through the arch. This means having them at a flatter angle than 45 degrees. That might seem obvious (Fig. 10-11G).

Cut notches for the braces to fit on the other parts and let them extend an inch or so past each joint. You could nail these joints. Even if you use nails elsewhere, these places would benefit from having bolts through (Fig. 10-11H).

Chapter 11

Outdoor Cooking

OUTDOOR FURNITURE IS OFTEN ASSOCIATED with eating and drinking. Tables and chairs are regularly used for open-air meals, but there are some things particularly used for food—either its preparation or transport. With barbecues and other ways of actually preparing the food outdoors there comes a need for furniture associated with them.

Some of the items described in this chapter are portable and might not be left out in the same way as other furniture. They do not have to be as weatherproof as other furniture, but there is always the possibility of them being left out in dew or rain. It is best to prepare them in the same way as the heavier furniture that is intended to stay outside. Exceptions are things that could have uses indoors as well. For instance, a food trolley might be used indoors. It would be given a better finish, for the sake of its appearance alongside other indoor furniture, than something that will only be used with rustic things outdoors.

TABLE/TROLLEY

It is convenient to have a means of carrying food, crockery, and cutlery to where you need them outdoors; it can also be used as a table. Figure 11-1 shows a trolley with a flat top and a shelf underneath. It has handles at one end and wheels at the other. The sizes suggested (Fig. 11-2A and Table 11-1) are for a moderate-sized assembly that could be taken indoors for loading. It will pass through doorways on its way to the patio, yard, or garden. It could be made much bigger if it is intended for large numbers of people.

It is advisable to get the wheels and axle first, and then it may be easy to modify other sizes to suit. Wheels with 6-inch diameters are drawn, but any convenient size can be used. They should be metal with rubber tires for most situations, but you might use wide, solid-rubber wheels for soft surfaces or you could turn wooden ones. The axle goes through the front legs and you have to choose a size with just over 18 inches between the wheels.

Start by marking out the legs (Fig. 11-3A). The front pair of legs are kept 1 inch short for ground clearance. The lengthwise lower rails are kept low, but the crosswise ones are higher so that they will prevent things being carried from slipping off (Fig. 11-2B). Most joints should be doweled, but you could use tenons.

Fig. 11-1. A table/trolley is useful for transporting and preparing food outdoors.

The four lower rails are central at the legs (Fig. 11-3B), but the long top rails have to be treated differently because of their extending handles. One way is tenon or dowel centrally to the front legs (Fig. 11-3C), and then notch them through the rear legs (Fig. 11-3D). Do not cut too much from the rails or that will weaken them where they take the load when the table is moved. Notching ⅛ of an inch on each side is enough; therefore ¾ of an inch is cut from the leg. Alternatively, have the rails level with the outsides of both legs. At the front you can use dowels. At the rear, notch the rails around the tops of the legs in a form of halving joint. Do not cut too much away from the rails (Fig. 11-3E). When these joints are assembled (whichever method is chosen), the dowels from the crosswise rails can go right through to strengthen those joints.

Shape the handles so that the grip part is about 1½ inches deep. Then round its section and ends (Fig. 11-3F). Make up the other rails and assemble the framework in two stages. Put the opposite long sides

together first and see that they match and that they are square. When the glue has set, add the crosswise members and again leave for the glue to set.

Arrange the shelf slats to come to the edges of their rails and space them evenly. Attach them with two screws or nails at each crossing. This is more easily done before you add the top.

There are several possible ways to make the top. It could be made of wider slats put across in a similar way to those on the shelf. Allow for a 2-inch overlap all around. It would be possible to use solid wood, probably made up by gluing two or more pieces to make up the width, with the grain the long way. An interesting variation of this is to use a butcher-block top. Many fairly narrow strips can be glued together to make up the width. It would also be advisable to use a few dowels between adjoining boards. In any case, the glue should be fully waterproof.

A simpler top can be made from a single piece of plywood or particleboard. Edges can be left true and rounded, but a better edge has a strip around it (Fig.

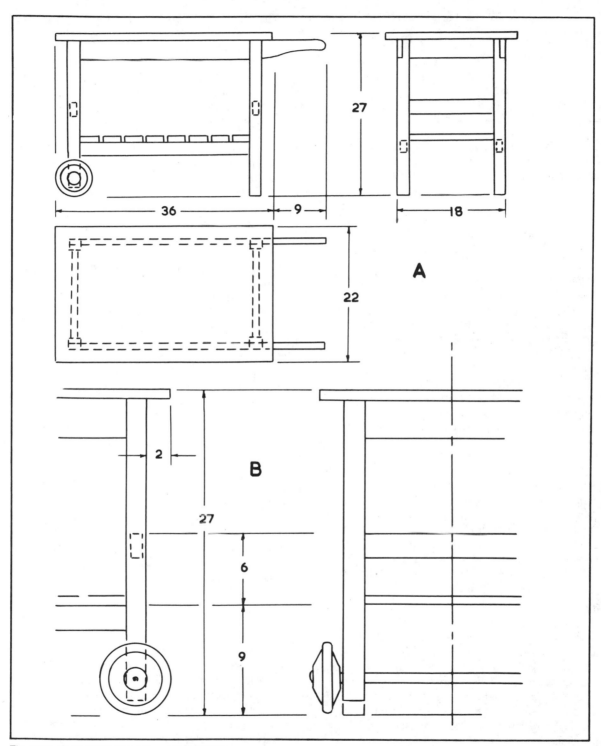

Fig. 11-2. Suggested sizes for a table/trolley.

Table 11-1. Materials List for Table/Trolley.

4 legs	1½ × 27 × 1½	
2 top rails	3 × 45 × 1	
2 top rails	3 × 18 × 1	
2 lower rails	2 × 32 × 1	
2 lower rails	2 × 18 × 1	
1 top	20 × 36 × ¾	
8 shelf slats	3 × 19 × ¾	

11-4A). The best edge, if you have the equipment to work it, uses a tongue and groove joint (Fig. 11-4B). For the preparation of food, a Formica surface or a similar surface can be used as a facing and a lip can be put around the edges. If you do not expect to cut on or otherwise treat the surface roughly, there are softer plastic-faced particleboards that you can buy as stock-sized panels. The edges will already be treated in the same way.

You can attach the top with screws driven down through into the rails, counterbored and plugged (Fig. 11-4C). The plugs can form a decorative treatment on a wood top, but they would not look right on other surfaces. One way of avoiding marking the top surface is to screw strips inside the top rails and screw upward through them (Fig. 11-4D). Pocket screwing is often used in furniture (11-4E); a hole is opened below for the head. The screw pulls up and the head goes below the surface (Fig. 11-4F). Instead of chiseling, you can use a large drill at an angle to make the recess for the head (Fig. 11-4G). In most assemblies, you will not need many screws to hold the top: two at each end and three at each side should be sufficient.

The top is shown with a flat surface and that is what is needed for a table. If the transport of a load of food or equipment is more important, the edging of the top could be carried upward to fully frame the top or to be cut back at the corners for ease in cleaning (Fig. 11-4H). It may be simpler, with some top materials, to put the border strips on top with screws up through (Fig. 11-4J).

FOOD TROLLEY

This trolley has similar uses to the previous one, but it is not intended to also be a table. The top has sides to keep things in place and it can have compartments for cutlery and other small items. The lower shelf is arranged as a tray that will slide in and it can be removed completely. This can be open to take a variety of things or it can be given compartments if you have certain pieces of equipment or boxes of food that you always want to carry. It could be arranged to take glasses or cups in individual positions.

The general assembly (Fig. 11-5) has sloping legs and is arranged with wheels at one end and handles at the other. This is another piece of portable furniture that could be made of an attractive hardwood, with a varnished finish, so it would also be suitable for use indoors. If it is only for outdoor use, painted softwood might be satisfactory. Nevertheless, the strength of hardwoods would be an advantage. The sizes shown (Fig. 11-6 and Table 11-2) would suit hard or soft woods, but sections could be reduced slightly for an indoor trolley. The construction suggested is nearly all simply nailed. While that is satisfactory, you could choose to dovetail corners and cut other joints for what amounts to a piece of cabinetwork for use indoors and only occasionally for use outdoors.

The wheels and axles should be obtained first. Those shown are 7 inches diameter, but the exact size is not crucial. The axle height on the legs can be adjusted to suit. If you have a lathe, you could turn wooden wheels, but metal wheels with rubber tires provide some slight cushioning and reduce vibration of the load.

The slopes of both pairs of legs are the same. If you are using power tools that can have their angles adjusted, the legs are at 15 degrees vertical. In any case, it is advisable to set out a full-size side view (Fig. 11-7A) using just the centerlines of the legs. You can take the lengths of the legs from this. Notice that the location of the legs on the sides are different at each end, but their angles are the same.

Make the pair of sides for the top (Fig. 11-7B). Locate the positions of the ends. This includes the bases that go under the plywood (Fig. 11-7C). Between these are lengthwise base pieces (Fig. 11-7D) that have to be notched to take the legs. Get their angles correct from your full-size drawing and make them a close fit on the wood that will be used for the legs. Shape the handles before going further.

Cut the plywood for the base of the top part. Then glue and nail it to the four strips that go under it and inside the framing. Plane the edges true and fit the sides and ends around it to complete the top.

Make the legs and mark on them the location of the shelf rails. The legs are paired and the ones that take the wheels should be drilled to suit the axle. Cut them off to clear the ground, but do not make them too short or the end grain below the axle might split in use.

The tray has a plywood base that extends at the sides to run in the grooved shelf rails (Fig. 11-8A). Plow the grooves about halfway through the rails and make them an easy fit on the plywood. Allow for the thickness of paint, but you should be able to slide the tray in and out without

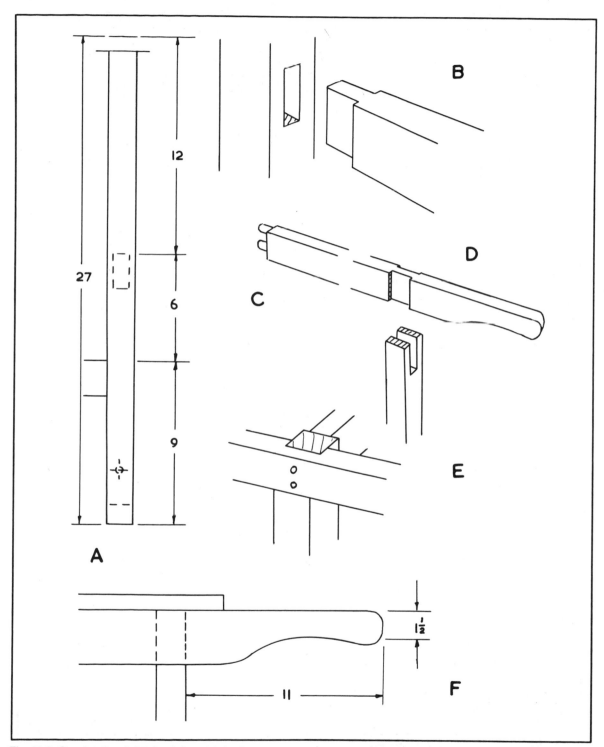

Fig. 11-3. Constructional details of the table/trolley.

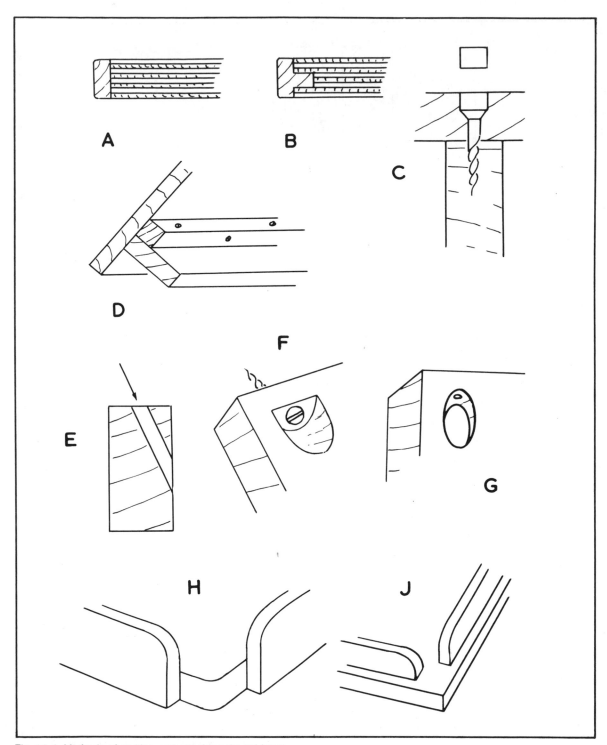

Fig. 11-4. Methods of making and attaching the tabletop.

Fig. 11-5. A food trolley with compartments and a tray.

trouble. It should not be so loose that there is a risk of it slipping out when the trolley is being wheeled. If the ends of grooves are widened a little, positioning the tray when replacing it will be easier. Assemble the tray as a box on its base. Keep the sides a short distance in from the shelf rails.

Fit the legs into the sockets in the top framing and screw the shelf rails to them. Sight across to check that they are parallel. Getting a twist in the relative positions of the grooves will cause the tray to stick when you try to move it. In end view the legs should be upright. Have the tray in position to keep the legs at the correct distance apart. Then fit the cross rails to the legs under the top and three under the shelf rails. They keep the sides at the correct distance apart and stiffen the whole trolley. Round and sand the edges of the plywood that fit the

grooves. Later, if there is too much stiffness there, rub the edges with wax or candle fat.

Temporarily fit the wheels and axle to check that the whole assembly is as you want it. Then remove the wheels and tray so that the wood can be painted or varnished.

There are a few possible modifications or improvements that you can incorporate during construction. If the trolley gets rained on or liquids are spilled on it, draining and cleaning can be difficult. If you drill holes (⅜-inch holes will do) near each corner of the top and tray, liquids will drain away.

The tray is shown with straight ends, but it will help in lifting if metal or plastic tray handles are added to them. Another way of providing handles without projections is to make the ends from wider wood shape hand

233

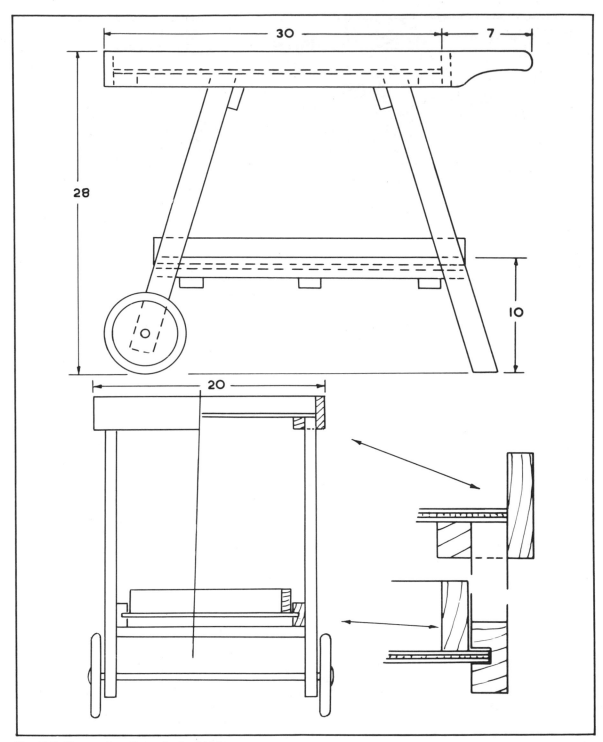

Fig. 11-6. Sizes and sections of a food trolley.

Table 11-2. Materials List for Food Trolley.

4 legs	2 × 30 × 1		
2 sides	3 × 38 × ¾		
2 ends	3 × 20 × ¾		
2 top bases	2 × 30 × 1		
2 top bases	2 × 20 × 1		
1 top base	20 × 30 × ¼ plywood		
2 shelf rails	2 × 30 × 1		
5 cross rails	2 × 20 × 1		
2 tray sides	2 × 27 × ¾		
2 tray ends	2 × 17 × ¾		
or			
2 tray bottoms	17 × 27 × ¼ plywood		
1 top partition	1½ × 20 × ½		
3 top partitions	1½ × 12 × ½		
1 tray divider	17 × 27 × ¼ plywood		
2 tray dividers	¾ × 27 × ¾		
2 tray dividers	¾ × 17 × ¾		

holes (Fig. 11-8B). The holes do not have to follow a curve, but they look better shaped that way. Draw the shapes—a half template insures accuracy—and then drill the ends of the openings and cut the waste out with a fine jigsaw. Thoroughly round the edges of the wood and the holes.

The tray and top can be divided into compartments. You could divide across or lengthwise, but too many divisions could interfere with changes in the load. Divisions at the end of the top will separate cutlery and other small items (Fig. 11-8C). The pieces should be kept just below the top edges and be rounded. They can be held in with fine nails.

If you want to carry glasses or cups, possibly with liquid already in them, it will help to give the top or tray a second piece of plywood—pierced with holes (Fig. 11-8D). Let this piece rest on strips around the inside of the tray (Fig. 11-8E), either all over or only part of it. If this plywood is loose, you can put your hand through a glass hole to remove it when not needed.

TAKE-DOWN TROLLEY

A food trolley that is always full size can sometimes be difficult to store. There is an attraction in one that folds or can be disassembled. This trolley is about the same size as the two previous ones, when prepared for use, but it can be partially disassembled and partially folded so that it reduces to about the thickness of the two trays (while keeping the same length and width). The flatter package can be stored in a space about 7 inches deep or hung on a wall until it is needed again.

The trolley shown in Fig. 11-9 consists of two trays joined by crossed legs, held in place with nuts and bolts.

There are wheels on one pair of legs and handles on the top tray at the other end. The sizes suggested (Fig. 11-10 and Table 11-3) can be altered to suit your needs. The main parts are 1-×-3 inch wood. That should be strong enough for a larger trolley if you want to increase sizes. Recommended wheels have a 7-inch diameter. They should be obtained, with their axle, before deciding on the width of trolley. The stock axle length will determine the width to make this.

Except for the handle extensions, the two trays can be made almost the same (Fig. 11-11A). The legs bolt on at different places. Make a full-size drawing, showing the trays in full, but with only the center lines of the legs (Fig. 11-11B). This will show you the sizes of the legs and the positions of the bolt holes on them and on the trays.

Make the sides of the trays and mark on the positions of the bolt holes. Also mark out the pairs of legs. Mark where the axle holes will come, but it is best to leave cutting the other legs to length until after a trial assembly. Then you can trim that pair of legs to bring the trays level with the legs on level ground.

Drill small holes at each bolt position of a size that will allow nails to be pushed through. Using nails, assemble one side to check that the two trays are parallel and that the feet will bring them level when the wheels and axle are in position.

The bolts can be 5/16 of an inch in diameter, but it would not matter if you went up to ⅜-inch bolts or down to ¼-inch bolts. With the bolts there should be enough washers and nuts. You can use butterfly nuts if you expect to be unscrewing frequently. If the parts are only to be taken down at the end of a season, plain nuts are less obtrusive. Drill to suit the bolts in all positions.

Make up the trays. Simplest would be nailed or screwed corners, with plywood nailed underneath (Fig. 11-11C), but the exposed edges of plywood do not look good. Moisture entering the end grain of plywood can cause damage even if it is exterior or marine grade. It is better to have the plywood inside. The best way of arranging this is to plow grooves in the sides (Fig. 11-11D), but then you have to choose corner joints that hide the groove ends. You could leave them exposed and glue in filler pieces. A simple nailed or screwed corner to hide the grooves can be made by rabbeting one piece (Fig. 11-11E).

Another way of enclosing the bottom is to put strips around and nail into them (Fig. 11-11F). Instead of plywood, there could be slats attached to the strips, with narrow spaces between (Fig. 11-11G). Shape the handles before assembling the top tray. Check squareness and that the two trays match.

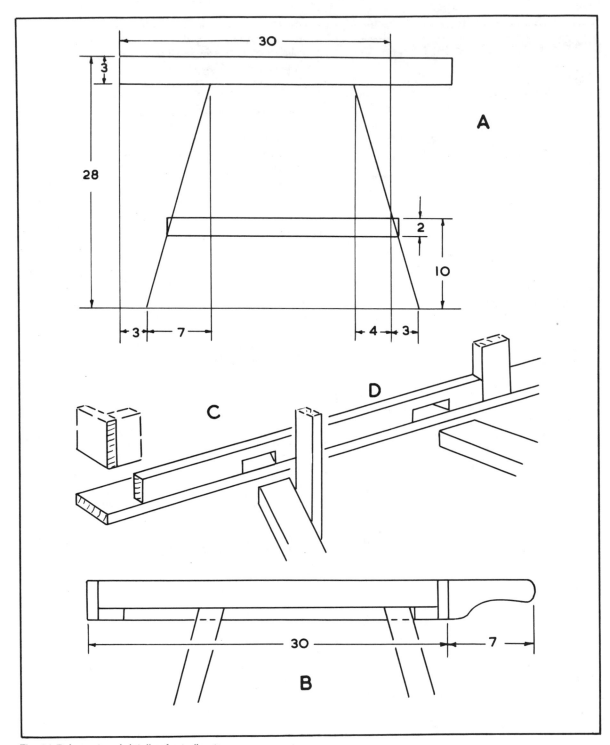

Fig. 11-7. Layout and details of a trolley top.

236

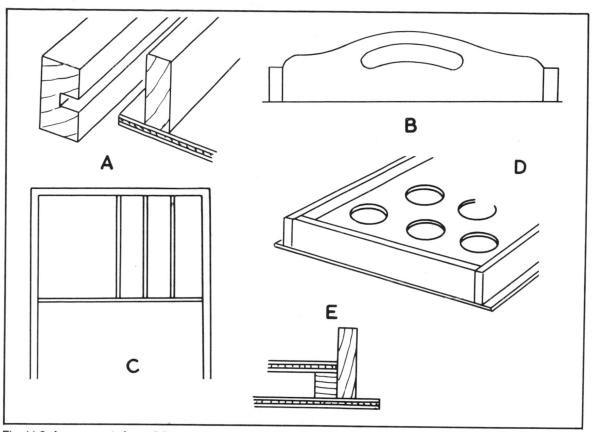

Fig. 11-8. Arrangements for a sliding tray and the top compartments.

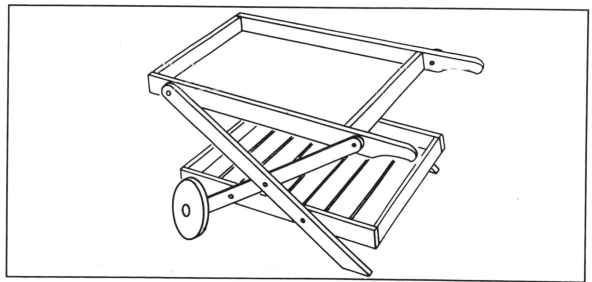

Fig. 11-9. A take-down food trolley.

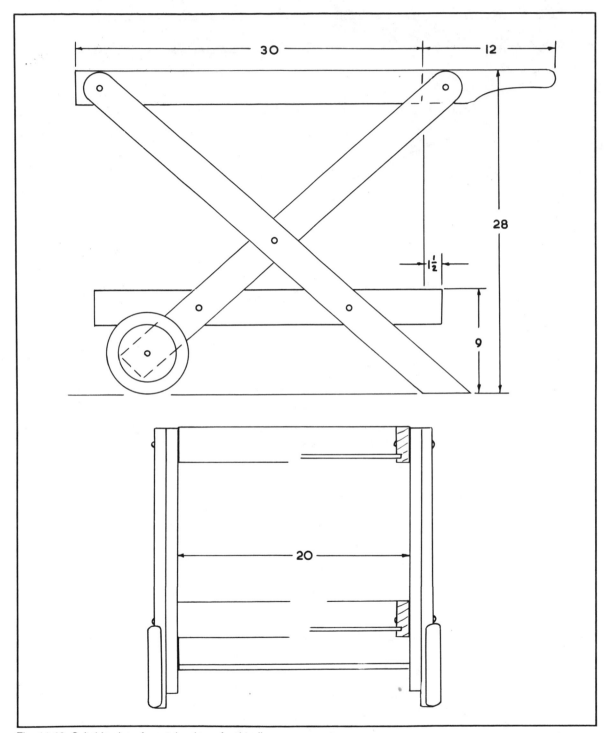

Fig. 11-10. Suitable sizes for a take-down food trolley.

Table 11-3. Materials List for Take-Down Trolley.

4 legs	3	× 42	× 1	
2 tray sides	3	× 43	× 1	
2 tray sides	3	× 31	× 1	
4 tray ends	3	× 20	× 1	
2 tray bottoms	20	× 30	× ¼	plywood
or 16 slats	3	× 20	× ½	

Arrange the pair of inner legs to be the ones with the axle through. Their bolts into the trays have washers between and under the nuts (Fig. 11-12A). The other legs cross with similar bolt arrangements at the leg crossings, but at the other joints there must be packings. These can be pieces of 1-inch dowel rod drilled through (Fig. 11-12B). Use metal washers at each end of the dowel rod and make the total length to suit the leg clearance.

Take the pieces apart for painting and then reassemble. For storage, there will be no need to take out all the bolts. You can leave the tops of the wheel legs bolted to the top tray and the other legs bolted to the lower tray. In both cases they will swing into line. To avoid losing the other nuts, bolts, and washers, put them in a bag tied to the woodwork or replace them in vacant holes. You can tie the parts together and hang the bundle from the axle.

BARBECUE BENCH

The bench shown in Fig. 11-13 is intended to be a substantial working place for a barbecue. It has a support for a barbecue grill at the center, a spacious shelf underneath, a rack for your tools and equipment at one side, and a strong butcher-block chopping area at the other side. Hooks can be added at the ends or sides for hanging many cooking implements.

The central recess is sunk slightly and it is provided with a number of square strips across, with plenty of air space between. How this part is planned and used depends on the type of barbecue grill fitted. In the bench shown in Fig. 11-14, there is a space 18 inches wide and 14 inches from front to back. Most grills need an air space around them. They should not fit tightly. Some grills need mounting on a metal plate or a sheet of asbestos. Check on the grill you intend to use and work out the dimensions of the bench around it.

Nearly all the main parts are 2-inch square wood. See Table 11-4. For a bench that is to stay outside, the wood should be a durable hardwood. If there is some shelter, many parts could be softwood, but the working surfaces—particularly the butcher block—should be a close-grained, clean-looking hardwood that will not splinter if you use a cleaver or hatchet over it.

Although the general form is the same as many tables, there are double rails around the top and the legs are set in from the corners. It will be best to make the top as a unit. Then build the supporting framework to match it. The framework forming the outside can be joined at the corners with bridle joints (Fig. 11-15A). If necessary, dowels can be put through them when you glue the top. Mark and cut the joints now, but there are other things to do to the top before assembly. The intermediate crosswise pieces can be tenoned or dowelled to the long sides (Fig. 11-15B). At the side where the slats come (shown on the left, but could be either side), nail in strips for the slats to be nailed or screwed to (Fig. 11-15C).

There is another possible method of fitting the slats. It depends on how the butcher block is fitted. For the butcher block, join enough pieces to make up the width (keeping them overlong at this stage). You can depend on glue alone or include dowels between meeting surfaces. A simple way of holding the joints close is to nail each piece to the next as you glue it (Fig. 11-15D). Each pair of nails will be covered by the next piece.

The butcher block assembly should have its top trued. The simplest way to fit it is to enclose it in the framing and nail through the sides. A better way, if you have the facilities for cutting the joints, is to groove the sides and cut the butcher block ends to fit (Fig. 11-15E). If you use a ½-inch groove ½ inch down from the top, it can be taken the full length of each side and the ends of the slats at the other end can be joined in a similar way (Fig. 11-15F).

The positions of other parts at the legs are shown on the general drawing (Fig. 11-14). To the side, there are two long rails: one supporting the grill strips, and the other supporting the shelf. At the ends there are two rails to provide stiffening. The shelf slats add strength in that direction (Fig. 11-15G). The tops of the legs can be doweled, but it is better to use stub tenons into the long parts of the top (Fig. 11-15A).

Use the assembled top as a guide to sizes of the supporting framework so that the legs will stand upright when they meet their joints in the top. It would be possible to use dowels between most of the framework parts, but tenons will be stronger. When marking the legs, position the mortises for the second top rail just far enough below the top to take the 1-inch square strips (Fig. 11-15C).

Assemble the framing like a table (preferably in two stages). Get the two ends squared and clamped tightly so that they match. Let their glue set. Then add the long

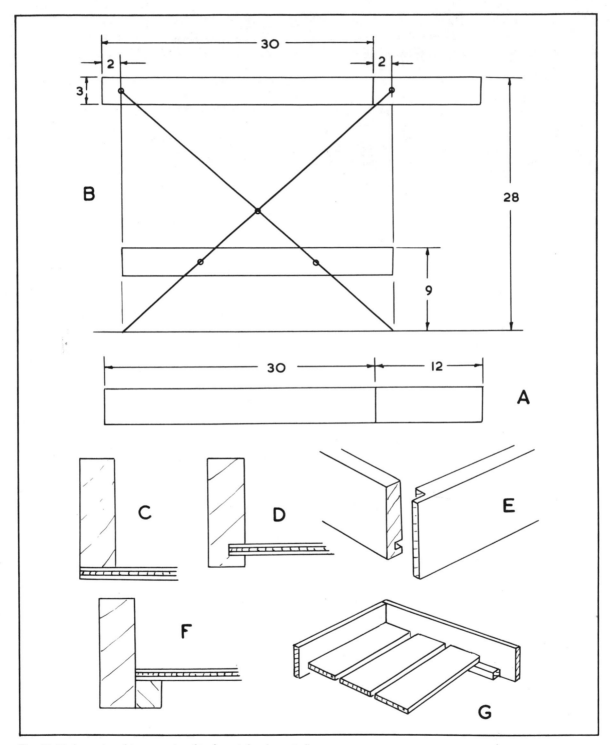

Fig. 11-11. Layout and tray construction for a take-down trolley.

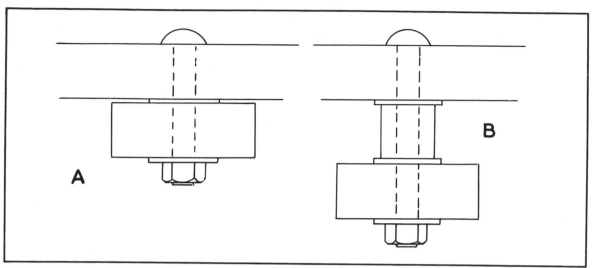

Fig 11-12. Two parts of the bolted construction of a take-down trolley.

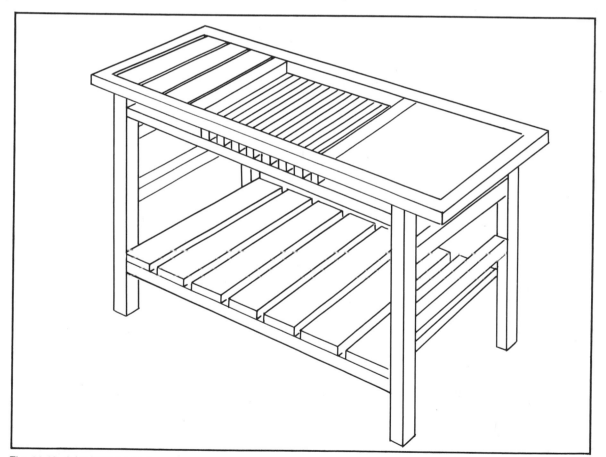

Fig. 11-13. A barbecue bench.

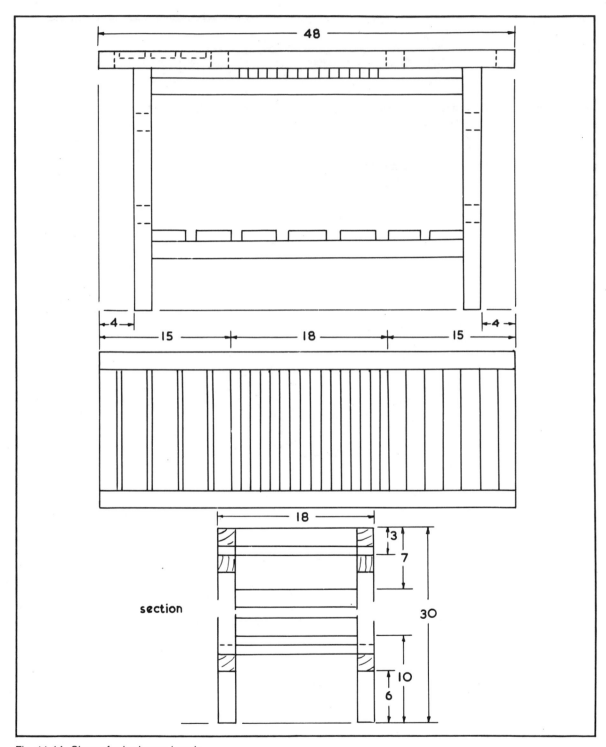

Fig. 11-14. Sizes of a barbecue bench.

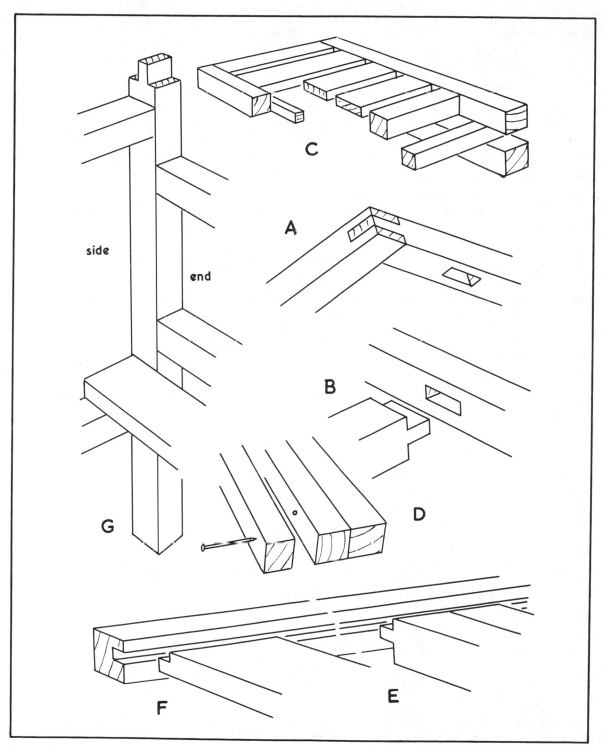

Fig. 11-15. Constructional details of parts of a barbecue bench.

Table 11-4. Materials List for Barbecue Bench.

4 legs	2	×	31	×	2
2 top frames	2	×	49	×	2
4 top frames	2	×	19	×	2
5 butcher blocks	2	×	19	×	2
3 top slats	3	×	15	×	1
2 slat supports	1	×	12	×	1
4 long rails	2	×	40	×	2
4 short rails	2	×	18	×	2
8 grill slats	1	×	19	×	1
7 shelf slats	4	×	19	×	1

parts (Fig. 11-16A) and introduce the leg tenons into their mortises in the top before the glue in the other joints has started to set.

Put the grill strips between the top rails and space them evenly. They can be held by glue only or you can put long thin nails upward into them from below.

The shelf is shown in Fig. 11-16B with slats across. Screw them to their rails to provide strength as well as a place to store things. There are other forms of shelving you can arrange. It is a fairly large storage area. Part of it can be boxed in to keep some items in place. There can be fitted compartments to secure frequently used equipment. There can be a bin for charcoal built in. There can

be a ledge or rail at the back to prevent things from falling. You might prefer a shelf without gaps. Enough slats could be used to fit closely or a piece of exterior plywood could be substituted.

If the bench is to be left outdoors unattended, you might want to enclose a part underneath, with a door, so that animals cannot reach inside. If you do that, the best place is under the butcher block (which will act as a top).

Metal hooks can be driven into the ends or sides of the top, for hanging tools on, but it is advisable to experiment with the bench before settling on hook positions. The hooks must be accessible yet not likely to snag clothing. Any metal should be corrosion resistant. An alternative is to use pieces of dowel rod driven into holes that make them slope upward slightly.

If you are in a windy climate, you can hinge a piece of plywood as long as the bench and about 18 inches wide to the back of the top so it normally hangs down behind. If it is needed to prevent drafts it can be swung up and held with hooks. You could arrange similar pieces at the ends.

Although paint is the usual finish for outdoor furniture, paint in a hot position will blister. It would be better to keep painted parts away from the grill. Let the wood there and the butcher block be left bare and occasionally scrub it clean.

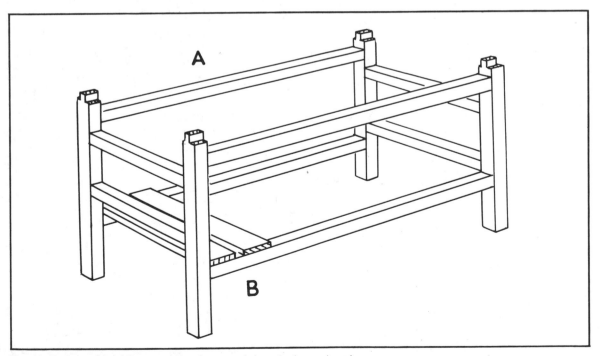

Fig. 11-16. Assembly of the supporting framework for a barbecue bench.

Chapter 12

Butcher-Block Furniture

THE TRADITIONAL BLOCK ON WHICH A BUTCHER chops meat is made up of many pieces of wood joined together with their end grain upwards. The name is given to an assembly of pieces laid with their grains parallel to the surface and built up to the area required in much the same way as a wall is built by whatever number of layers of bricks are required.

Some furniture for indoor use is made in this way. The method is also suitable for outdoor furniture that can be made of softwood or hardwood. The effect is of a substantial and massive assembly. A complete piece of furniture is usually fairly heavy. This can be an advantage in outdoor seats and tables that have to be left out and will need to resist knocks or loads that might move them or turn them over. Nevertheless, they are not always as massive as they appear because parts are not as thick as outer ones.

For indoor furniture the parts are glued. Outdoor furniture can be glued, but for many things it will be enough to use nails. For softwoods of fairly large sections, nails alone are all that are needed. Each layer is nailed to the next (Fig. 12-1A). A zigzag arrangement of nails that go well into the lower piece will make a strong joint. For instance, 2-inch planed wood finishes about 1¾

inches thick. A 3-inch nail then goes 1¼ inches into the lower wood, which is adequate, but a nail much shorter would not be adequate. Of course, nail heads will show on the last piece in a series, but you can usually arrange for that to be at the back or be hidden by another part. Glue in a nailed joint would strengthen it further and prevent water seepage between boards.

If the wood has been completely seasoned, you might rely on glue only, particularly with hardwoods, but unseasoned wood or softwood still containing much moisture will not take glue reliably. In any case, you can strengthen a glued joint by using dowels (Fig. 12-1B). How many depends on the joint, but a dowel near each end will resist any tendency for the joint to open.

Joints in the length would be inappropriate in a small assembly, but in a long bench or similar thing you can include an occasional joint to use up shorter pieces. It could even be considered a design feature. The simplest joint is a plain butt (Fig. 12-1C). Make sure the meeting ends are square and forced close together. The meeting angle need not be square so long as both pieces are the same (Fig. 12-1D). If you cut them to a long angle, it becomes possible to nail through during assembly (Fig. 12-1E). Even with a wider angle, a nail can be driven

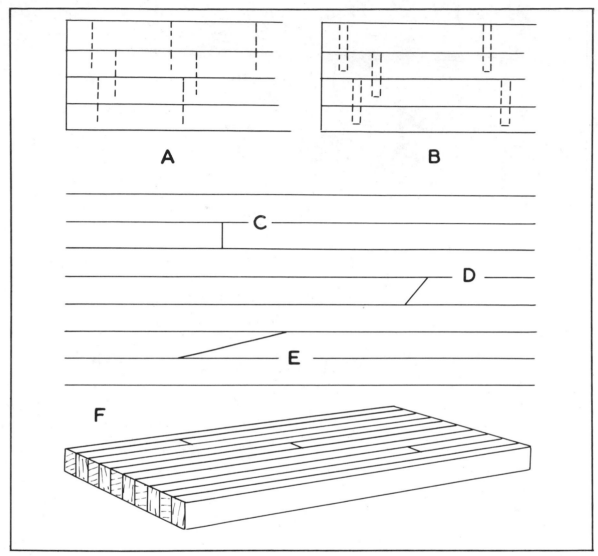

Fig. 12-1. In butcher block construction, the parts can be glued, doweled, or nailed and can be assembled with occasional lengthwise joints.

diagonally across the joint. Most nailing of softwoods can be direct without drilling. Near the ends and in places where accuracy is important, drill undersize almost as far as the nail is to go.

Do not have many joints in the length and always arrange short pieces between others going full length. Even then it looks better and is stronger if you stagger the joints (Fig. 12-1F).

You can use stock sizes of softwood; 2-×-4 inch is the obvious selection. What quality you choose depends

on the project, but occasional knots can be regarded as decoration. The method of construction provides mutual support. You can sometimes include a piece with flaws that might not be suitable for an assembly where it has to form a part unaided. Straight wood is usually the best choice, but a curved piece could be cut for shorter parts or could be cut and butted between other layers that would flatten it.

Hardwoods need not be as massive as softwoods; 2-×-2 inch sizes would suit many things. Much depends

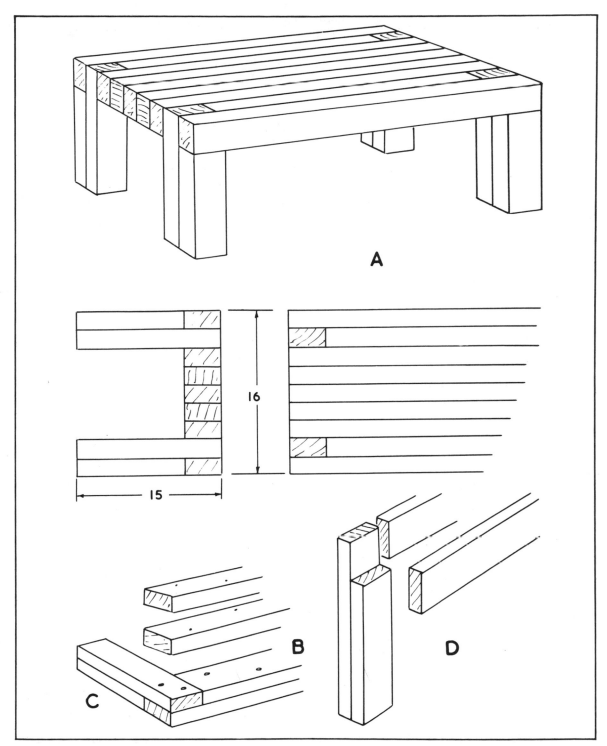

Fig. 12-2. This bench is built up from standard sections of lumber.

on the wood. You could use one wood throughout, but you can get an interesting effect by mixing two or more of different colors. There are alternate strips of dark and light colors or some other arrangement that can give an unusual effect.

SOFTWOOD BENCH

A simple bench, sometimes called a *parson's bench*, can be made with the legs included in butcher-block layers (Fig. 12-2A). A short bench is shown, but the method can be used to build up any length bench when you want to provide seating all around the edge of a patio. Intermediate supports would be needed for a length upwards of 8 feet.

For a simple bench, have enough pieces ready to make up the width you want and mark across the ends of all of them to get matching lengths. Cut them squarely. You might have to plane the ends after assembly. If you get them fairly accurate first, not much will have to be removed to level them. Alternatively, leave the wood too long and trim all the ends together after nailing. Whichever method is used, there have to be two pieces cut short by the width of the legs (Fig. 12-2B). Squareness in both directions is important in their ends because it affects the squareness of the legs.

Nail the strips together and include the legs as you progress (Fig. 12-2C). Make up the thickness of the legs with pieces on the outsides (Fig. 12-2D). The tops of the legs are best left very slightly too long so that you can plane them level. Cleanly planed end grain looks good between adjoining long grain.

If the bench is to remain in one place, possibly

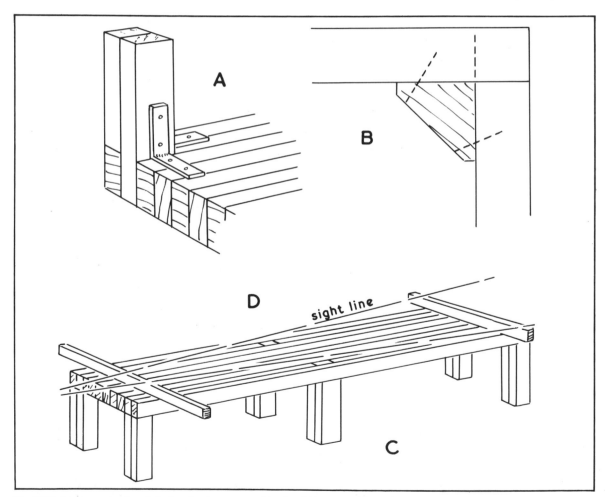

Fig. 12-3. Legs can be bracketed and a long assembly should be tested for twist.

against something else, legs nailed only should be strong enough. If the bench can be moved about or it might get rough usage, it would be better to provide brackets. They can be simple iron angle or shelf brackets that extend both ways underneath (Fig. 12-3A). If you prefer an all-wood construction, wood brackets can be nailed or screwed in (Fig. 12-3B).

If the bench is long enough to need intermediate legs, include them during assembly (Fig. 12-3C) at back and front. Thickening pieces should be the same as at the ends.

During the assembly of any bench, watch that it is going together with the top flat and without twist. So far as possible, assemble the top downward on a flat surface, but you will want to tilt the work sideways for convenience in nailing. Bring it back to the inverted position after each series of nails and see that the top still rests close to the flat surface. You can also check by standing the bench

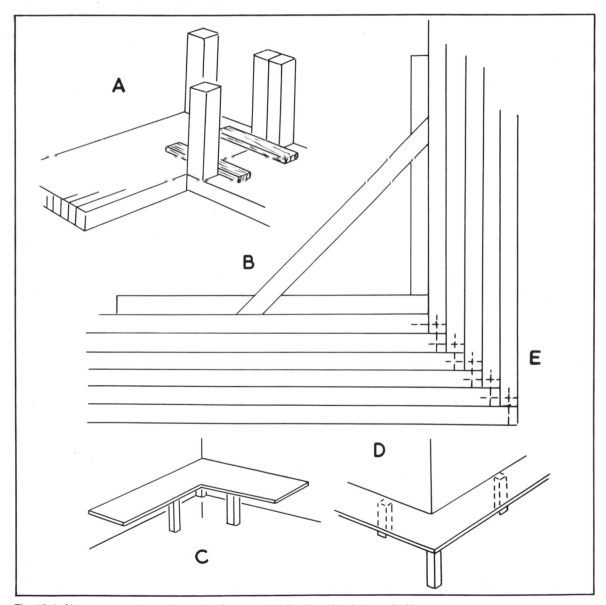

Fig. 12-4. At a corner, parts can butted or they can be joined in a herringbone fashion.

on its legs and sighting along. This check for twist can be helped by having long straight strips across the ends to exaggerate any twist (Fig. 12-3D). An old-time carpenter called these "winding strips" and a twisted assembly was "in winding."

CORNER SOFTWOOD BENCH

If you want to arrange bench seating around the edge of a patio or if you need to angle the seats for any reason, one way is to merely make separate seats and bring them together. If it would be better to join them, there could be strips of metal or wood underneath (Fig. 12-4A). That allows you to disassemble them later if you want to rearrange seating. If there is no doubt that the seating will remain where it is made, you can build the seat tops into each other.

It will help to have a frame against which you can assemble the butcher-block strips. This could be made from pieces that will be later cut and used in the assembly. Make that frame to match the angle the seat will be. Even if it is apparently 90 degrees, there is no point in carefully getting your bench square when the deck below or the corner of a house is a degree or so different. Make the frame to the actual shape and brace it with a diagonal strut (Fig. 12-4B).

Decide where you need legs. Their location will vary according to sizes and situations. If the seat fits inside a corner, you can put one leg near the corner at the back and two front legs a short distance each way from the angle (Fig. 12-4C). If the seat goes around an outside angle a leg can come right at the corner, and back legs need not be as close (Fig. 12-4D).

The corners could be made straight and butted, with straps below, but they look better with a herringbone arrangement. Using the frame as a guide, bring the ends together in alternate ways as you nail them in layers. Then add nails into the corners (Fig. 12-4E). Bring in the legs as you progress. Work upside down, as with a straight bench, checking flatness and that legs are upright as you go. Use brackets at the legs. Once the assembly has progressed to many layers, there is little risk of it going out of shape. You can remove the temporary frame and use its parts in further assembly work.

OPEN SOFTWOOD BENCH

The solid benches have smooth, level tops and an attractive massive appearance. They are also heavy and rain water can settle on top. It might be better in some situations to have gaps between the strips. In a given width, that would be lighter than a solid top and water

would be able to run through. In the simplest construction, alternate pieces can be cut short. That would leave rather wide gaps that would be uncomfortable to sit on and even cushions would become caught in the spaces. It would be better to have thinner spaces (1-×-4 inch is a suitable stock section).

The small bench shown in Fig. 12-5A has a full-length, 2-inch widths alternating with short sections of 1-inch width. The legs are made up to 5 inches thick. Ends could be left showing the end grain (Fig. 12-5B) or a strip could be put across between the outer sections of the legs (Fig. 12-5C).

Decide on the lengths of filler pieces. They should be shorter than the spaces between them (Fig. 12-5D). Plan the layout to suit the size bench you are making, but fillers between 6 inches and 12 inches will do. Make enough fillers for the whole bench so that you get them the same length.

Legs have the inner and filler pieces the full depth of the bench, but the outer piece is cut back (Fig. 12-5E). Nail the parts of the legs together. It will be best to make all the legs so they are ready for fitting to the other parts as you come to them. Set back the tops (Fig. 12-5F) if there is to be a strip across the end of the bench.

Mark on the first outside piece where the legs and spacers will come. Join this to the legs and the first set of spacers. As you add more strips, use a try square to mark across so that all the spacers are fitted level. Also watch the squareness of the ends if there is to be a strip across them. If the end grain is to be exposed, it would not matter if you left some excess length to be trimmed after complete assembly.

The simplest, closed end has the strip square between the outer pieces (Fig. 12-5G), but you can make a neater corner by mitering (Fig. 12-5H). Although all the parts are shown with sharp angles, the outer edges and corners should be rounded. You could round the lengthwise strips and arrange the spacers a short distance below the top level.

For an angled corner of an open bench, there are several ways of arranging a herringbone effect. You could treat each layer, whether full length piece or a spacer, separately (Fig. 12-6A) and alternate the laps. You could regard a long piece and its spacer as a unit and alternate these pairs (Fig. 12-6B). Whichever way you do it, the spacers could be all the same length. They should form a diagonal line with the inner ones getting closer to the next spacers (Fig. 12-6C) or you could arrange their lengths so that they come square across (Fig. 12-6D). Keep spaces along the bench the same.

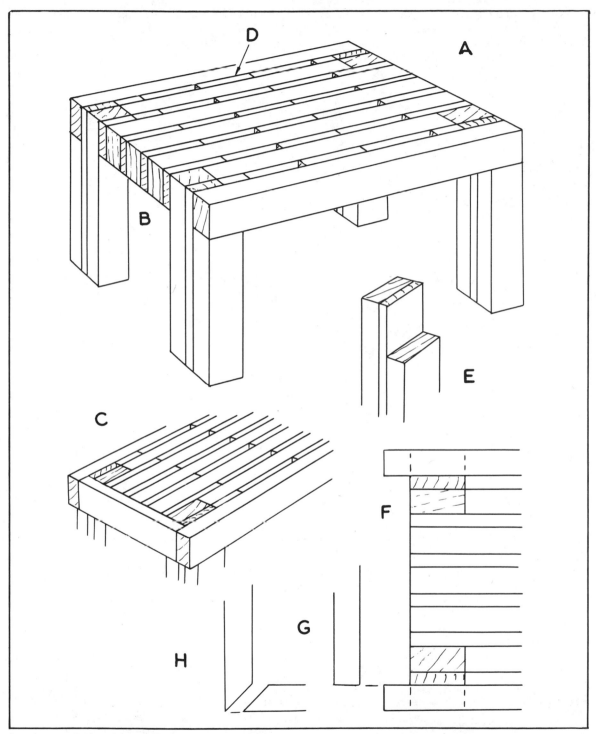

Fig. 12-5. An open butcher-block assembly will shed water.

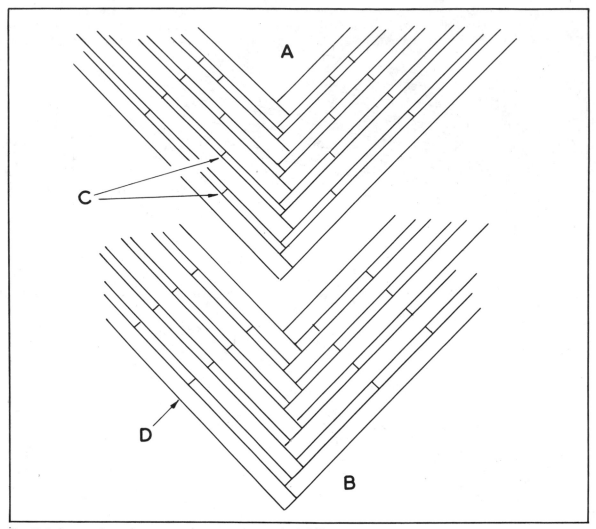

Fig. 12-6. An open-topped corner can have equal or graduated fillers.

If you want to put a leg at a corner, whether inside or outside the angle, cutting its top away to allow the outer seat pieces to go right through takes rather a lot from the leg. It could be strengthened to allow for this by increasing the wood section to 2 × 6 inches. In any case, there should be wood or metal brackets underneath. Another way would be to cut off the leg below the seat—allowing the top assembly to go right through to the corner—and then secure the leg with angle brackets in both directions to as many top pieces as can be included.

HARDWOOD BENCH

Any of the softwood bench designs could be made in hardwood, but that would result in great weight, increased costs, and a construction far stronger than required. A reasonable section for most benches built solidly is 2 inches square. This finishes after planing to about 1⅞ inch square. The tops can be of that size throughout and legs can be the same or larger section.

In the simple bench shown in Fig. 12-7A, the top is made up in the usual way. It could be of different woods for an unusual appearance. The exposed end grain adds to the effect (although it would be possible to frame across there). The legs are set in from the ends and are braced with framing (all have their joints to the top hidden). It is possible to do some assembly with nails, but cut joints are more appropriate to good hardwoods. Joints to build up the laminations could be nailed, but elsewhere glued cut joints are better.

Start by making the two assemblies that each consist of a lengthwise piece with legs attached (Fig. 12-7B). Set out the shapes at one leg. For a short bench, the bracing strut can be at 45 degrees. If the bench is long, it is better to take the strut further along (Fig. 12-7C).

Use a mortise and tenon joint at the top of a leg (Fig. 12-8A), but do not take it through the top piece (1 inch or slightly more will be long enough for a tenon). Tenon the strut into the leg (Fig. 12-8B). There could be a tenon at the other end of the strut, but it is easier to halve it—either straight (Fig. 12-8C) or dovetailed (Fig. 12-8D). There will be a rail between each pair of legs. You cannot make the rail yet, but you can cut its mortise in readiness (Fig. 12-8E).

With these two assemblies made up, further assem-

bly is just a case of starting at one side with a plain strip outside one legged piece, and more layers until you are ready to take in the other legged piece. Glue each joint and then nail it to its neighbor. Doweling is easy. Clamp the glued joint. Then drill through it at about 10-inch intervals so that you can drive in glued dowels (Fig. 12-8F). If you keep the dowels short, they will hold just as well. But you will not have to level their tops after driving. Stagger the dowel positions as you progress.

When you reach the stage of bringing in the second long piece with legs attached, measure the length between shoulders of the lower crosswise rails. Make these rails and glue them in at the same time you build in the legged piece.

If you want to close the ends of the top with strips, make the outer strips long enough to enclose the end pieces (Fig. 12-8G). These can merely fit between or be mitered (Fig. 12-8H). If the size of bench you want to

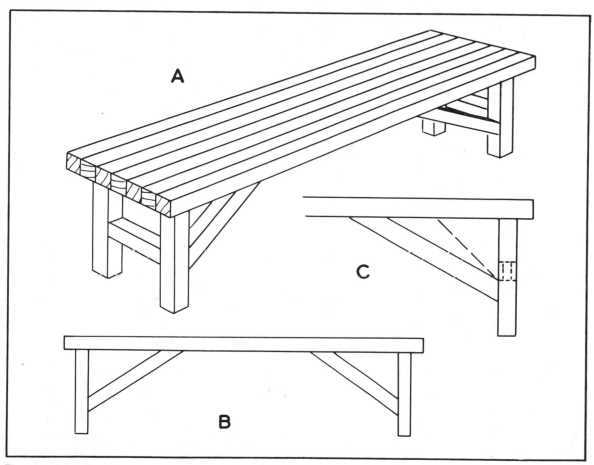

Fig. 12-7. A butcher-block top to a bench can have braced legs.

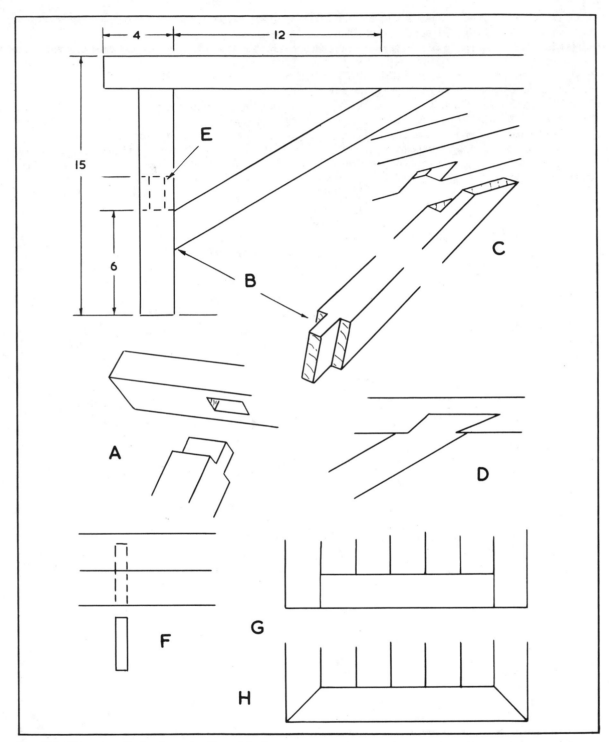

Fig. 12-8. Different methods of constructing a bench.

make would be better with thicker legs, there is no difficulty in making them any reasonable section. All that is necessary is to cut a suitable tenon at the top and arrange the rail and strut joints centrally in the leg.

BUTCHER-BLOCK TABLE

A tabletop in the butcher style could be made of thick pieces as described for the benches. The result would be quite heavy This might be an advantage in a permanent situation. If the table is to be used for outdoor hobbies, then a stiff solid top would be an advantage. For the more common outdoor use of a table, it would be better to lighten construction—while retaining the typical butcher block appearance—so it could partner forms or chairs made in this manner.

The table shown in Fig. 12-9 is moderate size, with the usual sturdy butcher-block appearance, but with a top that is not as heavy as it appears. The sizes given in Fig. 12-10 and Table 12-1 are suggestions. They can be varied according to needs and available wood. Most of the parts are 2-inch square and 1-×-2 inch sections. They are shown without allowance for planing, but the wood should be

planed all around. The final sizes will be less than shown.

It is the central area of the top that controls other sizes. Make this part first. If you work the other way and have to fit the top into a frame, you will have to cut the width of one strip. Join enough strips together (Fig. 12-11A). It might be sufficient to rely on glue only. If so, assemble all the parts of the top face downward on a flat surface covered with paper to prevent glue sticking to it and pull them together with bar clamps. You will have to put weights on the assembly to prevent it from buckling. A safer way of keeping it flat is to assemble the strips, in groups of two or three that have their tops planed true, before joining them to other groups.

You could use nails between the parts in predrilled holes or dowels across in a similar way (three along each joint should be enough). Have all the pieces too long at this stage so that you can trim the whole assembly as if it is a single board. How the ends are dealt with depends on your equipment. The best way is to rabbet across so that a tongue goes into a plowed groove in the frame (Fig. 12-11B). This could be done with a router, two passes on a table saw, or with a hand fillester plane.

Fig. 12-9. A butcher-block table.

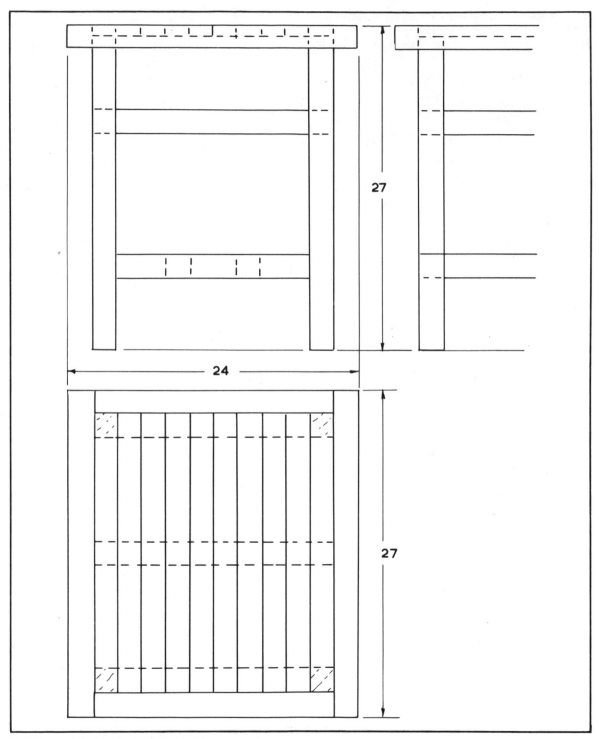

Fig. 12-10. Sizes for a butcher-block table.

Table 12-1. Materials List for Butcher-Block Table.

10 tops	2 × 24 × 1
2 tops	2 × 28 × 2
2 tops	2 × 21 × 2
1 top stiffener	2 × 21 × 1
4 legs	2 × 27 × 2
4 rails	2 × 20 × 2
4 rails	2 × 24 × 2
2 rails	2 × 20 × 1

Alternatively, you can use dowels in square-cut ends (Fig. 12-11C). At the sides, the joints can be glued or there could be a few dowels there. In the 1-inch thickness, the dowels could be ¾ of an inch in diameter.

There are three ways of making the frame. The ends can go right across with the sides taken into the same plowed grooves (Fig. 12-12A). The sides could be carried through so that the ends are covered, and there could be dowels in the joint (Fig. 12-12B). They could be only partly into the sides or taken through. Exposed dowel ends can be regarded as a design feature in this type of construction. The corners could be mitered and dowels could be taken through diagonally (Fig. 12-12C).

The top could be stiff enough as it is, but there also could be a piece across under the center, tenoned into the sides (Fig. 12-11D). Complete the top before starting on the framing. Clean off surplus glue where the legs and their top bars will come underneath.

The legs and rails are all square in order to match the solid appearance of the top. Four rails go around the table a short distance down from the top. Then there are two rails between the legs at the ends and lengthwise rails between them. At the tops of the legs, there are rails across to take screws upward into the tabletop.

Mark out the legs (Fig. 12-11E). Use mortise and tenon joints for the rails. The tenons can go about halfway through the legs and the lower ones will have to be mitered where they meet. Doweled joints could be used if you prefer, but tenons are more appropriate. The thinner top rails to take screws could be tenoned, but they are better dovetailed into the tops of the legs (Fig. 12-11F). Drill for screws before assembly, but angle them slightly so that there is clearance for your screwdriver past the main rail. Get the lengths of the rails such that the legs will come closely inside the top frame.

Make up the two end leg and rail assemblies. See that they are square, flat, and match as a pair. Join them with the rails the other way and fit the framework to the tabletop.

RADIAL TABLETOPS

Butcher-block tops do not have to be just parallel strips. You can make interesting tables with the tops divided into segments that are all in the same wood or in different woods so that the colors alternate. It is possible to make tops using narrow strips and a large number of segments. That would give you an opportunity of showing your skill. For the usual purposes of an outdoor table, a more simple arrangement would be appreciated just as much. It will usually be sufficient to divide the top into four segments.

An example is a square top with or without a border (Fig. 12-13A). This is shown with 2-×-4 inch pieces with the greater width on the top, but 2 inch square pieces, or even narrower ones, could be used. Join enough pieces to make up the width of a side, with the outside edge cut squarely, but enough extended to mark the miter (Fig. 12-13B). The safest way to get an accurate shape is to set out the final square full size on a piece of scrap plywood or hardboard, with diagonals drawn, then cut and plane the miter edges to that. In any case, you will have to do some careful planing for final close fitting. Mark adjoining surfaces so that they go back in the same place. Then drill for a few dowels.

Exposed ends of hardwood look attractive with their different grain patterns. This is particularly true if woods are mixed and the ends are sealed with varnish. Softwoods are better covered and you can make a border (Fig. 12-13C) with mitered or lapped corners. The top can be attached to legs and framing and made in the way described for the previous table.

A very similar top is easily converted to round (Fig. 12-13D). This is shown with square strips. The best plan to get a good shape is to start with the outline of a square table and draw the circle when the parts are joined. You could draw curves on each segment, but cut oversize, so there can be a final trimming to a true circle later.

The strips used do not all have to be the same widths. An interesting effect can be obtained by using random widths. This is a way of using up oddments left from other work. You can alternate wide and narrow pieces. Dark narrow pieces between lighter colored ones can be very attractive. An example is shown with an octagonal outline (Fig. 12-13E), but the design could be used in other shapes.

Any top with straight edges can be bordered with strips glued and nailed or screwed on. An alternative to a square unbordered edge is to make it semicircular or to bevel around top and bottom edges.

The usual assembly is with pieces to the full thickness of the top (Fig. 12-13F), but there is an alternative

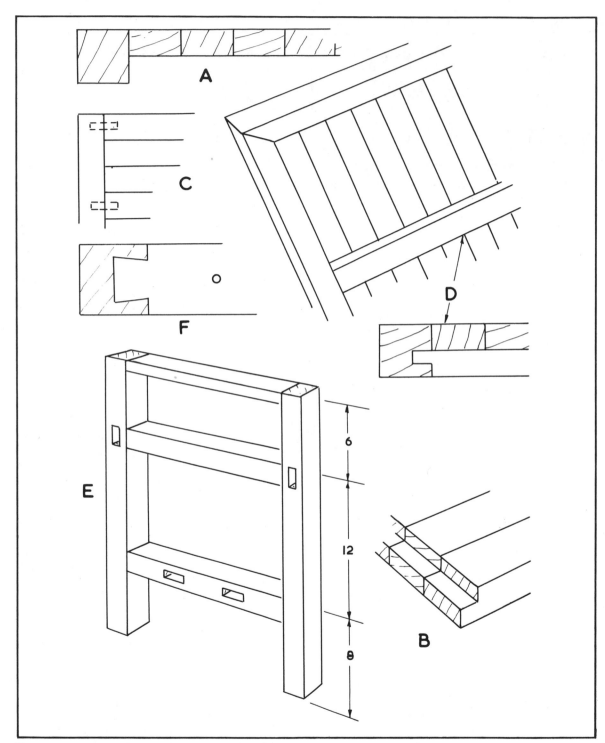

Fig. 12-11. Assembly details of the top and leg construction.

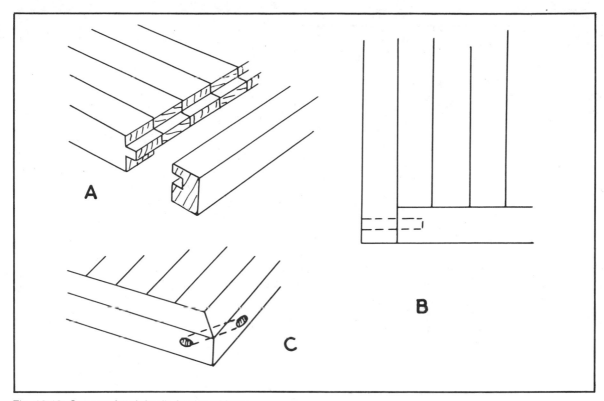

Fig. 12-12. Constructional details for the tabletop.

way of getting a similar top appearance using thinner wood. The base is a piece of stout exterior grade plywood that is marked or cut to the shape the table is to be. On this, go thinner strips of wood to make up any pattern you prefer (Fig. 12-13G). Any of the patterns suitable for solid wood could be used, but in this case you can put the pieces in place over a penciled pattern on the plywood. The parts can be glued only or you can drive screws from below as well. Glue is advisable, in any case, as it steals the gaps and prevents water becoming trapped between and under the strips.

A variation in pattern that would be difficult with solid pieces is easier to do on a plywood base. That is to arrange the meeting pieces in a herringbone pattern (Fig. 12-13H) instead of straight miters. There should be a border added, bedded in glue, so as to prevent moisture being absorbed by the exposed end grain of the plywood veneers.

FLAT SEAT CHAIR

Chairs to match other butcher-block furniture can have their seats and backs made in the typical manner, but otherwise they follow the usual construction. This is a plain chair with a flat sloping seat and a similar back (Fig. 12-14). The butcher-block parts are made up from strips 1⅜ inches square (Fig. 12-15). The design is intended for hardwood that will match a table. Like other assemblies, you can use a mixture of woods that will look good when varnished.

It is the butcher-block parts that control some of the other sizes. Start with the seat. Make up enough pieces to give a total width of about 15 inches. You could use glue only or nail or dowel through as you add each piece (as described for some of the benches). Square the ends to length. Round what will be the rear edge, but leave the front square because it will receive a cover strip.

The ends of the seat are joined to the sides with dowels (Fig. 12-16A). For accurate drilling, mark where the holes will come in the sides and drill through both together. Then put a side against the set and use its holes as a guide to drill into the end grain. Have the front end of each side square with the seat, but leave the rear end too long at this stage. Cut it against the rear leg later. Join the seat and sides. Trim the dowel ends later.

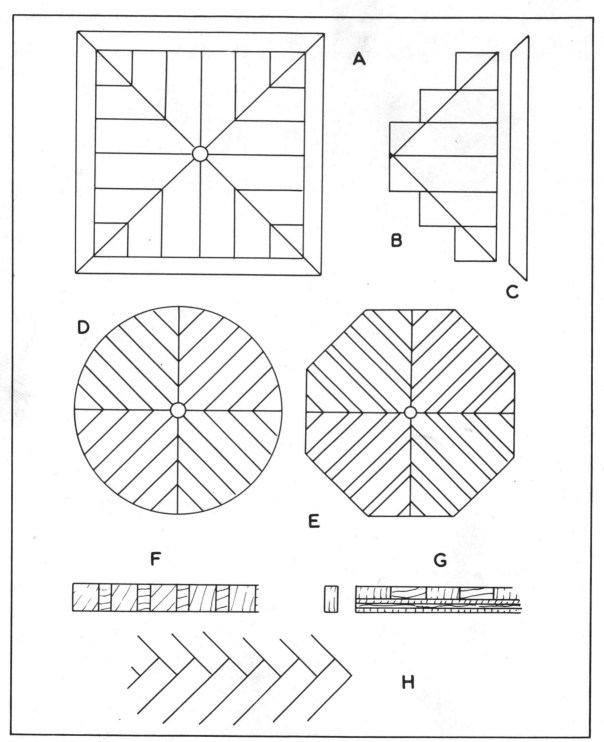

Fig. 12-13. Suggestions for radial butcher-block tabletops.

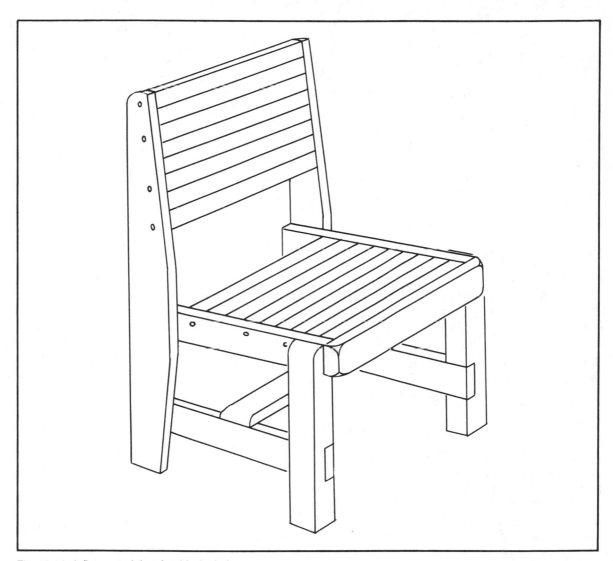

Fig. 12-14. A flat-seated, butcher-block chair.

The length of the back is the same as the distance across the seat and its sides. Make the butcher-block back and mark where its dowels will come.

Make the back legs (Fig. 12-17A). They taper to the ends, but are kept parallel where the seat sides will be attached. The seat is given a slope back. Set this out full size so as to get the position and angle of the seat side on the legs (Fig. 12-17B). Make the front legs (Fig. 12-17C). They are square, but must be notched to take the seat sides and the lower rails (Fig. 12-16B).

Fit the butcher-block back between the rear legs in the same way as the seat is doweled to its sides. Use your full-size setting out as a guide to the position and angle of the seat sides on the rear legs. Then join with glue and screws driven from inside. Fit the front legs and see that they are parallel to the straight edges of the rear legs. Well round the exposed edges at the tops of the front legs.

Add the seat front (Fig. 12-16C) and well round its edges and ends. The lower rails at the sides fit into the front leg notches (Fig. 12-16D) and are screwed inside to the legs parallel to the floor. Add a rail across between their centers to help rigidity. Take off sharpness of edges and remove surplus glue before varnishing.

261

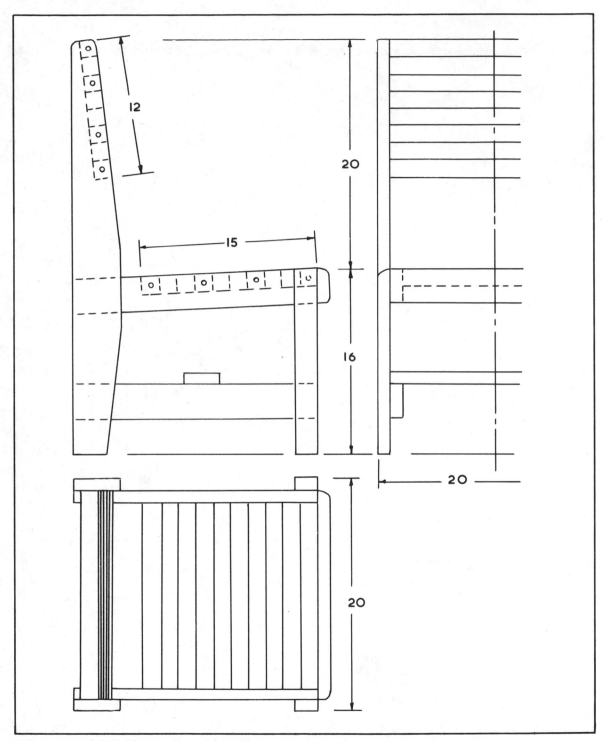

Fig. 12-15. Sizes of the flat-seated, butcher-block chair.

FLAT-SEAT ARMCHAIR

The open seat can be converted to an armchair during construction. Sizes can remain the same or the seat area might be increased by one or two inches in both directions if you prefer.

The general design remains the same, but the front legs are carried up to hold the arms (Fig. 12-18). Instead of square front legs, use a 1-×-3 inch section that is screwed to the outsides of the seat sides in the same way as the rear legs. At the tops of the front legs, arrange a 1-×-2 inch rail to the back legs (Fig. 12-18A). This is screwed outside both legs and parallel with the floor—not with the sloping seat.

The 1-×-3 inch arms go above these strips and are notched round the rear legs. You could curve the outline of an arm, but for the solid butcher-block appearance they are better straight (Fig. 12-18B) with rounded edges and

corners. Screw downward and into the back legs preferably with the screw heads counterbored and plugged. If you screw outward from the rear legs, the heads will not be very obvious.

SHAPED-SEAT CHAIR

If a chair is to be comfortable for long use without padding, it needs some shaping. Ideally, there should be compound curvature in the set, but that is almost impossible to produce in wood without considerable careful work. The most important need is shaping from front to back. This can be arranged fairly easily with the butcher-block technique. It helps to have some curve across the chair back and that is also fairly easy to make. See Table 12-3.

The chair shown in Fig 12-19 is intended to be rather more advanced than hammer-and-nail construction or

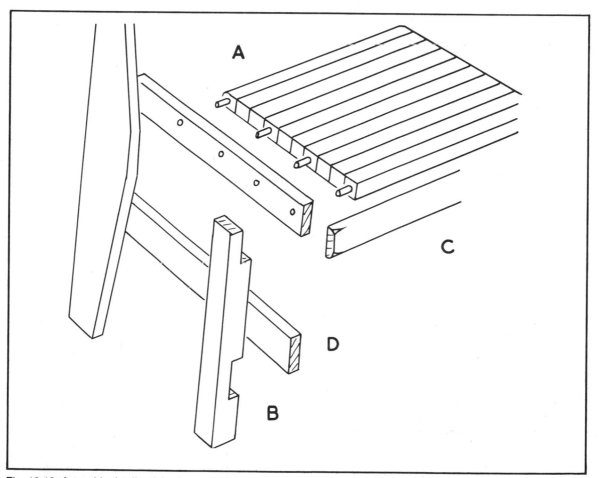

Fig. 12-16. Assembly details of the flat-seat chair.

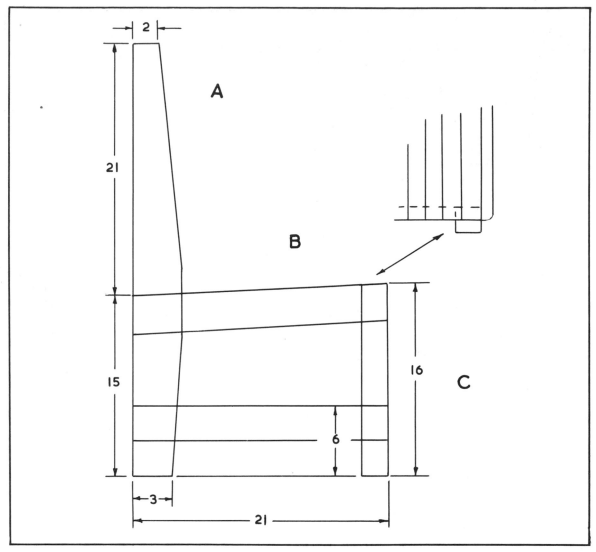

Fig. 12-17. Layout of a flat-seat chair.

even dowel construction. It is an example of cabinetwork taken outdoors. The finished chair can have uses in the house as well as outside (if it is given a good finish). If made of hardwoods—probably of mixed colors—and finished with clear varnish, it becomes a very attractive piece of furniture for use anywhere. The general drawing (Fig. 12-20) shows a chair of fairly roomy proportions. Sizes could be reduced slightly if it is to be used indoors with other smaller chairs, but outdoors a large size will often be appreciated.

The rails that support the seat slope back for economy in cutting the curve. Make a full-size outline drawing of a side view (Fig. 12-21A). From this, get the shape of a rail and mark on it the angles of the cuts and joints. Then draw the curve of the top edge. Use the pattern of 1½ inch squares as a guide (Fig. 12-21B). Cut the curve on the two matching sides.

Mark out the front legs so that you can cut the joints between them and the seat sides. They are best made with double tenons that are cut back about ½ inch from the front (Fig. 12-21C). They can go about 1¼ inches into the seat sides. Cut the mortises in the seat sides before

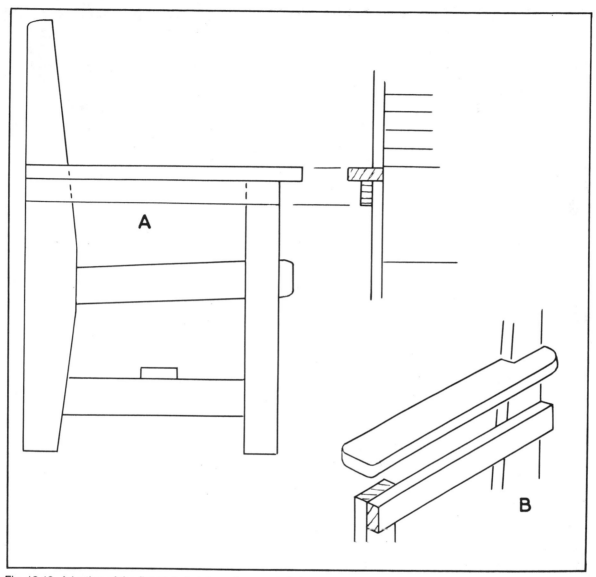

Fig. 12-18. Adaption of the flat-seat chair to make an armchair.

cutting the wood to length in order to reduce the risk of short grain breaking out.

The curving of the top edge reduces the rear end of the sides to about 2½ inches. Make a mortise and tenon joint there to the leg—with double tenons similar to those on the front legs—but there is no need to cut back from either edge. Cut the tenons on the sides, but the matching mortises can be left until later.

With the two sides prepared, have ready the pieces that will make the seat. Because of the varying curve,

Table 12-2. Materials List for Flat-Seat Chair.

10 seats	1½ × 17 × 1½
8 backs	1½ × 19 × 1½
2 legs	4 × 37 × 1
2 legs	2 × 17 × 1
2 seat sides	3 × 22 × 1
1 seat front	3 × 21 × 1
2 bottom rails	3 × 22 × 1
1 bottom rail	3 × 20 × 1

Table 12-3. Materials List for Shaped-Seat Chair.

2 legs	4	×	35	×	1½
2 legs	3	×	16	×	1½
2 sides	3	×	20	×	1½
1 front rail	3	×	20	×	1½
9 seats	1½	×	21	×	1
12 backs	1½	×	16	×	1
2 back supports from	6	×	20	×	1

their edges have to be planed to meet as you fit each one in turn. This is not as difficult as you might think because one edge of each piece is always square in section. You will start at the front and work back. Take care to keep the assembly square. Although the joints will be glued, it helps in assembly to put one screw in the end of each piece as it is fitted. In the finished chair, the seat will look good with plugs over counterbored screw heads. At this stage, it will be simplest to use thin temporary screws. When the seat is fully assembled and the glue set, they can be removed and the holes drilled and counterbored for larger screws and plugs.

Start at the front with one piece having both edges square (Fig. 12-22A). Plane the edge of the next piece to fit against it closely. Leave its other edge square (Fig. 12-22B). Then glue and screw it in place. Do the same with the next one, and so on until you have made up

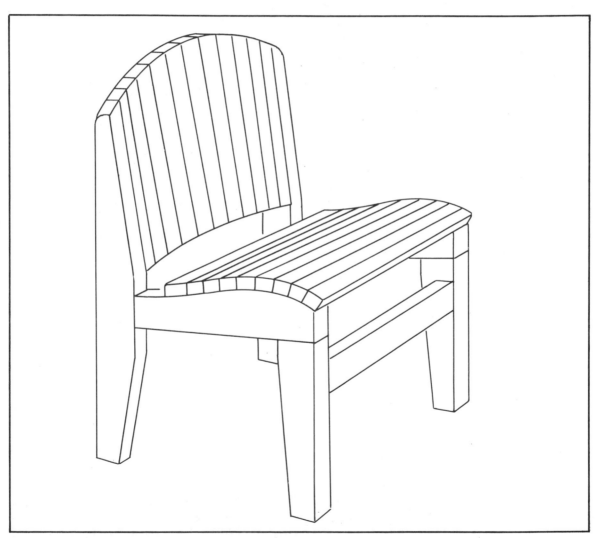

Fig. 12-19. A butcher-block chair with a shaped seat and back.

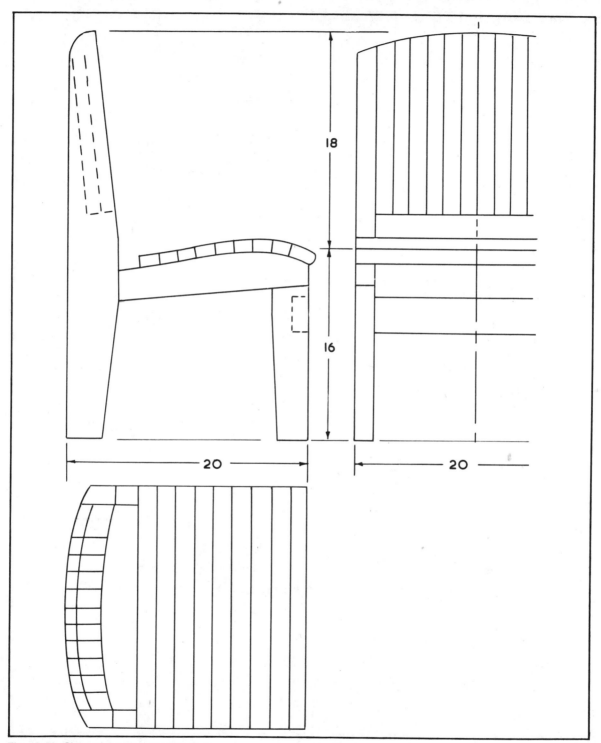

Fig. 12-20. Sizes of the shaped-seat chair.

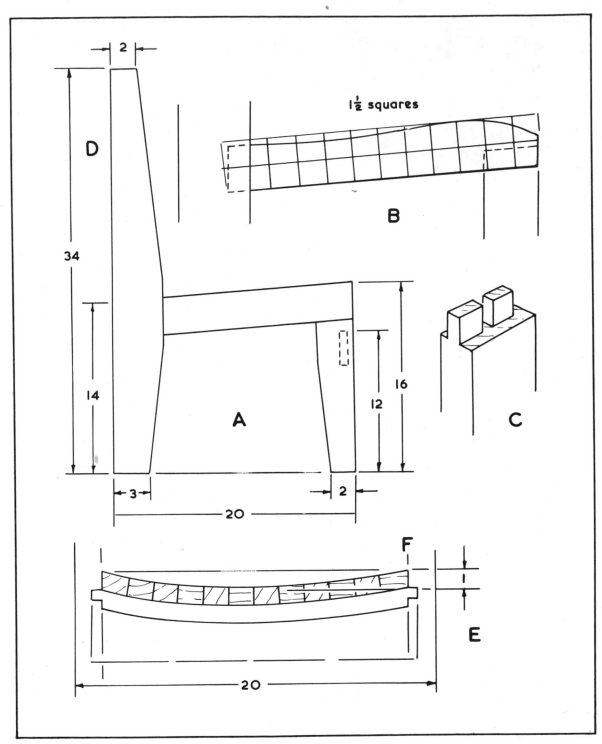

Fig. 12-21. Layout of the chair side and the curves of seat and back.

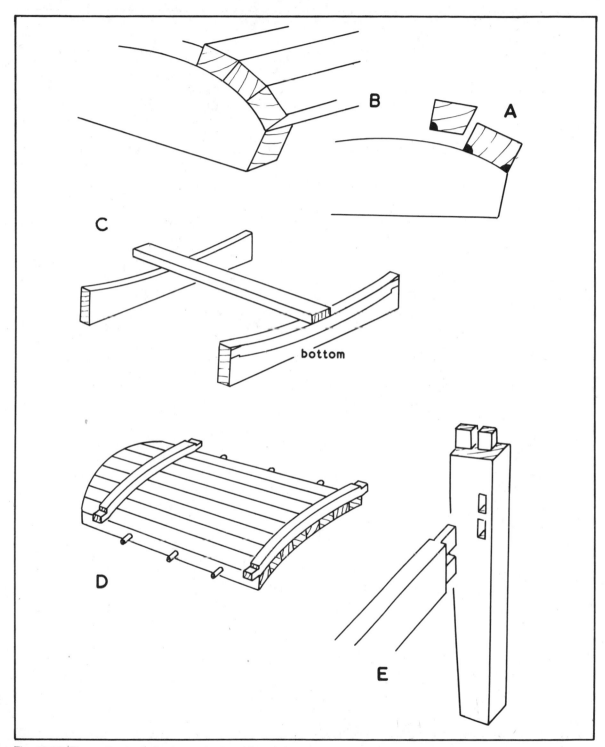

Fig. 12-22. The methods of shaping and assembling parts.

enough for the seat. Later you can plane and sand the top surface to a smooth curve, if you prefer, but the series of narrow flats will not be noticed when sitting and they help to give the butcher-block appearance. Level the outer ends of the strips and round the top edges. Well round the front edge of the seat.

Make the back legs (Fig. 12-21D). Cut the mortises for the seat sides, but leave preparation for the back until that is made up. The butcher-block back has to fit between the back legs—which will be the same distance apart as the sides of the seat—so use them as a gauge for the overall width.

In the finished chair, there are two curved pieces behind the back tenoned into the back legs (Fig. 12-21E). So as to get the curve of the butcher-block back true, these pieces are made too wide at first. They can be used as cradles in which to assemble the back. If made too narrow, they could buckle during assembly. They are shown about 6 inches wide, but that is not important. Mark on these pieces their final shapes and the tenons (which have to be cut after the strips have all been glued on).

Arrange one piece at what will be the bottom edge of the back and the other far enough down to allow for its curved top edge. Then put on the central strip (Fig. 12-22C). This has both edges square and must be square to the supports. Glue and screw it in the same way as the seat strips. Work outward from that and keep the bottom ends level. Plane the next pieces to match it, but leave their other edges square. Fit them in turn on opposite sides so that the width increases symmetrically about the center. When you reach the outside, you will have to plane the edges to size and to the angle that will fit them between the legs (Fig. 12-21F).

Cut off the surplus wood from the supports at the back. Trim them to a neat curve and round their exposed edges. Draw a curve over the tops of the strips and cut it. You can make it resemble anything you like, but keep it symmetrical and about 2 inches lower at the sides than the center. Besides the tenons and glue between the back and the legs, there should be some dowels (Fig. 12-22D). Use the back to mark where mortises and dowel holes have to come on the legs. Shape the tops of the legs to follow on the curve of the back and round the outer corners.

Complete the front legs. Make the front rail (Fig. 12-22E) that crosses far enough below the seat to avoid its joints and provide crosswise stiffness without interfering with a sitter's legs.

Assembly is best done in one process instead of in two steps as with many chairs. Fit the rail between the front legs and join them to the seat. Check squareness in the front view by measuring diagonals. Check the angle in side view by comparing with your full-size drawing. Assemble the back to the rear legs—preferably pulling tight with bar clamps—and then bring the rear legs to the seat. As you close those joints, check that the rear edges of the back legs are parallel with the front edges of the front legs.

Stand the chair on a level surface and look at it from all directions to see that it is true. Adjustments can be made before the glue starts to set. If any tenoned joints are not as good a fit as they should be, you can strengthen them by drilling across for ¼-inch dowels. Their exposed ends will form part of the patter made by the plugs over screws in the seat and back.

Chapter 13

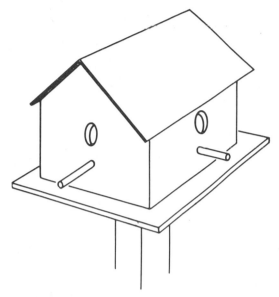

Bird Houses and Feeders

ALL OUTDOOR FURNITURE DOES NOT HAVE TO BE for human use. You can get a lot of enjoyment out of watching birds that feed where you have provided an eating place or nest in boxes or houses you have made. What you provide can vary from the absolute basics to the most elaborate equipment. The birds will get just as much satisfaction out of the simplest things, but you might enjoy making and watching something more advanced. An example is a feeder with a roof that makes it look more like a dollhouse.

There are a few key requirements. Most birds will not come too close to people. It is no use locating a feeder near where there is much human activity. The birds will stay away altogether or fly away everytime someone goes near. They will not frequent a feeder that is close to the ground because of their fear of animals.

Maybe they would like to place the feeder quite high, but then you have the problem of putting food on it, and it will be difficult to watch the birds. The table surface should be 48 inches or more above the ground. Birds tend to be wasteful and push food over the edge. A rim is helpful in keeping the food there. Whether a roof is

important is debatable, but it can provide shade in hot weather and keep off rain.

You will have to consider birds nesting habits. Some will nest close to buildings or even on them. Other birds always nest in trees. A bird house attached to a building might seem attractive to you, but you have to consider if it is attractive to the birds you hope will use it. Birds that nest in trees might be attracted to a bird house on a post, but they are more likely to use one mounted in a tree.

Birds are surprisingly concerned with the size of the access hole. You cannot just make a large hole with the idea that it will suit all birds. A small bird does not like a hole that will admit a larger bird that might attack it. The body size of a bird is smaller than you think because of the thickness of feathers that will compress. A bird is happiest with a hole that does not allow very much clearance as it passes through.

Most birds like a ledge or perch to alight on before entering a hole, but do not provide a large ledge on which you intend putting food. That would attract other birds. A nesting bird likes privacy.

The birds you hope to house will be different from

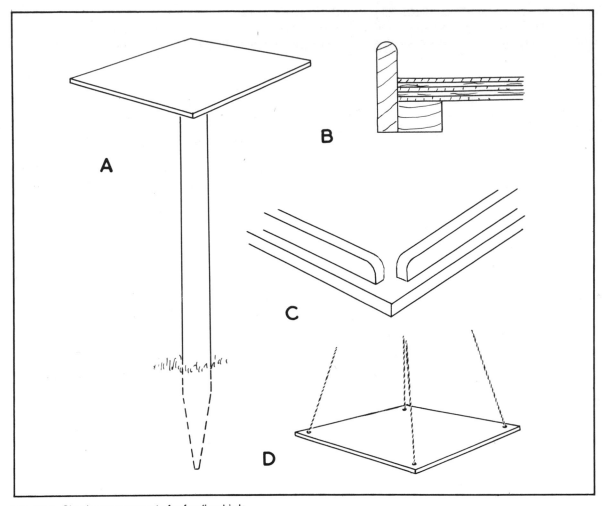

Fig. 13-1. Simple arrangements for feeding birds.

those someone elsewhere will want to house. You could get some advice from a local naturalist on the size of the box and hole that you should provide. If not, look at bird houses available in shops and measure or estimate sizes before making your own. This will also show you if it is worthwhile making single or multiple houses. Some birds like to nest in isolation while others are quite happy in groups. Some birds only use a nest long enough to lay eggs and rear their young. Then the whole family will fly away. Others will stay around a nesting place much longer. Your local naturalist can tell you which birds you are likely to have most success with and whether to make single or multiple houses or boxes. For instance, a wren will prefer a single house, but for martins you can make an apartment block—if you prefer.

SIMPLE FEEDERS

Birds will feed off a level board about 48 inches above the ground. If you make it too small, they will tend to push food over the edge. Most of them will not venture on to the ground to eat it and it will be wasted. A square of 15 inches is about the advisable minimum, but 24 inches would be better. This can be exterior grade plywood about ½ of an inch thick. It does not have to be square; a rectangle or circle can be used.

You can drive a post into the ground. Then cut its top level and nail the plywood to it (Fig. 13-1A). Strips around the edges will make a rim, forming a shallow box (Fig. 13-1B), and prevent water from being absorbed into the edges of the plywood if waterproof glue is used as well as nails or screws. You could put strips on top and cut

272

them short at the corners (Fig. 13-1C). This will make it easier to brush the table clean. Whatever rim you fit, round the top edges. Most birds perch on tree branches and their claws are adapted to a round surface rather than angular ones.

The board does not have to be supported from the ground. If there is a convenient tree branch, it could be hung from it using rope through holes at the corners (Fig. 13-1D). If the four ropes can go to different supporting places or be taken in pairs to different parts of a branch,

the board will not sway as much. An unsteady platform will scare some birds. You might be able to hang a board from a projecting arm from a building or other nearby object. If so, sling a rope and hang the board from it.

The feeder can be made portable. Instead of driving the post into the ground, it can have some sort of base. Then it can be lifted and moved easily. You can take it under cover in bad weather or it can be moved to different parts of a lawn for convenience in grass cutting.

Any base should extend far enough to ensure stabil-

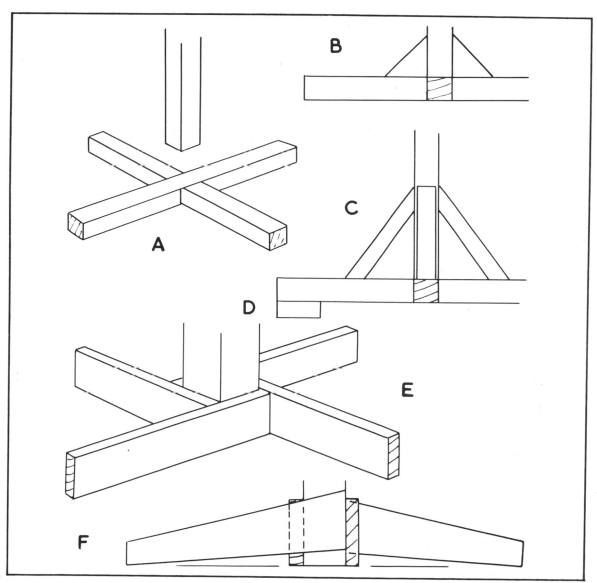

Fig. 13-2. Suggestions for feet to support bird tables.

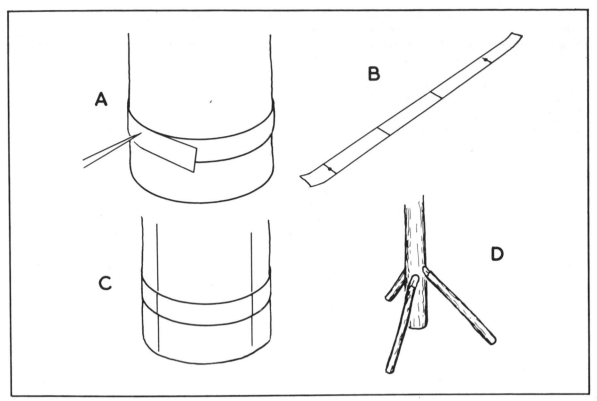

Fig. 13-3. Using a strip of paper to get three legs equally spaced round a post.

ity. Crossed legs ought to extend about 18 inches each way under a 48-inch post with a 24-inch square feeder. You could halve two pieces of the same section as the post (Fig. 13-2A). Then attach the post with a screw through and brackets all round (Fig. 13-2B). The brackets can be solid blocks or strips arranged further out (Fig. 13-2C). Nailing should provide all the strength needed, but you can cut joints if you want to show your skill. To allow for uneven ground, put feet under the ends (Fig. 13-2D).

Another arrangement of feet is made from flat pieces on the sides of the square post (Fig. 13-2E). They can extend squarely and either have feet attached or they might be given a slight slope (Fig. 13-2F) so that only the tips touch the ground and give support as far out as possible.

A round post could have similar feet to a square one or you could provide three feet with the advantage of freedom from wobble. To equally space three leg positions on a cylinder, wrap a strip of paper around and push a spike through the overlap (Fig. 13-3A). Open the strip and divide the distance between the spike holes into three (Fig. 13-3B). Wrap the paper around the post again and draw lines along it at the spacing on the paper (Fig. 13-3C).

You can arrange feet with rustic pieces to match a natural pole by tapering their ends to fit holes (in the manner described in Chapter 10). Do not join them in at the same level; otherwise the holes will run into each other. Use pieces that are too long. Then trim their ends to give level support after fitting (Fig. 13-3D). It does not matter if the slopes vary a little, but get a fairly even spread to the ends. The end of the post need not touch the ground.

ROOFED FEEDERS

A feeder should be kept fairly open all round. If you enclose a part, decayed food could accumulate there. Some birds will become suspicious of such an enclosure and they will stay away from the feeder. Another bird might decide that it is a good place for a nest, with resulting unhappiness for it and other visiting birds.

Support a roof on posts rather than on boards forming walls so that there is access all round. The simplest roof is flat, but give it some slope so it will shed water

(Fig. 13-4A). The minimum height under a roof should be 7 inches. Birds will be wary of too confined a space and they need height to throw their heads back when eating. If the roof is exterior plywood, posts about 1 inch square or round can be nailed through (Fig. 13-4B). Arrange the higher side toward the direction you want to view the feeding birds. If it is rain protection you are providing, make the roof at least as large as the platform. If it is shade from sun you are providing, it need only come over part of it.

A ridged roof is more attractive. A simple type can be made with exterior plywood (Fig. 13-5). Make the slope anything you prefer, but an angle of 45 degrees looks attractive. The roof shown is not as big as the table; birds like to have a surrounding area to alight on. Sizes shown are based on a 24 inch square platform, but exact sizes are not crucial and you can adjust them to suit available materials.

Cut a pair of roof ends; *gable* is the building term. Make the roof panels to overlap all round. Nail them to the ends. Then plane where they meet on the ridge so that you can put a strip on top and nail upward into it (Fig. 13-5A). Put a strip between the ends and attach this to two posts (Fig. 13-5B). These are held by screws driven upward through the platform (Fig. 13-5C). Be careful when squaring ends, so that the roof finishes level.

A central attachment only to a post will not be rigid enough. This is particularly true when you build up with a roof and other things. Brackets can be used. Metal shelf brackets can be screwed on or you can use strips of wood

with screws or nails through their beveled ends (Fig. 13-5D).

A roof of overlapping strips looks more like a full-size house and it has a more attractive appearance than pieces of plywood. In that case, settle on the size of strips. Then notch the ends to allow for them overlapping (Fig. 13-5E). Arrange the widths so one of the top strips overlaps the other and can be nailed to it. There will be a slight overhang at the bottom edges. You can put two narrow strips over the ridge (Fig. 13-5F) and let them project a little at the ends. If you can obtain sufficient, thin waney-edged pieces, they can be used on the roof to give an interesting effect—with wavy lines on the laps.

You could use slab offcuts from a mill to make a roof. Trim them parallel and use three or more overlapping on supports (Fig. 13-5G) instead of the steeper roof.

There are several additions you can make. Pieces of dowel rod can be extended from the roof ends as perches (Fig. 13-6A). Some birds like swinging perches. These could be lengths of ½-inch or ¾-inch dowel rod or you could remove the angles from square strips to make them approximately round. If they are slightly uneven and rough, they will be easier for claws to grip. Hanging can be by cord or fine chain. Chain looks better and will last longer. Arrange short or long hanging perches under the eaves of the roof (Fig. 13-6B). If they come at about half the height of the space, that should be about right. If you watch birds on the feeder, you will soon discover if the perches should be raised or lowered.

Some birds are attracted by hanging solid food or by

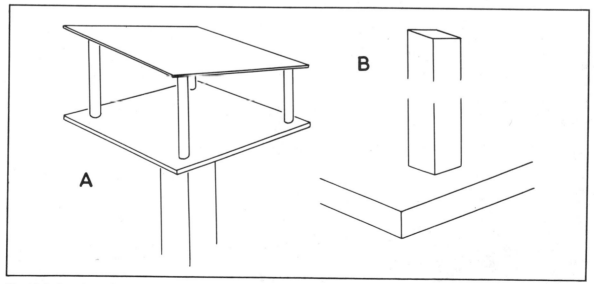

Fig. 13-4. A roofed bird feeder.

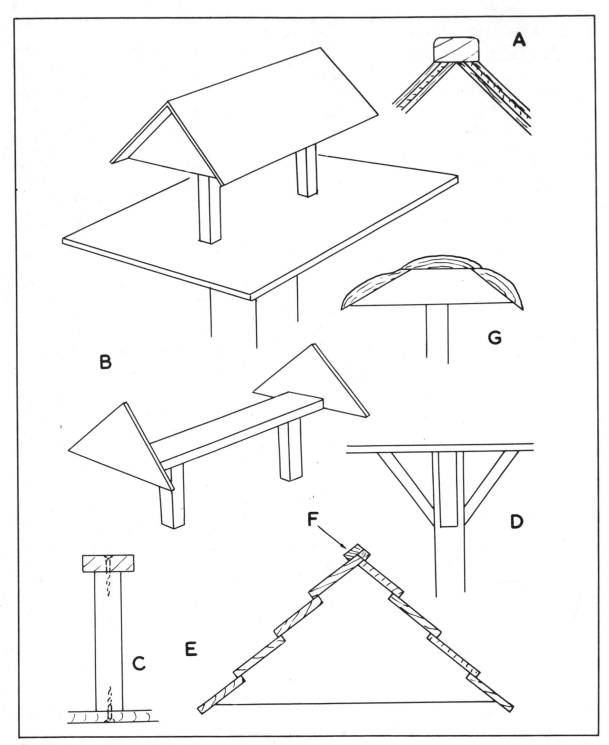

Fig. 13-5. Types of ridge-roofed bird feeders.

nuts enclosed in nets. You could arrange this on arms extending from the ends of the roof, but it would be better to keep the hanging food away from the surface of the platform (which may get congested). There could be diagonal pieces under the platform, extending a few inches with drilled ends for hanging food (Fig. 13-6C). These have a secondary use in preventing the platform from warping.

If the platform is made up of several boards, you will have to put cleats across. End ones can be extended and drilled for hanging food at the corners. (Fig. 13-6D). If there is a lip round the table, you could get similar results by extending the lips (Fig. 13-6E).

Other ideas for feeders might be described as whimsy. Examples are such things as having the covered part modeled on your own home or having dummy chimneys. You could include cutout trees on an extension of the platform. There could be a cutout of some other full-size feature nearby, but avoid anything that moves. Windmill sails rotating or a flag flying will drive birds away.

Coloring is a problem. Birds do not like the smell of varnish. If you can leave the feeder untreated, that will be best. If you want to treat it, the finish must be left to dry and then ventilated for quite a long time before birds will find it acceptable. Wood preservative has a smell that persists for a very long time. It is best not to use it. If you want to use paint, keep it for coloring the roof and the post. Leave the feeding surface untreated unless you are prepared to wait, possibly for months, for the paint to

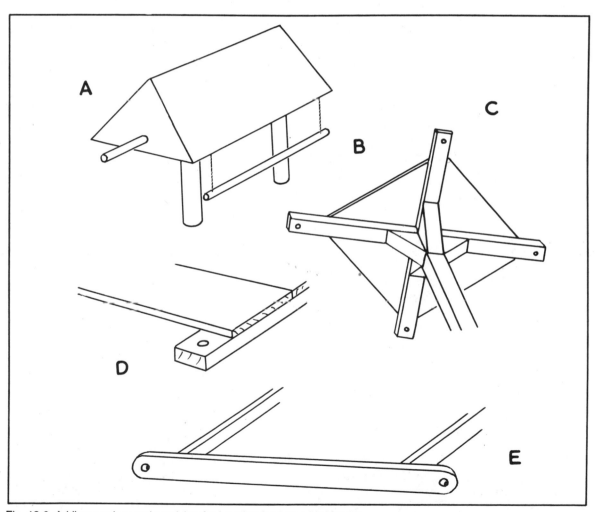

Fig. 13-6. Adding perches and provision for hanging food on a bird feeder.

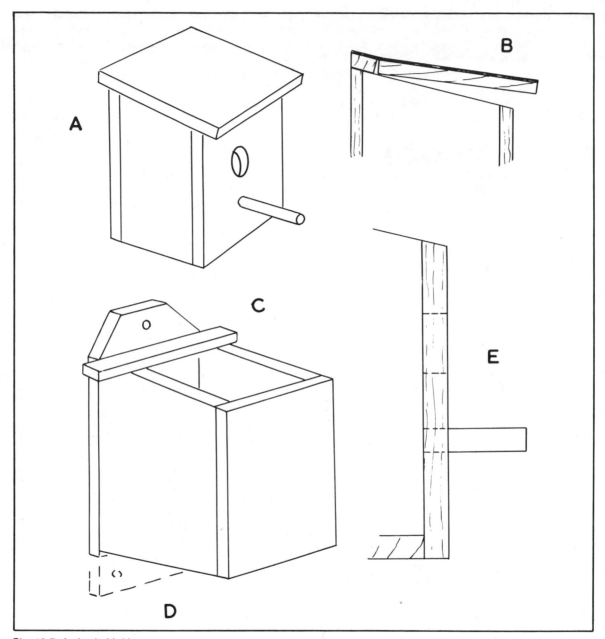

Fig. 13-7. A simple bird house.

become old enough for the birds not to bother about it. Do not use a high-gloss finish where they alight and eat. In any case, you only need paint the visible surfaces. Because of the need to allow a long time for paint to dry, the fall is the best time to do it. Then you are certain of the paint being free from odor in the spring.

SIMPLE BIRD HOUSES

A bird looking for a nesting place merely wants somewhere out of drafts, usually shaded from sunlight, and sheltered from predators. A box that has a big enough area, without being too large, and a hole of the right size should be attractive. Do not assume that there will be a rush of birds to move into the first house you provide. There is a certain amount of chance involved. You might not get a family in your bird house until next season.

One of the simplest bird houses is just a box with a sloping lid (Fig. 13-7A). Including the bottom within the sides is stronger than merely nailing it from below. With a sloping roof, there is less risk of rainwater settling and entering the house. If the roof is hinged, you will be able to open the box and clean it between seasons. Do not be tempted to visit an occupied box to inspect it. That would soon scare away the birds. One way of hinging the top is to cover it with rubber or flexible plastic (Fig. 13-7B) that will bend enough to act as a hinge and ensure waterproofness.

How the box is mounted depends on circumstances. If it goes on a post, you can nail down through the bottom. If it is to fit against a wall or tree, it helps to extend the back upward to take a nail or screw (Fig. 13-7C). A downward extension permits another nail to prevent swinging (Fig. 13-7D).

Most birds willing to accept a bird house for nesting only need a base about 4 inches square and an inside height not much more—say 6 inches. The size of the hole depends on the bird—and you should get local advice on this—but it will be about a 1-inch diameter. Arrange a perch about 1½ inch to 2 inches below this (Fig. 13-7E).

Some birds favor hollow trees. A box for them can be made from a log that has rotted through the center. It would not be impossible to hollow through a solid log, but having a hole already there permits fairly easy enlarging with chisels and gouges. You need to make a hole about 3 inches across, at least, so that you have to start with a log about 6 inches diameter. Cut a bottom to fit inside and hold it in place with a few nails. If the fit is not all it might be, put stopping around it. Avoid anything with a strong smell that will repel birds. Cut the top to a slope. If the lid is a section of log, the general effect will be rustic enough to fit a woodland setting (Fig. 13-8A).

The hole and perch can be similar to those for a box construction. Flatten the back of the house and its lid. One nail through the top of the log should be enough to hold it. A piece of leather or flexible plastic can be used as a lid hinge.

A compromise construction uses the outside offcuts from a mill. They can be left with bark on and the edges square enough to allow nailing together (Fig. 13-8B). The outside will then look much the same as a log and it will be suitable for blending into rural surroundings.

OTHER BIRD HOUSES

For your yard or a formal garden, it may be better to make a bird house that mounts on a post. Then you can design it as you prefer—with any decoration that suits the surroundings or your artistic ideas—providing you keep the needs of the birds in mind.

A variation on the box shape includes tapered sides and a roof sloping back from the front (Fig. 13-9A). This goes on to a post that can come below with a nail through the bottom of the box. It could go on the side of a post if you make it with the back upright and the tapers only at the sides and front (Fig. 13-9B). It helps to extend the back upward and downward to take screws (Fig. 13-9C).

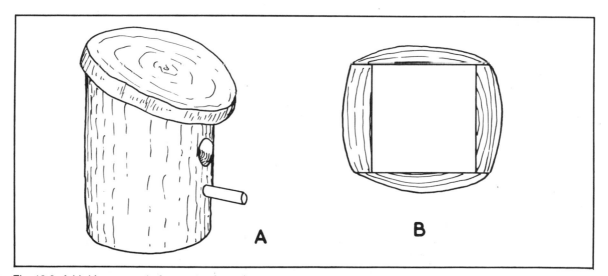

Fig. 13-8. A bird house made from natural wood.

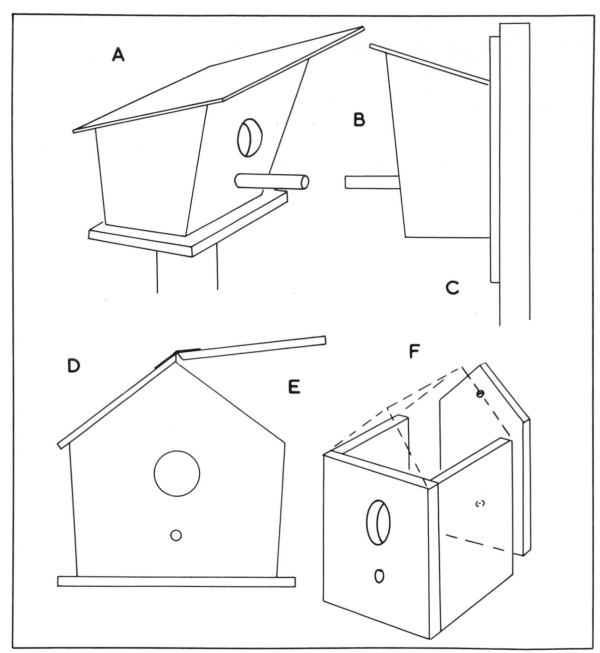

Fig. 13-9. Different styles of bird houses.

This sort of box looks good with a ridge roof (Fig. 13-9D). It can be made of plywood with one slope nailed down and the other hinged to it with rubber or plastic (Fig. 13-9E) to give access for cleaning.

A roof made of overlapping strips looks good, but you then have the problem of providing access for cleaning. You could make one side of the box removable by hinging it with a catch to keep it closed or by using noncorrodible screws so that it can be taken off occasionally. You could arrange the back to be screwed to the post. Then the rest of the house screws to it and can be drawn away (Fig. 13-9F).

The roof could be made up with the back and front notched to take the overlapping strips (Fig. 13-5E). It is also possible to make the whole roof into a lift-off lid, with the front and back overlapping the box part (Fig. 13-10D). It will stay there under its own weight or you can use two screws to ensure it will not come away in a high wind.

If you want to build a house to accommodate more than one nesting pair, it is easy to double up the basic box-type construction with two compartments alongside each other (Fig. 13-10A). Access can still be via a lid and the holes and perches should be for the individual birds. They may not like a communal perch.

A bird house on a post can be made square to accommodate four nests, but the compartments inside will

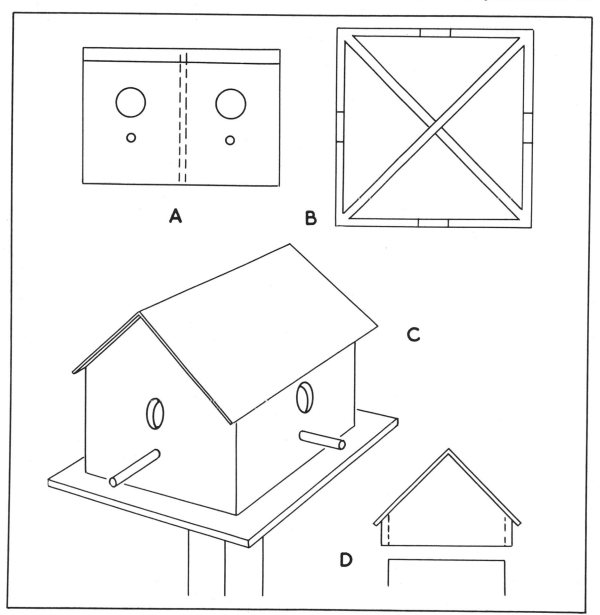

Fig. 13-10. Multiple bird houses.

281

have to be triangular (Fig. 13-10B). That will not matter providing they are large enough. The house would probably have to be 12 inches or 14 inches square for most small birds (Fig. 13-10C). A ridge roof could be made to lift off (Fig. 13-10D). It would probably be advisable to make the inside divisions high enough to provide privacy for each nest. If the birds like to nest close together they probably do not mind being accessible to each other.

A four-compartment bird house will be fairly heavy. The support needs to be strong. If it is a single post, have a base to the house like a feeder table. It could extend a short way all round for perching on. Join it to the post with metal shelf brackets or wood struts.

In some situations, it may be better to house two nests vertically. If it is against a wall, both entrances and perches will have to be on the front. Some birds, however, will cope with entrances on opposite sides. If the openings go on the front, they can be staggered toward the sides (Fig. 13-11A). The roof can be a single slope or a ridge.

If the two-tier box is to go above a post, the entrances can be at the back and front (Fig. 13-11B). Access to the top can be via the opening roof, but for the lower part you must arrange a door or removable panel.

If it is martins you want to attract, they will come in large numbers. If one pair find your box, many more will hope to move in as well. A martin house can have as many compartments as you would like to build. You could make a large structure on a central post, but it will usually be better to arrange tiers of compartments that might go against a wall. The birds will be attracted more if it is supported on posts away from buildings and fairly high. You could make two separate blocks of compartments and attach them on opposite sides of a pair of posts.

The compartments can be up to about 6-inch cubes and the holes can be fairly large. Other birds are unlikely to approach a resident flock of martins. You could put ledges for alighting on instead of individual perches. Such an assembly could then be made up of blocks of four or more arranged horizontally and mounted over each other (Fig. 13-11C). The top row could be protected by a separate lift-off sloping roof (Fig. 13-11D).

Not all birds want individual privacy. Some are happy to live communally. You might not want to encourage pigeons, because of the damage they do to crops, but our medieval forefathers kept pigeons as a source of winter meat. The birds lived in giant pigeon coops where there were many entrance holes and the building was lined with open nesting compartments.

If it is that sort of bird you want to attract, you can make something that looks like a dollhouse with several quite large entrances with flat shelves outside for landing on. Larger birds prefer that to round perches. The entrances can be about 4 inches high and 3 inches wide, depending on the birds, while inside the walls you make divided shelves to allow about 6 inches square space for each bird—all facing inward and without fronts. To be much use, this house has to be fairly large. It needs substantial supports, but arrange it high and make sure no animal can climb it and get into the house.

As with feeders, remember that most birds will not accept paint unless it is very old. So far as possible, let the insides be plain wood. In most cases, avoid glue that will leave an odor for some time. Paint might be needed to give the house the appearance you want. A white body and a green or red roof can look attractive, but you would need to do the painting a long time before birds will move in (many months before is advised).

WALL FEEDERS

A bird table on a post standing in isolation can be attractive as a garden feature, but some birds will favor a more sheltered position. There might not be space for a free-standing table, but you might be able to mount one on a house wall or against a fence. Of course, you should make sure that you do not choose a position where a cat or other animal could walk along a wall and get down to the table.

Wall feeders can be almost any size and you can make them to suit available wood. A small one could lose much of the food you put on it as birds scratch it and toss it about. There is also a possibility that a bird might take it over as a nest site. Some birds are not attracted by closed boxes with holes as entrances. They prefer a more open site. If you hope to appeal to them, you could make smaller versions of the feeders and see if you can entice birds to build a nest on them. You are unlikely to give birds the wrong ideas if the feeding area is upwards of 12 inches square.

Exterior plywood can be used throughout these feeders (although any available solid wood could be used). If you are using wide pieces of solid wood, there will have to be battens across to prevent warping. The designs shown are all suitable for ½-inch exterior or marine plywood. This is an opportunity for using up offcuts from larger work.

The first design is really a shelf (Fig. 13-12A). It is shown angular, but you could round the outlines of the back and brackets. The back could be about 15 inches square and the shelf could extend about 12 inches. Screw and glue the parts together. The border of the tray should

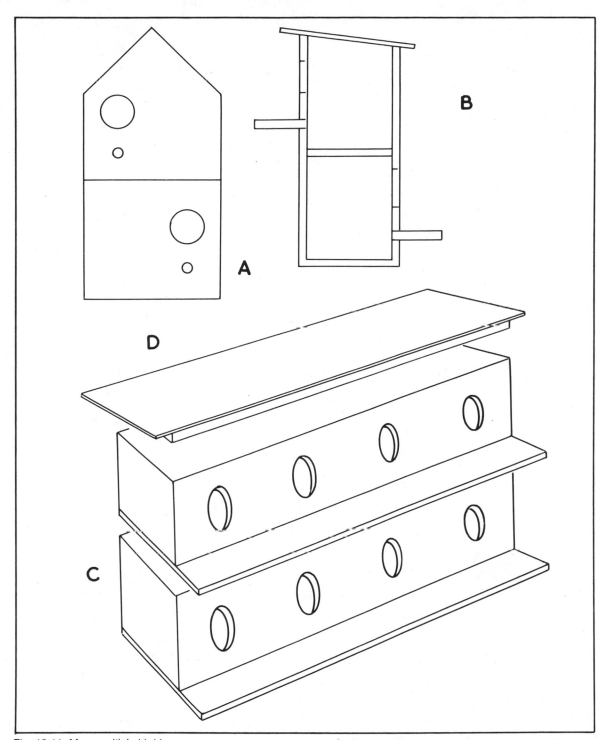

Fig. 13-11. More multiple bird houses.

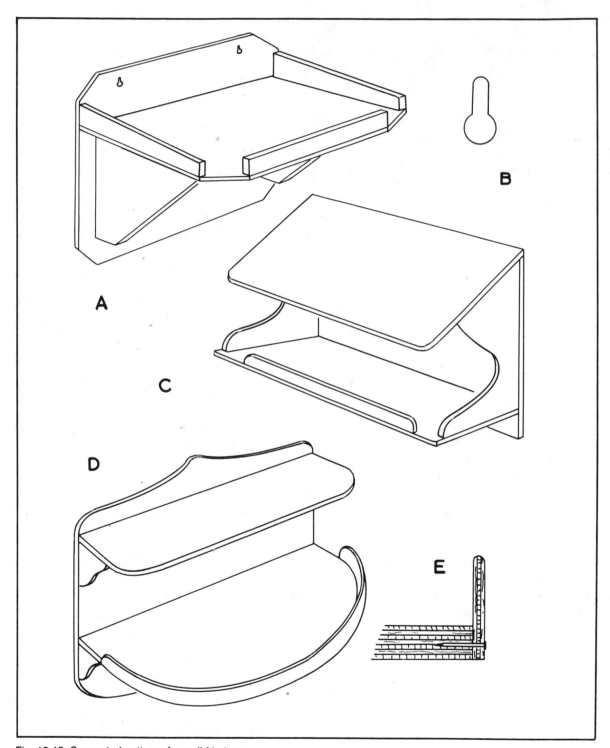

Fig. 13-12. Suggested patterns for wall feeders.

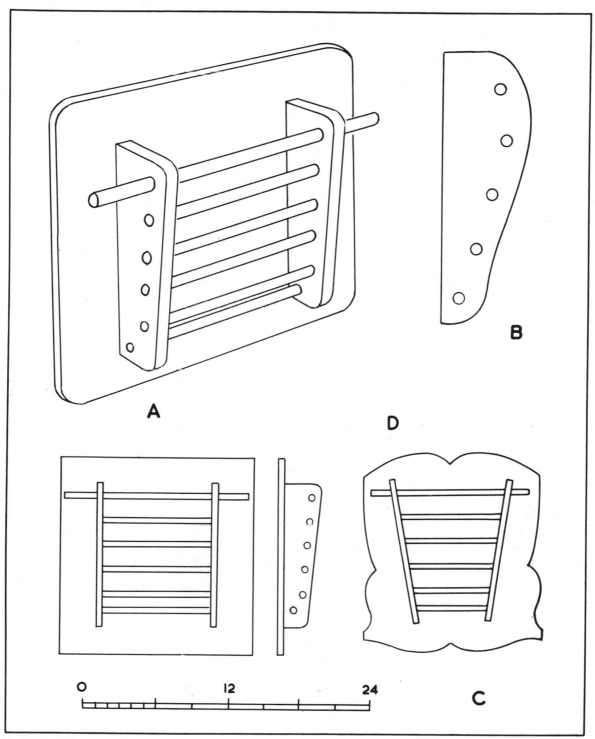

O 12 24

Fig. 13-13. Flat rod feeders.

not be less than ½ inch thick to provide a comfortable perching size for birds as they land. Round the top edges and corners. Leave the corners open for easy wiping out, but do not make the gaps too wide or food could be lost.

It is helpful to be able to take down the feeder for cleaning or storage. One way of arranging this without the need for tools is to hang it from two screws using keyhole slots (Fig. 13-12B). Use round-head screws projecting from the wall far enough to easily take the thickness of the back of the feeder. Drill large holes to easily clear the screw heads and make slots that will slide over the necks of the screws long enough not to allow the wood to be unintentionally released by a knock.

A roof over the feeder will shelter if from sun or rain (Fig. 13-12C). Do not make the roof too low or the birds will not like the rather confined space. Similarly, do not enclose the ends too much. Even if you do not curve the sides, as shown, cut them back so that there is easy entry all round. Take the roof over the back board so that there can be no gap for water to run through. Hanging can be by keyhole slots underneath the roof. With this and the first feeder, you could fit projecting dowel rods to act as perches at the sides.

A two-level feeder has the advantage of separating the birds. Ideally, smaller ones will use the upper shelf (Fig. 13-12D). Perhaps food falling from it will land on the lower shelf. This table could be made with straight edges, but if you have a jigsaw or a bandsaw you might prefer to make a curved outline. As shown, the top shelf is parallel, but it could be made as a smaller version of the lower one. There might be a rim to it, but if it is fairly large it could be left open.

The bottom shelf is shown elliptical. It needs a rim and it could be made with thin plywood, cut with the outside veneers having their grain upright, to ease bending (Fig. 13-12E). Nail fairly closely all around.

Some birds prefer to cling to an upright feeder and peck through openings. With the feeders just described, you could put hooks at the ends or front and hang net bags of food there. For some foods, such as pieces of suet or other fatty things, it may be better to have a series of rails that act as perches while feeding. Dowel rod is the obvious choice; ⅜-inch diameter rods will provide a grip for most birds' claws.

The basic design shown (Fig. 13-13A) has two uprights attached to a back about 16 inches square. The pieces that take the dowel rods are tapered. If they were parallel, the food would tend to settle at the bottom. One dowel rod is set in at the bottom to prevent food from falling right through. You could put a piece of solid wood across there if you think the food you intend to offer would fall past a rod. Drill through the two sides together to make them match. Assemble by screwing through from the back. Make two keyhole slots for hanging. Preferably they should be about one-fourth the distance down each side. The top dowels can extend to form perches, but the others are glued in and cut off flush.

There would be some advantage in shaping the outlines of the sides (Fig. 13-13B) so that the capacity near the top is greater and there would be less tendency for the food to settle lower. The supports could be mounted so that they slope toward each other (Fig. 13-13C). They can have straight or curved tapers that help to stop food slipping down and giving a greater capacity. This way you do not have to replenish the feeder as often. The only problem with that arrangment is drilling the dowel holes. You cannot drill through both sides together.

One way of getting them to match is to first drill straight through both sides pieces together with a small drill (less than ⅛ inch) to locate the positions. Then use a drill to match the dowel size entered at the required angle. With a drill press, you will be able to tilt the table or you can use an adjustable bevel standing beside the drill as a guide for freehand drilling. Utmost precision is not required.

The last example is shown with a shaped outline (Fig. 13-13D). If you have the means of cutting curves, you can use your own ideas about shapes. Work each side of a centerline. You can draw half the outline on a piece of paper and turn it over to get the shape of the other side.

With any of the designs, it will probably be best to leave the wood untreated so as not to scare birds by the smell of paint. With plywood you can lengthen its life by sealing the edges. You could use varnish and leave it long enough for the smell to disappear, but waterproof glue brushed on will also seal the grain.

Chapter 14

Children's Equipment

WHERE THE ADULT APPROACH TO OPEN-AIR AC-tivities is often directed towards resting—and outdoor furniture consists mainly of seats of many sorts—children want to be more active. There will be times when children are prepared to just sit, particularly when eating, but any equipment that helps them enjoy the expenditure of energy will have more appeal.

If you know that children will be using the furniture you are making, you can allow for their smaller size without spoiling the chairs, tables, and other things for adult use. Where a chair for an adult would be about 16 inches high, you could drop to perhaps 14 inches without making it uncomfortable for an adult while bringing it nearer the needs of a child. Similarly a table that would normally be 30 inches high could come down a couple of inches and be more reasonable for either user.

Loungers and other furniture where the user reclines will not usually need alteration. A child will happily stretch full length on a surface too big for him. Nevertheless, there is a case for making junior furniture. It can be justified for the satisfaction it gives to a child or his parents, but you must remember that children grow up—often too rapidly. If the thing can be passed on to a younger child, a smaller version of an adult furniture item could be worthwhile.

A child will probably treat his furniture more roughly than an adult would. If a seat or other item is scaled down, sections of wood should not always be scaled down as much as the general dimensions. A child can also find uses for the furniture that you never intended. Allow for a table or seat being found in any attitude because it might need to serve as a car, a boat, or perhaps a spacecraft, with the child's imagination playing the largest part. From the constructional point of view, this means that you have to build in strength in directions that would not apply in normal use.

One problem is keeping a child's toys within bounds. A playhouse might keep them together, but in fine weather a child will want to be outside and all his toys go out as well. You might find them in flower beds and other places you would rather they did not go. If you can make some sort of play place that appeals to the child your problem will be solved—at least partly.

PLAY ENCLOSURES

A simple box has limited appeal. If you make the box look

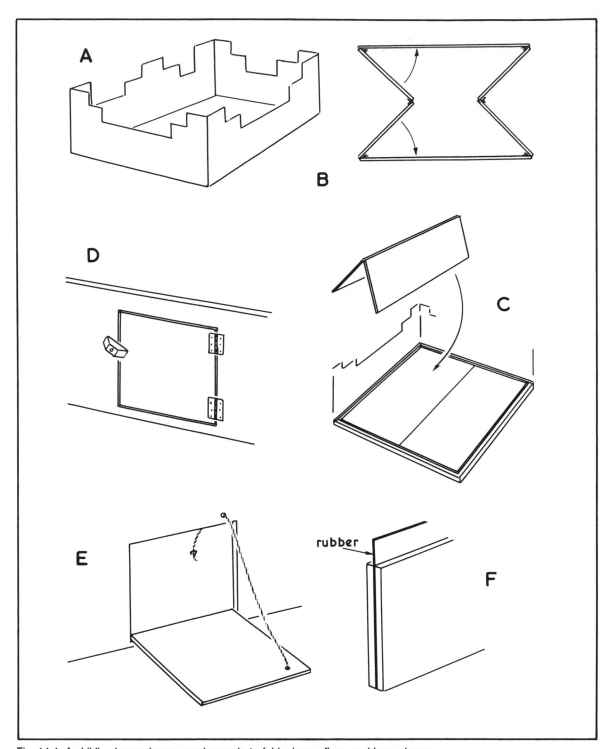

Fig. 14-1. A child's play enclosure can be made to fold, given a floor, and have doors.

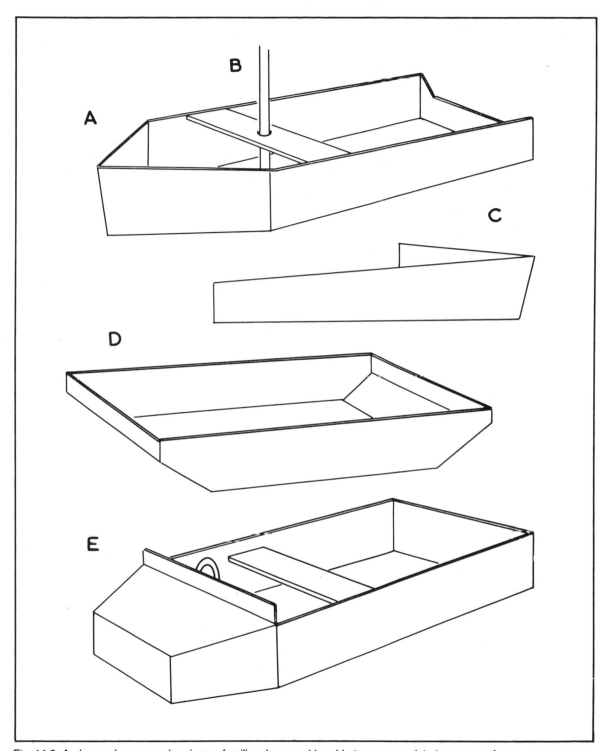

Fig. 14-2. A play enclosure can be given a familiar shape and be able to accommodate toys or sand.

like something else, its attraction is increased. It could have its edges cut to look like a fort or stockade (Fig. 14-1A), but be careful of including points or sharp corners on which a child could hurt himself.

You could make the box without a bottom or arrange it so that you could take it apart. It can serve as a playpen for a young child and it can be folded for storage. Be careful that any folding and securing arrangements cannot hurt a child or be operated by him. Bolts with nuts that require a wrench will be more trouble than butterfly nuts or other easier fasteners, but there will be no risk of the young occupant finding a way out.

You could make a sort of playpen that looks like a fort with opposite sides folding inward (Fig. 14-1B). Then a fitted floor folds in half for storage, but holds the walls out when it is in place (Fig. 14-1C). If it is a small child who you want to keep within bounds, that is all there is to it. If you want the child to be able to get in and out, there could be a door in one side. It could open at one side and be held with a simple catch. A fairly large turnbutton made of wood will be better for small hands than a more conventional fastener (Fig. 14-1D). The door could be hinged at the bottom so it could be pulled up by a rope like a drawbridge (Fig. 14-1E). It could hang from the top. That it could be pushed open and it will not need a fastener (Fig. 14-1F).

If the box is to hold sand or anything else in particle form, the bottom should be integral and there should be no gaps. The shape could follow the general lines of anything with which the child is familiar. There is no point in shaping it like an old-time steam locomotive if the child has never seen one. A boat outline is an obvious shape, but if you are in a place where boats are never seen that is not a good choice. It might be better to make the box look something like a car. You do not have to make any design very close to the original. A vague idea is enough to start a child's imagination working.

A boat shape can be just a box with a pointed end (Fig. 14-2A). You could put a board across to support a pole as a mast (Fig. 14-2B) or there could be a raised deck (Fig. 14-2C). The idea of going into a cabin under the deck might appeal to the young user, but make sure it is large enough for him to turn round and not get trapped.

That sort of boat box can be satisfactory as a play place. If you want it to be used with sand sometimes, it will be better if it is more open. A rectangular box can have sloped ends so it becomes more like a barge (Fig. 14-2D). There might be one or more seats across, but it would still be easy to empty when you want to clear it out.

A car or truck shape could have a taper forward, with a closed-in part and a steering wheel, then the area behind could be loaded with goods or passengers, possi-

bly on additional removable seats (Fig. 14-2E). The closed-in part could have a lid to give access to the "engine" or for storage.

CLIMBING FRAMES

Most children like climbing. They will climb trees, fences, and other places where you probably don't want them to go. If you provide some sort of climbing facility that presents a challenge, it brings their climbing under control. You can decide on the spacing of rails, the height, and the degree of difficulty involved. There has to be some skill, suited to the child's age, and often some apparent danger in his eyes even if you have arranged things so the risks are minimal.

You must make sure of stability by giving the frame such a broad base that a child could not tip it or by securing the frame to the ground. It could have feet driven into the ground or be bolted to brackets on a concrete base. A tapered frame has the advantage of bringing the child further within the base area as he climbs higher. The tipping effect would be greater as the child got higher on a vertical frame. The structure would be more dependent on attachment to the ground.

A tapered frame could be made from natural poles. This has the advantage of being inexpensive and it will fit in better with many surroundings. You have to design it to suit the available poles, but do not make it too small. See Table 14-1. Longer poles should not be less than 2 inches diameter, but do not use very thick poles for higher positions. Here small hands could have difficulty in gripping. Taper in all directions (Fig. 14-3A). You could have the end faces upright if the frame is to be more of an assault course for more than one child to cross over at a time.

Strip all bark from the poles. You need not aim at a sanded surface, but make sure that there are no splinters or rough spots that could harm soft skin. When you have cut a pole to the length you want, bevel all around any end that will be exposed. That does two things: it gets rid of roughness and reduces the risks of splitting.

It would be possible to assemble by merely nailing, but it will be better for securing the horizontal rails to the uprights to notch them so that the downward thrust from anyone climbing is taken by the wood to wood joint as well as by the nail (Fig. 14-3B). The notches need not make a precision fit, providing the load-carrying surfaces are in contact.

At the top, the sloping uprights will cross and be lightly notched into each other (Fig. 14-3C). Then the final rail can rest in the V, with nails to prevent movement.

Table 14-1. Materials List for Tapered Climbing Frame.

4 legs	4	×	120	×	2
1 top	4	×	74	×	2
2 rails	3	×	74	×	2
2 rails	3	×	82	×	2
2 rails	3	×	90	×	2
2 rails	3	×	50	×	2
2 gussets	7	×	14	×	1

If the frame will be permanently located, the bottoms of the posts can be set into the ground by pointing (Fig. 14-3D) and driving or by digging holes and refilling around the wood. Those ends will resist thrust in soft or loose soil better than pointed ones.

If you want to be able to move the frame, there could be pieces driven into the ground vertically for lashing or bolting to the posts (Fig. 14-3E). If the frame is to stand

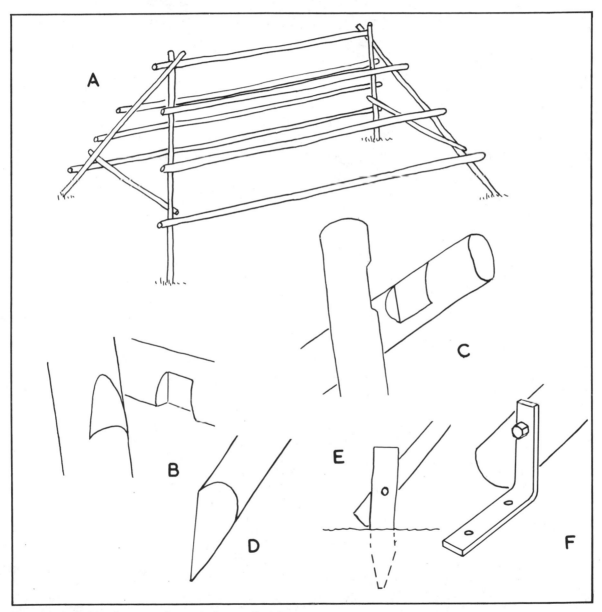

Fig. 14-3. A climbing frame can be made from rustic poles.

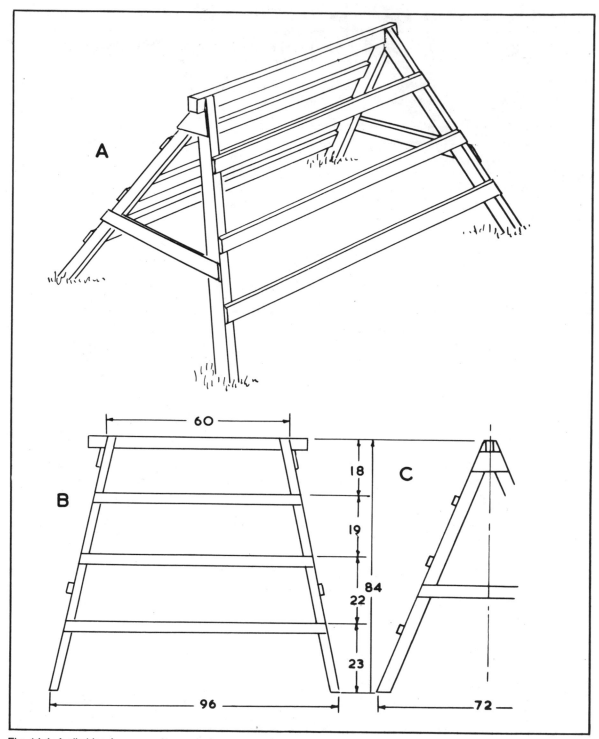

Fig. 14-4. A climbing frame can be made from squared wood.

on a hard base, angle brackets could take the bolts (Fig. 14-3F).

The frame of generally similar form could be made from standard sizes of planed wood (Fig. 14-4A). The sections you use will depend on the size of the frame, but do not use less than 2 × 2 inches for rails or 2 × 3 inches for the posts. For a large assembly, as illustrated in Fig. 14-4B, the posts are 2 × 4 inches and the rails are 2 × 3 inches. Choose straight wood without large knots. Plane off sharpness along all edges. When you have cut the wood to length, round all corners that will be exposed.

The spacing of rails should allow for a child standing on one rail and reaching for the second one above. Depending on the child, this means a spacing of somewhere between 15 and 24 inches. The spacing does not have to be the same all the way up. You can consider it safer to have rails closer near the top (Fig. 14-4C).

Although you can set out the intended shapes full size or to scale, it is simplest to set up the four uprights with the top rail and get the locations of joints and rail lengths from that temporary assembly.

At the top, allow for the legs being notched on each side of the top rail, with a strengthening piece across (Fig. 14-5A). The rail is extended and rounded.

Where the other rails come, there are shallow notches in both parts (Fig. 14-5B). Do not halve the parts together because that would cut too much away and could leave a weakness. The ends of the rails could be made a little too long and planed level after assembly.

At the ends it should be sufficient to use single rails, notched into the legs in the same way, unless you want to provide more rails for climbing there.

If the posts are to go into the ground, make points by tapering on the outsides only (Fig. 14-5C). That will bring the cuts near vertical and make driving easier.

If a climbing frame with vertical sides is to stand freely, it should be broad in relation to its height and be of fairly heavy construction so that a child climbing at one side cannot pull the whole thing over by his weight (Fig. 14-6A). You might be able to arrange a central crossbar that could be secured to the ground directly if it is at floor level or by a lashing (Fig. 14-6B).

A climbing frame does not necessarily have to be to a great height to provide enjoyment. It might be possible to have platforms so that a child can experiment with routes upward or pretend that a platform is a floor in his house or a lookout point. Rails in such an assembly could be of fairly light section (Fig. 14-6C) with tenoned joints at the ends or notches into the surface (Fig. 14-6D). In a small frame, you could use round rods taken right through the upright at some points (Fig. 14-6E).

Platforms need not be permanent. It might be possible to move them to other positions, but make sure that there are enough stops to locate them so they are unlikely to be knocked away in use. Plywood platforms with stiffening pieces underneath could be made (Fig. 14-6F).

A frame could be made in take-down form, with four sides assembled as units, so you can bolt through the corners (Fig. 14-6G).

SWING

A child's swing needs to be very securely mounted. The action of even a light body being swung puts a considerable backward and forward load on the attachment of the ropes (which is transferred to the feet). To be free-standing and safe, the feet should have a very large spread; probably more than could be accommodated in many places. It is better to regard securing to the ground as essential. Loads the other way—square to the direction of swinging—are not as great, but you must allow for some racking strains in that direction and build accordingly.

In a typical swing (Fig. 14-7A), the legs at each side are given a good spread. Then they slope toward each other in front view (Fig. 14-7B). Height has to be something of a compromise. A very low crossbar would obviously give too short a swinging stroke for the user to be satisfied. A very high crossbar would give a good swinging stroke, but possibly more than parents would want and the construction would be more lofty than would be acceptable.

A total height of about 8 feet should suit the needs of a young child. Construction is very similar to that of the climbing frame, but the joint between the crossbar and the legs needs stiffening to withstand probable sideways strains. There could be a metal bracket inside the angle (Fig. 14-8A) or the crossbar could be extended and a wooded strut taken to it at each side (Fig. 14-8B), to get the same effect. See Table 14-2.

The legs have a rail across at about the seat height. Besides bracing, it stops anyone from inadvertently walking into the swinging seat from the side. If you prefer, you could add another rail as a barrier higher up at each side.

The seat can be a plain board of solid wood or plywood, with battens across underneath where the rope holes will come (Fig. 14-8C). Drill to suit the chosen rope and countersink so the risk of chafing is reduced.

The seat has to be hung at a height that allows the young user to reach the ground for getting on and off and for stopping. Modern synthetic rope—which is very

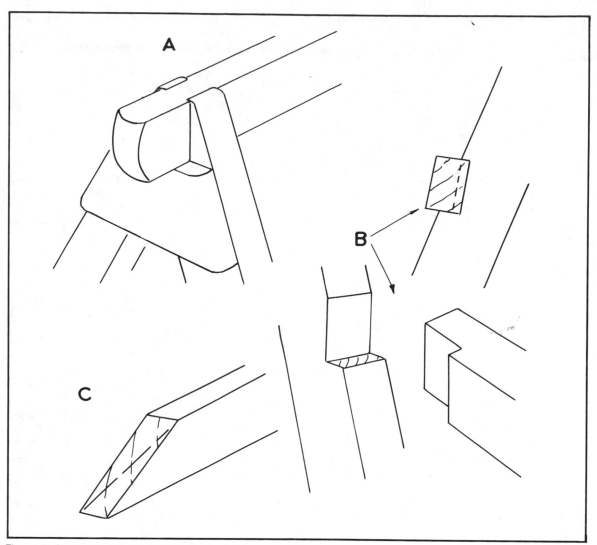

Fig. 14-5. Constructional details of a climbing frame.

strong and rot resistant—will suit most needs, but light chain could be used.

Ideally, the rope should be spliced. If you have to knot it, follow the same outline. The rope goes down through one hole in the seat and up the other side to be spliced or knotted back into itself about 24 inches above the seat (Fig. 14-8D). That is better than separately knotting underneath.

At the top, it is best to use eyebolts through the beam; ⅜-inch diameter eyebolts will do (Fig. 14-8E). The rope is best knotted or spliced round a *thimble*. A thimble is a grooved metal shape that protects the rope

from chafe (Fig. 14-8F). It is linked to the eyebolt with a *shackle*. The shackle is a D-shaped piece with a screwed pin (Fig. 14-8G). Use lock nuts on the eyebolts above large washers and burr the ends of the screws through the shackles to prevent them working loose.

SLIDE

A slide can be combined with a climbing frame, but you have to be careful how it is arranged—particularly for small children. There should be protection at the top so that the child is enclosed and has plenty to hold until he releases himself to slide down. An individual slide can be

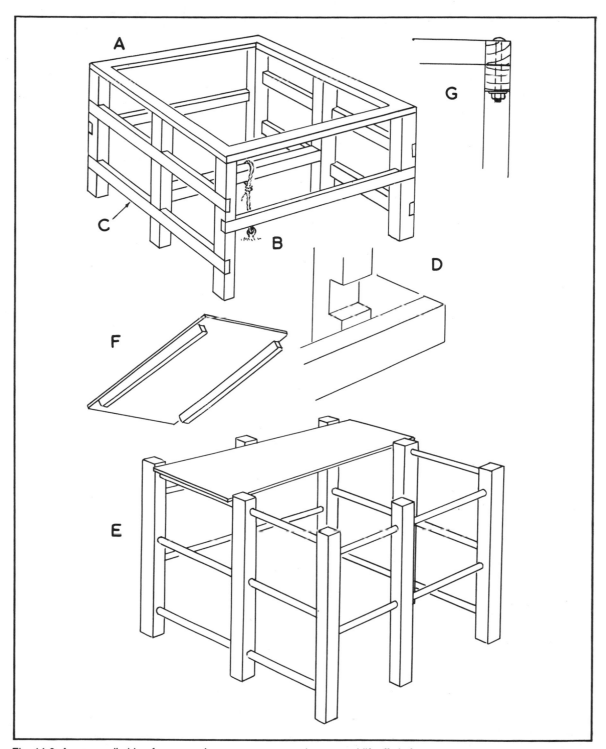

Fig. 14-6. A square climbing frame can have square or round rungs and lift-off platforms.

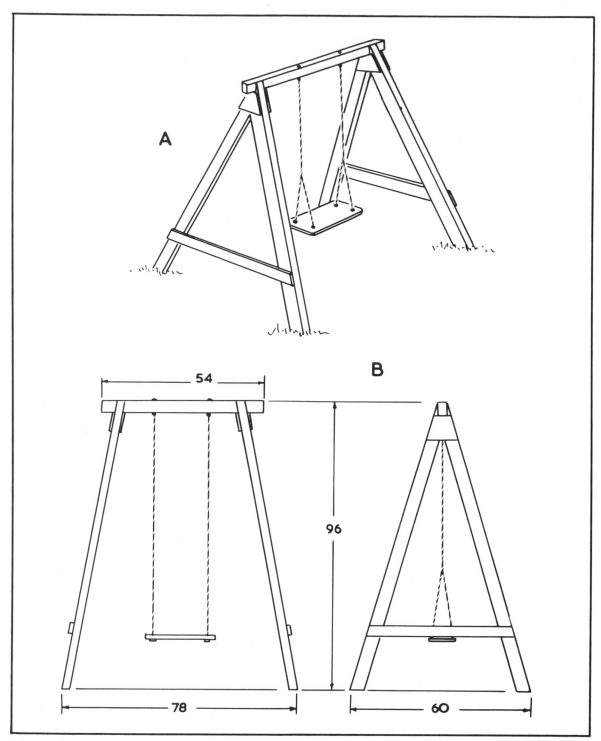

Fig. 14-7. Supports for a swing must be rigidly arranged.

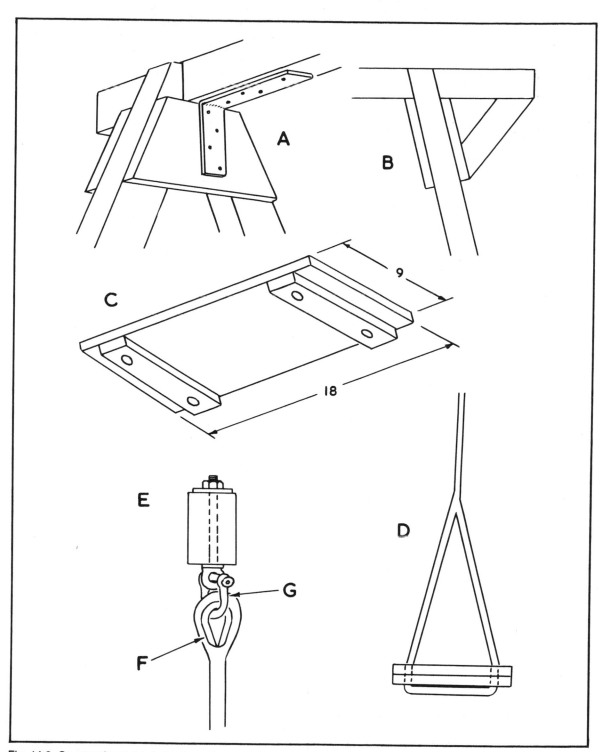

Fig. 14-8. Constructional details for the swing.

Table 14-2. Materials List for Swing.

4 legs	4	×	130	× 2
1 top	4	×	56	× 2
4 gussets	7	×	14	× 2
1 seat	9	×	20	× 1
2 seat battens	2	×	10	× 1
2 side rails	3	×	60	× 2

made as a tower from which it is possible to remove the slide part to reduce the size for storage.

This slide shown in Fig. 14-9A is big enough to give a young child a thrill, but not so high that his parents may get worried. As with swings and climbing frames, the posts ought to be attached to the ground. If that is impossible, there can be a broad spread of cross members under them.

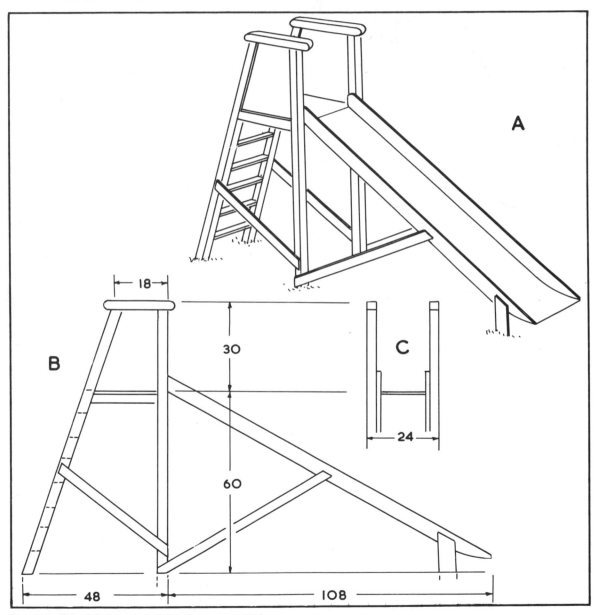

Fig. 14-9. This slide is intended to suit a young child.

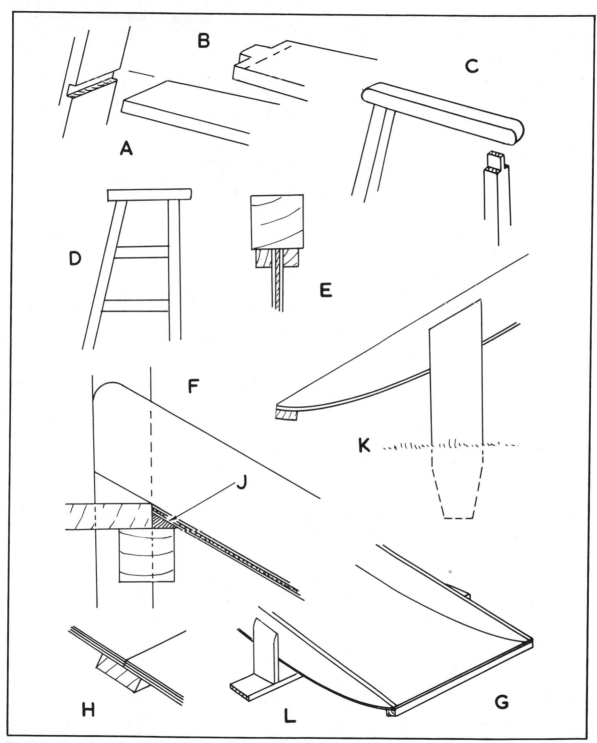

Fig. 14-10. Constructional details of the slide.

Table 14-3. Materials List for Slide.

2 legs	3	×	120	×	3	
2 legs	3	×	130	×	3	
2 tops	3	×	26	×	3	
2 platform rails	3	×	30	×	3	
2 platform rails	3	×	25	×	3	
1 platform	24	×	30	×	¼ plywood	
2 side panels	24	×	30	×	¼ plywood	
7 threads	4	×	25	×	1	
2 tower braces	3	×	50	×	1	
2 slide sides	5	×	140	×	1	
2 slide bottoms	19	×	70	×	½ plywood	
2 slide feet	5	×	30	×	1	
2 slide braces	3	×	70	×	1	
4 slide stiffeners	2	×	22	×	1	

Do not make the slide too steep. A more shallow slope gives a longer ride in a given height and brings the user down with less of a bump if he falls off the end. The sizes shown in Fig. 14-9B and Table 14-3 give a reasonable height and angle.

Treat the tower as a separate construction. The side toward the slide is upright while the other side slopes to form a ladder. Flat treads are shown; each goes into dado grooves (Fig. 14-10A). It will be strongest if the bottom tread also has a tenon going through and wedged (Fig. 14-10B). The platform is either plywood or several pieces of wood making up the width, supported on rails between the uprights. As you lay out the treads, arrange that every step the climber makes is the same height—all the way from the ground to the top of the platform—so that you have equal space between top surfaces.

The tower sides continue up to provide side protection at the platform and are tenoned into rails that extend slightly (Fig. 14-10C). You can put another rail at each side intermediately (Fig. 14-10D) or fill the sides with plywood. It could be merely nailed inside or fitted into grooves in the wood. Simpler than that is to enclose it between strips (Fig. 14-10E).

When the tower is erected, arrange diagonal braces from the center of the ladder sides to near the bottom of the uprights. They will have to clear other braces going to the slide.

The slide sides go between the uprights of the tower (Fig. 14-9C and 10F). The slide surface is plywood, with two pieces to make up the length, unless you can get material greater than standard lengths. Round the tops where they come between the tower sides so that there is nothing rough to hurt the user. At the bottom, make a long curve so the plywood sweeps to near parallel with the floor (Fig. 14-10G). You could build on a short flat section if you prefer. Otherwise, the child's feet hit the ground and he stands upright. If not, he only falls a few inches.

Join the plywood to the slide sides with glue and fairly close nailing. Where the plywood joint comes, put a batten across underneath (Fig. 14-10H) and other similar ones equally spaced—if more stiffness is needed.

At the top, the plywood should come level with the platform and will need a tapered packing underneath to make a firm joint (Fig. 14-10J). At the bottom, there could be two posts driven into the ground (Fig. 14-10K) or a support on the surface—with a cross piece (Fig. 14-10L). Put a strip across under the plywood to keep its end straight. Keep the top edges of the supports far enough below the tops of the slide sides to be clear of young hands. Arrange struts to the bottom of the tower and keep their edges equally low.

Round the top edges of the slide sides and go over the whole assembly to remove sharpness and roughness before painting or varnishing.

Chapter 15

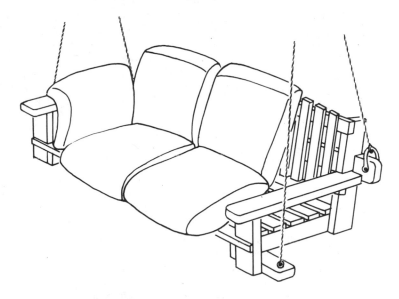

Other Items

ONE ATTRACTION OF MAKING OUTDOOR FURNI-ture is the scope for adapting and altering things that are already there or that can be moved around to suit. Tree stumps can be left after felling and their tops can be cut to make seats or leveled to support a tabletop or a plant holder. Trimmings from tree felling can be salvaged before they are thrown on a fire. Even bent branches can suggest some special construction.

The greatest use in outdoor furniture is for seating. This is closely followed by tables. There are also situations where you will want to provide shelves or even hooks for hanging clothing. You can make racks for hanging tools. What you make depends largely on what you visualize from the materials at hand.

There are several associated items that are not strictly called furniture, but they use similar constructions. These include tools for gathering grass or for other outdoor purposes. Some things can be made for an immediate purpose and then discarded. An example is a toasting fork for use at a campfire. Our rural forefathers made many things using the outdoor furniture techniques. They provide interesting items to reproduce.

SEATS AROUND TREES

Many tales from medieval times, and some not as far back, picture the oldest inhabitants or the village yokels sitting on seats around an old oak tree. A seat arranged around a tree is attractive. It does not have to completely encircle the tree, but that is common. If a tree is close to a fence, there might not be enough space. If there is space, no one would want to sit facing the fence. In such a case, the seat can be made only part of the circumference, but the method of construction is the same.

In general, it is inadvisable to use the tree as part of the construction. Driving nails into the tree could harm it. The tree is growing. As the tree gets bigger over the years, the seat built into it would become distorted or broken. The diameter of a hardwood tree does not increase very rapidly. If you are dealing with an established tree and allow a few inches clearance all around, that will probably be enough for the life of the seat—say 10 years. Younger softwood trees can grow more rapidly, but you would be starting with quite a small trunk and you would not make the seat a close fit to start. There would be more than enough clearance to allow for growth.

It would not be impossible to make a round seat, but you would then have to cut seat slats curved from wide boards (with a considerable amount of waste). You could not make the sections very long. Supports would have to be arranged fairly frequently around the circle to support the joints and to make sure no short-grained wood is projecting where it could be broken off in use. Making a fully circular seat is an interesting carpentry exercise, but it is wasteful of materials and not usually worthwhile. A multisided shape serves just as well and is easier to make accurately, with all straight parts, so waste is minimal.

How many sides to allow for depends on the size. People each need about the same area of sitting space and back whatever the overall size of the seat. If the seat is to go around a young tree, the hole in the center does not have to be very large. Even if that need is quite small, you have to allow for the width of a person's back. At the absolute minimum that should be 12 inches. For a small tree, you could make a small seat with a square outline (Fig. 15-1A). That allows for four people sitting with their backs supported. There will be space between them, for others who cannot lean back or for picnic or work materials.

If the tree is larger, a square is not a good choice. The corner projections become greater and the useful sitting space is not laid out efficiently. The projecting corners, besides being of little use, are obstructions to passage around the tree. This is particularly true for children playing and running around. The next logical step is a hexagonal seat for an easy shape to work. There is no reason why you should not use a pentagon if you are prepared to deal with the less convenient angles.

If you use a hexagonal shape, to get 12 inch widths for the backs the diameter has to be about 24 inches across the points (Fig. 15-1B). If the tree needs a larger space, you will get proportionately wider backs for six people and that would add to comfort. There is no reason for moving on to seven or eight sides until the tree calls for a much greater size. Seven sides introduces similar awkward angles to five sides. Eight sides uses variations on 45 degrees so it is more convenient (Fig. 15-1C).

It is unlikely that you will want to make a seat with more than eight sides around a tree. In most cases, that size will be enough, but the same idea can be used for other continuous seats. You can completely encircle a flower bed or a rocky outcrop. Then the diameter could be considerable and the number of sides could be whatever the design requires. You have to arrange a seat about 15 inches back to front and a back width for each individual about the same. If you find that a preliminary layout produces a shape going on to rather sharp corners,

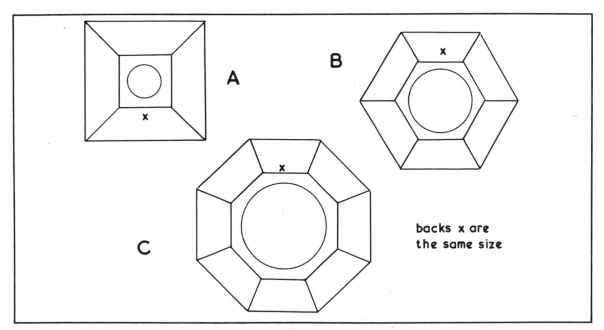

Fig. 15-1. Seats with backs of the same lengths cover different areas according to the number of sides, if arranged continuously round a tree.

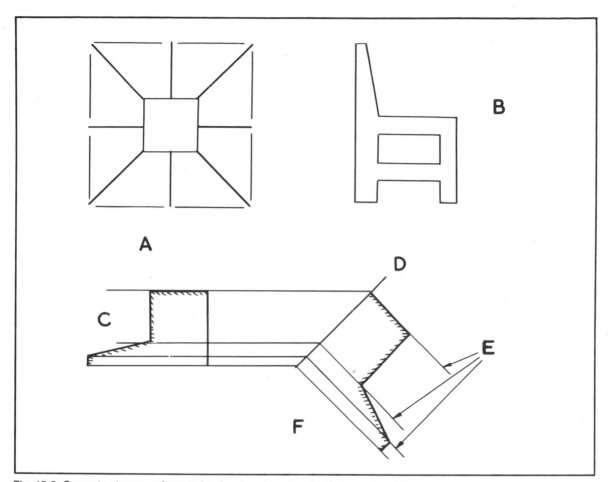

Fig. 15-2. Supports at corners have to be developed to allow for their greater widths.

some way each side of the space each person will need, it might be better to add to the number of sides and so reduce waste space and increase the comfortable seating capacity.

Unless a square seat is very small there will have to be supports square to each side and others at the corners (Fig. 15-2A). Those square to the seat are simple and can be laid out in a similar way to supports for chairs and benches (Fig. 15-2B). To get the sizes of matching corner supports is a matter of simple projection. Heights will be the same, but widths will be extended.

As a simple example, the section of a seat with back is shown in Fig. 15-2C. It allows for a level seat, but with the back inclined (Fig. 15-2C). What you must do is take the key parts of the square shape in side view and project them to a line at 45 degrees to the projection lines (Fig. 15-2D). Where the projection lines cut this line, erect

lines perpendicular to it (Fig. 15-2E). Using that miter cut as a base, measure heights the same as those on the square shape. Join the marks and you have the size and shape of the corner support (Fig. 15-2F). Include the projected shape of any sloping parts; keep them in the same plane. There is no need to project widths of wood that would then be wider than the squared parts. Increasing the wood widths on the corners is not required. Get the surfaces that will take lengthwise parts of the seat and back correct, and let the wood widths come as it will behind these lines.

In a typical square construction, draw a squared support and project the corners from it. The squared frame can be nailed or made with cut joints, as you prefer. The corner frames have to support joints in the seat and back slats.

The front and back legs can come central on the

303

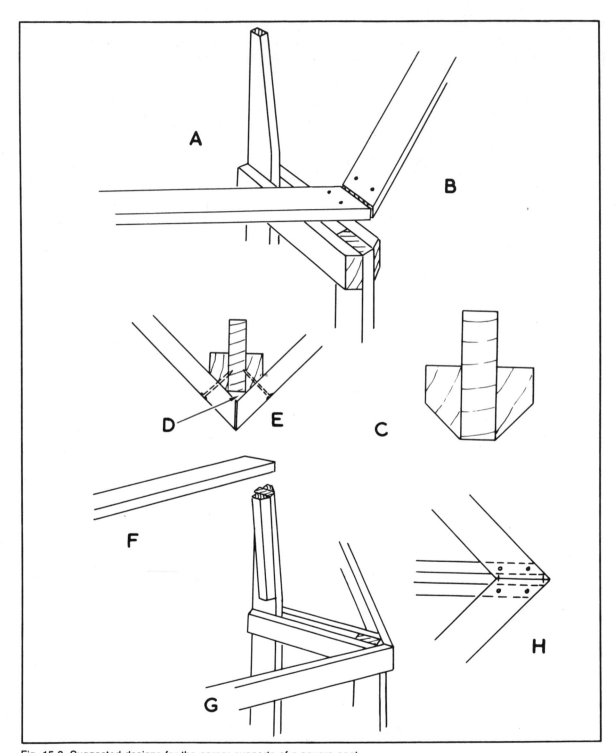

Fig. 15-3. Suggested designs for the corner supports of a square seat.

corner joint, but it helps to put a seat rail on each side of them (Fig. 15-3A). The seat slats can be cut to miter against each other and be nailed to their own rails (Fig. 15-3B). With a single rail, there is not much width for nailing unless it is very thick.

The back leg could be thickened with pieces on each side to give a better nailing area. Because the back slats cross at 45 degrees, the pieces should be planed to that before fitting (Fig. 15-3C). The slats will come above the surface of the leg, but that will not matter (Fig. 15-3D). For the neatest effect, the ends of the slats should be cut with a reasonable miter where they butt against each other (Fig. 15-3E). Cutting squarely should look satisfactory in most situations, but this is not precision cabinetwork!

One problem around trees is that the ground could be far from level. Roots can project or push up the earth. Each case will have to be dealt with according to the conditions. It might be possible to have a concrete base. There can be concrete or stone bases just where the legs come. You may be able to drive some legs into the ground. Other legs will have to rest on the ground or even be cut to fit over a root. It is usually best to make all the parts of a seat with the legs too long. Then you can trim them to suit as you assemble the seat.

You cannot do much prefabricating except for the frames. Other work has to be done in position. You have to get the assembly true to shape and with the seat surfaces reasonably level. It is helpful to have a capping piece over the backs (Fig. 15-3F). Make the capping pieces first (all the same and with their corners mitered). If you now make a temporary assembly with the capping pieces nailed to the frames, you can manipulate it until it looks square. Test with a try square as far as you can, but you cannot measure diagonals because the tree will be in the way.

With the frames all in about the right attitude, make the pieces that will form the front edges of the seat (Fig. 15-3G) or make the slats that will come at the front of the seat (Fig. 15-3H). They should all be the same length and mitered to each other. Attach them temporarily with partly driven nails. Again look at the seat and see that it is square. Up to this point, do not attach any legs to the ground—at least, not permanently.

You now have to level the seat with a spirit level laid along each of the sides. Do not worry about the correct height at this stage. Manipulate the seat with packings under the legs until you have it level. Now you can see how much you have to lower it to bring it to the position you want. Note what this is at every leg. It will help to

drive in a peg at each place and make register marks on the peg and its leg. Then you can check the relative positions as you cut off or sink the leg ends.

If you are making a hexagonal seat, the steps are very similar to making a square one. An exception is that you will probably not need to have frames square to the sides because the corner supports are relatively closer together. Nevertheless, you will still need to draw a frame square to the lines of a side so as to project the corner frame shape.

There is no need to draw the complete outline of the seat. One side with a small amount of the adjoining sides will be sufficient. Draw a part of a circle that will be sufficient to clear the tree trunk, but not less than 12 inches (and preferably more). Otherwise you will not get wide enough backs on each side. Draw a further part circle through where you intend the points of the seats to come (Fig. 15-4A), probably a further 24 inches, but you can modify that as you lay out the seat. At this stage it is merely used as a construction line in settling the lines of the corners. Use the radius of this circle to step off the same distance across the circumference (Fig. 15-4B). Join these points to the center of the circle (Fig. 15-4C). You have drawn the plan view of one side. The other five are repeats of it.

Draw what you intend the square section of the seat to be (Fig. 15-4D). Project this to the corner line and erect perpendicular lines (in the same way as for the square seat). With the key outline drawn, add the thicknesses of wood (Fig. 15-4E) to get the shape to make six corner frames. Angles that were 45 degrees on the square seat will now either be 30 degrees or 60 degrees. Set adjustable bevels to these angles when marking out and use these angles if you have a power saw that can have its guides adjusted.

If you use any other number of sides, it is advisable to make a reasonably large-scale drawing. You will have to divide 360 degrees by the intended number of sides to get the angle to project from the center to find the size of a side and the angles of the corners. If you decide on five, the angle at the center will be 72 degrees. If you decide on seven, it will be an awkward 51.43 degrees. With eight sides, it is much more reasonable at 45 degrees.

The angles between the frames and the seat slats are easily obtained, (the angles in any triangle total 180 degrees). If you take the center angle from 180 degrees, you have the total of the other two. Because they are the same, it is half this figure. For example, with five sides and a center angle of 72 degrees, you are left with 108 degrees to divide by two to get 54 degrees at each corner

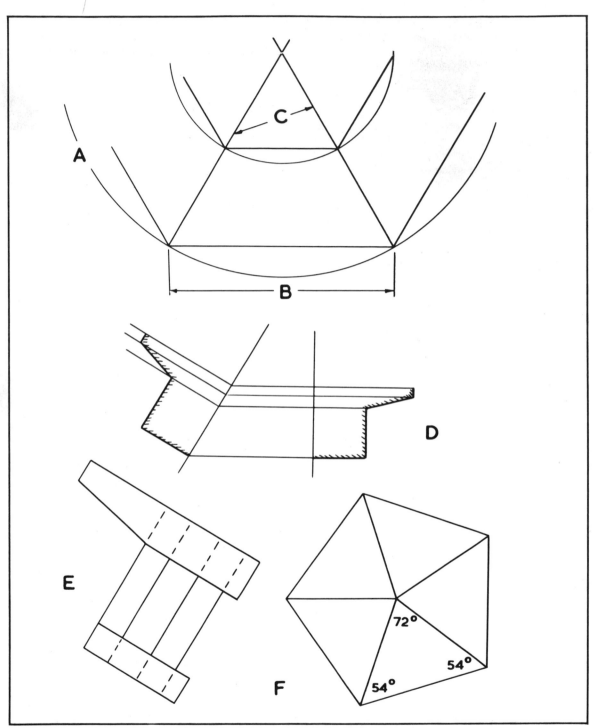

Fig. 15-4. The angles for seats with more than four sides have to be set out to obtain angles of parts and the widths of corner supports.

(Fig. 15-4F). With six sides, each corner is 60 degrees, with four sides it is 45 degrees, and then with eight sides it is 67½ degrees (or call it 1½ times a 45-degree miter).

Most seats around trees are basically as described. For a simple seat you can dispense with a back. A back can provide comfort, but it is also a structural part that helps to keep the seat in shape. If you leave it out, you will have to provide some more stiffening. If the legs all go into the ground, that will probably provide all the stiffening needed. Otherwise you will have to add lower rails around the inside legs or diagonal struts from the corner frames up to the seat level. Keep these out of the way of anyone swinging their legs.

You can make an interesting hexagonal or octagonal seat with arms at each angle. If you plan this, make sure the back panels are wide enough to give comfort when the arms have been added. If you are working on a small hexagonal seat, the individual seating positions might become too restricted. You need about 18 inches between the arms there. The arms can be supported by increasing the front leg lengths to hold the arm tops about 8 inches above the seat slats. The arms can be flat pieces with rounded fronts or thicker pieces cut to comfortable curves and thicker knuckles at the front.

Trees attract insects that might not harm the living tree, but they might attack the wood of the seat. If it is a tree with spreading branches and foliage, giving shade, the seat might be damp more than it is dry (although the amount of moisture will not be apparent to the touch). Because of this, treat the seat parts with preservative—preferably before assembly.

SUN LOUNGER

A support with an adjustable backrest for your full-length resting is attractive for sunbathing or just relaxing on the lawn or by a swimming pool. It can be used as a rather hard wooden lounger, but it is usually provided with cushions that are made to fit or a camping mattress or an air bed could be used.

This piece of furniture seems to have many names. Probably the most accurate name is *chaise longue,* which is French and means a long chair. The single word *chaise* is sometimes used, but that alone, in French, means a carriage. Talking about a "garden chaise" is incorrect. Chaise lounge is a peculiar mixture of French and English. It is probably better to talk of a *sun lounger*. This is a more appropriate description than long chair.

There are variations on the design, but all have wheels at the head end. The other end can have handles or you can put your hands under the framework and lift it to wheel the lounger to another position. The head end should have an adjustment so that the angle can be varied between two or three positions. Legs at the foot end support the flat part level and can be rigid or arranged to fold under. There can be arms that have to pivot with the tilting back.

As a full-length bed, a sun lounger is of necessity fairly long. You must be certain that you have adequate space for storage. It can be left out without its cushions, but it will have to be taken under cover during the winter in most parts of the country.

The sun lounger shown in Fig. 15-5 is of simple construction and suitable for leaving outdoors most of the

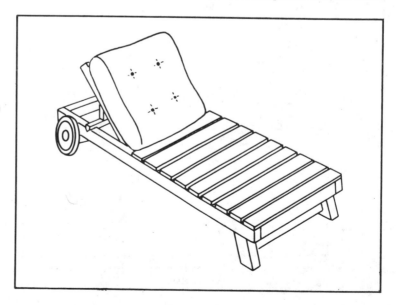

Fig. 15-5. A portable sun lounger with an adjustable rest.

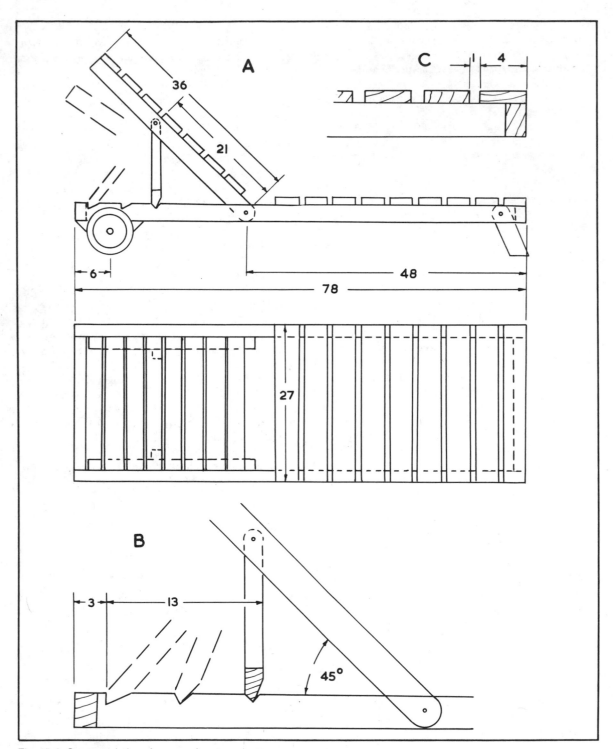

Fig. 15-6. Suggested sizes for a sun lounger.

Table 15-1. Materials List for Sun Lounger.

2 sides	3	×	79	×	2
or with handles	3	×	89	×	2
2 ends	3	×	28	×	2
2 axle blocks	3	×	13	×	2
2 backs	3	×	39	×	2
2 legs	3	×	12	×	2
1 leg rail	4	×	27	×	1
9 seat slats	4	×	28	×	1
7 back slats	4	×	24	×	1
2 struts	1½	×	18	×	1½
1 strut	3	×	28	×	1½
2 arms (optional)	4	×	37	×	1
2 arm supports (optional)	2	×	15	×	1

year if it is made of a durable hardwood. The sizes suggested (Fig. 15-6A and Table 15-1) should suit most purposes. A tall person might want a greater length. If you need to economize on size, it could be reduced by a few inches.

The main frame is a rectangle. It can have two sides extended to form handles if you prefer. Allow an extra 10 inches for handles. Mark out the sides (Fig. 15-7A). The crosspieces are plain strips. Corners can be open mortise and tenon or bridle joints (Fig. 15-8A). If there are to be handles, use ordinary through mortise and tenons (Fig. 15-8B). Stronger corner joints use dovetails (Fig. 15-8C). These are almost as simple to cut, in this construction, as bridle joints.

Shape the handles (Fig. 15-8D). Saw to the shape you want in side view. Then thin the ends. The 2-inch thickness is more than a hand can grasp and the end few inches should be not more than 1½ inch diameter. Remove the sharpness to get the end octagonal and follow by removing those angles so you can finish to a round section by pulling a strip of abrasive paper around the handle.

Make the back pieces (Fig. 15-7B). The lower ends are semicircular around the bolt hole. The tops are rounded on the sides away from the slats. Allow for ⅜-inch or ½-inch bolts.

Make the parts that form the struts (Fig. 15-7C). The crosspiece should be long enough to go over the main frame. The other parts are tenoned to it at a distance that will bring them between the back pieces (Fig. 15-7D). Measure the actual pieces of wood to get this spacing correct, but allow for washers on the bolts between all moving parts. The crosspiece must be shaped (Fig. 15-7E so that it will fit into notches without fear of slipping.

The drawing shows three notches (Fig. 15-6B). At

the highest position, the back is at about 45 degrees and the strut is upright. The other positions allow for further reclining. The notches in the sides of the main frame are slighty different at each position. You might make them an average shape. For the best arrangement, make a full-size drawing, showing each position, or have a trial assembly so that you can mark each notch to match the strut in that position. There is no need to cut the notches more than 1 inch deep.

How the axle blocks are arranged depends on the choice of wheels and axle. The drawings allow for 8-inch diameter wheels, but they need not be exactly that size. The axle will have to suit the wheels, but it will probably be a rod about ½ inch in diameter. It can go through the centers of the blocks (Fig. 15-7E). Glue and screw the blocks to the frame sides.

The front legs are inside the main frame and pivoted so that they will swing up. When down, they rest against the front part of the frame. Make them (Fig. 15-7F) so they support the lounger level. Their length depends on the height the chosen wheels lift it. Put a rail between the legs. It can be screwed at the ends, but the best joint is a double tenon (Fig. 15 7G).

Prepare all the strips for the seat and back slats. Round their top edges. Make them to come level with the outsides of their own frames. Space them evenly (Fig. 15-6C). Glue and two nails or screws at each end should be enough. Get the main frame square and see that the back slats hold the sides parallel and square.

Try the assembly with bolts loosely in each pivot place. See that the legs fold properly and the back adjusts without snags to each of the three positions. Check that the seat comes level when supported by the wheels and legs. If you are satisfied on all these points, remove the bolts and paint all the woodwork. Complete all painting before assembling again so that there is plenty of paint protection on surfaces that might not be accessible after bolting together. Put washers on the bolts between moving parts and under nuts. Use stiffnuts or other means of locking the nuts.

With plastic foam or rubber cushions at least 3 inches thick, the lounger will be very comfortable because the foam will conform to the body shape. If it is to be used without padding, comfort can be improved by shaping the seat. The 3-inch depth of the main sides do not permit much shaping as that would weaken them. It is better to cut sides from 2-×-4 inch wood.

On a 4-inch piece, draw the same layout as on a 3-inch piece, leaving the extra width on top. Allow for the ends being parallel and 3 inches deep. Where a sitter will rest with thighs slightly lifted, make a hollow to just

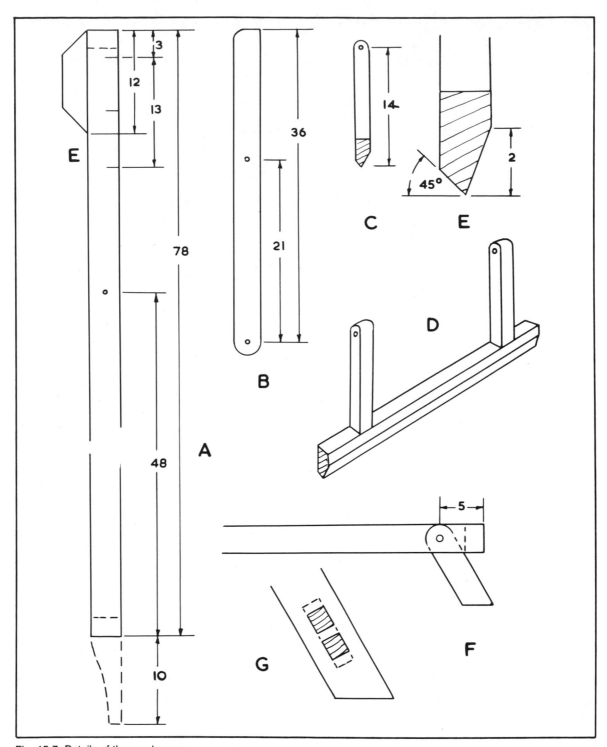

Fig. 15-7. Details of the sun lounger.

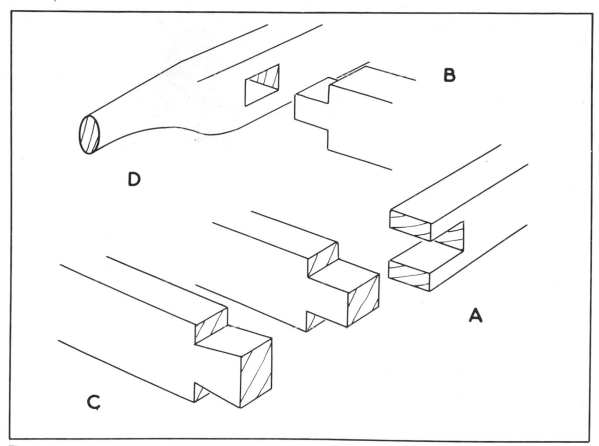

Fig. 15-8. Joints for the sun lounger.

below the 3-inch level and an upward curve to the full width above it (Fig. 15-9A). Let the curve be sweeping without any tight bends so that the slats will still bed down closely. Except for this change, the lounger can be completed in the same way as the one with a flat seat.

If you want to add arms, they must pivot with the back to its possible three positions. Each arm should be parallel to the seat and the support should be arranged parallel to the back (Fig. 15-9B). Because the back is pivoted inside the main frame and the arm supports must come outside it, you have to make arms that are shaped to take care of the different planes (Fig. 15-9C). The support has a bolt through the frame side. Its top pivots on a block glued and screwed under the arm (Fig. 15-9D). At the rear there is a bolt through the back. There should not be much strain on these bolts so a ¼-inch diameter bolt should work. Round the ends and edges of the arms. After a trial assembly, separate the parts for painting before final assembly.

UPHOLSTERY

The sun lounger should have cushions. They will probably have to be made specially because it is unlikely that any stock ones will fit. These are plain rectangular cushions that are not difficult to make if you have a sewing machine that will take the covering fabric. The assembly can be three parts linked together (Fig. 15-10A). The fillings are rubber or plastic foam, 3 inches or more thick. If you have to cut it, use a long-bladed thin knife such as a carving knife. If the material resists cutting, wet the blade.

The covering could be any floral or patterned fabric, but you must choose a water-resistant one if the cushions are to be left out in rain or dew. Plastic-coated fabric, as used in car upholstery, is water-resistant and hard-wearing material, but some of it will be too thick to sew with a domestic sewing machine.

The sewn joints can be simple seams made inside out and turned so the edges come inside (Fig. 15-10B) or you can include piping. This can be bought already prepared or it is possible to make it by sewing material around a cord core (Fig. 15-10C). If you make your own, cut the cloth diagonal to the weave. Then you will not be troubled so much by creasing due to lack of stretch in the piping when it is being sewn to other cloth. Piping is sewn into a seam inside out. Then it appears as a band around the seam (Fig. 15-10D). The piping should be in one piece all round a cushion, but the cloth used in it can be joined. With plastic-coated fabric, piping of a matching or contrasting color looks good. If you make up linked cushions, you need only include piping around the outer seams. If you use loose cushions that can be turned over, pipe around both seams.

The cloth for a cushion is sewn inside out. The top and bottom are single pieces and there are narrow pieces between them. Make the casing slightly too small so that the foam is compressed inside and the cloth will finish smooth. Have the cloth inside out and pin the parts together over the filling (Fig. 15-10E). Leave a seam open for the filling to be removed and inserted later. Arrange for this and the joint in the narrow piece to come on a side toward another cushion and for the top or bottom panels to extend about 2 inches extra there. Make the joint at the bottom of the seat cushions and the top between the seat and the back. If you are using piping, include that in the pinned seams with the cord inside (Fig. 15-10F).

Remove the filling and sew round the seams, except

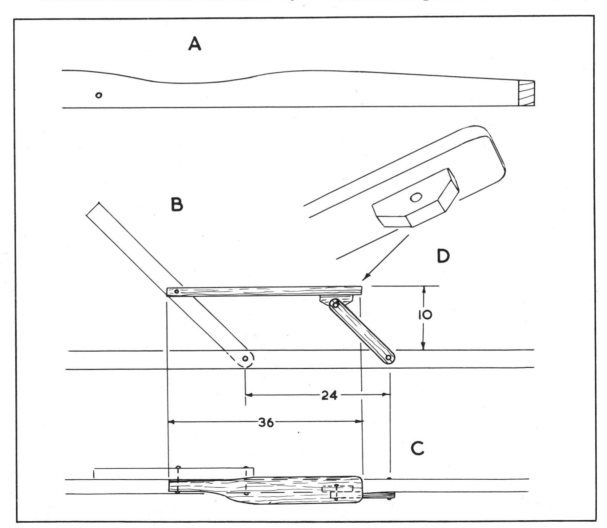

Fig. 15-9. How to modify the side shape and add arms to the sun lounger.

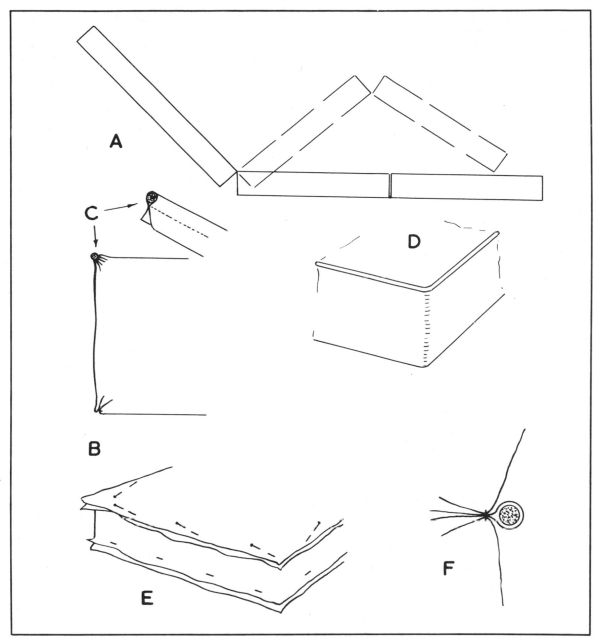

Fig. 15-10. Design of linked cushions for use with the sun lounger.

for the open part, keeping the rows of stitches on the pin line. Remove pins as you go and keep as close as the sewing machine foot will allow to the piping cord. Turn the cushion the right way and put the foam filling in.

The last seam has to be closed by hand sewing using slip stitches. If it is a seam without a flap to join to another cushion, have a length of thread doubled in a stout needle. Turn in the edges (Fig. 15-11A) and enter the needle up through one side (Fig. 15-11B). Go across to the other fold so that you can enter the crease directly opposite and go along a short way to come up again (Fig. 15-11C). Carry on like this for the length of the seam (Fig. 15-

11D). When you pull the seam tight, there will be very little of each stitch visible (Fig. 15-11E).

If the seam is one with a flap for joining to the next cushion, the slip stitches are very similar except you go through and back at the flap each time (Fig. 15-11F). When the three cushions have been made, sew the extending flaps closely to the other cushions near their seams. Leave only enough slack for folding and turning the edges under if you can sew through the extra thickness.

Traditionally, large cushions are buttoned. Over the surface there is a pattern of widely spaced buttons sewn through to the underside. The original purpose was to prevent the oldtime filling from moving. That was made up of hair, felt, and many other things that would move about and settle after use. There is little risk of foam filling moving. There could be four or more buttons in each cushion, mainly for appearance, to prevent the cov-

ering and filling from moving in relation to each other (Fig. 15-12A).

Buttons can be bought in colors to match most covering materials. It is possible to have your own materials put on buttons by a specialist upholstery supplier. Because both sides of the cushions will be visible, use similar buttons on both sides. On some upholstery, there are other attachments used where they will not show. You need a needle at least as long as the thickness of the cushion.

If possible, get both ends of the thread through the eye of the needle; otherwise you have to go through and back. Push the needle through (Fig. 15-12B). Take in the second button and tie the thread ends temporarily. Do not tighten until you have all the buttons ready. The buttons have to be pulled in uniformly so that they are just below the surface (Fig. 15-12C). Make a figure-eight slip knot. Take one end round the other part, under itself, and up

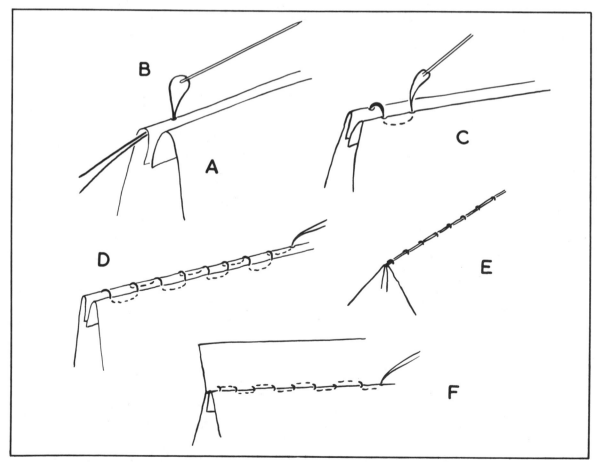

Fig. 15-11. Stitches used in making cushions for the sun lounger.

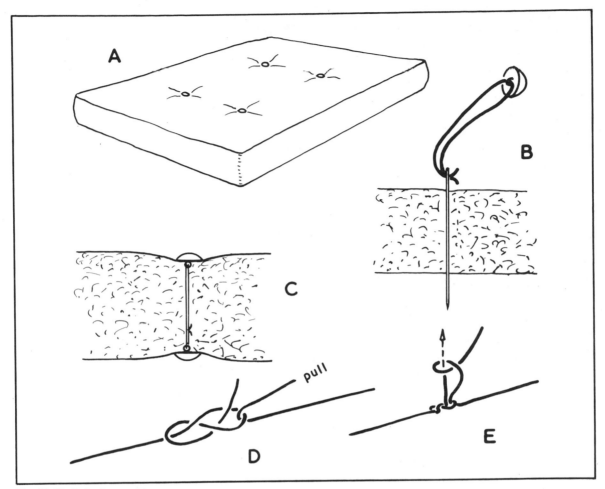

Fig. 15-12. Buttoning cushions.

through its loop (Fig. 15-12D). You can now pull the long end until both buttons have drawn in the right amount. When they are right, put a half-hitch over the standing end (Fig. 15-12E). That will lock the knot. Cut off the surplus ends. Compress the filling and work the thread around so that the knot is buried inside it. For more detailed information on upholstery see TAB Book No. 1004, *The Upholsterer's Bible.*

FOLD-FLAT SUN LOUNGER

This lounger shown in Fig. 15-13 requires a different method of construction to the previous one. Instead of the backrest having a strut assembly fitting into notches, the strut is permanently pivoted and different angles are obtained by moving the backrest to different spaces in the battens of the main frame. When the backrest is with-

drawn, it can be folded flat on to the main part. The legs and wheels also fold into the main frame so that the whole thing can be reduced in thickness for storage.

All of the parts can be softwood, except that the two struts are better made of hardwood to reduce the risk of breakage at the ends. The general drawing (Fig. 15-14) shows the wheel arms inside the main frame and the wheels inside them (Fig. 15-14A). This is necessary for the other parts to fold without interfering with the wheels stowing. The legs are also arranged inside (Fig. 15-14B). The struts pivot outside the main frame (Fig. 15-14C). The backrest is as wide as the main frame, but its up-rights are arranged to come inside the main frame sides (Fig. 15-14D) so as to slip between battens in three positions.

The main frame is made with pieces across the ends

(Fig. 15-14E). The corners can be tenoned or just nailed. Shape the handle extensions the same way as the other lounger. Drill the sides for bolts. The legs and wheel arms can be on ⅜-inch bolts, but ¼-inch or 5/16-inch bolts will be thick enough for the strut and backrest. All of the battens across the main frame are 1-×-3 inch section (see Table 15-2) and at the foot end they are about 2 inches apart. Get the spacing even after you have located the special positions near the other end. So the backrest will fit without excessive looseness in three positions, the battens across where it goes must have gaps of varying widths (Fig. 15-15A). With those located, space the others evenly for the rest of the length. Two nails or screws at each end of a batten should secure it and help to prevent the framework from twisting.

The wheel arms are simple pieces with rounded ends (Fig. 15-15B). The axle need not go right through, but set it deep enough to be secure. Wheels of 7 inches in diameter are suggested, but others can be used. The wheel arms bear against the cross member at the end of the main frame, but there is also a rail across them— resting there—to increase the bearing area and reduce any tendency to wobble when the lounger is moved.

The legs pivot on bolts in the same way as the wheel arms. They bear against the end cross member of the main frame and have a rail similarly arranged (Fig. 15-14F). Leave the legs too long until after assembly. Then they can be cut to hold the lounger level when the wheels are fully extended. The legs will fold fully inside the frame, but the wheel arms are restricted by the wheel sizes from going right in.

The backrest is made up with battens across uprights with their 2-inch side toward them (Fig. 15-15C). Make the uprights to extend about 3 inches below the lowest batten and round the ends so that they will fit easily between the main frame battens. Have the lengths of the battens the same as those on the main frame, but set back the uprights to a width that will drop easily between the main frame sides. Note that there is a wide gap near the center of the assembly. That is to give clearance for the ends of the struts. This is particularly true when the assembly is folded flat.

Make the struts (Fig. 15-15D). They go outside the main frame sides, but the backrest they support has its uprights inside. To allow for this, put packing pieces outside the uprights at the hole positions (Fig. 15-15E) so that long bolts can go through.

Try the action of the backrest and its struts with a

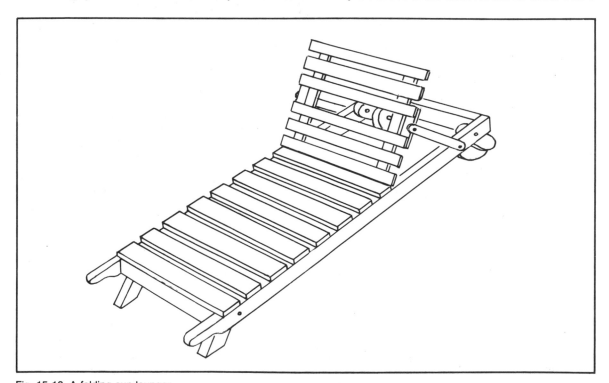

Fig. 15-13. A folding sun lounger.

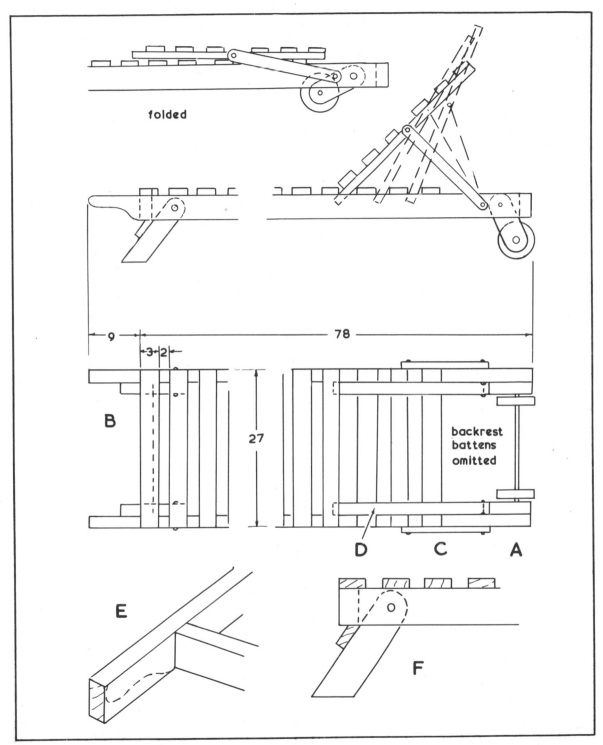

folded

B

9

3 2

27

78

backrest
battens
omitted

D   C   A

E

F

Fig 15-14. Sizes of a folding sun lounger.

Table 15-2. Materials List for Fold-Flat Sun Lounger.

2 sides	4 × 88 × 2
2 ends	4 × 24 × 2
2 legs	4 × 18 × 2
2 wheel arms	4 × 14 × 2
2 rails	3 × 24 × 1
20 battens	3 × 28 × 1
2 uprights	2 × 34 × 1
2 packings	2 × 8 × 1
2 struts	2 × 24 × 1

temporary assembly, going into all three positions. Also make sure that the legs and wheel arms will fold and extend properly. If all is satisfactory, separate the parts for final cleaning up—particularly the removal of sharp edges and corners—before painting and final assembly. Similar cushions to those for the previous lounger can be made and fitted.

GARDEN KNEELER

A padded kneeler can serve several purposes besides the obvious one of making kneeling on the ground more

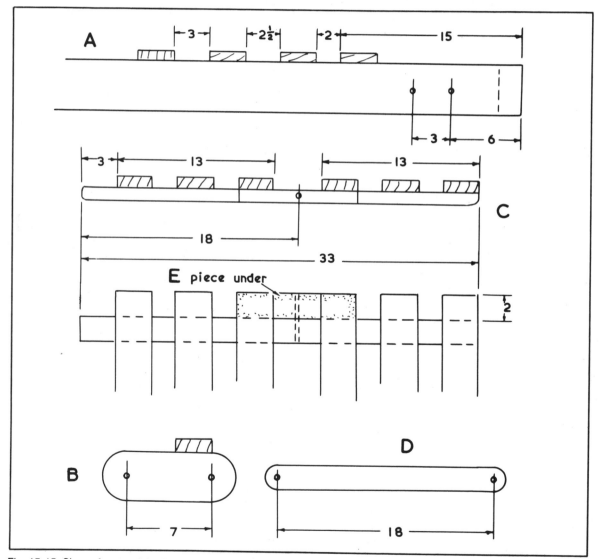

Fig. 15-15. Sizes of parts of the folding sun lounger.

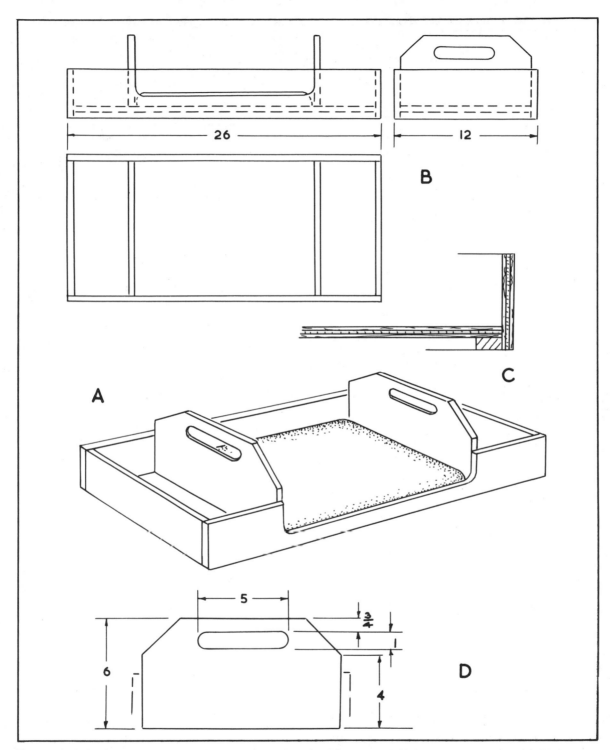

Fig. 15-16. A garden kneeler with compartments for tools and seeds.

comfortable. It keeps you off a damp surface and spreads the load. It can also be made to accommodate small tools and seeds or bulbs. It can have lifting handles. Dealing with gardening chores on your hands and knees can become a pleasure instead of something to be endured.

The kneeler shown in Fig. 15-16A will be found a reasonable size for most gardeners. It can be reduced slightly, if you want to keep it compact, or the end boxes could be left off. The padded center can be cut from a larger piece of foam plastic or rubber. If you find a stock size that can be used, then the box dimensions can be planned round it. See Table 15-3.

The working drawing (Fig. 15-16B) allows for most

of the parts being made of ½-inch exterior plywood. There are some solid wood strips below the bottom (Fig. 15-16C).

Start by making the two handled parts (Fig. 15-16D). You can make the handle slots by drilling two 1-inch holes at 4-inch centers. Then the waste can be removed with a jigsaw or by more drilling. Well round all the edges of the slots and the parts above them to make comfortable grips. The box ends must be the same length as the handle pieces, but deep enough to overlap the bottom.

Make the bottom the same width as the pieces that you have cut to go over it and 25 inches long, framed round with ½- × -1 inch strips underneath (Fig. 15-17A). All of the assembly can be done with waterproof glue and ¾-inch nails that are punched below the surface and covered with stopping. Most ½-inch plywood should be stiff enough with only the edge framing. If you think the bottom will flex too much under load, you can place another strip across under its center.

The back (the side away from you when kneeling) is a parallel strip. The front has to be cut down between the

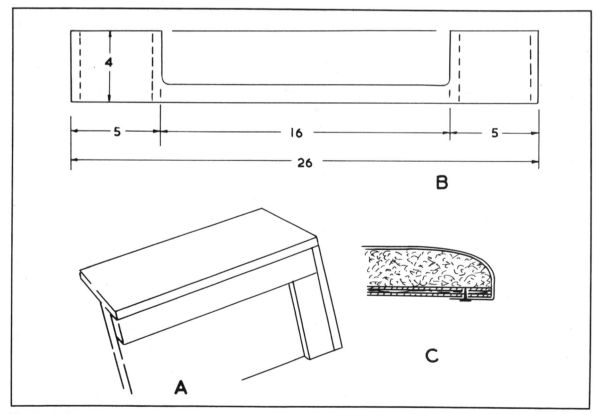

Fig. 15-17. Details of the garden kneeler.

handle pieces, but it should stand up enough to retain the padding. It should not be so high as to make a hard edge against your legs when the cushion compresses. Round the corners of the reduced part (Fig. 15-17B). Join the handled parts and the ends to the bottom and add the back and front. Glue and punched nails should be sufficient, but you could use a thin screw as well near the top edge of each joint.

The cushion is a piece of foam about 1 inch thick, mounted over a piece of plywood, with plastic-coated fabric stretched over it and tacked below (Fig. 15-17C). It should be loose enough in the kneeler to be removable. Cut the plywood to fit loosely in place and drill a few ¼-inch holes through it to allow air to move in and out. Cut the foam about ¼ inch too big so the covering material compresses it as it is stretched on to get a neat rounded edge. Tack as necessary below, but spacing will probably be about 1½ inches. Lap the fabric corners underneath and trim the surplus fabric parallel with the plywood edges inside the lines of tacks.

LOG FLOWER TROUGH

A hollowed piece of natural wood makes a decorative holder for growing flowers or plants. Several of them can be positioned alongside paths or as borders for gardens. They have the advantage of being portable—if they are not too large—so you can rearrange a garden layout or lift the container on to a deck or other solid surface. You can also take a trough indoors so that plants can be started early in the season and put outside when the weather gets better.

The main need is for a suitable log. It should have a reasonably straight grain so that you can split it in two. If you can be certain of hitting where you aim, you can split the log with an ax. Otherwise it would be safer to use a steel wedge and hammer. If the split follows a slightly wavy line, that can be ignored and treated as a decorative feature. Any large lumps should be leveled off.

If the trough is to be used without legs, make a flat surface underneath parallel with the top (Fig. 15-18A). That will give you an easier hold when you start hollowing. If legs are to be added, they can be dealt with later.

Hollowing does not have to be done with a great deal of precision, but you have to get a sufficient amount of wood removed to allow plenty of soil to be put in. In cross section, the shape follows the outline (Fig. 15-18B). In the length, there will have to be a curve down (Fig. 15-18C) to leave more thickness at the end grain—for the sake of strength.

Drill into the wood to near the depths you expect to go. A penciled outline on the top will serve as a rough guide. The more holes you drill, the easier it will be to remove the waste. For most of the work, use the largest bit your electric drill will drive or your muscle power will stand, (if you use a brace).

A large gouge sharpened on the outside is the best tool for hollowing (Fig. 15-18D). You can manage with chisels used with their bevels downward. In both cases, the tool goes where you direct it without the tendency to pull deeper that goes with a tool used bevel upward. Do all chopping toward the center of the log with the grain or diagonal to the grain. All cuts should slope down toward the center. A cut the other way would lift the grain and start a split. Driving a chisel in line with the grain would have the same effect, but a gouge would be less troublesome.

Remove the waste in the central area first. Go almost as deep as the final hollow is to be. Further chopping can be toward it. As you progress, you might find you want to go deeper than was drilled originally. You can drill again. That requires less effort than more work with a chisel or gouge.

One problem is holding the log. If it is fairly large and you have made a flat underneath, its weight will be enough to hold it against the tool being hit with a mallet. It does not have to be on a bench. You might find it easier to work at a large log on the ground. You could even dig a hollow for it so it will stay put as you work on it. If it is smaller, you might find an angle somewhere into which it can be put (Fig. 15-18E). Perhaps you could use a porch doorway while you kneel or sit on a step to work.

Feet can be short lengths of natural wood tapered to go into holes (Fig. 15-18F). You could use pieces across that are partly in grooves and partly shaped to the log (Fig. 15-18G).

Although anything planted in soil in the trough will need water, you have to guard against too much water. Drill a few holes through the bottom. To prevent the soil from falling through, put stones over the holes. The stones should not fit so tightly the water cannot get out.

FLOWER BOXES

Flowers and plants can be grown in pots or they can be planted directly in boxes you make. The use of boxes in a garden allows you to alter the layout. They give you extra growing space because boxes can be put on decks, patios, or other hard surfaces. They could go on top of a wall for plants that can then hang down. Construction needs to be fairly substantial because enough soil for plants to grow in is quite heavy.

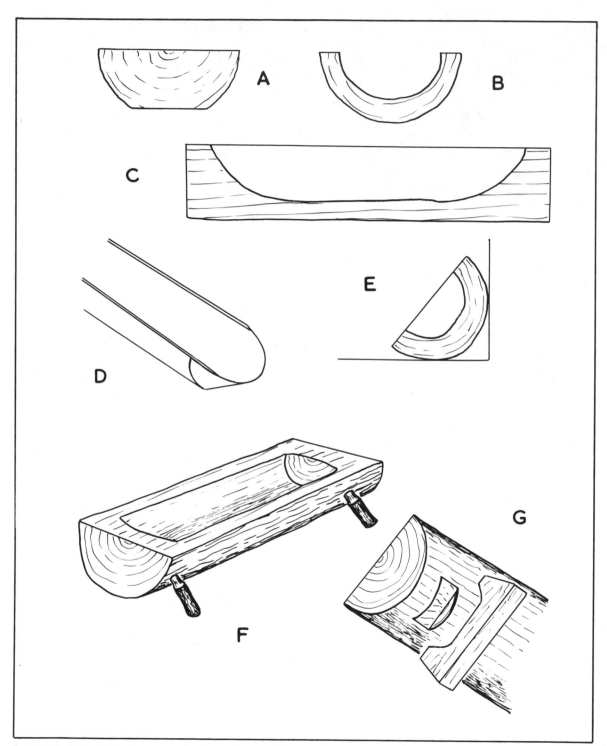

Fig. 15-18. A trough for flowers or plants can be carved from a log.

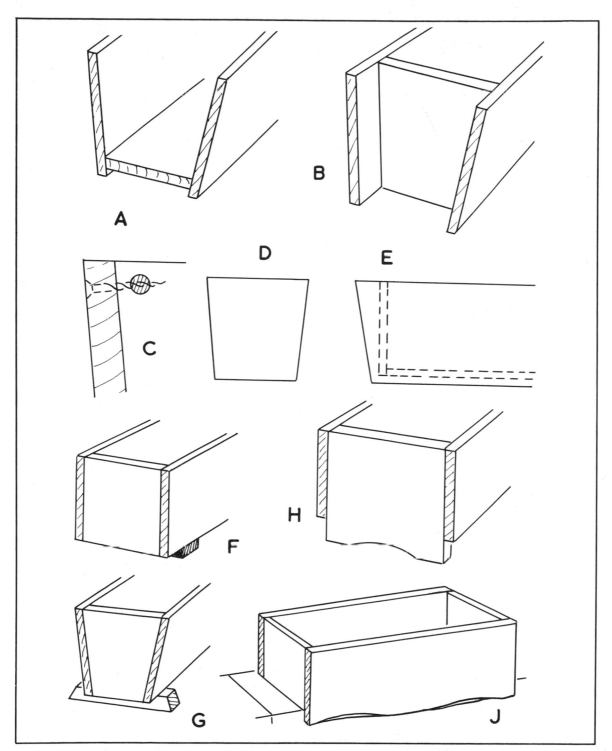

Fig. 15-19. Flower boxes can be constructed in several ways from flat boards.

The size of a box will be suggested by available boards or the space where it is to be put. If it is to contain plant pots, their size will control the inside measurements. If several pots are to be used, the length will then be a multiple of the width, and the depth has to suit the pots. Do not settle on too tight a fit. You need to be able to lift the pots and they are not always exactly the same size.

A plain box might be all you need. If the foliage is to hang all over the box, there is no point in making the box itself very decorative. It is stronger to include the bottom inside the sides (Fig. 15-19A), so that the load on screws or nails does not come in the direction that tends to withdraw them. It is stronger at the end grain if sides overlap the ends (Fig. 15-19B). The greatest bursting loads come near the top. Even if the sides are nailed to the ends for most of their depth, it helps to use screws near the top. They will be even stronger if you put dowels across the ends for the screw threads to grip (Fig. 15-19C).

There are places where a plain rectangular box is all that is needed, but tapers always look better than square corners so the box could be made to flare out toward the top. That is easy to arrange at the ends (Fig. 15-19D), but if you slope them out as well you have a compound angle at the corners. If the flare is not much, you can ignore it and cut the parts square across. Another way is to leave the ends upright, but bevel extending sides (Fig. 15-19E).

In most situations, it is better to raise the box off the ground. Simplest is to put strips across underneath (Fig. 15-19F). If the box is tall or tapers, let the feet extend a little for stability (Fig. 15-19G). A long box will need some intermediate feet. You could get a similar effect by extending ends downward (Fig. 15-19H). If the box is very wide, cut away at the center so support is only at the sides and steadiness on an uneven surface is easier to get.

Drill holes in the bottom of a box for drainage even if the contents will be pots. Pots are best stood on strips of wood so that their drainage holes are not obstructed.

Waney-edged boards can be used for box sides. If the waviness is not much, it could be upward as well as downward. Packings under the bottom will have to be high enough for the uneven edges to clear the ground. If the box is to be placed on a wall, its front could have a straight top. But the waney edge could overlap the wall (Fig. 15-19J).

FLOWER BOX ON STAND

The boxes described so far are intended to be at ground level or on a wall. One attraction of putting flowers or plants in boxes is that they can be arranged at a more accessible height for anyone to view, but particularly for those who have difficulty in bending. A raised flower box is also attractive among benches on a deck or against the house wall. See Table 15-4 for a materials list.

The box shown in Fig. 15-20A is designed for three 12-inch pots on a stand that brings their tops about 30 inches from the ground. Before you start construction, check the sizes of pots and the types of plants. If you are choosing plants that grow quite high, it will be better to lower the box. If the plants will hang over the sides plentifully, it will be better slightly higher.

The box and stand are separate, with the box fitting into the framed top of the stand, so it cannot be pushed off (Fig. 15-21A). Make the box first so that the stand sizes can be matched to it.

For a tapered construction with a slope both ways, the true depth of a side or end is rather more than the vertical depth. In this case, that and the resulting angles at the corners are so slightly different that they can be ignored and regarded as the same as if the box was made upright.

Start with the two sides (Fig. 15-22A). Make the two ends with similar slopes (Fig. 15-22B). The bottom is raised a little and fits inside these parts (Fig. 15-22C). Mark its position on them and the laps of the sides over the ends. That will give you the sizes of the bottom that will have to be beveled to fit. Screw the ends to the bottom using the sides as a guide to their angles. True the sides of the bottom to match the ends; then screw on the sides. It will probably be satisfactory to leave the screws level with the surface. If you are making something that

Table 15-4. Materials List for Flower Box on Stand.

Box .				
2 sides	14	× 46	× 1	
2 ends	14	× 18	× 1	
2 tops	2	× 46	× ¾	
2 tops	2	× 19	× ¾	
1 bottom	14	× 41	× 1	
Stand				
4 legs	2	× 17	× 2	
2 tops	2	× 43	× 1	
2 tops	2	× 18	× 1	
2 rims	2	× 45	× ¾	
2 rims	2	× 19	× ¾	
2 top rails	2	× 41	× 1	
2 top rails	2	× 16	× 1	
2 lower rails	2	× 45	× 1	
2 lower rails	2	× 19	× 1	
3 shelf slats	3	× 45	× 1	

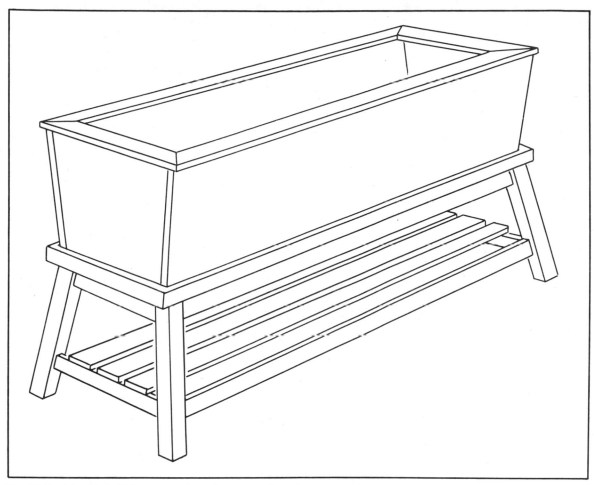

Fig. 15-20. A box to hold flowers or plants in pots can have its own stand.

will grace an entrance porch or some other important place, it would look better if the screw were counterbored and plugged. In any case, strength would be improved if the top screws went into dowels (as suggested for a simple box).

Use a straightedge across the top in all directions and plane the edges to take the top rim pieces (Fig. 15-22D). Miter their corners and screw down into the box edges. Plug over the screws if the importance of the work justifies it. The mitered corners can be strengthened with dowels arranged diagonally (Fig. 15-22E). Drill drainage holes in the bottom of the box to complete it.

The stand is made like a table, but with strips to take the box instead of the usual tabletop. As with the box, the amount of flare is not enough to need different heights and angles. Nevertheless, you might want to adjust the

shoulders of tenons slightly to get a close fit.

Lay out one end full size (Fig. 15-23A). The width at the top has to allow for an easy fit on the box (Fig. 15-21B). The slopes are the same the other way so an adjustable bevel can be used for the angles of all joints. Mark out the legs and rails from that drawing. Allow for mortise and tenon joints or dowels (Fig. 15-23B). At the same time, mark and cut the mortises in the other direction. Assemble the two ends; check that they match as a pair.

Make the rails the other way. Allow for the same clearance on the box and the same slope for the legs. A temporary partial assembly will show how the tops of the legs and the rails have to be cut to give a flat bearing for the box. It will be easier to do this shaping, at least partially, before assembly. Put the stand together.

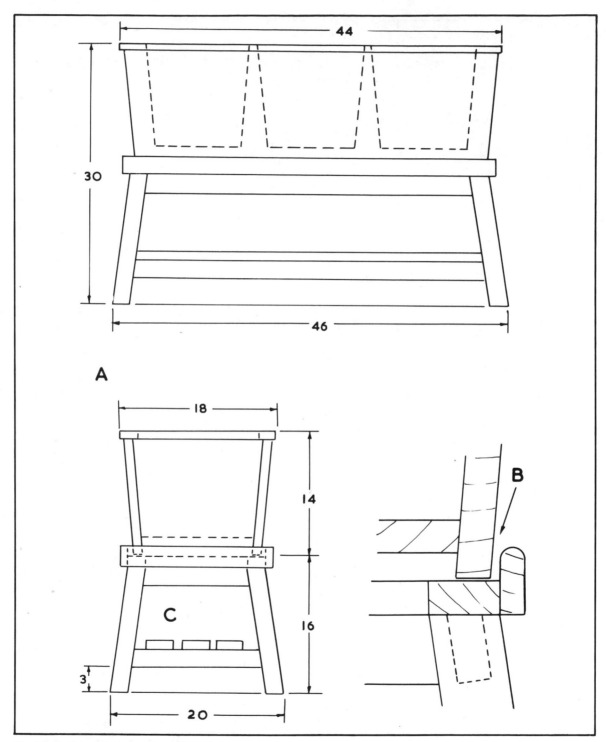

Fig. 15-21. Suggested sizes for a flower box and stand.

Checking that it stands level and that the top outline is a match for the box. It should go either way around, but if there are slight irregularities you will have to mark the better way.

When the glue in the stand has set, level its top and then put on the top strips. Their outsides are level with the tops of the legs (Fig. 15-22C) and the corners can be mitered. If screwed downward into the legs, there should be no need for dowels across the miters. Screw securely into rails and make sure outer edges are upright.

Add the rims that will locate the box (Fig. 15-23D). Round their top edges and miter their corners.

Lengthwise slats are shown in Fig. 15-21C to form a shelf. If they are not stiff enough, you will need one or two supports put across between the long rails. If you do not want a shelf the full length, slats can be put across the long rails to make up whatever area you need.

For normal outside use a painted finish would be best. The box could be painted a different color from the stand. If you have used an attractive hardwood, a clear

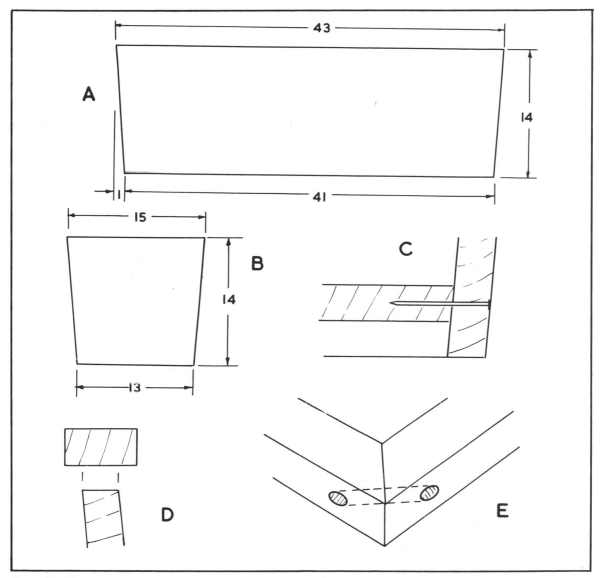

Fig. 15-22. The parts of the flower box.

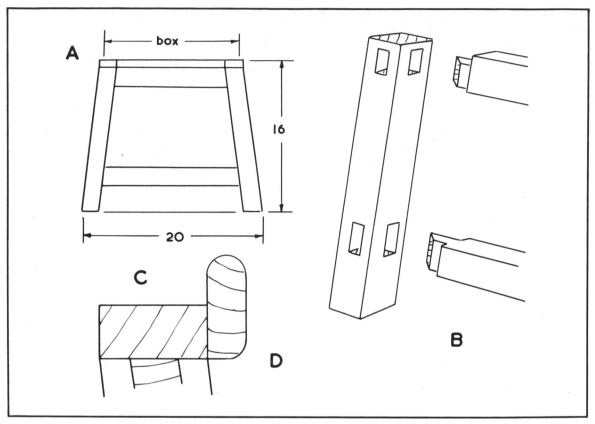

Fig. 15-23. Details of the flower box stand.

varnish finish would be attractive. The inside of the box can be treated the same as the outside—if it is to contain pots—but if you intend filling it with soil, it would be better treated with bitumastic or other waterproof paint and left to dry for some time before putting in soil and plants.

SINGLE PLANT POT

A small tree in a pot can be featured alone or as one of many. Similarly, you can have shrubs that produce large or high foliage. It needs to be in a fairly large container to take care of the roots and the base has to be stable. It can be in a pot that is decorative in itself, but if a wooden container is used the earth and roots can be put in something that has no beauty in itself (such as a cut-off oil drum or something similar). You could plant directly into the box, but most gardeners would prefer to have an inner container that could be lifted out. That would also make the wooden box longer lasting and more accessible for painting or maintenance.

Suitable containers could be made from slabs of sawn wood from a log (with or without a waney edge to the top). One way of making a plain box more interesting is to overlap the sides and cut them to uneven curves (Fig. 15-24A) so they look something like the waney edges along the grain. Such a box should be made with the bottom between the sides and ends above it. Then you can put strips across as feet, usually projecting slightly. The strips protect the bottom from direct contact with the ground (Fig. 15-24B) and allow water that drains through holes in the bottom to flow away. Sizes obviously depend on the container and the type of plant, but boxes about 18 inches each way are the sizes to consider for outdoor use.

Boxes do not have to be square or with vertical sides. Much depends on what has to be put inside. If there is a taper, 5 degrees from vertical should be enough (Fig. 15-24C) and the feet should extend far enough for stability.

One interesting variation has four identical sides. One end is cut square or to a slight taper and the other end is cut to irregular curves. They are put together to project in turn (Fig. 15-24D). The bottom should be fitted inside, given drain holes, and supported with feet.

PANELED PLANT POT

For a more formal display, such as a pair of small trees or flowering shrubs at the corners of a porch or deck, the containers would look better if they have more of a cabinetwork construction. They can be painted to fit in with the home frontage or the furniture on a deck.

The example shown in Fig. 15-25A has a stout framing with exterior plywood panels and a border at the

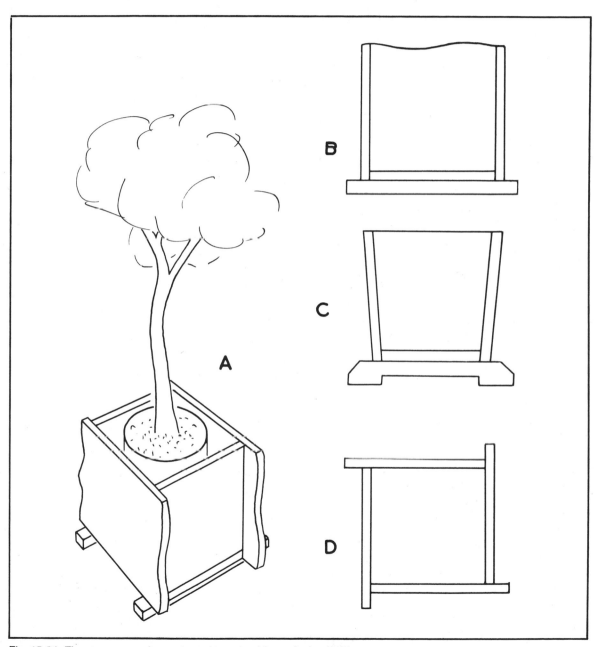

Fig. 15-24. There are several ways to make a stand for a single plant in a pot.

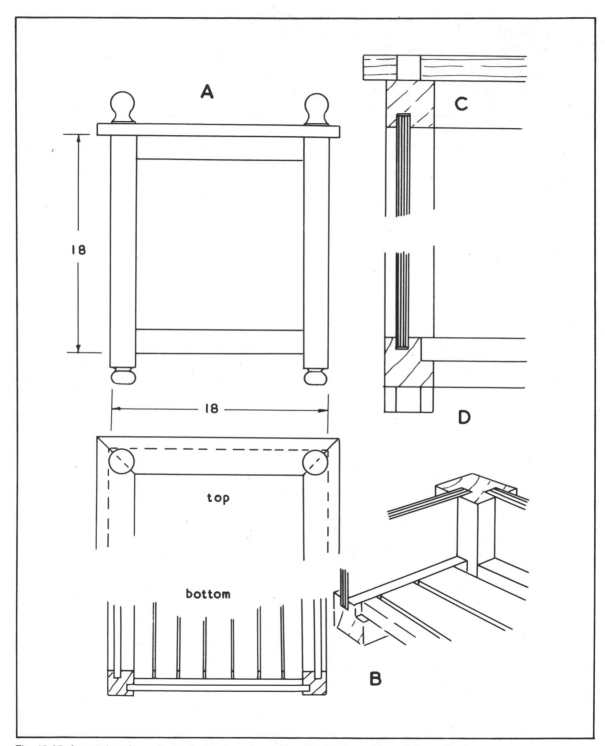

Fig. 15-25. A container for a single plant pot can be made with panels and turned decorations.

top. The bottom is made from slats to allow drainage. Turned parts are shown at the corners, top and bottom. If you do not have a lathe and cannot buy suitable finials and feet, the top border could be left plain and square blocks could be fitted as feet rather than let the end grain of the corner posts rest on the ground and absorb moisture that might cause rot.

All of the frame parts (Table 15-5) are 2-inch square section. That will be undersize after planing, but it does not matter as long as you allow for it in cutting joints. Plow grooves in all pieces to suit the plywood (Fig. 15-26A). This is shown as ½ inch thick, but it could be thinner. Two of the bottom rails must also be given rabbets to take the bottom slats (Fig. 15-26B). At this

Table 15-5. Materials List for Paneled Plant Pot.

4 posts	2 × 20 × 2
8 rails	2 × 18 × 2
4 borders	3 × 21 × 1
7 bottoms	2 × 18 × 1
Turned parts from	2 × 30 × 2
4 panels	16 × 16 × ½ plywood

stage, have all the parts too long to allow for cutting joints.

Tenon the horizontal rails into the corner posts. Cut back the tenons to the bottoms of the plowed grooves (Fig. 15-26C). The mortises will cut away the grooves

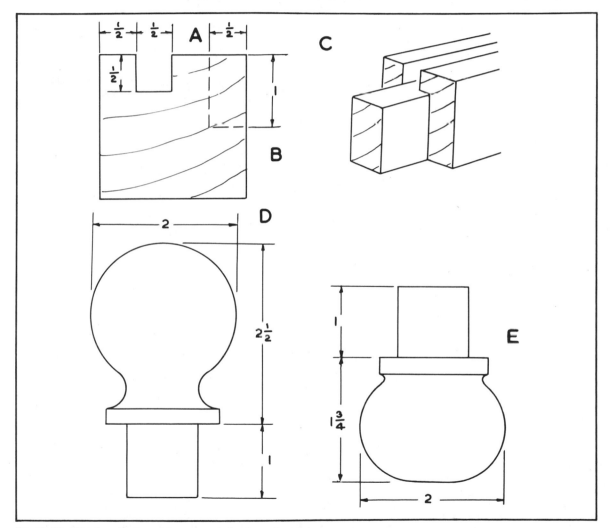

Fig. 15-26. Wood sections and turned parts for the pot container.

and the meeting grooves will suit the plywood panels. At the top, the border will cover the joints. It does not matter if you make the joints open at the ends of the posts. The posts project below the bottom rails so the mortises there are closed in any case. Make up two opposite sides. The plywood panels need not bottom in their grooves providing they are glued in. Allowing some play in the fit of the plywood ensures the corner joints will pull tight.

With the two sides squared and matching, add the parts the other way to complete the side assembly. For the bottom, space the slats to leave narrow gaps (Fig. 15-25B). The strips should be stiff enough. If you think there is risk of sagging, put another slat across the others underneath their centers.

Cut the pieces for the top border carefully as they are prominent features. Make them level with the insides of the framing, round their outer edges, and cut the miters closely. Glue and nail or screw the border on.

If you plan to use turned parts top and bottom, drill holes for the dowels on the finials and feet (Figs. 15-25C and 15-25D). They need not go far into the wood; 1 inch will be enough. The holes could be 1 inch in diameter, but any convenient bit up to that size can be used. At the same time, drill a similar hole in a thin piece of scrap wood to use as a gauge when turning the dowels.

You can use your own ideas for turning. Avoid points on the finials (Fig. 15-26D). Make the feet flat or slightly hollow underneath (Fig. 15-26E). Although the rest of the construction can be softwood, it is better to make the turned parts of hardwood. Hardwood is easier to turn accurately and less liable to suffer damage in use.

This sort of container looks best painted. The color could match its surroundings, but otherwise white is always a safe choice.

DOUBLE SWING

A swinging seat or glider for two or more people always makes a pleasant place to relax. It could be built as an independent unit or as the overhang of a porch (with no need for legs and beam).

The swinging seat shown in Fig. 15-27 has a completely independent assembly that would stand on any flat surface. If the seat only is required to be hung from an existing support, that part of the design can be used without alteration. There is enough spread of the feet to give stability under most circumstances, but it would be better to fasten them down if they are to stay in one place throughout the season. It would be possible to hang the seat with ropes. Modern synthetic rope fibers are strong and unaffected by dampness, but chains are better. Pref-

Fig. 15-27. A shaped, swinging seat.

erably the chains should be attached with shackles to the seat and to eyebolts through the beam.

See Table 15-6 for a materials list. The seat ends (Fig. 15-28A) control many of the other sizes. The legs (Fig. 15-29A) should be made to a reasonable height. Otherwise, lower supports will cause a shorter cycle of movement with a less restful action. The assembly is

Table 15-6. Materials List for Double Swing.

2 seat ends	6	×	22	×	1½	
2 upright ends	4	×	30	×	1½	
2 upright ends	4	×	22	×	1½	
2 arms	4	×	24	×	1½	
9 slats	2	×	64	×	1½	
1 beam	6	×	108	×	2	
4 legs	4	×	104	×	2	
2 feet	4	×	100	×	2	
2 rails	4	×	48	×	2	
4 gussets	6	×	15	×	1	

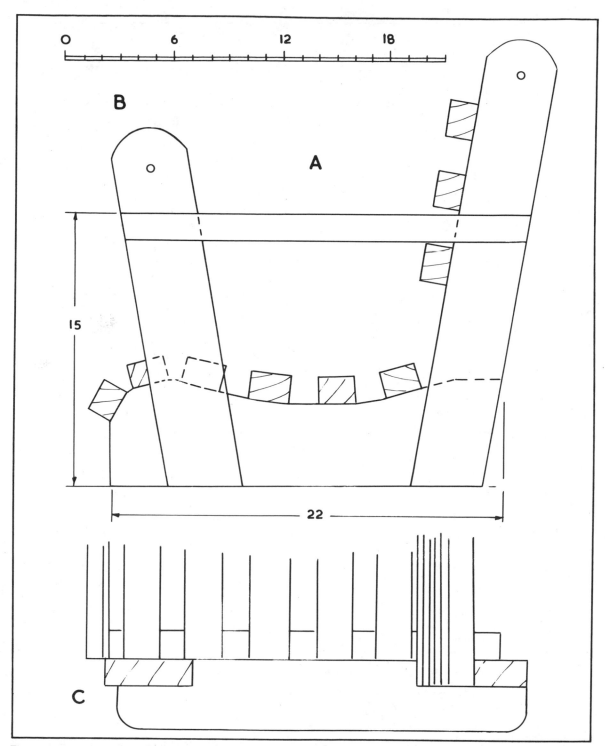

Fig. 15-28. Details of the end of a swinging seat.

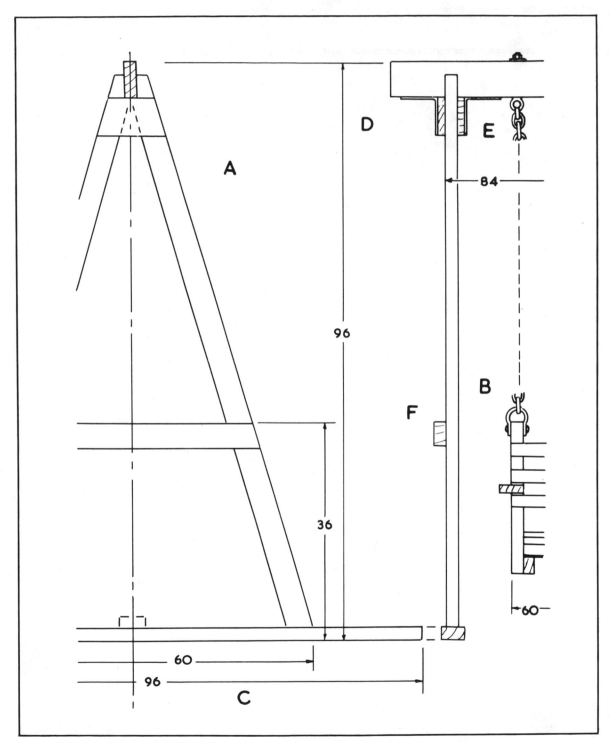

Fig. 15-29. Sizes of the supports for a double swing.

shown with a seat length of 60 inches. This provides space for two people and plenty of cushions. The sections of wood listed would still be suitable for a slightly longer seat. If you make the whole thing much longer, the seat slats would need some central support and the legs would be better rather thicker.

Start with the seat ends (Fig. 15-30A). Although the general effect is of a curve, you have to allow for the 2-inch wide slats bedding down. Arrange flat surfaces that will bring the pieces fairly evenly spaced on their outer surfaces (Fig. 15-30B).

The two ends, from which the seat hangs, should be without flaws. They slope outward at 10 degrees to vertical. The precise angle is not important so long as they match. At their tops, curve the ends (Fig. 15-28B). Do not cut away too much or the end grain that takes the load will be weakened. If chain is used, the attachment will be with shackles that fit over the wood (Fig. 15-29B) and the hole size must suit the bolt through the shackle. Do not drill it any larger than is necessary; it will probably be ⅜ of an inch.

Attach the ends to the seat with bolts through or with large wood screws long enough to almost go through the wood and driven from both sides. Check that the two assemblies match as a pair.

Mark where the arms will come on the upright ends, parallel with the bottoms of the seat ends. Notch the arms round the uprights so that the remainder of the width comes outside the seat (Fig. 15-28C). Round the exposed corners and edges of the arms. Glue and screw the arms in place. Again checking that the two assemblies match.

Prepare the seat and back slats by rounding the edges that will face outward. Drill for two screws at each end. Attach the seat slats to the curved seat ends. To ensure squareness during assembly, put one back slat in place. See that the seat slats make an even pattern. The back slats are about 2 inches apart. Arrange one below the arms and two above them.

Set out half of the leg assembly full size in order to get the sizes and angles of the legs (Fig. 15-29C). Choose a straight piece for the beam (Fig. 15-29D). Cut the tops of the legs to fit around it so that they can be screwed or bolted on. At the bottom, the feet are straight pieces with the legs tenoned into them (Fig. 15-30C) or held with metal brackets (Fig. 15-30D).

At the tops of the legs, the joint must be quite firm to resist any tendency to move sideways. Each joint can be strengthened with gussets (Fig. 15-30E). Then metal brackets added; these preferably should be stout iron brackets with legs about 6 inches long. Alternatively there could be wood struts at each side.

The rail (Fig. 15-29F) provides some strength, but it is also there to prevent anyone from walking between the legs—possibly when the seat is swinging—with a risk of harm to themselves.

For hanging the swing, there should be eyebolts—probably ½ inch in diameter—through the beam (Fig. 15-29E). Place large washers under the nuts to spread the load. Use locknuts or hammer over the ends of the bolts to prevent the nuts from coming off. The shackles on the seat should be large enough to project above the wood at least ¾ of an inch.

There are several sorts of chain suitable for hanging the seat. If it has plain links, the metal in them does not have to be very thick; under 3/16 of an inch should be satisfactory. The end link should slip over its seat shackle. If it will not, there should be another suitable small shackle to make the joint. At the top, the two links at each place can go over a small shackle that then attaches to the eyebolt. Arrange the chain lengths so the seat is level when at rest or tilted back slightly. Do not adjust it so that it slopes forward. Have the seat top between 15 inches and 18 inches from the ground.

The beam can be used as the central support for a roof or canopy to keep off rain or sun. End pieces determine the size of the roof (Fig. 15-31A). They can be screwed across the ends of the beams (with brackets inside if necessary). Shingles make an appropriate roof covering. In that case, add enough lengthwise strips to suit the sizes of shingles. The ends could be 1-×-6 inch strips and lengthwise pieces should be 1-×2 inch sections. You will find one intermediate strip (Fig. 15-31B) will be needed for stiffness.

Nail shingles starting from the bottom and work toward the top. Arrange to stagger the joints. At the ridge, there can be two overlapping strips nailed together and to the shingles (Fig. 15-31C). The shingles can be allowed to weather naturally or they can be treated with preservative in a different color from that used on the rest of the assembly.

You could have a removable canvas awning to fit over a framework that stays in place. In that case, arrange the ends as for the shingle roof, but put strips between their ends and other strips to the ridge beam. They will prevent the canvas from sagging and should not be more than 24 inches apart (Fig. 15-31D). If the ends of the eyebolts project upward, put some strips of wood along the top of the beam to keep the canvas clear of the bolt ends.

You could have a canvas cover made from paper patterns, but you can sew light canvas on a domestic sewing machine. Arrange the canvas with a border to

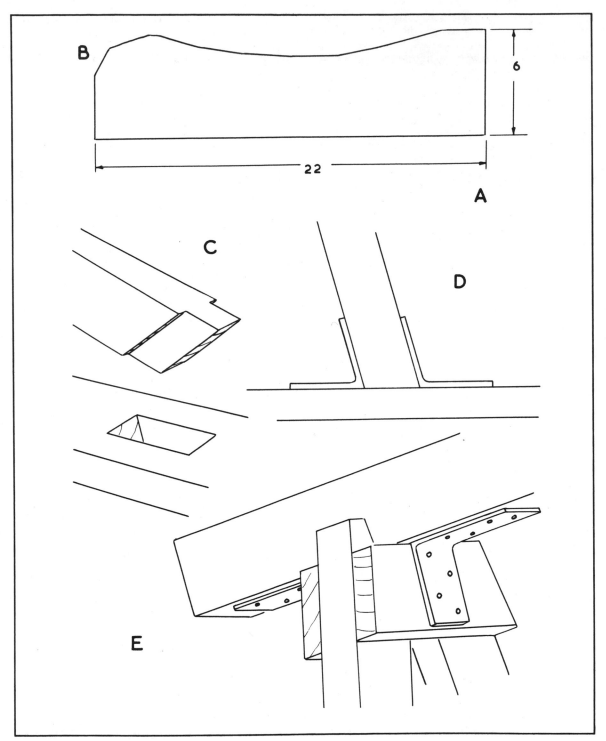

Fig. 15-30. Details of seat and support construction.

hang below the sloping part of the roof and put strings or pieces of tape inside to tie to the framing (Fig. 15-31E).

You could cover a framework with plywood and allow for a border vertically below the sloping roof. The general shape would then be similar to a canvas top. It could be painted brightly in contrast to a plainer paint on the rest of the structure. The whole roof could be made up as a unit to lift off. The ends would not be screwed to the beam, but there would have to be a stiff ridge piece to rest on top of it. If the ends of the eyebolts are long enough, it could have holes to go over them so that it can be held with additional nuts. Alternatively, there could be extra bolts with their ends upward for attaching the roof.

SWINGING SEAT

This is an alternative to the double seat just described. It

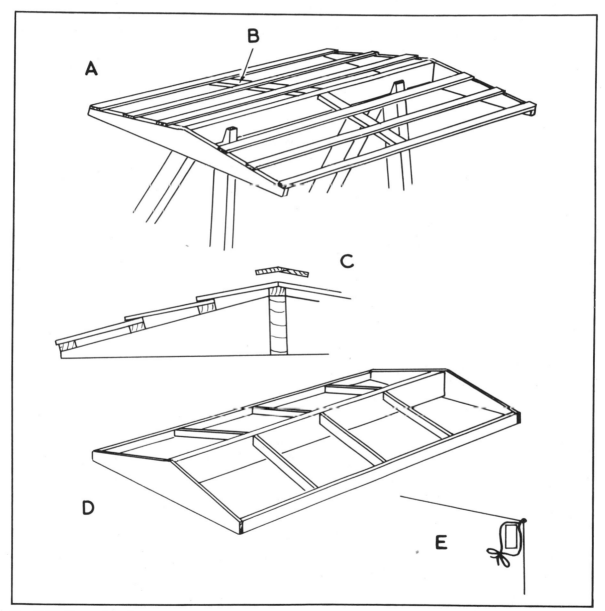

Fig. 15-31. Suggestions for a permanent or removable canvas canopy.

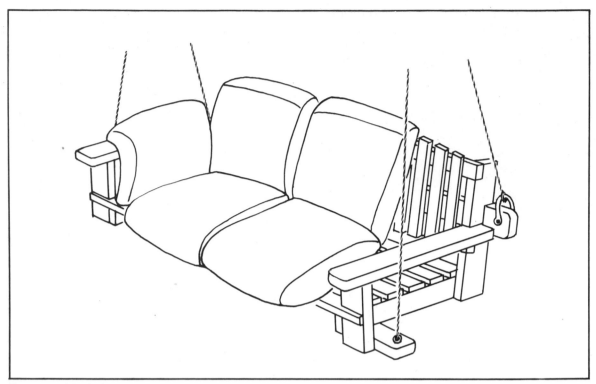

Fig. 15-32. A swinging seat.

could be used with a similar frame anywhere outdoors or it could hang in the porch. As shown, it is intended to be a roomy two-seater (Fig. 15-32). The sizes shown in Fig. 15-33 and Table 15-7 will suit softwoods. If hardwoods are chosen the sections could be reduced. The main supports are pieces that go under and behind the seat (Figs. 15-33A and 15-33B) and extend far enough to take the supporting chains or ropes. There can be an eyebolt through the ends of the piece under the seat. The one at the back can take a shackle over the wood (as described for the previous seat) or there could be another eyebolt through for the chain to be joined there with a small shackle. Support in this seat lifts toward the load instead of the load being suspended from the attachment points.

The seat has lengthwise slats, but the back is made up of vertical pieces attached to two lengthwise strips. The parts that make the ends are lapped and screwed together, but the supporting back piece is better let in. Letting in the lengthwise pieces behind the back uprights also makes a neater finish. Where screws are used, they should be fairly stout (12-gauge screws would be suitable) and long enough to penetrate the lower wood by at least 1 inch.

Start by setting out the shape of an end full size (Fig. 15-34A). The back should slope at about 10 degrees to vertical. You can alter that if you think another angle would be more comfortable. All of the parts on this drawing are 2-×-4 inch section, with the arm and its support edgewise.

From this drawing, make the seat and back supports so the pair match, but do not screw them together until you have cut the other joints in the back pieces. For the pieces that support the back uprights, cut half out of their thickness for each joint (Fig. 15-34B). For the supporting strip at the back, do not cut as much away from it in order to leave enough strength there. In a 2-inch thickness, the notch in the strip could be ½ inch deep; leave 1 inch to be cut from the upright (Fig. 15-34C). If you prefer, you can make the joint without cutting anything from the strip so that it stands out from the upright notch. Assemble the seat ends and see that they match as a pair. Add the supporting lengthwise parts and the back supporting pieces. Check that the whole assembly is square.

The seat slats should be rounded on their exposed edges. They rest on the ends except for the front one shown cut around the arm support for neatness (Fig.

338

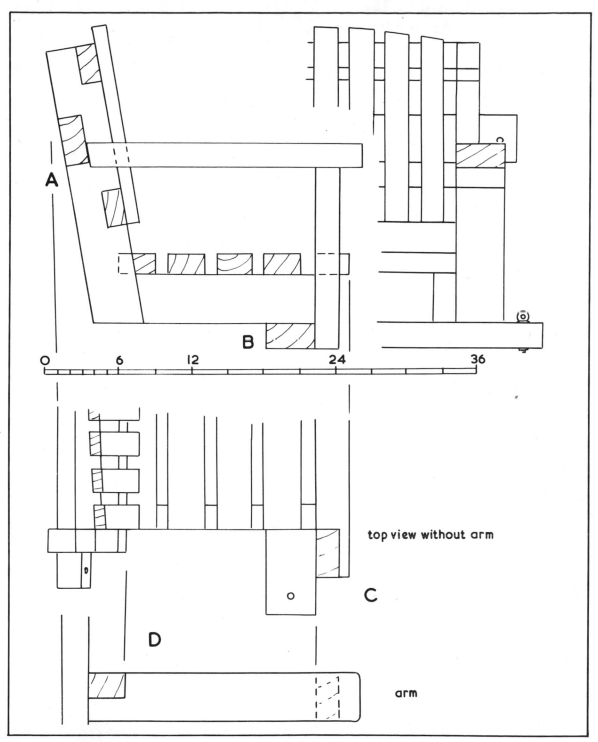

A

B

O   6   12   24   36

top view without arm

C

D

arm

Fig. 15-33. Sizes of a swinging seat.

Table 15-7. Materials List for Swinging Seat.

2 ends	4 × 25 × 2
2 ends	4 × 23 × 2
2 arms	4 × 27 × 2
2 arm supports	4 × 17 × 2
2 hanging rails	4 × 72 × 2
2 back rails	3 × 62 × 1½
4 seat rails	3 × 60 × 1½
1 seat rail	3 × 68 × 1½
20 back uprights	2 × 18 × 1

15-33C). You can cut it the same length as the others and then round its projecting corners. If you want to cut around the arm support, leave cutting and fitting it until the arm support is added.

The arm supports fit against the seat end and hanging rail so that it can be screwed securely in both directions. At the top, there can be screws downward through the arms, preferably counterbored and plugged, or you can use stub tenons (Fig. 15-35A). Let the front of the arms extend so they can be well rounded. At the back, each arm has to be cut round the upright and its end beveled to fit against the rear supporting rail (Fig. 15-33D). It can be secured by screwing both ways.

The back is made up of a large number of upright strips, that are shown as 1 inch by 2 inch section, but you could use any available widths. Space them evenly; gaps about 1 inch wide will do. You can increase that if the seat will always be used with cushions. The strips are shown with their tops cut to a curve. To get an even shape, it is best to have the strips too long and cut the curve after fitting them. You can then bend a lath over them and pencil where they are to be cut (Fig. 15-35B).

Cutting the back strips while in position on the seat would not be difficult. If you prefer to deal with them flat on the bench, the two lengthwise pieces that support them could first be put loosely in the end notches and the end upright pieces attached temporarily to them. This assembly can be lifted away so that the other pieces can be fitted and the tops can be curved before putting the lot back permanently on the seat.

Remove sharp edges and corners, but the general effect should be rather chunky and not excessively rounded. If the seat slats seem too flexible, place a front-to-back strip to link them under their centers.

TRASH CONTAINERS

You could make trash containers very similar to the boxes described for containing flower pots, but they should be deeper if they are to have a useful capacity. A square box that is taller than it is wide, with a shaped top or other decoration to relieve its plainness, should be satisfactory. It can be used as it is and the whole thing upended for emptying or it could have a liner of some sort that can be taken out without disturbing the outside. Because an attractive wood container will be fairly heavy, that is a better plan.

The container could be a plastic bag that is discarded with its contents each time it is filled, but that has to be supported at the top and a fold over the wood is rather unattractive. Rigid plastic or metal would be better. It need not be bought for the purpose. You can cut the top of a metal drum or plastic container. It will be hidden by the wood casing so it does not matter if its exterior is printed or otherwise marked.

Most of these containers are round. In a square box, there is a gap at each corner, inside, where small things will be dropped. Then you must clean out the box after removing the internal container. It would be better if the box is made nearer the shape of its liner. Your best approach to the job is to find the liner you want to use and build the box to suit it.

An attractive container can be made by coopering (like a barrel). Fitting a large number of sides together to make something that comes close to being a circle calls for small skill and patience than might be justified for this use, but you can use a similar method with eight sides and an octagon comes close enough to the circular liner to not leave any gaps large enough for anything but the tiniest things to fall through.

The container can be made parallel or it can be given a slight taper. Two sides can be extended to be slotted as handles (Fig. 15-36). This gives an appearance reminiscent of an old-time milking pail.

The angles involved are the same whatever size container you make. If you decide on a taper and keep it slight, the angles remain the same for all practical purposes. For a considerable flare, the angles you have to plane meeting edges would be different. With eight equal sides, a setting out (Fig. 15-37A) shows the angle of each triangle at the center is 45 degrees (one-eight of 360 degrees). Because the three angles in any triangle must total 180 degrees and the other two are the same, they are each 62½ degrees (half of 135 degrees). That is the angle you have to make the edges of the panels (Fig. 15-37B).

An adjustable bevel will serve as a guide, if you will be planing by hand, or that is the angle to set the fence on a jointer. To make sure the outsides of the container

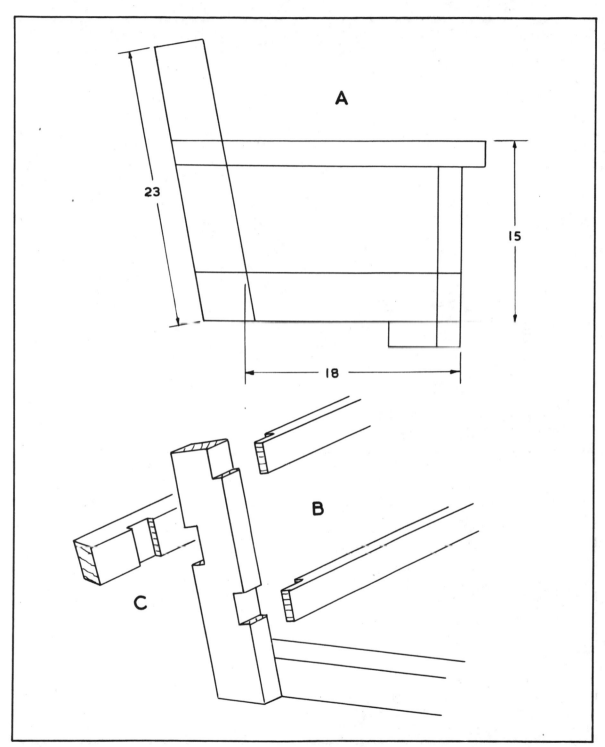

Fig. 15-34. Layout of the seat end and details of its notched joints.

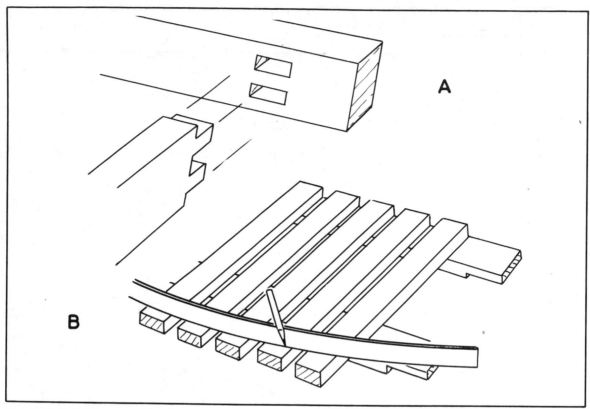

Fig. 15-35. A double-tenoned joint and drawing the curve on the back.

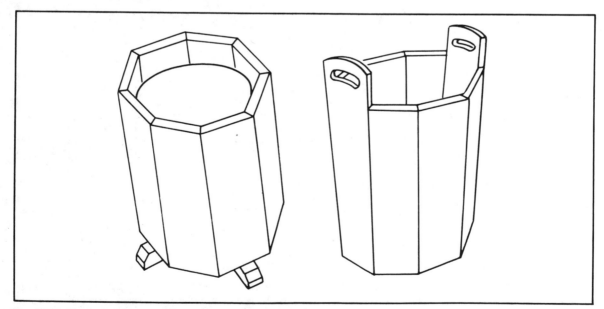

Fig. 15-36. Trash containers can be coopered around a metal or plastic liner.

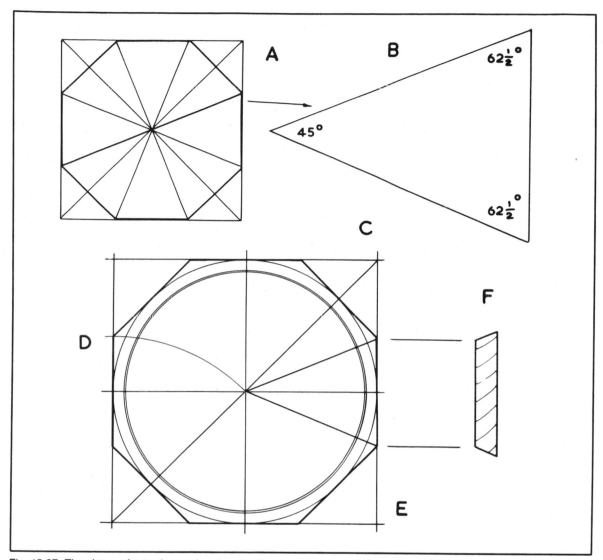

Fig. 15-37. The shape of a trash container is set out geometrically to get the angles of the wood panels.

come close, you can make the angles very slightly less by ignoring the ½ degree. If there is any discrepancy, it comes inside where it will not show.

Draw a circle of the outside size of your liner. Allow some clearance round it and draw two crossing lines square to each other. When they cross the outer circumference, draw lines square to them, long enough to meet and form a square (Fig. 15-37C). Check that the four lengths are the same. Measure from the center to a corner and use this length to mark along each side from each corner (Fig. 15-37D). If you join these points, the lines should make tangents to the circle and you should now have eight equal sides (Fig. 15-37E) representing the inner surfaces of each *stave* (the coopering term). If you mark the thickness of the wood, that will give you the section of a stave (Fig. 15-37F). You must prepare eight identical ones.

The thickness of wood has to be proportional to the overall sizes, but it should not be less than ¾ of an inch. It could go up to twice that size for a large box.

For a tapered container, set out the top and bottom to get the widths of staves at these levels. They are made

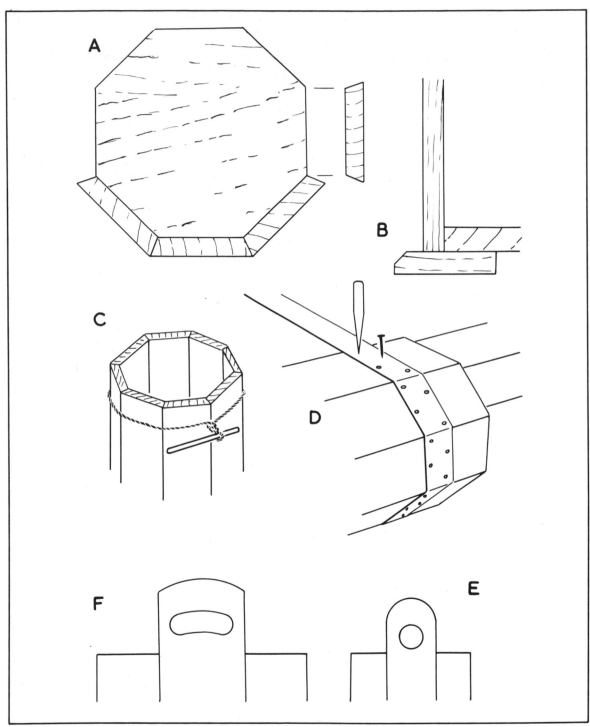

Fig. 15-38. The bottom fits inside and can have feet (A and B). The top may be drawn together with rope and a metal band put around (C and D). Sides can be extended as handles (E and F).

to this taper. Otherwise, the work is the same as for a parallel box. If you want to extend a pair of staves to make handles, remember to prepare them about 6 inches longer than the other six staves.

At the bottom, make an octagonal base to fit inside (Fig. 15-38A). Ideally this will be a perfect fit. What you have to avoid is making it too large because the staves could not then be drawn closely round it. Marginally too small is better than being oversize. The bottom might rest on the ground, but it would be better to provide feet. Four will do (Fig. 15-38B). Do not carry them right across. Individual feet are better able to stand firm on uneven ground.

In the barrelmaking tradition, the tops of the staves should be drawn together with a metal band. This can be a strip of any metal; aluminum is easy to work. Its width depends on the size of the box, but between 1 inch and 2 inches will suit most containers. Have a length ready that is a few inches longer than the circumference. Use a waterproof glue on all the meeting surfaces. Nail to the bottom and draw the tops together with a rope, twisted as a "Spanish windlass," with a piece of scrap wood (Fig. 15-38C). Keep that pressure on until the glue has set.

Pencil around where the metal band will come. Support the box over the end of a stout board that is narrower than the inner face of a stave, projecting over the edge of your bench. Nail progressively to the staves. Use a pointed punch to pierce the metal and hammer it over the angles as you work around (Fig. 15-38D). Let one end overlap the other on the flat of a stave.

Plane the tops of the stave level and round them on the outsides. You can extend a pair of opposite staves as handles. For a smaller container, you can use a round hole (Fig. 15-38E). For a wider stave, it would be better to make a shaped hole (Fig. 15-38F). You need at least 4 inches to put a hand through.

Glossary

THE MAKING OF OUTDOOR FURNITURE IS ONLY one branch of woodworking. It shares a very large large vocabulary of special terms, but a complete glossary of all such words that might be met would be too large for this book. The selection of words that follow are in use today, but there are a few obsolescent ones that might be met and not otherwise readily understood.

Alburnum—The botanical name of sapwood.

annular rings—The concentric rings in the cross section of a tree that form the grain pattern. One ring is added each year.

arris—The line or sharp edge between two flat or plane surfaces.

assymetrical—A shape that is not symmetrical or of balanced form about a centerline.

auger—A long drill, with its own handle, for deep drilling.

autumn growth—Part of an annual ring in a tree. It is formed as the sap descends.

balk (baulk)—A roughly squared block of lumber.

ball peen (pein) hammer—A hammer with one side of its head rounded like half a ball.

bamboo—Cane sometimes used for furniture. It differs from ordinary wood in that as it grows the new wood is formed on the inside of a tube.

barefaced tenon—A tenon shouldered on one face only.

batten—Any narrow strip of wood. A board fitted across other boards to join them (also called a cleat), cover a gap, or prevent warping.

batting—A cotton padding material used for upholstery.

bench stop—A wood or metal projection on a bench top. Wood can be pressed against it to prevent movement under a plane or other tool.

bevel—An angle or chamfer planed on an edge. Also the name of an adjustable tool used for marking and testing angles.

bias—Cloth cut diagonally to the weave.

blind—Not right through, such as a stopped hole for a dowel or a mortise for a short tenon.

bow saw—A small frame saw with a narrow blade for cutting curves.

bracket—An angular piece used to strengthen or support a shelf or flap.

burlap—Coarse-weave jute cloth used in upholstery. Also called hessian.

button—Round or shaped disc used on twine through upholstery for appearance and to retain the stuffing.

buttoning—Securing upholstery with buttons. Deep buttoning is used only on indoor furniture.

cast—Twisting of a surface that should be flat.

chaise longue—Literally, a long chair, but more like a bed with an adjustable head board. Sometimes called chaise lounge.

chamfer—An angle or bevel planed on an edge.

check—A lengthwise separation of the grain in a piece of wood.

clamp—A device for drawing things together. Used especially to draw joints together. Alternative name for a cleat.

cleat—Any small piece joining other parts together, but particularly a strip across other boards to hold them together and prevent warping.

clench nailing—Using nails long enough to go right through so the projecting ends can be hammered over.

coniferous—Cone-bearing. Most softwood trees are coniferous.

conversion—The general turn for cutting a log into boards and smaller sections of wood for use.

cotton—Natural material, woven in many ways, for upholstery covering and loosely compounded for stuffing.

cotton batting—Cotton upholstery padding material.

counterbore—Drill a larger hole over a smaller one so the head of a screw is drawn below the surface and it can be covered by a plug.

countersink—Bevel the top of a hole so a flat-headed screw can be driven level with the surface.

cramp—Usual British name for a clamp.

cross-lap joint—Two pieces cut to fit into each other where they cross.

cross-peen hammer—Hammer with one face of its head made narrow crosswise.

cup shake—A crack that develops in the growing tree and follows the line of an annual ring.

dado joint—A groove in wood, cut across the surface to support a shelf or other part.

dead pin—A wedge. Sometimes a dowel.

deal—Trade name for some soft woods, such as pine and fir, but now less commonly used. Can also mean a plank or board.

deciduous—A leaf-shedding tree and the source of most hardwoods.

dovetail—The fan-shaped piece that projects between pins in the other part of a dovetail joint. It is cut to resist pulling out.

dovetail nailing—Driving nails so they slope slightly at opposite angles and resist the boards being pulled apart.

dowel—A cylindrical piece of wood used as a peg when making joints.

draw bore or draw pin—A peg or dowel across a mortise and tenon joint to pull the parts together.

ellipse—The inclined transverse section across a cylinder. Often wrongly called oval, which is egg shaped.

fastenings (fasteners)—Collective name for anything used for joining—such as nails and screws.

feather edge—A wide, smooth bevel taking the edge of a board to a very thin line.

fillet—A narrow strip of wood used to fill or support a part.

fillister—A rabbet plane with fences to control depth and width of cut. Sometimes confused with a plow plane, which is used for cutting grooves.

firmer chisel—A strong general-purpose chisel with square or bevel edges.

folding wedges—Two similar wedges used overlapping each other in opposite directions so that they provide pressure when driven.

foxiness—The signs of the first onset of rot. It can be regarded as decoration.

foxtail wedging—Wedges arranged in the end of a tenon so it is spread when driven into a blind hole.

frame saw—A narrow saw blade tensioned in a frame.

gauge—A marking tool or means of testing. A definition of size such as the thickness of sheet metal or the diameters of wire or screws. Numbers are used in recognized systems.

gouge—A type of chisel that is rounded in cross-section.

grain—The striped marks seen in wood due to the annual rings.

groove—Any slot, cut in wood, such as a dado. Less commonly, a rabbet.

haft—The handle of a tool, particularly a long one.

half-lap joint—Two crossing pieces, notched into each other, usually to bring their surfaces level.

handed—Made as a pair.

hand screw—A clamp usually made entirely of wood.

hardwood—Wood from a deciduous tree. Usually, but not always, harder than softwoods.

haunch—A short cut-back part of a tenon that joins another piece near its end.

heartwood—The mature wood near the center of a tree.

hessian—Alternative name for burlap.

housing joint—Alternative name for a dado joint where a shelf fits into a groove in another part.

jigsaw—Fine hand saw in a metal frame. A hand powered saw with a projecting reciprocating blade.

jointing—The making of any joint, but particularly planing edges straight to make close-glued joints to make up a width.

kerf—The slot made by a saw.

knot—A flaw in wood due to where a branch left the trunk. A method of joining cords.

laminate—Construct in layers with several pieces of wood glued together. Used particularly to make up curved parts. Plywood is laminated.

lap joint—The general name for joints where one piece of wood is cut to overlap and fit into another.

laying out—Setting out the details of design and construction, usually full size.

mallet—Wood, hide, or plastic hammerlike hitting tool.

marking out—Indicating cuts and positions on wood before cutting, shaping, and drilling.

medullary rays—Radiating lines from the center of a log. These can be seen in some woods radially cut, but they are invisible in others. The markings are most prominent in oak.

miter box or board—Guide for the saw when cutting miters.

miter (mitre)—A joint where the meeting angle of the surfaces is divided or bisected, as in the corner of a picture frame.

molding (moulding)—Decorative edge or border that can be a simple rounding or an intricate section of curves and quirks.

mortise (mortice)—The rectangular socket cut to take a tenon.

mortise and tenon joint—A method of joining the end of one piece of wood into the side of another. The tenon projects like a tongue on the end to fit into the mortise cut in the other piece.

needle-leaf trees—Alternative name for cone-bearing trees that produce softwoods.

oil slip—A shaped oilstone used on the inside curves of gouges and carving tools.

oil stain—Wood coloring with the pigment dissolved in oil.

oil stone—A sharpening stone for edge tools, used with thin oil. Often called a whetstone.

peck marks—Penciled marks used to transfer points on one thing to another.

pedestal—A supporting post. A central support for a table or a support at each of its ends.

pedestal table—A table with a central support and spreading feet.

pegging—Dowels or wooden pegs through joints.

piercing—Decoration made by cutting through the wood. Similar to fretwork, but more robust.

pilot hole—A small hole drilled as a guide for the drill point, before making a larger hole.

pinking shears—Scissors that cut a serrated edge on cloth.

pintle—A dowel or peg on which a part pivots. The name is taken from the pivot of a boat rudder.

plain sawn—Boards cut across a log.

plow (plough)—A plane for cutting grooves. Guides control depth and distance from an edge.

plywood—Board made with veneers glued in laminations with the grain of each layer square to the next.

quartered (quarter-sawn)—Boards cut radially from a log to minimize warping and shrinking or to show the medullary rays in oak and some other woods.

rabbet (rebate)—Angular cut out section at an edge, as in the back of a picture frame.

rail—A horizontal member in framing.

rake—Incline to the horizontal.

rivet sett—Tool to fit over the end of a rivet and drive the parts together. Often combined with a rivet snap.

rivet snap—Tool for forming a rivet head after hammering to an approximate shape.

rod—Strip of wood with distances of details of construction marked on it. Used for comparing parts instead of measuring with a rule.

router—Power tool or hand tool for leveling the bottom of a groove or recessed surface.

rule—Measuring rod. A craftsman does not spell it "ruler."

run—In a long length. Lumber quantity can be quoted as so many feet run.

sapwood—The wood nearer the outside of a tree. Not as strong or durable as the heartwood in most trees.

sawbuck—Crossed sawing trestle. The name can be applied to table legs crossed in a similar way.

seasoning—Drying lumber to a controlled moisture content in preparation for using it in constructional work.

segments—Curved pieces of wood used to build up table rails and similar things in round work.

selvage—The manufactured edge in a piece of cloth where the threads turn back and the edge will not fray.

set—To punch a nail below the surface. The tool for doing that. The bending of saw teeth in opposite directions to cut a kerf wider than the thickness of the saw metal.

setting out—Laying out details, usually full size, of a piece of furniture or other construction.

shake—A defect or crack in the growing tree that might not be apparent until it is cut into boards.

shot joint—Planed edges glued together.

slat—Narrow, thin wood.

slip—A shaped, small oilstone for sharpening inside the curve of a gouge or similar tool.

softwood—The wood from a coniferous, needle-leaf tree.

Spanish windlass—A device using rope twisted with a lever to give a tightening effect.

splay—To spread out.

spline—A narrow strip of wood fitting into grooves. Commonly used to strengthen two meeting surfaces that are glued.

spud—A tool with a broad end like a blunt chisel. Used for removing bark from a felled tree.

staple—Two-ended nail forming a loop. Two-legged fastener driven by a special tool and used instead of tacks for attaching upholstery cloth.

star shake—A defect in a growing tree, with cracks radiating from the center.

stiffnut—A nut to fit on a bolt that incorporates a means of resisting loosening.

stile—Vertical member in chair framing.

stopped tenon—A tenon engaging with a mortise that is not cut through the wood. A stub tenon.

stretcher—A lengthwise rail between the lower parts of a table or chair.

stub tenon—Alternative name for a stopped tenon.

tabling—The turned-in edge of a piece of cloth, to strengthen it or prevent fraying.

tack—Small tapered nail with a large head. A temporary sewing stitch.

tang—The tapered end of a tool, such as a file or chisel, to fit into its handle.

template (templet)—Shaped pattern to draw round when marking out parts.

tenon—The projecting tongue on the end of one piece of wood to fit into a mortise in another piece of wood.

tote—A tool handle, particularly on a plane.

tusk tenon—A tusk tenon that goes through its mortise and projects at the other side. There it can be secured with a wedge.

twine—General name for thin string or stout thread used in upholstery.

underbracing—Arrangement of rails and stretchers to provide stiffness between the lower parts of a table or chair legs. Also called underframing.

varnish—A near-transparent paintlike finish, once made from natural lacs, but now usually synthetic.

waney edge—The edge of a board that still has bark on it or is still showing the pattern of the outside of the tree.

warping—Distortion of a board by twisting or curving because of unequal shrinkage as moisture dries out.

winding—A board or assembly is said to be "in winding" when it is not flat and a twist can be seen when sighting from one end.

working drawing—A drawing showing sizes—usually in elevations, plan and sections—from which measurements can be taken to make furniture. Not a pictorial view.

Index